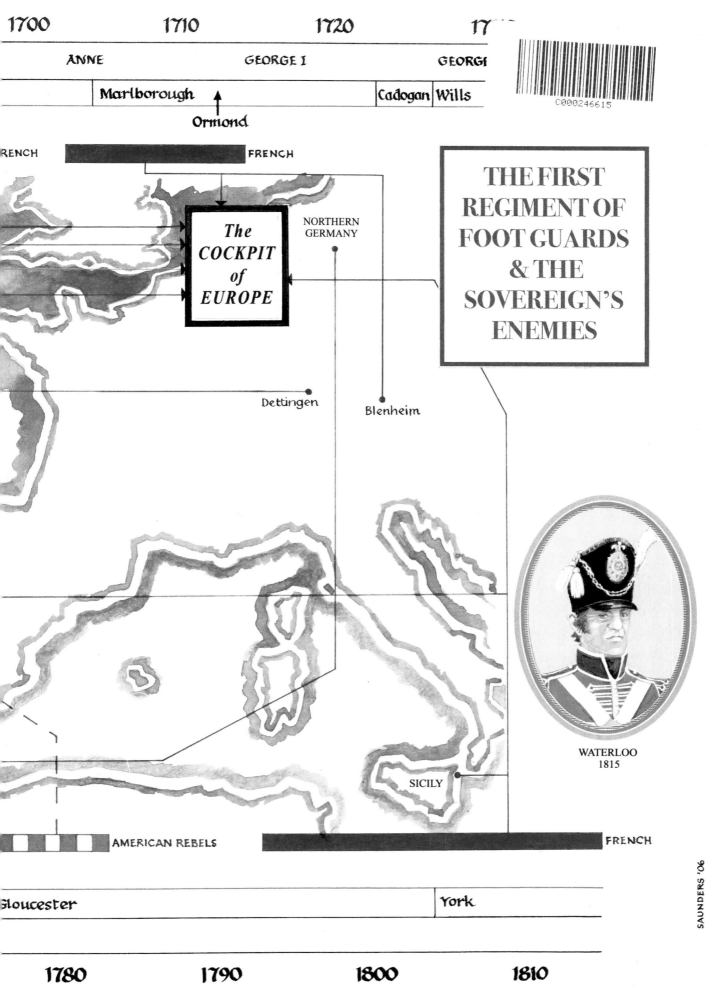

1700   1710   1720   17

ANNE   GEORGE I   GEORGE

Marlborough   Cadogan   Wills

Ormond

FRENCH   FRENCH

The COCKPIT of EUROPE

NORTHERN GERMANY

THE FIRST REGIMENT OF FOOT GUARDS & THE SOVEREIGN'S ENEMIES

Dettingen

Blenheim

WATERLOO
1815

SICILY

FRENCH

AMERICAN REBELS

Gloucester   York

1780   1790   1800   1810

SAUNDERS '06

C000246615

THE
BRITISH
GRENADIERS

COLONEL-IN-CHIEF

Her Majesty the Queen on 'Imperial' in the gardens of Buckingham Palace, 1962, by Terence Tenison Cuneo CVO OBE (1907-1996). Commissioned by Her Majesty the Queen in 1962.

The Royal Collection © 2005. Her Majesty Queen Elizabeth II
(Cuneo's characteristic mouse is under the tree on the right).

This painting is one of a very small number of paintings that Her Majesty has commissioned of herself. It marked ten years from her accession to the throne in 1952 and thus her assumption of the title of Colonel-in-Chief, and twenty years from when, on her sixteenth birthday on 21st April 1942, she became Colonel of the Regiment. It has been exhibited at the Summer Exhibition at the Royal Academy in 1963, at the Mall Galleries in 1987, and at Christies by the Society of Equestrian Artists in 1996 and 2000. It hangs in Buckingham Palace.

THE
BRITISH
GRENADIERS

THREE HUNDRED & FIFTY YEARS OF THE
FIRST REGIMENT OF FOOT GUARDS 1656–2006

HENRY HANNING

Pen & Sword
MILITARY

First published in Great Britain by
PEN & SWORD MILITARY
an imprint of
Pen & Sword Books Limited
47 Church Street, Barnsley
S. Yorkshire, S70 2AS

Copyright © Henry Hanning, 2006

ISBN 1 84415 385 1
ISBN 978 1 84415 385 5

The right of Henry Hanning
to be identified as Author of this Work has
been asserted by him in accordance with
the Copyright, Designs and Patents Act 1988

A CIP catalogue record for this book
is available from the British Library

Designed and typeset in 11pt Garamond Narrow
by Sylvia Menzies, Pen & Sword Books Ltd

Printed and bound in England by
CPI UK

Pen & Sword Books Ltd incorporates the imprints of
Pen & Sword Aviation, Pen & Sword Maritime, Pen & Sword Military,
Pen & Sword Select, Pen & Sword Military Classics,
Leo Cooper and Wharncliffe Local History.

For a complete list of Pen & Sword titles please contact:
PEN & SWORD BOOKS LIMITED
47 Church Street, Barnsley, South Yorkshire, S70 2AS, England
E-mail: enquiries@pen-and-sword.co.uk
Website: www.pen-and-sword.co.uk

CONTENTS

MAPS

Introduction
and Acknowledgements

In three hundred pages it is hardly possible to write a comprehensive account of what has befallen the First or Grenadier Regiment of Foot Guards over the three hundred and fifty years of their history. Indeed, a great deal has been written in the past and it has been my pleasant task merely to select, illustrate and present. I have drawn heavily on the work of Sir Frederick Hamilton, Rex Whitworth and Oliver Lindsay and the World War histories of Sir Frederick Ponsonby, Patrick Forbes and Nigel Nicolson. But there have been many other writings to consult, some of them very recent.

Special thanks are due to Major the Rt Hon the Lord Carrington KG CH GCMG MC PC, MB Mavroleon Esq, Major JFM Rodwell and Major AR Taylor MBE.

I make grateful acknowledgement of editorial assistance from numerous directions. Many will be evident from the bibliography. Tom Hartman, Sylvia Menzies, Jon Wilkinson and Henry Wilson, all of Pen and Sword Books, have been a delight to work with and deserve high recognition for the quality of this book. I have had special help from Edward Bolitho, Sir Hervey Bruce-Clifton, Barbara Chambers, Frank Clark, Michael Craster, Viscount De L'Isle, Richard Dorney, Andrew Duncan, Jim Eastwood, Lord Forbes, Ray Glasspell, Philip Hawkesworth, Philip Haythornthwaite, David Horn, Brian Lane, Oliver Lindsay, Hugh Lockhart, Paul Naish, Andrew Orgill (RMA Sandhurst), David Sewell, Conway Seymour and his staff at Regimental Headquarters Grenadier Guards, Sir John Smiley, Geoffrey Somerset, Joan Soole, Michael Springman, Ronnie Taylor, George Turton, Sir Evelyn Webb-Carter, Mark Whitehead and Bob Woodfield.

For illustrations I am especially indebted to Gary Gibbs. I also gratefully acknowledge the contributions of Michael Barthorp, Sean Bolan and Les Brown; Leonora Clark, Lisa Heighway and Karen Lawson (Royal Collection); Christopher Collins, Mary-Clare Denny, Andrew Fergusson-Cuninghame, Bryan Fosten, Algernon Heber Percy (Cattermole paintings), Peter Hartley (cigarette cards), Neil Hyslop (maps), the Imperial War Museum, Patrick McSweeney, The Orion Publishing Group (for Pierre Turner paintings in *British Infantry Uniforms Since 1660* by Michael Barthorp), Algernon Percy (certain Wymer paintings), Jeremy Pilcher, Gill Robinson, David Rowlands and Roger Scruton; Joanna Quill and Jenny Spencer-Smith (National Army Museum), Bob Marrion, the Pompadour Gallery, Clare and Paul Risoe, Alan Saunders (for the endpapers) and Roger Thompson; Andrew Wallis and Mary O'Keefe (Guards Museum) and Philip Wright.

Grenadiers and Guardsmen

Readers may sometimes find the use of these terms baffling. They will discover, if they succeed in penetrating a short distance into the book, that, in the early days, 'grenadiers' were specialist soldiers, to be found in all infantry regiments. As a result of their performance at the Battle of Waterloo, however, the First Guards were made an entire regiment of grenadiers. Since the middle of the nineteenth century, when this type of soldier was no longer to be found in the army, 'Grenadiers' have been recognised only as members of the Grenadier Guards.

'Guardsmen', in the broadest sense, are those soldiers, both officers and men, who have served at any time in the regiments of Household Cavalry or Foot Guards and who are entitled to wear the distinctive colours of blue-red-blue. Troops described in the narrative as 'guardsmen' may simply be members of those regiments. In 1918, however, private soldiers of the Foot Guards were given the formal title of 'Guardsmen' and, since then, the term has been used in that sense also.

Dedication

Dedicated to Elizabeth my wife, and to our children Matthew, Sally and Christopher, in most grateful appreciation of their loving help, support and encouragement, and in special recognition of their cheerful endurance, over many years, of the claims of my other, regimental, family..

Chapter One

IN THE BEGINNING
1656-1702

Exile and Restoration

The Formation of the Regiment, the Dunes

The regiment that was to become one of the most famous in the world was formed in inauspicious circumstances: by an exiled monarch who had several times been worsted in battle, in a foreign land, poorly equipped, barely paid, often starving, and with an uncertain future.

In earlier years the Stuart monarchs had formed troops for their own protection as and when they were needed. There was no money to pay for a permanent establishment, and indeed no standing army of any kind. Charles I had been executed and his son Charles II, after an abortive effort to regain the throne, went into exile. This took him first to the French Court, then to Cologne, and finally to Flanders, then under Spanish domination, where he set up his headquarters in Bruges.

In 1655 Oliver Cromwell formed an alliance with Louis XIV of France against Spain. In

Charles II in his oak tree: this camp colour was allotted in due course to the left-hand rifle company (No 4) of the 3rd Battalion, and now belongs to the Inkerman Company, which continues the tradition of that battalion.

1656 Charles tried to form an army at Bruges but, short of money and arms, managed to raise only five regiments. One of these, in which was collected some 400 of his most loyal supporters, was named the Royal Regiment of Guards and the command given to Lord Wentworth. His officers were chosen carefully from those who had served him well in the sorry circumstances of exile and whom he could fully trust. One of his captains was William Careless, or Carlos, who had had command of a regiment of horse in

1643, accompanied Charles throughout the action at Worcester and escorted him off the field under close pursuit. Knowing the neighbourhood well, it was he who guided the King through the forest of Boscobel and up into the branches of a great oak which, having been topped some three or four years before, had grown out thick and bushy. Fortified by a supply of bread, cheese and beer, the King slept soundly on the arm of his friend while soldiers beat the bushes below. At one point Careless's arm became so uncomfortable as to be useless and he was afraid that Charles would move suddenly and fall out of the tree, so he took his courage in his remaining hand and woke the King, terrified that he would cry out, and together they watched the activities of their pursuers below.

It fell to the Regiment to fight its first action against other Englishmen. It played a valiant part in the battle of the **Dunes** near **Dunkirk** in 1658. This was in effect the last battle of the Civil War, being fought between the adherents of the exiled king and the army of Cromwell with his French allies under the formidable leadership of Turenne. Alongside Scots and Irish regiments, the Regiment of Guards was under the command of Charles's brother, James, Duke of York, later to have a short and unhappy reign as James II. It took up a position high in the sand dunes between the seashore and the flat inlands. One company was sent forward to an outpost line, but the bulk of the

9

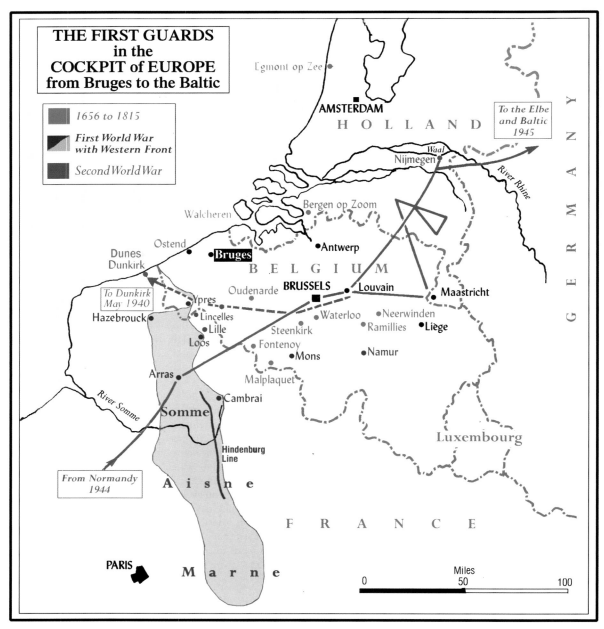

THE FIRST GUARDS
in the
COCKPIT of EUROPE
from Bruges to the Baltic

1656 to 1815

First World War
with Western Front

Second World War

To the Elbe
and Baltic
1945

To Dunkirk
May 1940

From Normandy
1944

body, some 400 strong, stood back behind the highest point in the dunes, where they could not easily see the progress of the fight. Very soon the Spanish and other allied troops were falling back under a fierce enemy assault. The Guards were invited to surrender but refused. 'We were posted here by the Duke of York and mean to hold our ground as long as we can' was the brave reply. Informed of the hopeless tactical situation, they remarked that they were not accustomed to believing their enemies, but two of the officers agreed to be led by a French officer to the top of the highest dune, from where they could see all too clearly the confusion and retreat of their comrades. They finally agreed to surrender provided that they

were not handed over to their English enemies or stripped of their clothing or possessions. These terms were scrupulously kept, and only a few days later they were released on half-ransom 'by which they fared much better than the men of other regiments'. Thus, early on, they won an immediate reputation for courage and steadfastness.

The Monarchy Restored

The 'Commonwealth' of Oliver Cromwell turned sour. As was to become so familiar in later revolutions across the world, the new regime turned out to be worse than that it had displaced. Cromwell was dictatorial and puritanical, and chose to dispense with parliament and exercise a military rule by major general. This provoked disgust in the populace, who decided that a king (under suitable control of course) could not possibly be worse and would very likely be better. After all, they were used to monarchs, not to military dictators, and abhorred standing armies. When Cromwell died in 1658 the way for restoration was open.

Royal Archer: the Golden Book of the Royal Guild of Archers of St Sebastian of Bruges, of which the exiled Charles II became a member.

In January 1660 General Monck (later to be Duke of Albemarle) raised a regiment across the Scottish border at Coldstream and marched to London. Charles II returned to England in May and was restored to the throne. One of his early commissions, dated 26 August 1660, confirmed the establishment of the Royal Regiment of Guards, which, however, for financial and political reasons, remained in Flanders as part of the garrison of Dunkirk. The regiment was brought up to 1200 strong, of whom 500 were buff-clad pikemen and 700 musketeers in red coats. The waiting time in Flanders was one of deprivation, hardship and sickness. There was little money or supplies, and in their desperation some soldiers were said to have resorted to highway robbery. However, this lean time lasted only until 1662, when the port was sold to the French for £385,000 ready money, of which Charles was short, as usual.

Meanwhile the King had decided that, for his own protection, there should also be a regiment of guards in England. On 23 November 1660, therefore, he commissioned Colonel John Russell to raise His Majesty's Foot Regiment of Guards, consisting of twelve companies, each of 100 men. The four senior companies in both regiments were rather larger than the others and

King CHARLES II
1630-1685

Founder of the
Regiment,
Restored Monarch,
'Father of the Nation'

Charles Stuart had a turbulent life, at a defining time of British history. His father, Charles I, had fought a bitter civil war with the forces of Parliament, which ended with his execution in 1649 and the exile of Charles and his brother James. The young King, however, made a further attempt to overthrow Oliver Cromwell in 1650, but was defeated, first at Dunbar and then at Worcester in 1651, after which battle he was forced again to flee, at one point taking refuge in an oak tree at Boscobel, while Roundhead troopers scoured the ground beneath. He made his way to Paris, then to Cologne, and eventually set up a ramshackle court in the Flemish city of Bruges.

It was there that in 1656 he formed a new regiment for his own protection, giving the commands to English supporters who had faithfully shared his trials. A similar regiment was raised at home on his restoration, the two being combined in 1665.

His reign, from 1660 to 1685, was full of incident. Political intrigue abounded, there were Catholic plots, the Great Plague and Great Fire of London, the Dutch wars and the growth of the navy. He founded the Royal Hospital at Chelsea.

'Good King Charles', though often vacillating and indecisive, emerged with an attractive reputation. He was easy and good-natured, and never lost the common touch. His queen provided him with no heir, but he saw action in a good many other bedrooms. His recognized mistresses numbered twelve and they provided him with the same number of acknowledged children, six of whom he made dukes. Unlike his Hanoverian successors, he got on with them all. He was not dubbed 'Father of the Nation' for nothing and indeed, centuries later, descendants of his were still to be found in his First Regiment of Guards.

See Fraser (Antonia)

named the King's, Colonel's, Lieutenant Colonel's and Major's companies.

Charles was determined that his original creation should not be disbanded, but when Wentworth's regiment was brought home there was bickering with Russell's officers, and Wentworth's companies were tactfully dispersed to garrisons in Berwick, Hull, Dover, the Channel Islands, Portsmouth, Cornwall and Windsor. In 1665, however, Wentworth died and on 16 March the two regiments were brought together under the command of Russell.[1] Now twenty-four companies strong, and in 1678 to be twenty-eight with the addition of four companies of grenadiers,[2] it became known from about 1685 as the First Regiment of Foot Guards. The senior company, on the right flank, became the Sovereign's personal company.

A musketeer of 1656: his cumbersome weapon was useful only at very short range.
Bob Marrion

Precedence, Organization and Double Rank

On 26 January 1661 the King signed a Royal Warrant which has been called 'the birth certificate of the British Army'. It established, in their original form, the regiments that were in due course to become the Grenadier and Coldstream Guards, and the Household Cavalry. The Scots Guards followed in 1666 in Scotland, joining the English army in 1686 and being dubbed 'The Kiddies' by the older regiments. The Coldstream had been fortunate. The last regiment of Cromwell's Commonwealth, it was about to be disbanded when called into action to suppress a wild rebellion that suddenly broke out in the City, thus proving itself indispensable and earning a reprieve.

Precedence was a tricky matter in view of the earlier origins of the Coldstream and Scots regiments, but the King determined that his own regiment should take first place. On 12 September 1666 he issued a Royal Warrant, setting down the order of precedence in the following terms: *First as to the Foot, that the Regiment of Guards takes place of all the Regiments.* Later this was further clarified by a similar Royal Warrant of

---

[1] Curiously, on the very day of Wentworth's death an order was signed to double the strength of Russell's regiment to twenty-four companies. When the two regiments were merged, however, the order was rescinded

[2] For a short time there were four battalions, each with one grenadier company. When the organization settled on three battalions, the number of grenadier companies was not reduced and the 1st Battalion had two

Pride of place: the memorial to Charles II in the Guildhall of the Archers, which he rented for his first headquarters.

February 1684 by which: *Concerning the Ranks of several Regiments of Foot, That Our Own Regiment of Guards takes place of all other Regiments of Foot.* The ruling provoked the Coldstream to adopt the motto of 'Nulli Secundus' – Second to None,[3] which sparked a rivalry between the two English regiments that has endured for three and a half centuries, and is certain to continue, to the great enjoyment of both parties.

From about 1672 companies of the First Guards would be formed from time to time into distinct battalions, to meet a particular need. Composite battalions, of companies from different regiments, would also be thrown together on occasion. The earliest example was the dispatch of such a force in 1676 to restore order in the colony of Virginia in America, returning two years later. From 1686 the battalion organization became more or less permanent.

The companies stationed in the capital suffered many deaths in the Great Plague of 1665, though encamped in Hyde Park as a precaution. They also gave their services in the Great Fire of the following year. Training was more realistic than might be supposed. In 1674 'On Saturday night, in one of the meadows at the foot of the long terrace below Windsor Castle, earthworks were thrown up to represent the city of Maastricht, which had recently been taken by the French. It was attacked by the Duke of Monmouth and the Duke of York; approaches were made, and all the formalities of a siege gone through.'[4]

In 1687 the regiments of Foot Guards received from the new King James II a distinction with regard to the rank of company officers. Captains were to hold the rank of lieutenant colonel in the Army and lieutenants were similarly to be captains.[5] This gave a welcome extra status to those officers, at no extra expense to the King as they did not receive the pay of the higher rank. It was also thought that His Majesty used the device to bolster the allegiance of his officers, which had been put under strain

Picked man of the infantry: a pikeman of 1656. Bob Marrion

---

[3] Grenadiers have preferred to further their cause by looser translations, such as 'Second to One' or 'Better than Nothing'

[4] Hamilton

[5] The privilege was to be extended to ensigns – ranking as lieutenants – following the exceptional performance of the regiments of Guards at Waterloo in 1815 – and did not fall out of use until the Cardwell reforms of 1871

THOMAS, Lord WENTWORTH
c 1613-1665

Loyal Servant to Charles II and Founding Colonel of the Royal Regiment of Guards in Bruges

*L*ord Wentworth, to whom Charles II entrusted the colonelcy of his newly raised regiment of Guards in Flanders, had been known to the King since the Civil War campaign of 1645-46 in south-west England. He then commanded a regiment of horse, of which Lord Hopton wrote to the Prince of Wales: 'Among them were gallant men but I cannot say they were exact upon duty'. Wentworth did not show himself to be a particularly successful commander; he appeared to be quarrelsome and rather too fond of the bottle – traits not uncommon in Cavalier circles.

He accompanied Charles in his unhappy campaign of 1650 and was present at the Battle of Worcester, escaping to France and subsequently joining his master in exile.

His father, Lord Cleveland, had been a more distinguished leader in the army of Charles I and the whole family were devoted Royalists. The many years of exile brought Charles II and Wentworth very close and the King clearly had full confidence in his loyalty. The reward for steadfastness in those hard times was the colonelcy.

Wentworth was described by Lloyd, a chronicler of most of the leading Royalists of the period, as a gentleman of a very strong constitution and admirable parts for 'contrivance, and especially for the dispatch of business, sleeping little and reading much; well acquainted with the affairs, interests, intrigues, the strengths and weakness of ports and garrisons, both of England and the neighbouring Continental powers'.

He brought his regiment home from Flanders in 1662 and continued to be indispensable to the King, serving in the Privy Council. He died in February 1665, in the midst of preparations for the Dutch war.

See Hamilton, Whitworth (2)

COLONEL
The Hon JOHN RUSSELL
1612-1687

Colonel of
His Majesty's
First Regiment of
Guards, later
First Regiment of
Foot Guards

*J*ohn Russell, son of the Earl of Bedford, was commissioned by the restored King Charles II to raise a new regiment of Guards in England in November 1660. Though Member of Parliament for Tavistock, he had long been an ardent Royalist and served as a colonel throughout the civil wars. From 1652 he became one of a secret band of loyalists names the *Sealed Knot*, who took part in no fewer than eight attempts to achieve the restoration of the monarchy. For his part in a rising in 1658 he was imprisoned in the Tower of London.

On the death of Lord Wentworth in 1665, Russell became Colonel of the new combined regiment of twenty-four companies. The appointment was disputed by the Duke of Richmond, one of Charles II's numerous illegitimate sons. The two fought a duel, much to the displeasure of the King, and Russell found himself back in the Tower for a few weeks, though consoled by knowing that the Duke was suffering the same punishment.

In 1675, when Russell had held the colonelcy for fifteen years, the Duke of Monmouth, who had acquitted himself well serving in the French armies, was anxious to take his place. The two negotiated an agreement, but James Duke of York was implacably opposed to the appointment and the King was eventually induced to withhold his sanction, though Monmouth was his favourite natural son. This no doubt fuelled Monmouth's hatred of James, which was to result in the rebellion of 1685.

In 1681 Russell was almost seventy years old and, not favouring the succession of the Catholic James, appeared to be losing the favour of the King. The time had come to pass on his colonelcy, and this he did to the nineteen-year-old Henry, Duke of Grafton, yet another of the King's progeny.

See Hamilton, Whitworth (2)

by his anti-Protestant measures.

A captaincy in the Regiment fetched around £1,000.[6] Pay for the rank was some fifty percent more than in the Line. Other officers of the Guards received higher pay in much the same proportion.

Action at Sea in the Dutch Wars

The shifting alliances of Europe drew England into war with the Dutch, a surprising antagonist in view of long-standing sympathy between the two nations, and indeed of the adoption of a Dutch monarch only a few years later. Naval rivalry was largely responsible and it was at sea that most of the action took place

It was customary, at the time, for the Admiralty to apply to the Commander-in-Chief for soldiers to serve as marines aboard ships of the Royal Navy. Three hundred of the First Guards took part in an action off Lowestoft in 1665, in which the Dutch were defeated. Several of the guardsmen, embarked in the *Royal Catherine*, drove off repeated attempts by the Dutch in the *Orange* to board. Eventually, after receiving several broadsides, she was forced to strike her colours. In 1667 Admiral Van Tromp, his broom lashed to the masthead to 'sweep the English from the seas', sailed boldly up the Thames, took Sheerness and penetrated the Medway as far as Chatham, burning and carrying off English ships. A company of the First Guards had been placed at Upnor Castle, and it gave the Dutch such a warm reception that they soon after retired down the river. Companies were constantly to be found on board ship or in coastal garrisons as the war continued. In May 1672 there was a major engagement at **Sole Bay** off Southwold, where The King's Company itself was embarked in the Duke of York's flagship, and in the following year another off the Dutch island of Texel.

Tangier 1680 – the First Battle Honour

Charles's queen, the Portuguese Princess Catherine of Braganza, was given the North African port of **Tangier** as part of her dowry. Men from the First Guards joined others from the Coldstream to form a composite force known as 'The King's Battalion' as part of the garrison, which was constantly under attack from the native Moors. 'Colonel Sackville, on riding up to the King's battalion, spoke to them some inspiriting words before going into

---

[6] Well over £100,000 at 2005 values

action, addressing them as "My good fellows". He told them that as Guardsmen much was expected of them... He doubted not but that they would overcome the rude and undisciplined attacks of the enemy, gain for themselves the favour of the king and the love of their country, as well as secure to themselves a glorious and everlasting fame, and the good reputation of all persons.[7] They drove back the encroaching Moors from trench to trench, on 20 September the musketeers emptying three or four collars of bandoliers. Various 'small affairs' continued through the following month and a major assault was launched on 27 October, the Moors being driven off at all points and the battalion taking two of their guns. Tangier became the first regimental battle honour, though Charles eventually decided that the port was not worth the effort and expense of defending, and abandoned it in 1684, the garrison being brought home.

[7] Hamilton

At the Tower of London: officers, drummers, pikemen and musketeers of the First Regiment of Guards.
Reginald Wymer

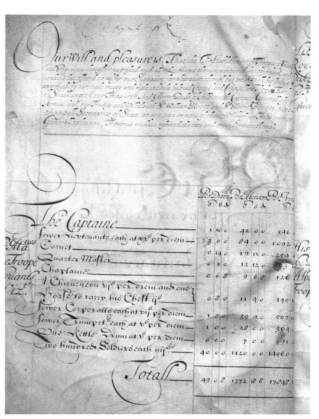

Our Will and pleasure: Charles II's warrant of 1660 giving formal 'Establishment of Troopes of Guardes and Regiments', with the first list of expenses and his signature of 26 January 1661 at the head.

A Crisis of Loyalty[8]

James II, Monmouth and Sedgemoor

The accession as King James II of the Duke of York, brother to Charles II, immediately provoked a rebellion by the Duke of Monmouth. Queen Catherine had not borne Charles an heir, but Monmouth (otherwise James Crofts) was the favourite of his many irregular sons and well liked in the country. He expected to succeed his father and took violent exception (as did many others) to the Catholic convictions of his uncle. He also, on several occasions, had coveted the colonelcy of the First Regiment of Guards, but had been prevented by James.

In June 1685 Monmouth landed at Lyme Regis in Dorset and proceeded to drum up support in the west. After a sharp engagement at Norton St Philip, involving a grenadier company of the First Guards and a body of Horse Grenadiers, he was confronted and beaten by the King's army at Sedgemoor in Somerset on 6 July. Two battalions of the Regiment were present, placed rather surprisingly in the centre of the line under command of their new young colonel, the nineteen-year-old Duke of Grafton, another of the King's numerous unofficial sons. Dumbarton's regiment, later First of the Line, was stationed on the right.

The victory was largely attributed to the talents of John Churchill, later to be Duke of Marlborough. Monmouth attempted to force the line with cavalry, but was unexpectedly checked by a dyke running across his front. His horsemen were shot to pieces by the guardsmen and their comrades, standing firm in line on the other bank. This was followed by a cannonade by Monmouth, which did considerable execution in the infantry ranks until silenced by guns brought up from the rear. The battalions then advanced across the stream and routed the rebels, who were armed largely with scythes, pitchforks and miners' picks. The First Guards suffered some seventy casualties; the number of dead among these was not recorded.

Monmouth was taken prisoner and executed on Tower Hill, the nervous headsman taking several blows, and some desperate butchery with a knife, to finish the job. The failure of the rebellion provoked a hideous revenge. Judge Jeffreys held his notorious 'Bloody Assize' in the west, sentencing great numbers of Monmouth's unlucky

adherents to execution or transportation to the colonies. By contrast, in the twentieth century the name of his brother's descendant[9] was to re-appear in the annals of the Grenadier Guards in the most honourable and distinguished circumstances.

William of Orange Takes the Field

It would be difficult in the twenty-first century to appreciate the passions roused by religious differences had they not been only too evident in the Northern Ireland of very recent times. In the seventeenth century Roman Catholics were widely viewed with suspicion and a number of loyal officers and soldiers in the First Guards were compelled to resign for their religious convictions alone.

Hapless king: the unpopular James II, though not deserted by his Guards, was forced to abandon his throne.

With the Catholic James, however, the boot moved smartly to the other foot. His reign became increasingly turbulent and difficult, and he quickly lost the confidence of most of his countrymen. This reached such a point that the Dutch Prince William of Orange who was married to Mary, daughter of James II[10], was invited to descend upon England and turn out the tiresome monarch.

William was already a renowned soldier and conducted his campaign with a great deal more skill than had the luckless Monmouth. In November 1688 he landed at Torbay in Devon. James's army, including two battalions of the First Guards, moved to Salisbury to check him. At this point many of the King's remaining adherents decided that his cause was lost and that the whole nation was ready to rise in defence of the Protestant religion. Churchill deserted, taking with him the young Grafton, Colonel of the First Guards.

This placed his regiment in a dreadful dilemma. They had sworn allegiance to James (as had Grafton himself). They had often served under his leadership, both in the field and at sea, since the early days in Bruges and felt bound to keep their word. They had bled for him at Sedgemoor. In 1686 he had honoured his Guards with a special review to celebrate his birthday, before going off on a wolf hunt.

---

[8] See Annex A 'Kings, Queens and Colonels'
[9] General the Lord Jeffreys
[10] Not, as schoolboys rather liked to suppose, the offspring of Charles II and Nell Gwynn with her orange basket

The King quickly appointed a new colonel, the Roman Catholic Earl of Lichfield (by chance brother-in-law to Grafton). The two battalions were drawn back to the outskirts of London, the third being already there, and awaited the outcome with trepidation. But at last, showing good sense, James concluded that he was lost. He instructed his Guards not to resist William and disappeared to France. Lichfield, after a brief three weeks as Colonel, went with him. By great good fortune blood had not been spilt.

The game was not quite over. James, encouraged by the French, made another attempt in the following year, this time in Ireland. William met him there, and on 1 July 1690 destroyed him at the Battle of the Boyne. The story of that epic encounter has echoed down through the centuries in Irish memories, and 300 years later Grenadiers were to be familiar with the huge murals in Belfast and Londonderry by which the hardline Protestants remembered 'King Billy' and taunted their Catholic opponents. The First Guards, however, were not at the Boyne. They had been carefully left behind.

Early Days under William III

Not a single member of the First Guards took part in the coronation of their new king and several senior officers were changed. They can hardly have been surprised not to enjoy his immediate confidence. Many had been ashamed

Uncertain colonel: the Duke of Grafton led his men bravely at Sedgemoor, but later went over to William of Orange without taking his regiment with him.

of the defection of Grafton without their consent and disgusted by the ease with which he turned up again at their head, re-appointed by William as Colonel. William might well have been nervous that, if the tide of battle had moved against him in Ireland, the Guards would return to their earlier allegiance. It was perhaps fortunate that he did not at once disband this regiment, which had been formed and maintained for the protection of the Stuarts. He did not do so, recognizing perhaps that their fighting qualities were likely to be useful to him. But for a time he supplanted them in the capital with his own Dutch Guards and dispersed the battalions to Gravesend, Portsmouth and Oxford, to their chagrin and annoyance. There was muttering in dark corners. And they were not the only ones. A visitor to London, Reresby, narrated how 'in coming to town in January, he was at once struck by the great change. He finds that, instead of English Guards – who, both from their personal appearance and their gallantry, were an ornament to the place – nothing but streets swarming with ill-favoured and ill-accoutred Dutchmen, and other strangers of the prince's army; and yet the people seem well pleased with their deliverers.'[11]

William soon had second thoughts about the reliability of Grafton. In 1690 the Duke returned to his first love, the

[11] Hamilton

Sedgemoor 1685: on these bloody fields the poorly armed rebels of Monmouth were cut to pieces. He himself was destined for a messy execution. *Adrian Amber*

On the Boyne 1690: here William III finally put paid to the ambitions of James II, having cautiously left his English Guards behind.

KING WILLIAM III.
Crossing the Boyne July 1st 1690.

navy, in command of a frigate, and was replaced as Colonel by Henry Sidney, later Earl of Romney, who remained in the post until 1704, with a short interruption between 1691 and 1693 when occupied with the government of Ireland. He was temporarily succeeded in the colonelcy by the Dutch Duke of Schomberg, who was killed in action leading a British force against the French in Italy.

King William's Wars 1691-1697

But, after all, it did not take the guardsmen long to recognize that they had in William a better king, and an incomparably better general, than James. In no time they were fighting his battles with as much gusto as ever. Between 1691 and 1697 they were constantly in Flanders, pitted once more against their traditional enemy, the French.

The **2nd Battalion** (Lt Col Lenthal Warcup)[12] particularly distinguished itself at **Steenkirk** in 1692. On 3 August the battalion, in nine companies (one of grenadiers), each 100 strong, was ordered with a battalion of Dutch Guards to lead a formation of six battalions in an assault on a powerful French force firmly entrenched in their own camp. The battalion advanced with such determination, and so far, as

to capture one of the enemy batteries in the camp, which the French were obliged to abandon. 'Colonel Warcup, in command, particularly distinguished himself and gave the battery in charge to a sergeant who would have brought it off the field had not the French led away their horses.' The attack was succeeding at all points when the French General Boufflers appeared on the right flank with a fresh and greatly superior force, who so outnumbered the allies (by more than four to one) that the advance was checked. The contest continued with a fierce artillery duel. King William formed his battalions into line and over a period of two hours they received the charge of large bodies of the enemy, pouring volley after volley into them, but the continued advance of the French reinforcements, and the approach of darkness, induced him gradually to withdraw his troops. The return to camp was conducted in an orderly manner, the grenadiers of the army bringing up the rear.

The 2nd Battalion lost very heavily, having almost 400 casualties, and were withdrawn from the field army for the rest of the campaign. Colonel Warcup and four captains of companies were among the dead. There was much criticism in the army for the failure of the Dutch General Solmes, commanding supporting troops, to come to the aid of the beleaguered battalions. He hated his allies and was heard to remark, 'Damn the English; if they are so fond of fighting, let them have a bellyful.' But in this first action the battalion established a tremendous reputation for the determination of the attack and the weight of its musketry fire. As the battle was not counted a victory, however, it was not awarded to any regiment as a battle honour, though well deserved by the First Guards.

As part of a greatly outnumbered force, the **1st Battalion** (Lt Col Sir Charles O'Hara) defended the village of **Neerwinden** near Landen in 1693, and in June 1694 a composite battalion of Guards took part in a commando-style raid on the port of **Brest**, which unhappily failed, largely, it was thought, because of treachery. The French, evidently forewarned and well prepared, repelled the attack with resolution.

In 1695 the Regiment won a second battle honour emblazoned on its Colours at **Namur**, a formidable fortress on the River Meuse. Both 1st and 2nd Battalions were engaged. William besieged and took the town in an operation where assaults were carried out with great

---

[12] Two other officers of the battalion were splendidly named Ventris Columbine and Alway Sergeant

18

Steenkirk 1692: the first battle of the 2nd Battalion, which was cursed by the Dutch general for its enthusiasm. *Richard Simkin*

gallantry and distinction. On 18 July, preceded by the grenadier companies and fusiliers carrying fascines,[13] the two Guards brigades advanced steadily with shouldered arms across half a mile of flat, open country, against the murderous fire of the French defenders. On reaching the first line of palisades, they thrust their flintlocks through, fired a volley and then flung themselves over the palisades and stormed the defences. 'The British Guards had now effectively performed all that was expected of them; but they were flushed with success, and eager to advance still further against the enemy's works. Having gained the first covered way, they could not be restrained; another covered way was in their front, also protected by palisades; on they went in their victorious career, and, after a short dispute, gained possession of this second line also, forcing the enemy in consternation to retire. Many of the Guards then pursued the enemy sword in hand amongst the forts scattered on the brow of the hill; and the most forward advanced to the very counterscarp of the town, opposite the Porte de Fer, killing the enemy at their palisades. Several Guardsmen were,

The palisades of Namur 1695: the Guards, flushed with success, making one of several violent attacks. *Faulkner's Celebrated Cigarettes*

however, here made prisoners, by advancing too far; others pursued, and made great slaughter of the French....'[14] The Guards brigades had 584 casualties, including some forty prisoners, and sixteen officers of the First Guards.

Another violent attack, made chiefly by grenadiers of the army, was made on 30 August, and a few days later the fortress capitulated.

By the time Queen Anne (another daughter of James II) came to the throne in 1702, the 'Glorious Revolution' of William and Mary had firmly taken root and the First Guards had fully re-established their reputation. Thereafter no difficulties of allegiance were to trouble either regiment or monarch, and the special place of the First Regiment of Guards in service to the sovereign was to be strengthened as the centuries rolled on.

Principal sources: Hamilton, Whitworth (2), Fraser (1), Paget, Regiment

---

[13] Bundles of sticks for crossing ditches
[14] Hamilton

THE SOVEREIGN'S OWN COMPANY

The particular attachment of the Regiment to the person of the sovereign takes its closest form in the Sovereign's Company. On the formation of the Regiment under Lord Wentworth in 1656, King Charles II reserved to himself the command of the First Company, which was designated the 'King's Own Company'. The executive command of the company was entrusted to the 'Captain Lieutenant', literally, the officer lieu tenant or 'taking the place' of the Captain, who was the King himself. When a second regiment was formed under Colonel John Russell, the same arrangement was made, and thus there was a 'King's Own Company' with each

regiment until the two were amalgamated in 1665.

It was not long, however, before the 'Captain Lieutenant' was known as 'The Captain', and so he has been described ever since. In the 1st Battalion today, 'The Captain' means 'The Captain of the Queen's Company' and no other, despite his actual military rank of major. Except where impracticable in wartime, appointments as Captain are approved personally by the monarch. His deputy is the 'Second Captain'. Past and present officers of the Queen's Company have their own dining club.

This personal attachment has occasionally had unforeseen results. The Captain of the King's

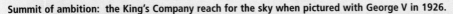

Summit of ambition: the King's Company reach for the sky when pictured with George V in 1926.

Company at the time of Edward VIII's abdication in 1936 was said to have declared that he would follow his monarch into exile and take the entire company with him. The immediate accession of George VI effectively stymied this improbable outcome.

The tallest men are normally chosen for the Sovereign's Company, though the height standard has varied over the years in response to the demands and successes of recruiting. Since 1908, the average height has varied between 6 ft 1in and 6 ft 4 in, the lowest being in 1980 and 1986, and the highest in the Tercentenary year of 1956.

One of the early ensigns was John Churchill, later Duke of Marlborough. When battalions were regularly established, the company became the senior one of the 1st Battalion and stood on the right of the line.[1] The Sovereign's Company has its own Colour, also named the Royal Standard of the Regiment, which is distinct from the Colours of the 1st Battalion.

Caped for a Queen: the new Colonel-in-Chief with her company shortly after her accession to the throne in 1952.

Three cheers: a rousing acclamation for Her Majesty in 2003.

[1] In the very earliest days it was not a grenadier company, but it probably became one before the end of the eighteenth century. The Regiment had four such companies, of which two were in the 1st Battalion and one in each of the others. In lists for the 1st Battalion going to war in 1806 and 1808 Hamilton shows 'Kings, Grenadier, No 3 to 10, two Light Infantry', a total of twelve companies. The other battalions had only ten, one grenadier, one light and eight battalion companies. In his three volumes Hamilton very rarely makes specific mention of the Sovereign's Company

company to guard the coffin until the lying-in-state. The duty of the bearer party is in the most literal way a heavy one and carries responsibility of a very high order. The camp colour belonging to the company is buried with the sovereign.

The company is reviewed by the monarch from time to time. Since the Second World War the Queen's Company has been reviewed by Her Majesty at intervals of ten to twelve years. Each review has provided the occasion for a major parade, after which past captains and company sergeant majors of the company have been presented to her.

In all other respects the Sovereign's Company takes its place in the order of battle of the 1st Battalion. Indeed it is said that a good Queen's Company means a good 1st Battalion.

The Colour passes: the Queen's review at Windsor Castle in 2003.

The Sovereign's Company is on duty at Westminster Abbey during a coronation, and on 11 November 1920 it was men of the King's Company who mounted guard upon the body of the Unknown Soldier, also at the Abbey.

It is, however, the funeral of a monarch with which it is now most closely associated and where it comes most prominently to public attention. Nowhere is its particular duty to the King or Queen more personal and more highly charged. It is the privilege of the

Down the Champs Elysées: a party of the Queen's Company lead the parade in Paris to mark the centenary of the _Entente Cordiale_ with France in 2004.

Chapter Two

THE EIGHTEENTH CENTURY
1702-1793

The Marlborough Wars

The 18th Century saw a succession of campaigns, almost invariably against the French, in which the First Guards won new renown.

The first engagement of the century, however, was fought against Spain, as an abortive raid on **Cadiz** in 1702, in which a composite battalion of Guards took part. It was followed by action at **Gibraltar**, which had been taken from the Spaniards in 1704 by Admiral Rooke. Two hundred of the First Guards were in a composite battalion as part of the garrison. The former occupants made a determined attempt to recover their property in 1705, but were repulsed, and a new battle honour was emblazoned on the Colours. A foray into Spain was made in the following year, when Barcelona was taken, but two years later the entire British force was forced to surrender

at Almanza. A further attempt on Gibraltar, also while the First Guards were present, was made by the Spaniards in 1727, and repulsed.

The War of the Spanish Succession 1702-14

The year of 1704 marked the first of a series of battles in which the Duke of Marlborough (who became Colonel of the First Guards that year) made an undying reputation. Until 1708 the **1st Battalion** (Maj Gen Henry Withers[1]) was the sole representative of the Foot Guards and it remained under his command throughout.

Louis XIV was attempting to decide the succession to the throne of Spain and thereby to increase the power of

[1] Withers also commanded a brigade of the Line

Forlorn hope: grenadiers lead the assault on Schellenberg – only a quarter of them emerged. *Reginald Wymer*

FIELD MARSHAL

JOHN CHURCHILL,
Duke of MARLBOROUGH

KG *1650-1722*

Ensign of the
King's Company,
Victor of Blenheim,
Colonel of the
Regiment

John Churchill, Duke of Marlborough, was incomparably the greatest soldier to have served in the ranks of the First Guards.

Born in 1650, the eldest son of Sir Winston Churchill, whose descendant of the same name was to be a dominating figure of the twentieth century, he quickly entered the profession of arms, and in the best possible way. He became ensign of the King's Company in the First Guards in 1667 and served as a volunteer in Tangier in the following year. In 1672 he was embarked with his company in the Duke of York's flagship at Sole Bay, an indecisive though bloody action against the Dutch. Thereafter, using his impeccable connections at court, he quickly rose to a colonelcy in the Line, gained further experience in the field against the French and was soon marked out for high command.

In 1685 he played the leading part in the suppression of the Duke of Monmouth's rebellion, two battalions of the First Guards coming under his command at Sedgemoor. James II rewarded him with the appointment of lieutenant general, which virtually gave him the chief command of the army.

But in 1688, despairing of the King's ability to hold the confidence of his people, he deserted him and transferred his allegiance to Prince William of Orange, shortly to relieve James of his throne. Created Earl of Marlborough, he fought successfully for William in Ireland. But the King was jealous of his military talents and wary of his loyalties. He fell out of favour and for a short time was imprisoned in the Tower of London.

His time was to come, however, with the accession of Queen Anne in 1702. Between 1702 and 1711, by which time he was over sixty, though still up to the rigours of hard campaigning, he conducted a series of resounding operations against the French. His famous victories of Blenheim 1704, Ramillies 1706, Oudenarde 1708 and Malplaquet 1709 were destined to be remembered by generations of schoolboys as the 'history telephone number', BROM 4689.

He was Colonel of the First Guards from 1704 until his death in 1722, with a short interval between 1712 and 1714. He built Blenheim Palace in Oxfordshire.

He lost favour again through the plotting of his political enemies, though he returned to advise King George I on meeting the 1715 rebellion of James II's son, the Old Pretender.

Marlborough was undoubtedly an opportunist, and often cunning and devious. He went hard in pursuit of honours, social position and wealth – which he was frugal, not to say mean, in dispensing. He was certainly admired, though 'the flame of his spirit served for light, not warmth'.

But to his men he was much more. 'He never fought a battle he did not win, nor besieged a town he did not take', wrote an early biographer. He was brave to a fault, and more than once came close to being killed. He was energetic and tireless, a fine strategist, a brilliant tactician and a first-rate administrator. His judgement was flawless. One of his soldiers, waiting to make an assault ordered by his own commander, which he felt to be ill-advised, wished earnestly that 'the Duke might take a nearer view of the thing'. To his great relief up he rode, quite alone 'and posted himself a little to the right of my company of grenadiers... It is quite impossible for me to express the joy which the sight of this man gave me at this very critical moment...He stayed only three or four minutes and then rode back. We were in pain for him while he stayed, lest the enemy might have discovered him, and fired at him; in which case they could not well have missed him. He had not been longer from us, than he stayed, when orders came for us to retire... inasmuch that there was not a single man of all the grenadiers hurt.'

See Chandler (1)

A scrambling over: crossing the Nebel stream en route for Blenheim. *C du Bosch, After Laguerre*

France on the continent. The war saw the 'Grand Alliance' of Britain, Holland and the Holy Roman Empire (Austria) pitted against France and Bavaria. The campaign began with the famous march from the Low Countries to the Danube, where the French hoped to crush Austria. In July they came up against the **Schellenberg** hill fort, overlooking **Donauwörth** on the Danube. It was a formidable obstacle, and well defended by Bavarians, allies of France. Marlborough decided that an attack could not be delayed without placing later success at risk. The troops, who had only just completed a forced march of sixteen hours, had to assault uphill, cross ditches and storm the breastworks behind them, all the time under the direct fire of cannon. The spearhead, the 'forlorn hope', in the most

Schellenberg: close action at the trenches. *Faulkner's Celebrated Cigarettes*

dangerous position, was found by the grenadier company of the First Guards. Every soldier, beside his musket, carried a fascine to help him across the ditches. The musket, carried over the right arm, could not be used while the fascines occupied the left. A steady advance began just before six o'clock in the evening. The enemy batteries inflicted heavy casualties, but the lines moved on. A short distance from the breastworks heavy musketry fire at a few yards range tore great gaps in the advancing infantry and the Bavarians came tearing out in counter-attack. The First Guards lost all their senior officers and about half their strength. The grenadier company of eighty-two men emerged with only twenty-three. But they re-formed, faced the counter-attack and drove the Bavarians back to their trenches.

About to lay the myth of French invincibility: approaching the burning battlefield of Blenheim. *Richard Simkin*

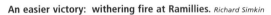

An easier victory: withering fire at Ramillies. *Richard Simkin*

For over an hour desperate hand-to-hand fighting continued on the parapets, but eventually the first attempt failed. It was not until Marlborough had launched two further assaults that the combined efforts of the Allies prevailed. Unable to escape across the river, three-quarters of the French army were destroyed.

James Deane, a 'private sentinel' of the First Guards, paid his opponents due respect: 'But no sooner did our Forlorn Hope appear but the enemy did throw in their volleys of cannon balls and small shot among them and made a brave defence and a bold resistance against us as brave loyal-hearted gentlemen soldiers ought to for their prince and country ...'[2]

Six weeks later, on 13 August, came Marlborough's greatest victory at **Blenheim**. The First Guards were normally held in reserve, under his personal control, but on this occasion he launched them in the open with four battalions of the Line against a position at Blenheim strongly defended by elite French troops. Twice they assaulted with great gallantry and, while unable to penetrate the defences, accomplished what was required of them by preparing the way for the cavalry, which broke through and inflicted a crushing defeat on the French. The casualties of 12,000 were very high, but the enemy lost 40,000, besides 100 guns and 300 colours and standards. The battle put paid to the myth that the French were invincible.

The First Guards marched back to Mainz, where they embarked in barges and sailed down the Rhine to the Netherlands. In the following January 120 pikemen of the Guards regiments bore the captured Colours past Queen Anne in St James's Park, on the way to laying-up in Westminster Abbey.

The remaining campaigns took place in the Low Countries where 'it was undoubtedly the superior

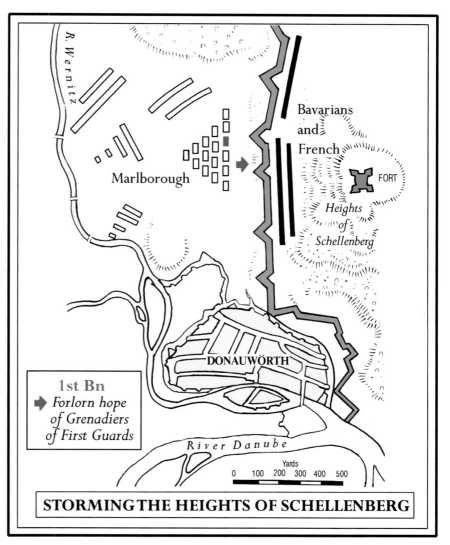

1st Bn
➡ *Forlorn hope of Grenadiers of First Guards*

STORMING THE HEIGHTS OF SCHELLENBERG

discipline and musketry of the British infantry that made possible the great cavalry break-throughs of the day, though the battles became ever more bloody until the holocaust in the woods at Malplaquet called in question the continuing purpose of Marlborough's strategy'.[3]

At **Ramillies**, in May 1706, the enemy suffered great loss in men and equipment for little on the Allied side. The great encounter battle of **Oudenarde** followed in July 1708. 'As the evening drew on the contest here also became very severe, and the infantry after a hard struggle drove the enemy from hedge to hedge. After a time, the brigade of Guards and two other brigades, in advancing upon the French, received their fire without it

[2] Holmes (Richard), from Chandler (2)
[3] Whitworth (2)

A dreadfully hard engagement: Malplaquet cost the victors more than the enemy. *Richard Simkin*

doing much damage, upon which the Guards returned a murderous volley into the enemy's ranks, causing them to turn and retreat from the field.[4] Deane (now a sergeant) wrote how 'two battalions of the Guards, supported by two British brigades, advanced and put the enemy to the right-about by fire, having received theirs without much damage'.[5] Only two officers were killed, but the casualties among the men, though the number was not recorded, were reported as severe. **Malplaquet**, in September 1709, was a dreadfully hard engagement, the battalions assaulting entrenched positions in wooded country. The allied army of 93,000 lost 18,000, more than those incurred by the defeated enemy.

The First Guards were also heavily involved in the sieges of Ghent, Tournai, Mons and Lille. It was at **Lille** in 1708 that Sergeant William Lettler was one of a party of five who volunteered to release the

The drawbridge at Lille: William Lettler hacks away at the chains. *Faulkner's Celebrated Cigarettes*

chains of a drawbridge spanning part of the works. This was no small order, the city being one of the most elaborate and formidable of all the fortified towns in an age when the science of such defences was at its peak. They swam across the ditch under a galling fire and three of the party were killed, but Lettler, hacking away at the chains with an axe while bullets parted his hair, succeeded in his task and enabled the troops to charge across the bridge and take the town. For his gallantry he was commissioned, and eventually he rose to be captain and lieutenant colonel of a company of grenadiers

In 1712 the Duke of Marlborough temporarily fell out of favour and for two years his colonelcy was given to James Butler, Duke of Ormond.

[4] Hamilton
[5] Deane

The House of Hanover

When Queen Anne died in 1714, all her seventeen children had pre-deceased her. Her cousin the Elector of Hanover, descended from the sister of Charles I, came to the throne as George I. He introduced several reforms into the army, including annual inspections, and attempted to check the worst abuses, such as officers drawing their pay but seldom appearing for duty. Britain, however, paid a price for a German monarch, who never in fact managed to learn English, and in succeeding years her armies were often to be embroiled in defence of Hanoverian rather than British interests. In 1714 the Duke of Marlborough resumed his colonelcy, being succeeded in turn by Earl Cadogan (1722-26), Sir Charles Wills (1726-42) and the Duke of Cumberland (1742-57). The Regiment was not called upon to suppress the '15 Jacobite Rebellion of the 'Old Pretender', son of James II.

In 1727 George II succeeded his father and times became quieter. The First Guards continued their royal duties in London, sending detachments to Hampton Court and Windsor from time to time. There being no police force, they were also often employed in the preservation of order. This included guarding criminals at the courts, assisting customs officers to prevent smuggling and checking poaching in the royal preserves, including Enfield Chase. In addition 'a guard of 100 men, under a captain and lieutenant-colonel, a lieutenant and an ensign, was always furnished to the king's theatre in the Haymarket whenever balls were given there, when, amongst other orders the sentries received, was one not to permit any persons whatsoever to enter the said theatre in habits worn by the clergy.'[6]

Even the guardsmen did not always defer to royalty. They were so disgusted with the scruffy appearance of the king's sister that they refused to lower their Colours to her.

It seems that in December 1739 'six regiments of marines were to be raised, and 120 corporals and privates were ordered to be drafted from the Guards to be made sergeants in them'.[7] That they could supply so many for promotion was a clear indication of the high standard of training given to the rank and file.

[6] Hamilton
[7] McNair

Grenades flying: grenadiers in action at Fontenoy. *Richard Simkin*

On several occasions there was more serious work to be done. Even at the coronation of George III in 1760 the crowd pressed so hard that the Foot Guards had to get to work with musket and bayonet. Companies were called out to subdue rioters in the docks and elsewhere. A show of force usually had the desired effect, but sometimes weapons had to be used. The Gordon riots of 1780 were serious enough for sharp measures and the 3rd Battalion was compelled to fire volleys on a huge mob outside the Bank of England[8] in order to restore calm to the capital. Three hundred were killed.

The War of the Austrian Succession 1740-48

War with France resumed in 1740 and in 1742 an expeditionary force, including a Guards brigade, was sent to the Continent. In the same year the Duke of Cumberland became Colonel. At **Dettingen**, on 27 June 1743, the army was under the personal command of George II. It was the last time a British monarch led his forces in the field, which he did with great courage and rather less skill. As part of the infantry of an English, Hanoverian and Hessian force, the **1st Battalion** (Lt Col Charles Russell) was at first in reserve, but later it contained an assault, counter-charged and helped to drive the French in retreat across the River Main and beyond the Rhine.

The Battle of **Fontenoy**, on 11 May 1745, was a more famous engagement although, not being counted a victory, it was not entered as a regimental battle honour, as it certainly should have been. The twenty-five-year-old Duke of Cumberland had been given the command by his father, with an Austrian deputy aged seventy-three. It was a most bloody engagement, which, however, supplied the supreme example of the good manners that sometimes distinguished these brutal proceedings. The British infantry, with the 1st Battalion of the First Guards properly placed on the right of the Guards brigade, advanced towards a much stronger body of French deployed unseen behind a ridge. Great gaps were torn in the line by cannon fire and on breasting the ridge they found, directly to their front thirty yards away,

A notable Colonel of the Regiment: Field Marshal Earl Ligonier had a remarkable career and became Commander-in-Chief. *Late 18th/early 19th century school*

four battalions of French Guards, their opposite numbers. The situation was later to be mirrored in a striking way by the attack of the French Imperial Guard at Waterloo, and happily on both occasions the honours went to the British.

The Captain of the King's Company, Lord Charles Hay, stepped forward and doffed his hat. He pulled out a flask, raised it and drank a toast to his astonished opponents. 'Gentlemen of the French Guard', he said in French, 'I hope that you will wait for us today, and not swim the Scheldt as you swam the Main at Dettingen.' Then he

---

[8] The Bank Picquet (or Guard) was mounted permanently thereafter until 1973

turned to his own company and said, 'Men of the King's Company, these are the French Guards and I hope you are going to beat them today.' The company gave a hurrah, and after what was described as a half-hearted cheer in response, French commands rang out. 'For what we are about to receive, may the Lord make us truly thankful' muttered a guardsman. The French, shaken no doubt by such a show of confidence, released a ragged and ineffectual volley, mostly firing too high. The First Guards marched forward and delivered volley after volley, six platoons at a time, at point-blank range, the officers tapping down the musket muzzles to avoid the mistake made by the French. Their opponents were destroyed in a matter of minutes.

The British infantry moved right forward into the enemy camp, but their allies failed to come up in support and finish the job. The French Life Guards charged repeatedly and for three hours the guardsmen stood firm against them. But the enemy continued to reinforce and finally the British were forced to withdraw, the Guards brigade acting as rearguard, though by then they had lost half their strength.

In July 1745 came the **'45 Jacobite Rebellion**. Charles Stuart, the 'Young Pretender' and popularly remembered as 'Bonnie Prince Charlie', was the son of the 'Old Pretender', whose own rebellion had failed in 1715, and grandson of James II. He landed in Scotland, gathered up support and, having defeated the English at Prestonpans, marched boldly into England. The grenadier companies of the Guards battalions in London assembled hurriedly to defend the capital, while the Guards brigade in Flanders was quickly ordered home. Charles's nerve failed him and, having advanced as far as Derby, he began to retrace his steps. Cumberland went in pursuit with a force of cavalry supplemented by a scratch body of mounted volunteers, including 400 of the Foot Guards. These returned after relieving Carlisle, but Cumberland pressed on into Scotland, where on 16 April 1746 he crushed the Jacobite threat for good at Culloden Moor. To their great disappointment, he was without the benefit of his guardsmen. The best that could be done by the First Guards was to stage reconstructions of the battle in Hyde Park for the edification and amusement of the Londoners.

In the following year Cumberland returned to Flanders with a fresh Guards brigade, which included the 2nd Battalion of each regiment, and in 1748 the war

Grenadier Gallery

FIELD MARSHAL

HRH WILLIAM AUGUSTUS, Duke of CUMBERLAND
KG *1721-1765*

Colonel of the Regiment, Captain-General of the Army, Scourge of the Jacobites

William Augustus, Duke of Cumberland, was a grandson of George I. The King remained a German all his life and was barely able to converse in his adopted tongue. Cumberland did rather better than that, but was Germanic by nature and a martinet. He took no care that orders should be 'softened by gentle persuasive arguments by which a gentleman, particularly those of a British constitution, must be governed'. But as the last Captain-General of the army he showed understanding, energy and good sense by the very necessary reforms he introduced.

He was Colonel of the First Guards from 1742 to 1757 and was quick to see the value of using their non-commissioned officers to instil proper military standards into other parts of the army. He made much use of them as a cadre for the Highland regiments raised at the time of the '45 rebellion and also for the Royal American Regiment.

Cumberland was advanced swiftly to high rank, being a major-general at only twenty-one, but showed plenty of aptitude. He performed well at Dettingen, where he was wounded in the leg, and was in command at Fontenoy, it being generally agreed that the disappointing result of that battle was attributable to his Dutch allies rather than to himself.

His enduring reputation was, however, to be forged by the barbarity of his army after defeating the Jacobite rebels at Culloden. He is still known as 'Butcher' Cumberland. However, largely through the efforts of his Grenadier biographer, it is now clear that he did everything in his power, by the rough standards of his time, to curb such excesses, and that the Jacobite claim that he organized systematic reprisals was a false one.

See Whitworth (3)

Cool courtesy at Fontenoy: two views of the famous incident, one showing the King's Company as a battalion company and the other as a grenadier company – which version is correct is not certain. *Richard Simkin (above), Reginald Wymer (below)*

March of the Guards at Finchley in 1745: an unflattering depiction by Hogarth.

ended and they came home. Before then, however, the 3rd Battalion had an adventure in the form of an abortive raid on **Port L'Orient**. Encountering no resistance, the soldiers burned and pillaged enthusiastically before an uncomfortable journey home, 'exposed to a very severe gale off Dungeness, which committed great havoc both amongst the ships and the arms and accoutrements of the men on board'.[9]

In 1750 the Horse Guards building, where the Commander-in-Chief and the Secretary of War resided, was re-designed. It was opened by the King in the following year and is still to be seen very much as it appeared then.

The Seven Years War 1756-63

This was the war best remembered for splendid feats of British arms in Canada, where Wolfe took Quebec, and in India, where Clive triumphed. The French were effectively subdued and two enormous dominions added to the British Empire. The First Guards did not campaign in those parts, but there was work for the 2nd Battalion in the British contingent led by the Marquis of Granby, marching and counter-marching in northern Germany with their allies against superior French forces. The Guards brigade in which they served was commanded by a Coldstreamer with the resounding name of Julius Caesar. In 1761 the three grenadier companies were drawn together into a fourth battalion of the brigade, a practice which was often to be repeated in subsequent years.

In September 1758 there was a disastrous raid on the French port of **St Malo**. The rearguard of four companies of the First Guards, together with the grenadier companies of all three regiments, was cut off by superior enemy forces and fought a gallant running battle among the sandhills while covering the re-embarkation at **St Cast**. They had no redoubts for protection and the struggle at close quarters masked the gunfire of supporting ships. Eventually, out of ammunition, and having lost half their number killed or wounded, they were compelled to surrender.

In 1757 Field Marshal Earl Ligonier became Colonel. Although not much associated with the First Guards in earlier years he had had a remarkable career and was Commander-in-Chief from 1757 to 1766.[10] He was succeeded in 1770 by HRH William, Duke of Gloucester.

The American War of Independence 1776-83

The triumph of British arms over their French rivals was not matched by similar success in the colonies of North America. In fact the episode has often been passed

[9] Hamilton

CANADA AND THE AMERICAN COLONIES

Composite bns 1776-83
2nd Bn 1838-42
1st Bn 1861-65

over by historians as too embarrassing to recount. A ramshackle army of settlers (admittedly, in the main, of good British stock) prevailed over the starched tactics of the redcoats where the disciplined continental armies had failed. It was ungentlemanly and unfair; the King's Company of Fontenoy days would never have approved. It marked the beginning of a new reality and taught lessons similar to those painfully learnt at the hands of the Boers over a century later.

The war was caused by growing outrage by the American colonists at increasing taxation on trade from England. The touch-paper was lit in Boston, which

General Howe was forced to evacuate in March 1776. In August he received substantial reinforcements from England, including a Guards brigade. The Guards were formed into two composite battalions, fifteen men being taken from each of the sixty-four companies of which the three regiments were composed. For the first time a light company was formed in each battalion, and later a third battalion was formed of the grenadier companies

---

[10] See Whitworth (1)
[11] The Coldstream had assisted in taking New York, formerly New Amsterdam, from the Dutch in 1665

and a full brigade thereby established. After a voyage which took all of five months, the force disembarked thankfully on Long Island to join Howe. Following a lively battle for **Brooklyn**, General Washington was chased out of New York.[11] Under General Cornwallis the British force then drove the Americans across the Delaware and pursued them to Trenton before returning to winter in Brunswick.

In the following year they took part in the Battles of **Brandywine** and **Germantown** and then occupied Philadelphia, the capital, where they received news that the northern British army had capitulated at Saratoga. The French had now entered the fray, naval supremacy was lost and the struggle continued in Virginia and the Carolinas in an increasingly unpleasant guerrilla war. The Guards brigade, however, spent the next two years of garrison duty in New York.

The brigade was then attached to Cornwallis in the south. It distinguished itself at the taking of **Charleston** and, in February 1781, at the crossing of the flooded **Catawba River** in North Carolina, which the guardsmen had to wade across waist high for 500 yards, under heavy fire from the opposite bank. The light and grenadier companies crossed first. 'The Guards behaved gallantly and, although fired upon during the whole time of this crossing, never returned a shot until they got out of the river and formed,' wrote Cornwallis, who had special confidence in the brigade. The march led on to the furthest point of North Carolina, some 600 miles from the point of departure, but the colonists managed to withdraw almost unscathed into the interior.

Six weeks later both battalions took part in the inconclusive Battle of **Guilford Court House**. Both sides claimed victory and losses had been equally heavy, the Guards losing almost half their strength. The force was compelled to withdraw and eventually the Guards battalions were holed up with the rest of the army in Yorktown. There, heavily outnumbered by Americans and French, and hemmed in by land and sea, Cornwallis surrendered to Washington on 19 October 1781. The American colonies had already declared their independence in November 1776. It was the birth of the United States of America.

On picquet: outpost duty by one of the new light companies in the American colonies. *Richard Simkin*

Largely because of irresolution and feeble support from home, the outcome of the long campaign was disastrous and a dreadful blow to British prestige. But, in a purely military sense the Foot Guards had in fact performed extremely well and with great courage, over five years of marching and fighting over long distances, and against an unfamiliar enemy. They had every reason to be proud.

Principal sources: Hamilton, Whitworth (1),(2), (3), Fraser (1), Paget, Regiment

Eighteenth Century Soldiering

Tactics, Drill and Organization

A force moved naturally in column, to follow what roads and tracks there were, but had to deploy into line in order to deliver fire, whether in a defensive position or, having made a suitable approach march, in the assault.[12] Moving from column to line, at exactly the right intervals to form an uninterrupted front, and without delay, was therefore crucial. It takes a little skill on Horse Guards Parade, but it demanded a good deal more over muddy, broken, interrupted ground, especially under fire. Exact and repetitious drill was required to achieve this and any nervousness in the ranks had to be suppressed by the most rigid discipline lest it provoke unease or even panic.

And once in the firing line the same discipline had to be firmly applied. The mere handling of arms had to be done with extreme care. The weapons themselves were cumbersome and sometimes unpredictable, and bad handling often caused accidents. When men in the front rank knelt to fire and then sprang up to load they were sometimes shot by men in the rank behind. Men were terribly burned when cartridge boxes blew up, eyes were poked out by bungled movements with bayonets, and ramrods left in barrels would be fired off. After firing a few shots, face and uniform would be smutty with powder smoke and mouths black with gunpowder from biting open the cartridges.

In barracks, drill would take up most of the day's work. For arms drill, recruits would follow the movements and timing of the fugleman, a trained soldier standing in front of the squad. Their skills improved and the Duke of Cumberland 'was very pleased to see the Guards Brigade carry out the first twenty-two movements of their drill in impressive silence, without a word of command, relying just on drumbeat, flam or ruffle.'[13] The results of this unimaginative though very necessary process were

---

[12] In the French army, cocked hats were described as *en colonne* when worn front to back, and *en bataille* when fore and aft
[13] Whitworth

Ceremonial of 1780: on duty at St James's Palace. *Reginald Wymer*

Heroes recruiting at Kelsey's: another uncomplimentary observation. *James Gillray*

certainly good. It carried British troops through countless campaigns and engendered a bloody-minded doggedness and determination to stick together that later led one of Napoleon's marshals to complain: 'There is no beating these British soldiers. They were completely beaten and the day was mine, but they did not know it and would not run'.

Companies were each commanded by a captain, assisted by a subaltern (lieutenant) and ensign. There were usually two sergeants, three corporals, a drummer and up to 100 privates. The establishment of companies varied considerably: peacetime economies could reduce them to sixty or so, and augmentation in time of war increase to some 120. On campaign, sickness and battle casualties could quickly reduce a company to a few dozen men. Disease normally caused far more casualties than battle. A colour sergeant to each company was established by a General Order of 6 July 1813. Platoons were not fixed in the organization, but denoted a body of men marked for a particular task, such as ranks firing volleys in sequence.

Billets, Barracks and Beef

There were very few barracks anywhere in the army. Most soldiers were billeted (often two to a bed) in 'inns, livery stables, alehouses, victualling houses, and all houses selling brandy, strong waters, cider or metheglin[14] by retail to be drunk upon the premises, and no other'. This extract from the annual Mutiny Acts reflected the right of an Englishmen not to accept the billeting of soldiers upon him except by his consent and with proper payment. In the English Civil Wars the excesses of soldiers billeted in private houses had been deeply resented and had reinforced the general aversion to any kind of standing army. The use of public houses was therefore the norm and the arrangements closely controlled by paymasters. Food and small beer (weak stuff, brewed largely to make the water safe and palatable) was received from their hosts at contracted prices set by justices.

Officers followed the same arrangements, though they messed together and paid rather more for better rations in the inns where they lived out of trunks in sparsely furnished rooms. On duty there were improvements and the officers' mess at St James's Palace was built for them in 1793.

Because of these billeting arrangements, companies were normally dispersed. In 1726, for example, the two battalions of the First Guards in London had nine companies spread about Holborn, two in Clerkenwell, two in St Giles Cripplegate, one each in Spitalfields, Whitechapel and St Sepulchre without Newgate, one each in Shoreditch and Folgate, Smithfield and St Katherine's, and ten more south of the Thames in Southwark.

Where there were barracks, from about the 1790s, men were packed tight and cooking normally had to be done in the barrack rooms. A soldier would be appointed cook for a 'mess', a small group of comrades. Two large copper pans were provided for every twelve men. Meat, almost always beef, would be boiled in one and potatoes in the other, the main meal always being provided at midday. The meat ration was weighed regardless of the amount of bone or gristle, and sometimes fairness in distribution would be achieved by the cook standing with his back to the mess, inviting men to bid for whatever he had, unseen, in the tin mug used to dole it out. The cooking, unwashed feet, foul breath and wet clothing made barrack rooms extraordinarily smelly, even by the

---

[14] A spiced variety of mead

NAAFI break: a rest in the 1750s. *Reginald Wymer*

pungent standards of the time. They were not improved by the 'sip pot', a large wooden tub used as a night urinal. When smoking became universal it was possible to enter a barrack room without being able to see a single one of its inhabitants for the thick fug of smoke.

Flogging, Prejudice Against the Military

Flogging, administered under the supervision of the drum major, was widely used. Sometimes sentences of over a thousand lashes were given, though a few hundred were usually enough to finish off the victim for good, despite the presence of a surgeon who was supposed to judge when a man's life was in danger, and then to halt the proceedings.

One of the few who recorded his experience of a flogging was a cavalryman, Alexander Waterfield. He was tied up and heard the RSM order: 'Farrier Simpson, you will do your duty. Simpson then took the cat as ordered, at least I believe so: I did not see him, but I felt an astounding sensation between the shoulders, under my neck, which went to my toe nails in one direction, my finger nails in another, and stung me to the heart, as if a knife had gone through my body. The sergeant major called in a loud voice "one". I felt as if it would be kind of Simpson not to strike in the same place again. He came on again a second time a few inches lower, and

then I thought the former stroke was sweet and agreeable compared to that one. The sergeant major counted "two". The cat was swung twice round the farrier's head again, and he came on somewhere about the right shoulder blade, and the loud voice of the reckoner said "three".' After twenty-five strokes Simpson handed over to a youngster who had never flogged before, but had practised on a stable post of sack and sawdust, and 'gave me some dreadful cuts about the ribs'. Simpson then took over again, and he 'got up among the old sores; the strokes were not so sharp as at first; they were like the blows of heavy weights, but far more painful than the fresh ones...'. His commanding officer spared Waterfield after a hundred strokes, as he was a young soldier.

It has long been characteristic of the British view of their soldiery that they are more popular the further from home. The 18th Century was no exception. In 1723 Private William Hawksworth was marching through St James's Park with his battalion of Foot Guards when he heard a woman shout an insult about his regiment. He left the ranks and punched the man accompanying her, who fell over, fracturing his skull, and died. Though the luckless guardsman clearly had no intention to kill the man, he was found guilty of murder rather than manslaughter, and hanged.

Grease, Powder and Moustaches

Until the 1760s officers usually wore wigs, in keeping with civilian practice, although on campaign many simply clinched their hair back into a ponytail or cropped it short. Men wore their hair greased, pulled back into a thick queue and powdered. The process took about an hour. One complained that, when dressed thus for parade, the skin of his face was pulled so tight that he could not so much as wink an eyelid. With an enormous high stock pushed under his chin, he felt as if he had swallowed a ramrod or a sergeant's halberd. It was hardly surprising that the infantryman in his red coat was nicknamed 'Thomas Lobster'.

Continental guardsmen, especially grenadiers, made moustaches and lovelocks their hallmark, though most pictures of British guardsmen of the time show them clean-shaven.

Recruiting, Pay and Travelling

Men were pulled in by recruiting parties, sometimes no more discerning than the notorious naval press gangs, who would dazzle with the beat of a drum, fine uniforms and tall stories, and ply the victim with drink until he accepted 'the King's shilling' as a sign of commitment. James Boswell, the journalist, once took a drink to a Foot Guards sentry who told him that he was a tailor, enlisted to escape imprisonment for debt.

Guardsmen and cavalrymen were paid more than infantrymen of the Line, who for most of the period received a shilling (12d)[15] a day. This, after stoppages, would be worth a good deal less and did not go very far when beer cost 2d a pint and a dinner of cold meat, bread and cheese 7d.

Travel by sea to the theatre of war was rough and uncomfortable. A guardsman who sailed to the Low Countries in 1708 described his voyage as 'continued destruction in the foretops, the pox above-board, the plague between decks, hell on the forecastle and the devil at the helm'.[16]

Officers, Wives

In 1771 it was decreed that commissions should not be allowed under the age of sixteen, but in 1751 Lord George Lennox had become an ensign at thirteen and was lieutenant colonel of a regiment of the Line at twenty. In November 1795 *The Times* alleged that 'several young gentlemen of the Guards ... have sent for the alphabet, in gingerbread, as preliminary education'.

Thomas Lobster: a starched, powdered and tightly constricted private of the 1790s. *Bryan Fosten*

However, the Duke of York, when commander-in-chief, raised the age to eighteen.

The social origins of officers and men differed very widely, but the experience of active service often brought them much closer. A sergeant wrote that the fondness of the officer continues with the man who fought under his command, to the remotest period of his declining years, and the old soldier venerates his aged officer far more than perhaps he did in his youthful days; it is like friendship between schoolboys, which increases in manhood and ripens in old age.

For much of the period most sergeants and some seven per cent of the rank and file were permitted to marry. Once barracks became established, only those wives on the regimental roll were allowed to live there, where they often earned some money washing for the soldiers. Only a small quota was allowed to accompany husbands overseas.

Principal sources: Holmes, Paget

---

[15] About £4.50 in 2005
[16] Deane

GRENADES, GRENADIERS AND BEARSKIN CAPS

The Grenade

Primitive grenades, containing some kind of incendiary material, were to be found way back in the Dark Ages, and new forms were developed slowly from about the 15th Century as gunpowder came into use in Europe. The name of 'grenade' has been attributed to two possible sources: the first regular manufacture having been at Grenada in Spain in about 1530, or its likeness to the pomegranate (which seems more probable).

Grenades in their natural state: pomegranates, complete and burst.

Grenades of the 17th Century generally consisted of a hollow cast-iron sphere filled with gunpowder and sometimes a few lead balls as well, about 3½ inches in diameter and weighing about 2½ lbs. Four of these were normally carried. There was a lighter version, about the size of a cricket ball, of which eight were carried. The fuse, secured by a wooden plug, was some form of burning match, such as hemp dipped in saltpetre. The slow-burning match used to light the fuse was contained in a tube perforated with holes to conceal the light and fixed on the belt. The burning time of the fuse was very uncertain and the timing of the throw a matter of the nicest judgement and considerable risk. If thrown too early, the enemy might toss it back; too late and the grenadier himself would be the victim. One, indeed, who was badly burnt when a grenade went off in his hands in an attack on a French fortress, reported the effect: 'Killing several men about me, and blew me over the Pallasods [palisades]; burnt my clothes so that the skin came off me. [I was] flayed like an old dead horse from head to foot. They cast me into water to put out the fire about me.'[1]

As firearms improved in the 18th Century these hair-raising devices fell out of use. Grenadiers could too easily be picked off before coming within throwing range. They were used by other armies during siege operations, tossed from the fighting tops of warships at Trafalgar (especially by the French) and experimented with in Africa, where jam tins were filled with black powder and quartz pebbles 'held in place by clay from an anthill'.[2] But in the First World War they were ideal for trench warfare, and more jam-tin grenades were knocked up by the Royal Engineers workshops, though they could be almost as alarming as their early ancestors:

'I carried in my pocket a tin box containing a dozen or so little red fuses. The method we were instructed to employ was as follows: "Take one fuse from the box, put it in the hole already prepared in the jam-tin grenade (taking care not to press it in too hard or the grenade might explode), then cut off a bit from the protruding end, light a match, apply the match to the said end, hold until the fuse was about to act, and then throw the damned thing at the Huns." ... Imagine an ink-black night and soppy rain, and you will realize the weapon had its faults.'[3]

The properly designed Mills 'bomb' was introduced in 1915 and some 75 million were made in Britain during the war. Since then the essential design has changed very little, though a variety of explosive and pyrotechnic fillings have been developed and ingenious means of projection invented.

Hard and heavy: an early grenade ready to be filled.

[1] Holmes (Richard)
[2] JSAHR 1999
[3] Buchanan

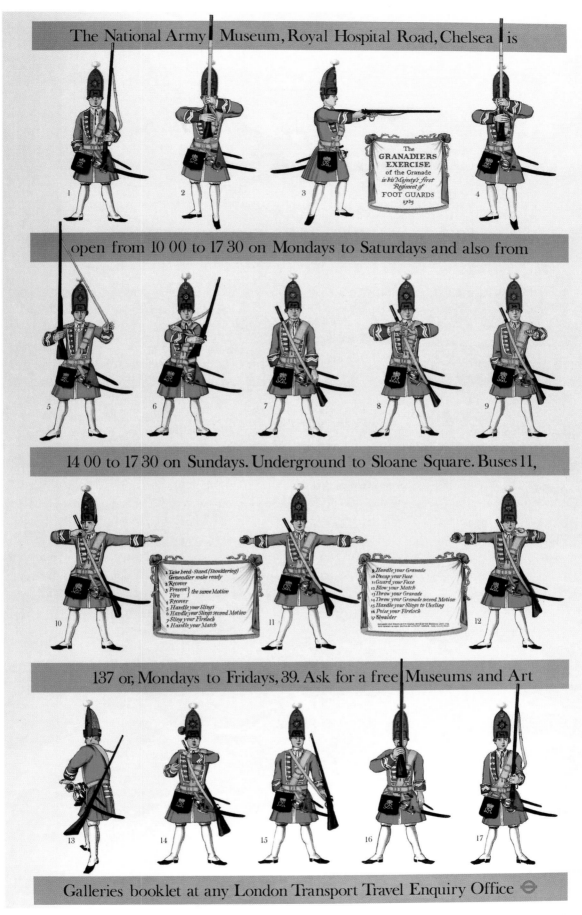

Throwing by numbers: the 'Granadier's Exercise' of 1735; seventeen movements made up into a poster for the National Army Museum in 1972.

The Grenadier

In May 1677 'a certain Captain Charles Lloyd was directed ... to instruct in the grenade exercise a squad of fifty-four men'[4] taken from the King's Regiment of Guards and the Coldstream. This was to be the first introduction of grenadiers to the Army. The diarist John Evelyn described at a review in 1678 'that new sort of soldier, who with a pouchful of grenades was skilful at throwing them at the enemy'. In that year six further regiments of infantry formed grenadier companies, and the practice was extended to the infantry as a whole in the time of James II. The grenadier had replaced the pikeman as the superior soldier.

Folk songs of the time applauded the 'bold grenadier', and they did not exaggerate. It was not as if he could wait behind cover, in some sort of security, with reasonable time to prepare his hazardous ordnance before tossing it over the parapet at his assailants. He was a storm trooper. The grenadier was already burdened with an uncomfortable uniform (designed rather to impress the enemy than to allow easy movement), bulky equipment, a cumbersome musket and sword, a hatchet and his bag of grenades. Thus laden, he was required to lead the assault and cut away or surmount obstacles, and it was in these already desperate circumstances that he had to light his fuse by blowing on the slow match and applying it to the wick, and make a cool judgement on the right moment to throw.

In each regiment the grenadier company contained the tallest, strongest and most courageous men, and stood on the right flank.[5] Long after the grenade itself fell out of use this company retained its senior status and was often selected (or grouped with grenadier companies of other battalions) for particularly difficult tasks. The appointment in 1815 of the First Guards as an entire grenadier regiment was

Prepare to throw: the captain of a grenadier company in 1685 about to light the fuse of his dangerous weapon.
Pierre Turner (from British Infantry Uniforms Since 1660 by Michael Barthorp – Orion Publishing Group)

thus an accolade of the highest order. It was not until 1860 that the titles and dress distinctions of grenadier (and light) companies were abolished throughout the Army and from that time 'grenadier' meant the Grenadier Guards alone.

However, the re-introduction of grenades in the First World War provoked an interesting challenge to this special position. It was proposed that the name 'grenadier' should again be applied to a soldier of any regiment whose business it was to throw grenades. It set off a furious correspondence between the Adjutant General at General Headquarters in France and Lord Cavan, commanding the Guards Division. Finding GHQ immovable, Cavan appealed to the King as Colonel-in-Chief to protect the position of his First Guards. He was successful, the Army Council stating on 28 March 1916 that: 'The term "Grenadier" will no longer be applied to men trained or employed in the use of hand grenades. Such men will in future be designated "Bombers".'[6]

The Bearskin Cap

In 1678 Evelyn described the new grenadiers as having 'furr'd caps, with coped crowns, like Janizeries,[7] which gave them a fierce expression; while some wore long hoods hanging down behind, as fools are pictured. Their clothing was pie-bald, yellow and red'. These new caps, arranged in a vertical rather than a horizontal attitude, were necessary to allow the grenadier to sling his firelock and then to throw his grenade successfully (the bowling action required could without much difficulty sweep off the broad-brimmed hat). This close-sided hat was unimpressive,

[4] Hamilton

[5] From this time until 1788 there were also **Horse Grenadier Guards**, who were horsemen throwing grenades rather than grenadiers mounted on horses. Formed from the Household Cavalry, they were sometimes confusingly termed 'Grenadier Guards', though nothing to do with the First Guards. They became the 2nd Life Guards in 1788 and were amalgamated with the 1st Life Guards in 1922

[6] Ponsonby

[7] The Janissaries (as normally spelt) were the dreaded crack troops of the Ottoman Turks

however, and evolved in the 18th Century into the well-known mitre shape, with all sorts of extra embellishments. This became the mark of grenadiers in many European armies, the Prussians, in their efforts to achieve the tallest manageable impression, probably over-topping the others. In the British battalions the grenadiers became known as 'tow rows', the light company men with their low jockey caps as 'light bobs' and the eight battalion companies with hats turned up in three corners into a tricorne as 'hatmen'.[8]

The bearskin cap, in something like its present form, though rather more shaggy and considerably more decorated, seems to have made its first appearance in the early 1760s, becoming regulation from 1768. By this time the mechanics of grenade-throwing could safely be ignored. The bearskin was a development of the tall mitre cap and worn by the grenadier companies of all three regiments of Foot Guards (First, Coldstream and Third Guards).[9] However, it was treated as full dress and not worn in the field in the Napoleonic campaigns.

Tall, tough and tenacious: a bold grenadier of 1751 in mitre cap. *Courtesy Brian Fosten – The Pompadour Gallery*

Here the shako was adopted by each battalion, that of the grenadier company being marked by a white plume on the left hand side, a brass plate and a decorative cord, the light company by a green plume, and the remaining battalion companies (usually eight) by a red and white one.

Shaggy hat: the bearskin cap, with a fine prominent plume, worn by the Duke of York in the early nineteenth century.

On 29 July 1815, six weeks after the Battle of Waterloo on 18 June, the *London Gazette* published the order of the Prince Regent that the First Guards would in future be known as the 'First or Grenadier Regiment of Foot Guards' as a reward for their decisive part in the battle. Thus, by definition, every man in the Regiment was entitled to wear the insignia of a grenadier. The two battalions who had fought at Waterloo remained in France, the 2nd until January 1816 and the 3rd until November 1818, while the 1st remained at home. At some point they would all have adopted the white grenadier plume for the shako and in full dress the grenadier bearskin cap. The grenade was also adopted as a badge. Exactly when all this was finally accomplished is in some doubt, though there is a clue in a mishap to the Duke of Wellington: 'At a military review in May 1829, wearing the tall and top-heavy cap of the Grenadiers which the King had introduced, he fell off his horse at the feet of the Duke of Clarence, much to the amusement of the ultra-Tories.'[10]

The grenadier companies of the Coldstream and Third Guards continued to wear bearskins, with the white plume. In 1831, however, a major change took place. Both regiments were awarded the title of 'Fusilier'.[11] The Coldstream, feeling perhaps that

---

[8] Holmes (Richard)
[9] And also by drummers, pioneers and fusiliers of the Army and by the Scots Greys, a cavalry regiment originally formed as grenadiers
[10] Hibbert. As he got older Wellington, though a fine horseman, regularly fell off hunting and sometimes on parade (JSAHR 1965)
[11] Fusiliers, originally established to protect the artillery on the line of march and armed with the lighter 'fusil', which was less likely to ignite powder, were superior to other regiments of the Line, though not of course to the Guards. The title was given to certain regiments as a reward for distinguished service

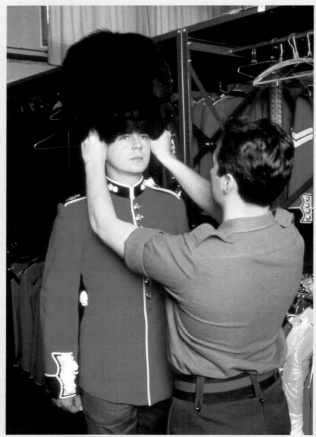

Tender care: this lance corporal treats his bearskin like a friend. It should look like an apple from the front and a pear from behind. *Roger Scruton*

If you want to get ahead, get a hat: a good fit for this young Grenadier is essential. The bearskin must be secure but not so tight as to hold the head in an iron grip and induce unconsciousness. *Roger Scruton*

Airhead: this dissection of a bearskin cap reveals the framework of its cage. The space has sometimes been called upon to compensate for the small capacity of pockets in the uniform.

Magnificent quality: two of these three Crimean veteran pioneers are perfectly comfortable in their caps while attending to their pipes and beer.

'Fusilier' was rather too clear a statement of inferiority to 'Grenadier', declined to use the title, but the 'Scots Fusilier Guards' were known as such until 1877. As a consequence of this change the bearskin was adopted by these regiments between 1830 and 1832, thus bringing them into line with the First or Grenadier Regiment.

Extraneous decoration on the bearskins of all three regiments was abolished, the result being caps that were very much like those worn today, though of finer quality as the furs were taken from young black bears in prime condition, killed just before going into hibernation, and mostly from British Columbia. In those days, of course, shooting was unlicensed and conservation unheard of. Today bearskins still come from Canada, but the annual quantity required is very small and a negligible proportion of the overall market for the pelts. Attempts to find a synthetic alternative continue, though so far they have failed.

The Bearskin Plume

Grenadiers had always worn a white plume in their cap, almost always on the left-hand side. It was said to represent the smoke of a fizzing grenade. The Coldstream naturally chose a distinctive plume of their own, coloured red as the most emphatic contrast to their Grenadier rivals, and worn on the right-hand side in order to be visible from the centre when occupying their position on the left of the line. The Scots Fusiliers, being in the centre of the line, needed no plume.

Hide or display? The bearer party at Queen Victoria's funeral seem to do as they please with their plumes.

At some stage, though quite when has not been well established, Grenadiers adopted the strange, not to say perverse, custom of brushing the fur over the white plume in order to make it as inconspicuous as possible. The custom seems to date from the late 1950s and reached a point at that time when new, larger plumes were prescribed for warrant officers but never drawn up, those senior Grenadiers preferring to retain their smaller versions because easier to hide. The new plumes languished in store and eventually were thrown away.

Various explanations have been offered for this bizarre procedure, including ancient Jacobite sympathies, the avoidance of embarrassment to the Regiment if misbehaving when walking out, and fashionable shaping of the bearskin by brushing it into a tail at the neck, which was not supposed to obscure

The red Grenadier capband: Lance Sergeant Paul Roberts of the Regimental Police in No 2 Dress at Windsor in 2005. *Roger Scruton*

the plume from the side but very often did. None of these explanations are very convincing. And a photograph from Queen Victoria's funeral in 1901 compounds the riddle. Here Grenadiers, marching with arms reversed, are seen flanking the principal mourners directly behind the coffin. Six appear in the picture. The two in the foreground have their plumes more or less concealed. Of the four in the background, two reveal no plumes at all, while the other two sprout them in full flower. Even the roots seem to be prominent. A greater variation between six men could hardly be imagined and it gives the impression that personal taste may have decided how the plume was worn. This seems an unlikely explanation for so highly regimented a body as the Grenadier Guards (and the King's Company[12] at that), but another is hard to find. The habit of concealing the plume is a good example of bizarre variations in dress, and indeed in customs, which seem rooted in fashion and for which no sound basis will probably ever be uncovered.

The Red Grenadier Capband

The riddle would hardly be complete without a mention of the capband worn with the forage cap. Why did not Grenadiers wear a white band, and the Coldstream red, to match their plumes? Before 1829 a soldier's

'undress' or working uniform was largely a matter of regimental choice, but in that year new directives on dress were issued from the Commander-in-Chief at Horse Guards. These prescribed a blue forage cap with bands of various colours, red being that for 'royal' regiments and duly adopted by the Foot Guards. When, however, the Coldstream and Scots Fusilier Guards were put into bearskin caps they were allowed to adopt new colours for capbands. The Coldstream chose white and the Scots Fusiliers their diced arrangement, the Grenadiers alone retaining the royal red.[13]
And so they have endured into modern times.

---

[12] Probably it remained 'The Queen's Company' until after her burial, as on later occasions
[13] Wild accusations of Grenadiers and Coldstream stealing each other's colours (like schoolboys squabbling over sweets) have from time to time appeared in the journals of the Household Division and the Society for Army Historical Research

BEARCUT!

Philip Wright

Chapter Three

THE LONG STRUGGLE WITH FRANCE
1793-1815

The French Revolution and its Aftermath

The violent revolution that broke out in France with the storming of the Bastille on 14 July 1789 sent dreadful shocks through the other nations of Europe. Not only were the monarchy and the nobility knocked off their perch, in many cases deservedly so, but the revolutionaries fought among themselves over several years. There was great disorder and brutality, and in due course revolutionary fervour spilled over the national borders and offered opportunity to the ambitions of a military genius – Napoleon Bonaparte.

The British had hardly been behind in the matter: after all, over a century earlier Charles I had been beheaded after a cruel civil war. But they would not submit to the balance of power in Europe being upset, and their own maritime empire threatened, by the ambitions of France, the old enemy. The result was a war spanning twenty-two years, the whole engagement period of an ordinary soldier, in which England was twice threatened with invasion and British arms were engaged in several parts of the continent. The nature of warfare changed from the rigid rules of earlier years and France was for the first time to enlist the 'nation in arms' by forming huge armies of conscripts against the standing armies and professional mercenaries of her enemies. It was a most formidable challenge.

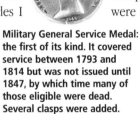

Military General Service Medal: the first of its kind. It covered service between 1793 and 1814 but was not issued until 1847, by which time many of those eligible were dead. Several clasps were added.

The Regiment of Guards

The soldier of the Guards was still well drilled, strictly disciplined, highly trained and well administered, though the state of the army in general was nothing short of disgraceful. The First Guards found three battalions, the Coldstream and Third Guards two apiece. Each battalion (whose strength could vary from a few hundred to well over a thousand) usually had eight 'battalion' companies; one, sometimes two, grenadier companies; and, in due course a light company of marksmen, taught to skirmish and act more independently after the fashion of the skirmishers formed in the earlier American campaigns. The grenadier and light companies were described collectively as 'flank' companies (the grenadiers on the right of the line and light infantrymen on the left) and were frequently removed from their parent and drawn together to fight as battalions under separate command.

Flanders and Lincelles 1793-95

In 1792 the French Republic was established. Early in 1793 Louis XVI was guillotined and war declared upon Great Britain. A British expedition was raised under the Duke of York to help the Dutch allies. He assembled all eight battalions of Guards on Horse Guards Parade and invited volunteers to serve with him. Every man stepped forward. The **1st Battalion** (Maj Gen Samuel Hulse) was selected, the first battalions of the Coldstream and Third Guards, and a composite battalion of their grenadier companies, all four being brigaded together under Major General Lake, Lieutenant Colonel of the First Guards. The expedition was so ill-equipped, with no transport, little

The COURSE of the FRENCH WARS for the FIRST GUARDS

The Wider War		Periods in Theatres of War in Bold Colours			
Details	Year	1st Bn	2nd Bn	3rd Bn	Composite
French Revolution	1789				
	1790				
	1791				a. Grenadier & (later) light companies
French Republic declared	1792	a.			
Louis XVI guillotined. French Revolutionary	1793	Flanders LINCELLES			Flanders LINCELLES
Wars begin	1794				
	1795				
Napoleon's Italian campaigns	1796				
Napoleon's invasion plans thwarted	1797				b. Light companies
	1798			b.	Ostend
Napoleon lands in Egypt	1799			Ireland Holland EGMONT-op-ZEE	Holland EGMONT-op-ZEE
	1800				
French defeated in Egypt	1801			c.	c. Grenadier companies
Peace of Amiens	1802				
War resumed	1803	1st Gds Bde	3rd Gds Bde	1st Gds Bde	
Napoleon threatens invasion again	1804				
Napoleon Emperor					d. Flank (grenadier and light) companies
Nelson's victory at Trafalgar	1805	d.		d.	
Napoleon victories at Austeritz and Jena	1806	Sicily		Sicily	Sicily
Napoleon defeats Russia at Friedland	1807				
Napoleon invades Spain and Portugal	1808	Spain CORUNNA Walcheren		Spain CORUNNA Walcheren	e. Flank (grenadier and light) companies
Napoleon defeats Austria at Wagram	1809		e. Composite Bde		Walcheren
	1810		Cadiz	Composite Bde	
	1811		BARROSA	Cadiz	Period of PENINSULAR WAR
Napoleon retreats from Moscow	1812	Spain San Sebastian NIVE Bayonne		1st Gds Bde	
Napoleon defeated at Leipzig	1813		3rd Gds Bde		
Napoleon abdicates and is exiled to Elba	1814		Bergen-op-Zoom	San Sebastian NIVE Bayonne	
		Not brigaded	1st Gds Bde		
The Hundred Days	1815		WATERLOO	WATERLOO	

reserve ammunition and few stores, that the prospect of victory seemed remote. Indeed, shipping was so short that they had to sail to Holland in Thames coal barges. And, once arrived, the allied commanders quarrelled and missed every opportunity, the French growing daily stronger.

The composite battalion was strengthened by light companies, raised in England, hastily trained before despatch to Flanders, and later formed into a battalion of their own. By the time they arrived the whole force had moved south to the area of Lille and had fought a number of minor engagements. And here, on 18 August, there was a moment of glory when the Guards were sent to support the Dutch Prince of Orange at Lincelles. Lake boldly decided to launch a frontal attack in the fading light, though the enemy numbered 5000 to his mere 1100 and were strongly entrenched. The assault up a steep slope, in the face of heavy artillery and musketry fire, was carried out with great vigour and the position taken. The Dutch, whose earlier feeble attempt had come to nothing, 'were so much ashamed of their conduct and so crest-fallen, that they slunk about, avoiding the British soldiers as much as possible'.[1] Neither were the British impressed by their enemies. 'In physique there is no doubt that at this time the French troops were inferior, for the better part of the population had not yet been drawn into their ranks. The Guards, instead of killing them when they got into the redoubt, rather treated them as a mob in London, striking them with their fists, and frequently calling out, "Let him alone, the little animal can't do much harm".'[2] The First Guards suffered twenty-two killed and forty-six wounded.

The campaign dragged on until April 1795, after further lesser actions, much marching about, one season in winter quarters and a second winter in which the French had occupied most of Holland and the allied force was compelled to retire behind the Rhine, marching through Nijmegen and Arnhem. By this time half the army was sick and the rest exhausted, and the winter was one of the most severe seen that century. After a long and arduous march they embarked eventually at Bremen and reached Greenwich in May, to their great relief. There they were met by the King himself 'who welcomed them back with much earnestness, and shook many of the private soldiers by the hand. They all received on their return eight days' leave of absence to visit their friends'.[3]

Ostend, Ireland and Holland 1798-99

The Duke of York was now Commander-in-Chief and demonstrated that his skills in administration were distinctly superior to those in strategy and tactics. The deficiencies of the army, in everything save fighting power, had been too clearly exposed in Flanders to be ignored and he set out resolutely to repair them. He established a training camp at Warley[4], where the 2nd and 3rd Battalions of the First Guards spent four months in 1795, and greatly improved the supply and medical services. This took several years, but by the time the Peninsular campaign opened in 1809 the whole system had been transformed.

In the meantime the young Napoleon had won dramatic victories in Italy and the French government

---

[1] Hamilton
[2] Hamilton
[3] Hamilton
[4] Later to precede Caterham as the Guards Depot

FIELD MARSHAL
HRH FREDERICK AUGUSTUS, Duke of YORK
KG GCB GCH *1763-1827*

Ill-Fated Expedition Leader, Military Innovator, Colonel of the Regiment, Commander-in-Chief

The second son of King George III, the 'Grand Old Duke of York' was condemned to be remembered by generations of children as having led his ten thousand men up to the top of the hill and down again. In fact there were few enough hills to be found in Flanders in 1793, but certainly there was plenty of marching to and fro for his expedition. His efforts were not crowned with success, he missed opportunities and his army suffered grievously from dreadful weather. He was no more successful in the Dutch expedition of 1799, where his army ground to a halt in the sand dunes and he was compelled to negotiate an armistice. There is certainly truth in the claim that 'he was not always well advised on the field, and he was always clumsily interfered with from home', but his relations with other allied commanders were often sour.

However, he was a brave man and a dedicated soldier, and as architect of Wellington's army he made a real mark as military administrator. The demands on the British Army over the years of the French wars were extreme and he was energetic in establishing proper camps of exercise for training, promoting military education (he founded the military school at Dover, Sandhurst and the Staff College) and making large improvements to the lamentable administrative and medical services.

He was Commander-in-Chief from 1798 to 1815, with an interval from 1809 to 1811 after he had resigned because of the conduct of his mistress, who had been taking bribes in exchange for exercising influence over promotions.

In 1805 he became Colonel of the First Guards and held the post until his death in 1827.

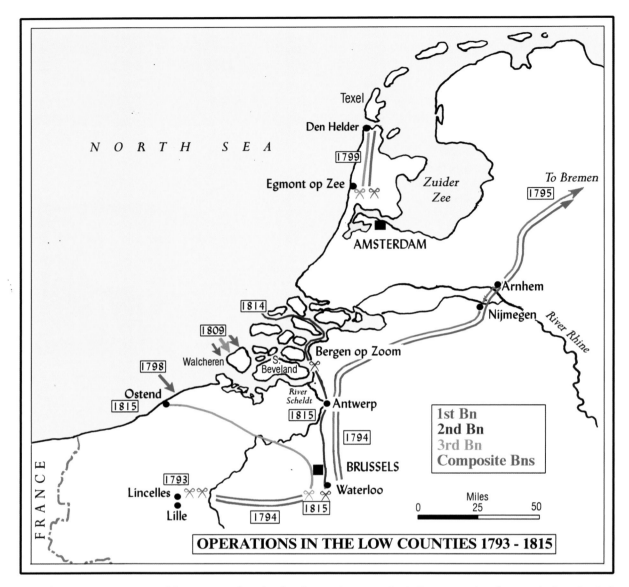

OPERATIONS IN THE LOW COUNTIES 1793 - 1815

turned its attention to a possible invasion of England and Ireland. In order to disturb preparations, a raid was made on **Ostend** in May 1798 by a force which included eight light companies of the Guards. Those of the Coldstream and Third Guards landed successfully, destroying several boats and lock gates, but high surf prevented their re-embarkation and they were pinned on the beach by a superior force and compelled to capitulate. By good fortune, however, the captain of the *Minerva*, carrying the four companies of the First Guards, arrived too late to land with the others and the surf then prevented them from doing so. They were therefore able to return home unscathed and were spared the six months of captivity suffered by their comrades.

Almost at once the French attempted to threaten England by supporting insurgents in **Ireland**, then in a seditious and rebellious mood. A force including the 3rd Battalion of the First Guards arrived at Waterford in June. However, French support for the rebellion evaporated on news that the French fleet had been destroyed in Egypt and after various manoeuvrings the battalion returned home in February 1799.

In August the **3rd Battalion** (Col Augustus Maitland) was off again, this time to **Holland**, where an attempt was to be made by General Abercrombie to seize the Dutch fleet (then under French control) at the Texel, land on Den Helder, advance on Amsterdam and restore the ousted Prince of Orange. Once more the grenadier companies of the Guards battalions were formed into a composite battalion, but a similar battalion of the light companies remained in England and was not ordered out until too late. After a successful landing, not seriously opposed, progress towards Amsterdam was painfully slow, despite a large force of Russian allies, but the two brigades of Guards took their objectives at Bergen after a battle of thirteen hours. West of Alkmaar the 3rd Battalion penetrated some six miles below the sand dunes along the beach and on 3 October turned the French out of **Egmont-op-Zee**. But in the sandhills all impetus was soon lost and casualties were severe. The absence of the light companies, which could have kept at bay the enemy marksmen in the dunes, was keenly felt. The soldiers also suffered terribly from heat and thirst, aggravated by their rations of salt meat, though it did not prevent them from encouraging their commanders: 'Give us some cartridges and we'll see what we can do', said one.[5] Torrents of rain then fell, there was no shelter in the sandhills and provisions were difficult to procure. The Duke of York, who had come out with reinforcements and assumed command, abandoned the strategic aim and concluded an armistice. It had been a bloody and useless campaign.

Lincelles, the first major battle: the Dutch allies, ashamed of their own performance, slunk about avoiding the British soldiers. *Faulkner's Celebrated Cigarettes*

A Six-Year Interval 1800-06

In November 1799 the regimental strength was considerably increased, each company being raised to 150 men. The establishment was then greater than it had ever been: 140 officers, 224 sergeants, 3 staff, 75 drummers and 4800 rank and file, making a grand total of 5242 men, at an annual charge of £158,000.[6]

In 1800 battalions of the Coldstream and Third Guards were sent to join Abercrombie's army in Egypt, but the First Guards remained at home for the next six years. The 2nd Battalion, indeed, did not go abroad until 1810, as it served, along with the second battalions of the other regiments, to act as a training depot for supplying the other battalions with reinforcements. They consisted principally of those unfit for active service and of raw recruits, who were constantly being drilled, and were nicknamed the 'bone-drivers' by always having pieces of bone in their flintlocks

An elegant figure: officer of the 1st Guards in 1808. *Pierre Turner (from 'British Infantry Uniforms Since 1660' by Michael Barthorp – Orion Publishing Group)*

rather than flints. One of their peacetime duties was to guard George III during his seaside jaunts to Weymouth.

In 1803 the 1st and 3rd Battalions were formed into the 1st Guards Brigade and for most of the remaining campaigns fought side by side. The 2nd Battalion joined the other second battalions in 3rd Guards Brigade, while the 1st Battalions of the Coldstream and Third Guards formed the 2nd Guards Brigade. Hereafter it was more usual for the flank (grenadier and light) companies to be deployed with their parent battalions. In 1805 the Duke of York, still Commander-in-Chief, became Colonel of the Regiment.

Napoleon's failure in Egypt had been followed by the uneasy Peace of Amiens in 1802, but war resumed in the following year. By 1805, having conquered Italy, pole-axed Austria and Russia, and crumpled up Prussia, he was at the height of his power and had asserted his dominance by crowning himself Emperor. He assembled a great fleet of barges at Dunkirk and the spectre of invasion loomed again. Martello towers (still to be seen today on the south coast) were built, military canals constructed and chains of beacons prepared, but the danger was averted. In a victory that was to rank in British history alongside Waterloo, Horatio Nelson destroyed the French and Spanish fleets at Trafalgar on 21 October 1805, dying himself in the moment of victory.

Sicily 1806-07, An Observant Sergeant Major

True to tradition, Britain used her sea power to strike at the enemy and in December 1806 1st Guards Brigade was sent to reinforce the occupation of the vital Mediterranean base of Sicily. The voyage was eventful. In the Bay of Biscay the *Christopher*, a collier brig carrying part of the battalion of light companies, lost her foremast in a gale and the captain sailed on for three weeks by his own reckoning, though in fact hopelessly lost. One evening just before dark the acting quartermaster,

[5] Jeffreys (4)
[6] About £15 million in 2005, an average of under £3000 per head

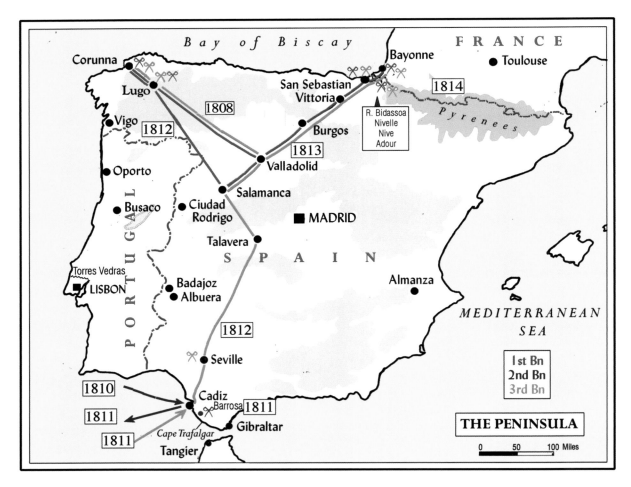

Sergeant Major Colquhoun, reported to the commanding officer that he thought the sea had very much changed colour during the day. The captain scoffed at the idea, declaring that they were at least a hundred miles out to sea, but on sounding with the lead, discovered to his great astonishment that they were in only ten fathoms. They were found to be off the Spanish coast and almost under enemy guns. They extricated themselves carefully and arrived safely at Gibraltar. Colquhoun's powers of observation had certainly saved many lives.

While in Sicily the light companies were inspected by Sir John Moore, second in command on the island. It was he who had formed and trained the light infantry that was to win such renown in later battles. He declared that the light companies of the First Guards moved better than any others he had seen (except of course the 52nd Regiment, his own creation). It was a high compliment.

The French made no attempt on the island. At the end of 1807 the two First Guards battalions were called home and returned via Gibraltar to prepare for more serious work.

Corunna 1808-09 – A Triumph of Discipline

The campaign of Corunna that followed was to be an epic in the annals of the First Guards. Napoleon had turned against Spain, his old ally, and in February 1808 poured his armies across the Pyrenees, unseating the king and replacing him by his own brother Joseph Bonaparte. He then invaded Portugal also. But he had under-estimated the spirit of a nation oppressed by a foreign invader. The Spanish people rose in revolt and waged a bitter *guerrilla* (little war) against him. To support them the British government sent an army under Lieutenant General Sir Arthur Wellesley, then thirty-nine years old, who promptly drove the invaders out of Portugal. Encouraged by this, a second force was ordered to land at Corunna in October and link up with others in the Lisbon area, the whole coming under command of Sir John Moore. The 1st Guards Brigade, still composed of the **1st Battalion** (Col Hon Philip Cocks) and **3rd Battalion** (Col William Wheatley) of the First Guards, was part of this force and marched inland to a point near

52

'Spare your powder, but give them steel enough': the 2nd Battalion, at last in the war at full strength, gives a fine account of itself at Barrosa. *Richard Simkin*

Well protected in heavy weather: officer, private and sergeant in the Peninsula.

Pipe and sticks in the Peninsula: a workmanlike private of 1809 to 1811. *Bob Marrion*

Coup-de-main by night: over frozen ditches and up ladders on to the walls of Bergen op Zoom. *Faulkner's Celebrated Cigarettes*

Bayonne, the tragic and expensive last battle of the Peninsular campaign: Napoleon had already abdicated but the news had not reached the combatants. *Faulkner's Celebrated Cigarettes*

Backs to the sea at Corunna: these finely turned out and disciplined guardsmen show few signs of the harrowing retreat they had just endured. *Reginald Wymer*

REGIMENTAL SERGEANT MAJOR
WILLIAM MIDDLEDITCH
1781-1834

Suffolk man who
fought through the
French wars and was
borne to his grave by
six Waterloo heroes

William Middleditch was born near Bury St Edmunds. At the age of twelve he was apprenticed to a bricklayer and developed into a tall, strong youth. In 1800 he walked twenty-eight miles to Colchester to join the First Guards. Compared to his later marches it was a short distance.

He served with the 3rd Battalion in Sicily from 1806, and two years later sailed with the battalion to Corunna with Sir John Moore's expedition, suffering dreadful hardship. He went on as a sergeant to Walcheren, where fever convulsed the army, and he probably suffered the effects for the rest of his life. He then fought through Spain and on the field of Waterloo.

After the war he became Sergeant Major of the 1st Battalion, where he remained for five years before being medically discharged. He suffered from arthritis, due in part no doubt to the arduous campaigns in which he had fought. He became a publican at 'The Ram' in Bury St Edmunds, which became a meeting place for Waterloo veterans. He died in November 1834 after a short illness, a well-known and respected citizen of the town. Just before his death he requested that he should be borne to his grave by six Waterloo heroes.

His epitaph in the Great Churchyard reads:
A husband, father, comrade friend sincere,
British Soldier brave lies buried here
In Spain and Flushing and at Waterloo,
He fought to guard our Country from the foe;
His Comrades Britons, who survive him say,
He acted nobly on the glorious day.

See Clark (1)

Salamanca, where Moore concentrated his army and then, in November, boldly marched north to attack Marshal Soult near Valladolid. But, on Christmas Day, came disastrous news. Napoleon himself had marched into Spain at the head of 200,000 veterans and, having re-occupied Madrid, was heading north with 50,000 men to cut off Moore from his base at Corunna. Outnumbered two to one, Moore had no option but to withdraw, in order to save what was virtually the only effective allied force opposing the emperor. So began the grim retreat to Corunna.

The magnificent rearguard actions fell chiefly to Moore's own light infantry and the cavalry, though the First Guards, notably the light companies, had the satisfaction of repelling a French attack at **Lugo** directly after a forced march of thirty-six hours. Where they particularly distinguished themselves, however, was in discipline and leadership. With deep snow and freezing wind, the conditions were appalling. There were almost no supplies, clothes or comforts, and many of the troops were soon famished and barefoot. In the demoralization of retreat, 'sullenly, like a flock of sheep',[7] many regiments began to fall apart, their men looting, drinking themselves into a stupor or collapsing dead by the roadside. But, as one observer noted, 'The conduct of the officers and soldiers of the Guards was highly to their credit from the time they disembarked; fewer excesses were committed by these men than many regiments of similar numbers and their officers preferred sharing with them their quarters to profiting by the billets offered them'. Another observed, 'The Guards were the strongest body of men in the army, and consequently suffered least from fatigue; besides, they are strictly disciplined, and their non-commissioned officers are excellent'. Even so, their losses during the march were all too great, sixty-nine of the 1st Battalion and fifty-six of the 3rd, and others beside who later succumbed to the exhaustion of the campaign. Most of the Spanish citizens, for whom these trials were being endured, barred their doors to the soldiers.

At last, sixteen days later, on 11 January 1809, the desperately weary troops came within sight of Corunna, to find that the fleet that was to evacuate them had not yet arrived. It was here that Sir Robert Arbuthnot was standing near Moore, watching the regiments come in,

---

[7] Jeffreys (4)

weary, starving, ragged and in many cases barefoot:

'Sir John called his attention, saying: "Arbuthnot, look at that body of men in the distance; they are the Guards, by the way they are marching." They watched them and saw them march into Corunna by sections, their drums beating, the drum-major in front flourishing his stick, the sergeant-major at the head, and the drill-sergeants on the flanks keeping the men in step, exactly as if they were on their own drill ground at home. Sir Robert said it was a fine sight, and one he would never forget.'[8] With the enemy at their heels and in the midst of a disintegrating army, they had covered the last 150 miles in eleven days, with three days' rest, and yet that is how they came in.

Soult, in command of the French forces, was held off by the thin British line for the few days before the ships arrived and embarkation could be accomplished. At the height of the final battle Moore was struck by a round shot, which tore away his left arm. He was carried from the field by six soldiers of the First Guards and the 42nd Highlanders, those nearest to him when he fell, and there a chaplain of the First Guards buried him.

Walcheren 1809 – Defeat by Fever, A Gallant Grenadier

Hardly had the battalions of the 1st Guards Brigade returned home than they were despatched on another disastrous expedition to the Low Countries. The **1st Battalion** (Col William Anson) and **3rd Battalion** (Col William Wheatley) were accompanied by a composite battalion formed by the flank companies of all three battalions (the first time men of the 2nd Battalion had been sent abroad). This time it was to the island of Walcheren, from where a large British force struggled in vain through the swamps along the

The enterprising John Skinner, who unspiked the guns at Fort Batz: how he managed it nobody knows.

Scheldt in an attempt to open a passage to Antwerp. They might perhaps have succeeded were it not for the fever that brought the army to its knees. After only two months they pulled out, the First Guards losing 230 men, most of whom died on return home. The miserable venture was enlivened only by the enterprise of a grenadier, John

Skinner. The French had abandoned Fort Batz on South Beveland, leaving their guns spiked (put out of action by driving a soft nail into the touchhole and filing it smooth). Skinner found some means of unspiking all twelve of them with tools made by himself. How he did it nobody knows – and moreover under fire with the knowledge that any heat applied to the guns would very likely set them off, the French having left them loaded for that very purpose. There were no gallantry medals at that time, so a special one was struck and presented to him by the Duke of York and the officers of the Regiment.

Cadiz and Barrosa 1810-12

The French were by now almost fully in possession of Spain, and the defence of the port of Cadiz became critical. It was at last the turn of the 2nd Battalion to make a larger contribution and in February 1810 six companies joined a composite Guards brigade to garrison it. Much of the work consisted in building fortifications and it is good to note that the soldiers were given an extra allowance in recognition of the hard labour and wear and tear involved in the strenuous work.

In March 1811 they added a battle honour to their colours at Barrosa. A force was withdrawn from the town and landed further up the coast to engage the rear of the encircling French army. Separated from their Spanish allies, this body found itself facing a fresh enemy in twice its strength, but after a long march of fifteen miles drove them from a strong position. Their commander, General Graham, had decided that a bold offensive was required. 'Now my lads,' he told his men, waving his hat, 'There they are, spare your powder but give them steel enough.' In they went, with great determination, led by the Guards, and the position was won. It was one of the most stirring actions of the Peninsular War.

The cost, however, was very high, a total of 216 killed and wounded, and two months later the battalion was sent home and replaced by the 3rd Battalion, who remained at Cadiz until August 1812.

Wellington's Victorious Advance 1812-14

The stage was now set for the final, decisive operations in the Peninsula. Wellesley, now Viscount Wellington, had been campaigning with mixed success since 1809. The 2nd Guards Brigade, with the 1st Battalions of the Coldstream and Third Guards, were with

[8] Hamilton

Grenadier Gallery

PRIVATE

JOHN COLLETT

1781-1849

Private of the First
Guards for twenty
years, survivor of
Corunna, the later
Peninsular campaign
and Waterloo

*J*ohn Collett was born in Gloucestershire in the town of Bibury, where he became a labourer, and enlisted in the First Guards in September 1803 at Winchester.

Serving first with the 1st Battalion, he went to Sicily and then served through the campaign of Corunna. On the retreat six of his company of 100 were taken prisoner (being unable through sickness or fatigue to keep up) and twenty-one died at that time or later. Whether or not he then went to Walcheren is not certain, as he was sick during that period, as most of the army was, but this may have happened at home. At any rate he then returned to Spain where they again endured dreadful weather and disease. At the end of a punishing winter only seven of the original company were still on strength, including a young drummer who somehow managed to survive.

Collett moved to another company and, after Wellington's final drive through Spain, where he took part in several engagements, was transferred to the 2nd Battalion which was in Belgium during the short peace of 1814. When the Waterloo campaign opened he marched to Quatre Bras with his battalion and there was wounded in the foot. The wound turned out not to be serious and he returned to duty, the battalion then being part of the occupying force in France.

In 1818 he was at last given furlough and he seems to have spent the rest of his service in England before retiring in 1823 with his two campaign medals (the General Service with a bar for Corunna, and Waterloo) and the princely sum of 1s 0d a day. He died at the age of 68, a good score for that time.

See Chambers (1) and (2)

him. The battles of Talavera and Busaco had been fought and the famous defensive lines of Torres Vedras occupied. Albuera, Ciudad Rodrigo and Badajoz had been added to his roll of victories and in July 1812 he took Salamanca.

This caused the French to raise the siege of Cadiz and accordingly the **3rd Battalion** (Col Peregrine Maitland) marched 650 miles north with the liberated garrison and joined the main army at Salamanca, having fought a stirring action at **Seville** on the way. The **1st Battalion** (Col Darby Griffith) landed again at Corunna in September and marched south to rejoin its fellow in the 1st Guards Brigade. Both then settled into winter quarters, where they were badly stricken by sickness. This seems to have been a virulent low fever, from which the unacclimatized 1st Battalion suffered particularly severely. Despite being sent to Oporto on the coast, by the time the summer broke the two battalions had buried 800 out of 2500 men.

In May 1813, however, Wellington was ready to drive the French out of Spain altogether and his advance began. On 21 June, and before the 1st Guards Brigade was called forward, he all but destroyed the French army at Vittoria, but could not pursue them into France before dealing with the fortress of **San Sebastian** which stood in his way. The siege lasted three months and was accomplished only with heavy loss to a storming party of 200 taken from the Guards battalions. Some 150 became casualties.

The obstacle finally removed, the army crossed the rivers of Bidassoa, Nivelle, Nive and Adour. During the advance Lord Saltoun, commanding the light companies of the First Guards, saw one of his men approach some of the French wounded lying by the roadside and, after a moment, put his bayonet through one of them. Saltoun immediately rushed at him to inquire what he was doing. 'It's no Frenchman, sir,' was the reply, 'it's that Evans who deserted the night before the battle of Corunna'. It was true. The man, who died shortly afterwards, had deserted in January 1809 and taken service with the French. He gave himself away, and invited his death, by recognizing the uniform of his old comrades and calling to them for a drink.

On the **Nive**, on 9 December 1813, the enemy had to be forced back while contesting every inch of ground, every hedge and every bank, and then on the 11th made a powerful counter-attack which caused a running battle

to rage across the front of the Guards for most of the day.

On 5 April 1814 Napoleon, heavily pressed after being defeated by the allies at Leipzig, abdicated, but final battles were to be fought by Wellington at **Toulouse** before the news reached the French armies there, and then at **Bayonne**. This was a tragic affair. The French commander refused to believe that Napoleon had abdicated and made a last desperate sortie. He was met by the two Guards brigades and, after fierce, confused fighting in the dark, was finally repulsed. It cost the Guards over 500 casualties.

Now, at last, the fighting in the Peninsula and southern France was over and in August the battalions of the First Guards returned home. The campaign had been long and hard, in harsh winters and burning summers. To the end transport and supplies were normally inadequate and haphazard. The Guards had also found it frustrating to have remarkably little opportunity, compared to other regiments, to show their mettle in battle. They had demonstrated on many occasions, however, how crucial to success were the qualities of discipline that they displayed and in which they had earned the admiration of the whole army.

A well-covered head: this officer of the period 1809 to 1811 in the Peninsula, who appears to be wearing an absurd-looking tea cosy, was using a make-shift expedient for keeping the rain off his hat. There was no need for him to risk the wrath of the Great Duke by resorting to an umbrella. *Bob Marrion*

Bergen op Zoom 1814

The long series of operations would hardly have been complete without yet another attempt on that graveyard of good intentions, the Low Countries. It was to be the business of the 3rd Guards Brigade, containing the **2nd Battalion** (Col Lord Proby) and the other second battalions of Guards. In order to threaten Antwerp a plan was made to take Bergen op Zoom by coup-de-main on 8 March. A force of four columns was formed, one of which, 1000 strong, was found from the Guards. Each column approached by night from a different direction, but only that of the Guards succeeded in making an entry over frozen ditches and up ladders to scale the walls seventeen

feet high. Supported by men of other regiments, they maintained themselves through the night on the ramparts, though exposed and under constant fire. Eventually, the other columns having failed, they were ordered to withdraw, which they did with difficulty though in good order.

The attempt was soon followed by news of Napoleon's abdication, the terms of peace were signed on 23 April and the expedition moved to occupy Antwerp, evacuated by the French. Napoleon was exiled to the island of Elba in the Mediterranean. It seemed to be the end of the war, but the final act was yet to come on the bloody field of Waterloo a year later.

Ridiculous in the Rain and Courageous under Suffering

In 1813 when Wellington had observed several officers of the Guards under umbrellas he sent them a message: 'Lord Wellington does not approve of the use of umbrellas during the enemy's firing, and will not allow the gentlemen's sons to make themselves ridiculous in the eyes of the army.'

'Adair [a captain of the First Guards] was struck towards the end of the day by a cannon ball, which shattered his thigh near the hip. His sufferings during the amputation were dreadful; the shot had torn away the flesh of the thigh, and the bones were sticking up near the hip in splinters. The surgeon, Mr Gilder, had much difficulty in using his knife, having blunted it, and all his other instruments, by amputations in the earlier part of the battle. Poor Adair during the operation had sufficient pluck to make one last ghastly joke, saying, "Take your time, Mr Carver". He soon afterwards died from loss of blood.'[9]

Principal Source: Hamilton

A bearskin of modest size: full dress from 1812 to 1815 for this officer of a grenadier company. *Bryan Fosten*

---

[9] Gronow

Waterloo – Winning a Name, 18 June 1815

On 18 June 1815 the open fields of Waterloo, just outside the boundaries of Brussels and still to be seen in very much their original state, were to be the scene of one of the most important battles of history. The significance of this long, violent and extremely bloody engagement can hardly be over-stated. All arms, infantry, cavalry and artillery, fought ferociously in the hardest of encounters. It was the last battle fought between British and French after centuries of intermittent conflict. It ended twenty-two years of French military dominion over Europe and after it British troops did not return to the continent until the First World War a hundred years later. It set an allied army, containing soldiers of Britain, the Netherlands, Belgium, Prussia and several other German states, against the feared warriors of France, once invincible, and destroyed them. Face to face, in their first and only contest, were two of the greatest military leaders in history: Arthur, Duke of Wellington, the infantryman, and Napoleon Bonaparte, the artilleryman. Both were aged forty-six. The outcome of the battle was to shape the future of Europe for decades to come. And the margin by which it was won was very close – very close indeed.

Moreover, for our First Regiment of Guards it had very special significance. Through years of fighting we had never faced the core of Napoleon's cherished Imperial Guard, a body of soldiers who, in a hundred contests, had not known defeat. The moment came at the climax of the battle, when thin lines of guardsmen, exhausted and much depleted after two days of heavy fighting, battered by artillery and staggered by the shock of mass cavalry charges, got to their feet to face three full battalions of French veterans, fresh and undamaged, and throw them back down the slope. It won for the Regiment the name of 'Grenadier', the only title ever won by a British regiment as a direct result of its performance in battle.

The Hundred Days of Napoleon

After his abdication in April 1814 Napoleon was exiled to Elba. But in March 1815 he escaped with his small

Waterloo Medal: the first to be awarded to all ranks for a particular campaign.

The green plume: private of one of the light companies.
Bob Marrion

escort of Grenadiers and Chasseurs, and moved swiftly to Paris, collecting more and more of his old adherents on the way and turning out the restored monarchy. In no time he had reconstituted a large body of his Imperial Guard, including four regiments each of Grenadiers-à-pied and Chasseurs-à-pied (divided into 'Old Guard' and 'Middle Guard')[10], and two each of Tirailleurs and Voltigeurs ('Young Guard'); a total of twenty-two battalions of his most formidable troops. With these at the heart of a large army of 124,000, he marched north against Brussels in June.

The Allies were not well prepared to meet him. Wellington had great difficulty in gathering an army of 90,000, of very mixed quality and missing many of his veteran regiments from the Peninsula. He did have, however, a brigade of Household Cavalry and two brigades of Foot Guards. The **2nd Battalion** (Col Sir Henry Askew) and the **3rd Battalion** (Col Hon William Stuart) of the First Guards[11] formed the 1st Guards Brigade under Sir Peregrine Maitland, and the second battalions of the Coldstream and Third Guards the 2nd Guards Brigade. Maitland, Cooke (the 1st (Guards) Division commander) and Clinton (commanding the 2nd Division) were all officers of the First Guards. All the Guards battalions were over 1000 strong.

Quatre Bras (the Four Arms)

Much depended on Blücher's army of 116,000 Prussians linking up with Wellington from the north before Napoleon had a chance to deal with them separately. In his usual way, the Emperor moved with speed and decision, and it was not until the early morning of 16 June that Wellington heard that the French were within two and half miles of the crossroads at Quatre Bras, south of Waterloo, where

---

[10] These terms were used in different ways, but it mattered little to their enemies. 'They could have been Old Guard, Middle Guard, or anyone's Guard at all', commented one, 'they were ugly enough for anything'

[11] The 2nd Battalion had been quartered in Brussels since 1814, the 3rd Battalion being sent out to join it in April

Hougoumont: the light companies engaged in the long and furious struggle for the farm.
Richard Simkin

Complete over-throw: *The Times* reports the Duke of Wellington's despatch four days after the battle.

Pike and sword: a sergeant of a battalion company with red and white plume. Sergeants had to use their spontoons (half-pikes) to steady the line under the furious attack of the Imperial Guard.
Bob Marrion

Like hailstones on a window pane: the sound of bullets against the cuirasses of the French cavalry as they strove vainly to penetrate the squares of the two First Guards battalions. *Reginald Wymer*

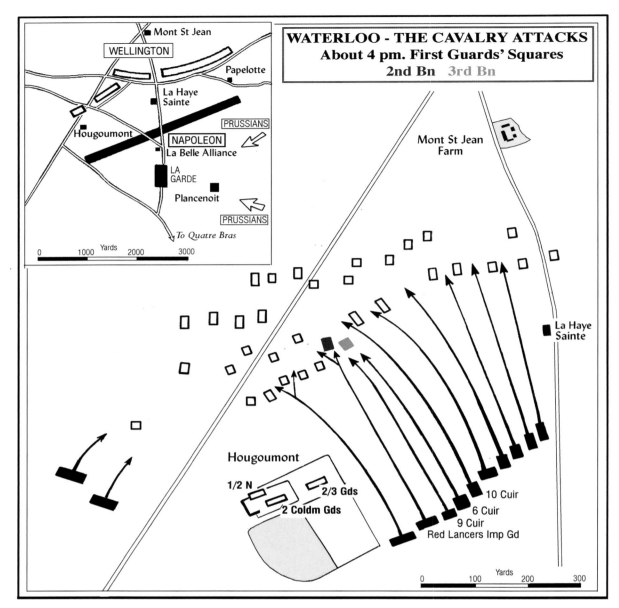

WATERLOO - THE CAVALRY ATTACKS
About 4 pm. First Guards' Squares
2nd Bn   3rd Bn

Mont St Jean
WELLINGTON
Papelotte
La Haye Sainte
PRUSSIANS
Hougoumont
NAPOLEON
La Belle Alliance
LA GARDE
Plancenoit
PRUSSIANS
To Quatre Bras

0   1000   Yards   2000   3000

Mont St Jean Farm

La Haye Sainte

Hougoumont

1/2 N   2/3 Gds
2 Coldm Gds
10 Cuir
6 Cuir
9 Cuir
Red Lancers Imp Gd

0   100   Yards   200   300

he had already determined to meet him. As dawn broke a force of 8000 troops, mostly Dutch, faced three times as many French, but the enemy did not press their attack and the allied line held. In the meantime the Guards marched twenty-six miles in thirteen hours from their initial position to the west, through a flaming hot June day. The start was not entirely auspicious. Joseph St John, an ensign, wrote, 'By the time that we got three miles out of the town [Brussels] I began to feel ashamed of the Guards, half the men were so tipsy that they kept tumbling into the ditches, but really it was so ridiculous that I could not help laughing,'[12]

They reached Quatre Bras at 5 pm, just as the French had gained possession of a vital feature, Bossu Wood. The light companies, and then the other companies of the two battalions of First Guards, were flung straight into the battle as they arrived. They drove the French steadily out of the difficult and tangled woodland, though suffering heavily in doing so, and helped to restore the line.

On the same day Blücher's Prussians had been heavily attacked at Ligny, and withdrew to Wavre, ten miles east of Waterloo. On hearing this, Wellington decided to pull back from Quatre Bras to his main position, and on 17 June the army moved to occupy it. The First Guards, having already lost 548 of their number at Quatre Bras, went with them.

---

[12] *Household Brigade Magazine,* Summer 1936

The Battlefield of Waterloo

The battlefield of Waterloo consisted of two ridges some 1200 yards apart, and the two armies faced each other across the shallow intervening valley along a front of some 4200 yards. The allied position was centred on Mont St Jean, with the village of Waterloo just behind it. The two farms of Hougoumont and La Haye Sainte were the only important buildings in this part of the valley and at dusk on 17 June the four light companies of Guards were sent to occupy Hougoumont. Behind them, the two Guards brigades were formed up, towards the centre of the allied line. Wellington posted most of his troops on the reverse slope, where they were to some extent sheltered from artillery bombardment, and where their exact number and disposition were concealed from the French.

Rain fell during the night of 17 June and the troops awoke cold, wet and muddy. The French were, of course, in a similar condition. Napoleon, at the inn of La Belle Alliance, decided to wait until noon to launch his main attack, so that the sodden ground could dry out for his cavalry and guns. In the meantime he directed his left-hand corps to capture Hougoumont, which he expected to be easily done. He was mistaken.

Advancing in square: it is probable that the Middle Guard battalions trudged up the slope in this formation, rather than in a vulnerable dense column. It would have allowed them to open out into an assaulting line in the last stages. As it was, the First Guards rose so unexpectedly in front of them that they had no chance to do so.

The Defence of Hougoumont

The light companies of the Coldstream and Third Guards held the buildings, which they had barricaded for defence, and those of the First Guards, under Lord Saltoun, the walled garden and orchard, There were also considerable numbers of 1/2 Nassau Regiment. The French attacked without success at 11 am and made a second attempt an hour later. Surrounding the buildings

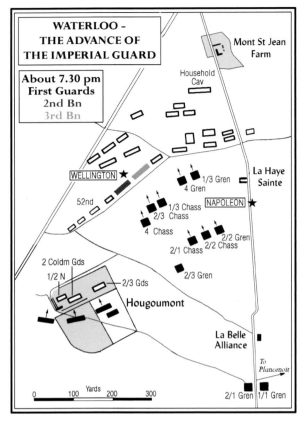

**WATERLOO –
THE ADVANCE OF
THE IMPERIAL GUARD**

**About 7.30 pm
First Guards
2nd Bn
3rd Bn**

Mont St Jean
Farm

Household
Cav

WELLINGTON ★

52nd

La Haye
Sainte

1/3 Gren
4 Gren

NAPOLEON ★

1/3 Chass
2/3 Chass
4 Chass
2/1 Chass 2/2 Chass
2/2 Gren

2 Coldm Gds
1/2 N
2/3 Gds
2/3 Gren

Hougoumont

La Belle
Alliance

To
Plancenoit

Yards
0   100   200   300

2/1 Gren 1/1 Gren

on three sides, they attempted to force the north gate, which was open to admit guardsmen withdrawing from outside the walls. A party succeeded in penetrating, but they were all killed and the gates forced shut against a wall of enemy by ten gallant officers and NCOs of the Coldstream and Third Guards. Further attacks followed throughout the day and counter-attacks were launched by the battalions of the 2nd Guards Brigade. The light companies of the First Guards threw the French out of the orchard several times, but were horribly mauled by an artillery piece at close range. The few survivors were eventually relieved and rejoined their own battalions on the ridge. Hougoumont held, at a cost of 540 casualties, while the French, increasingly desperate, lost 8000 in the attempt.

Napoleon's Main Infantry Attack

Napoleon had hoped that Wellington would weaken his centre to reinforce Hougoumont. He did not, and the farm had held. Two elements of the Emperor's plan had

Sweeping down the slope: the final rout of the Imperial Guard and the destruction of Napoleon's ambitions. *Faulkner's Celebrated Cigarettes*

already failed. Now the Prussians were moving towards the battlefield and not far away. Eighty-four guns had been pounding the allied lines since midday and Napoleon therefore decided to launch his main infantry attack on Wellington's centre at 1 pm. It was thrown back by a resolute infantry defence and the charge of two brigades of heavy cavalry, including the Household Cavalry, who, however, lost heavily in the process.

The French Cavalry and the Allied Squares

The French infantry had failed. Now it was the turn of the cavalry. After another intensive bombardment of the allied centre from 3.30, Wellington ordered his forward troops to pull back behind the reverse slope. Marshal Ney, Napoleon's cavalry commander, took this to indicate a general withdrawal and ordered an attack by 5000 cavalry to take advantage of it.

The First Guards, with the other infantry battalions, formed square. Wellington took his own place in the square of the 2nd Battalion, where he sat unmoved on Copenhagen, his favourite charger. Captain Gronow described the scene vividly: 'You perceived at a distance what appeared to be an overwhelming, long moving line which, ever advancing, glittered like a stormy wave of the sea when it catches the sunlight ... They were the famous Cuirassiers, almost all old soldiers, who had distinguished themselves on most of the battlefields of Europe. In an almost incredibly short period they were within twenty yards of us shouting *Vive L'Empereur!* The word of command "Prepare to receive cavalry" had been given, every man in the front ranks knelt, and a wall bristling with steel, held together by steady hands, presented itself to the infuriated Cuirassiers... [The square was] a perfect hospital, being full of dead and dying and mutilated soldiers. The charges were in appearance very formidable but in reality a great relief as the artillery could no longer fire at us. The noise of our bullets against the cuirasses of Kellerman's and Milhaud's squadrons was like hailstones on a window pane.'[13]

Five times, for over an hour, the French attacked and

---

[13] Gronow

FIELD MARSHAL
ARTHUR WELLESLEY, Duke of WELLINGTON
KG GCB GCH* *1769-1852*

Victor of India, the Peninsula and Waterloo, Colonel of the Regiment, Commander-in-Chief, Prime Minister

*A*rthur Wellesley, Duke of Wellington, is the most celebrated military figure in British history.

The fifth son of the Earl of Mornington (he spelt his name Wesley until 1798) he rather perversely received his military education in France, at Angers, there being no equivalent school in England. He was a dreamy and languid youth, devoted to his violin, but being unhappy in love he threw the instrument on the fire and took himself off to war, where he quickly discovered his vocation.

He commanded the 33rd Foot in the Duke of York's Netherlands campaign of 1794-1795, where he learned a good many lessons in how not to run a war. Moving on to India, his brother the Governor General gave him the opportunity of a larger command, in which he greatly distinguished himself, especially at Assaye in 1803 where he crushed the Mahrattas. He advanced rapidly in rank, in the early stages by purchase, as was the system, but later by sheer merit.

By 1808 he was a lieutenant-general and a viscount, and was entrusted with the command in Portugal. Over the following five years, with several shifts in fortune, he fought Napoleon's marshals in Portugal and Spain and won a string of victories: Vimiero, Talavera, Busaco, the defence of the lines of Torres Vedras, the storming of Ciudad Rodrigo and Badajoz, Salamanca, Vittoria and the battles of the Pyrenees, Bayonne and Toulouse.

Finally, he met Napoleon himself on the field of Waterloo and won Britain's most famous victory.

It was, by his own admission, 'the most desperate business I ever was in. I never took so much trouble over a battle, and never was so near being beat. Our loss is immense, particularly in that best of all Instruments, British Infantry. I never saw the Infantry behave so well'. And he was no more than acknowledging the truth when he said, 'By God! I don't think it would have been done if I had not been there'.

A superb horseman, his favourite charger was the renowned Copenhagen. On one occasion in Spain he was forced to retire rapidly from a bold reconnaissance, with French bullets peppering his retreat and his own men rising to their feet and cheering him home.

His career was by no means over in 1815. Though loaded with honours and riches, he had a high sense of public duty and an immense capacity for work. It even led him to accept twice, though reluctantly, the responsibilities of prime minister. It was not a success and brought him unpopularity at a time of great political turbulence. And it was different from soldiering. 'I gave them their orders,' he is reported to have complained after an early cabinet meeting, 'and they wanted to stay and discuss them.'

He was three times Commander-in-Chief, occupying the famous office over the arch of Horse Guards, twice briefly in 1827-1828 and then from 1842 until 1846. He was Colonel of the Regiment from 1827 until his death. This did not give him unalloyed pleasure. He was harassed by applications for commissions. 'I have a list ... as long as my arm,' he wrote with some petulance. 'We and our fathers could serve in the Line. But now everybody must place his son in the Guards, in the Grenadiers "par preference" because I am Colonel of that Regt. And everyone has a right to apply to me.'

He managed to create victorious armies from the most unpromising material: the sweepings of jails, poorhouses and taverns. He called them 'the scum of the earth', but because of their origins, not their quality, adding 'it is really wonderful that we should have made them the fine fellows they are'. His soldiers were devoted to him. One said, 'We would rather see his long nose in a fight than a reinforcement of ten thousand men any day'. The 'Great Duke', the 'Iron Duke', he was indeed.

Principal sources: Haythornthwaite, Longford, Paget

* Knight Grand Cross of the Hanoverian Order

CAPTAIN
REES GRONOW
1794-1865

Veteran of the
Peninsula and
Waterloo, Author of
voluminous
recollections and
anecdotes

*R*ees Gronow was commissioned ensign in the First Guards in December 1812. He was just in time to go to Spain in February 1813 and take part in several engagements with the 1st Battalion in the subsequent campaign. Threatened with being left behind in England with that battalion in 1815, he promptly went on leave and made his way to Belgium, where he turned up with the 3rd Battalion in time to play his part at Waterloo.

Between 1810 and 1860 he wrote a long series of *Reminiscences and Recollections, being Anecdotes of the Camp, Court, Clubs and Society*, many of them set in Paris after the war. These include a vivid account of Waterloo, notably the cavalry charges on the British squares, the agonies of wounded men and horses, and the approach and destruction of the Imperial Guard. He also captured several aspects of life on campaign in the Peninsula. He was impressed by the civilized form of the French encampments, well drained, with streets, squares and places of amusement, while the British soldiers were crammed into small tents with nothing to do. 'The pipeclay system of tormenting our men, by requiring them to keep their kits clean and punishing them by extra drills if the firelock or belts were not as spotless as on parade at the Horse Guards, was (to say the least of it) extremely injudicious' echoes complaints of a later age. He commented on avoiding dysentery by drinking a small glass of brandy or rum every morning, and on his soldier-servant's excellence as a cook and his 'too great admiration, unqualified with respect, for the charms of the fair sex' (he once had to be removed from beneath a bed with poker and tongs).

See Gronow

five times they were beaten off. The steady accurate musketry of the infantry struck them and their mounts with deadly effect, and they also suffered severely from the grapeshot fired at close range by Captain Mercer's troop of horse artillery, close to the ever-dwindling squares of the First Guards.

The Defeat of the Imperial Guard

Following his earlier attack, Napoleon had had some success against Wellington's centre and by 6.30 had taken the farm of La Haye Sainte. This enabled him to bring his artillery closer, and with it he pummelled the centre unrelentingly. If he had followed up at that point he might well have broken through. But he waited half an hour too long and allowed Wellington to reinforce the centre from his left, as the Prussians had begun to appear from that flank and were bringing the French right under pressure at Plancenoit. At last, however, the Emperor made his final throw.

Many of the twenty-two battalions of the Imperial Guard had already been committed. The Tirailleurs and Voltigeurs of the Young Guard, and later two battalions of the Old Guard, were sent to Plancenoit on the right flank to hold back the Prussians. The remainder of the Old Guard took no prominent part in the battle at all, being concerned largely with covering the eventual retreat and seeing the defeated Emperor safely off the field. The six Middle Guard battalions (two each of the 3rd Grenadiers and 3rd Chasseurs, and the single one of each of the two 4th Regiments) were left to mount the assault on Wellington's line. They were led by Napoleon himself, who then handed them over to Ney at the bottom of the slope. One battalion was held back in reserve, while the remaining five were launched up the rise. There is no exact authority for which battalion took which route, but there seems every reason to suppose that they deployed in the same order as originally formed, the Grenadiers being in the place of honour on the right of the line. It is also probable that they advanced in square formation, in preparation for opening out into a more extended line when close to their enemy in order to bring the maximum fire to bear.

Thus it would have been the two fresh battalions of the 3rd Chasseurs, closely followed by the 4th Chasseurs, that assaulted the two exhausted battalions of the First Guards. Gronow, again, saw them come, 'their red epaulettes and crossbelts put on over their blue greatcoats [giving] them a gigantic appearance, which was increased by their high hairy caps and long red feathers, which waved with the nod of their heads as they kept time to a drum in the centre of their column'.[14]

The guardsmen, lying down as ordered just over the crest, could not at first see the enemy advancing on them. But they heard the tramp of their feet, getting ever closer, and the confident roars of *En avant! Vive L'Empereur!* Wellington, however, on horseback directly behind them, could see the Imperial Guard closing in steadily, while across the valley stood Napoleon, watching them fade into the dusk and smoke. Wellington waited calmly until the enemy were only some forty paces away, then he called out to the brigade commander, 'Now, Maitland, Now's your time', and a moment later, 'Stand up Guards. Make Ready. Fire!' The First Guards rose to their feet as the French columns breasted the slope and the antagonists saw each other for the first time. The surprised Frenchmen had no time to extend their formation or even to press forward before the first deadly volley tore into them. The Guards were in four ranks to gain the maximum fire effect, and they overlapped the frontage of the French

Spiritual comfort in the agony of battle and wounds: the silver chalice used by Stonestreet, chaplain to the Guards at Waterloo.

column. They fired from the hip and the effect was terrible. Packed so close, it was almost impossible for the French to retaliate. For about ten minutes they tried to advance, but could not. Two hundred yards to a flank, Bolton's battery joined in with a barrage of grape-shot.

Colour Sergeant Charles Wood of the 3rd Battalion wrote, 'The fight at one time became so desperate with our battalion that files upon files were carried to the rear from the carnage, and the line was held by the serjeants' pikes, placed against the rear: not for want of courage on the men's part (for they were desperate), only for moments our loss so unsteadied the line'. In a later letter he described how 'the serjeants placed their pikes [lengthways] against the men's backs ... and bore them upon their shoulders by main strength'.[15]

At last the enemy wavered. 'Now's the time, my boys,' called Lord Saltoun, echoing his general, and the First Guards charged with the bayonet. For a moment

---

[14] Gronow
[15] Chambers (2)

'The most desperate business I ever was in': Wellington and his First Guards at the climax of the great victory. *Robert Hillingsford*

the French faced them and then they broke. Meanwhile the 4th Chasseurs, coming up rather behind the 3rd and to a flank, threatened to imperil the right flank of the 1st Guards battalions. A moment of confusion arose as Maitland checked his right-hand battalion (the 2nd) and reformed. They did so successfully and at that moment the 52nd Light Infantry on the right executed a brilliant enfilading movement, pouring fire into the flank of the 4th Chasseurs. They also turned and fled.

The onlookers in the French army could not believe their eyes. The shout went up, 'La Garde recule – the Guard recoils'. And it was true. It was the first time they had ever suffered a defeat. The panic spread. Wellington saw it and, raising his hat, he waved it in an unmistakable signal towards the French. With a resounding cheer, the entire British line, now only 40,000 strong, swept forward and drove the demoralized enemy headlong down the slope into the valley below and up the opposite side. The cavalry joined in with relish. Napoleon himself took shelter inside a square of Grenadiers of his Old Guard, who escorted him off the field. It was just 8.30 and the sun was setting, blood-red through the thick smoke.

The British were too exhausted to pursue far, but fresh Prussians harried the French ruthlessly into the night. It was the most complete victory, but at an enormous cost. Some 40,000 men and 10,000 horses lay dead or wounded on the battlefield that night. The First Guards alone had lost over a thousand, half of them at Quatre Bras. But, with the exception of a short fight at Péronne, the war was over and the allies moved in to occupy French territory.

The Title of Grenadier, the Bearskin and Plume, the Grenade Badge

On 29 July, just a few weeks after the battle, the Prince Regent granted the title of *Grenadiers* to the First Regiment of Foot Guards. By the same token the bearskin with a white Grenadier plume would be worn by the whole regiment, and the grenade itself would take its place alongside the royal cypher as the regimental badge.

The Reward and the Riddle

The *London Gazette* of that day reads:

War-Office, July 29, 1815

The Prince Regent, as a mark of His Royal approbation of the distinguished gallantry of the Brigade of Foot Guards in the victory of Waterloo, has been

Napoleon's pride: Chasseur-à-pied (left) and Grenadier-à-pied, in slightly different orders of dress. It would have been hard to distinguish between the two in the fury and murk of a battlefield, and neither Wellington nor his Foot Guards had encountered them before.

pleased, in the name and on the behalf of His Majesty, to approve of all the Ensigns of the three Regiments of Foot Guards having the rank of Lieutenants, and that such rank shall be attached to all the future appointments to Ensigncies in the Foot Guards, in the same manner as the Lieutenants of those Regiments obtain the rank of Captain.

His Royal Highness has also been pleased to approve of the 1st Regiment of Foot Guards being made a Regiment of Grenadiers, and styled 'The First or Grenadier Regiment of Foot Guards', in commemoration of their having defeated the Grenadiers of the French Imperial Guards upon this memorable occasion.

It was a tremendous honour, the grenadier companies throughout the army being considered the elite. No greater accolade could be bestowed than being made an entire regiment of grenadiers.

How the award came to be made is not clear. There is no documentary record of the proposal. Wellington himself was heard by a gunner officer to say on the battlefield shortly after the Imperial Guard turned tail, 'Guards, you will be rewarded for this', and no doubt this was the result. However, in his famous Waterloo Despatch, written shortly after the battle and before any detailed gathering of records by his staff, Wellington was very sparing in giving praise to one regiment rather than another and made no specific mention of the First Guards, even though he was on the very spot of their historic action and indeed gave the command that launched it. Neither did he mention the 52nd, whose intelligent action he clearly saw and admired. He did, however, allude to Hougoumont twice, and the Coldstream and Third Guards also received rewards in the terms of the *London Gazette* of 29 July and later (in 1831) were given the bearskin cap. The Waterloo Despatch gave rise in subsequent years to almost as much heat as the battle itself, as regiment after regiment, commander after commander, pressed their claims for greater credit than their fellows.

As late as 2005, 190 years after the battle, a new book appeared alleging that, to all intents and purposes, the 52nd Light Infantry had disposed of the Imperial Guard on their own and that Wellington had fudged the record and silenced senior commanders with honours in order to preserve his own reputation.[16]

A dispute has also raged about whether they really were *Grenadiers* of the Imperial Guard that the First Guards saw off so decisively and whose name they assumed. By a careful examination of the evidence almost two centuries later, it seems virtually certain that they were in fact regiments of *Chasseurs*. But riddles still remain. Gronow refers to the French figures conspicuous by their high bearskin caps, adorned with red feathers. Lachouque, the principal French historian of the Imperial Guard, tells us that, bearskins being in short supply, the 3rd and 4th

Mark of approbation: the page of the *London Gazette* with the famous entry.

A little tidying up en route for Paris: the final action at Péronne. *Faulkner's Celebrated Cigarettes*

regiments of both Grenadiers and Chasseurs had none at all. Even if they had, the French guardsmen were accustomed to wear small plumes in battle, rather than the full-sized ones. Despite the length of the war the British regiments had never before met either the grenadiers-à-pied or chasseurs-à-pied, who were kept close to the Emperor's side and used in his own battles. In the din and smoke and exhaustion of the battle, it was perhaps an easy enough assumption to have made, and it fitted the picture very nicely when it was decided to give the Regiment a signal honour – the name of *Grenadier*.

Principal Sources: Adkin, Hamilton, Lachouque (1) and (2), Paget, Whitworth (2)

---

[16] Sale

COLOURS OF THE REGIMENT

The Colours form the spiritual core of a regiment. In earlier times the rallying point in battle, they are consecrated emblems and treated with great care and reverence. To lose Colours to the enemy was the ultimate disgrace: to capture them the ultimate triumph. When they pass on parade soldiers salute and civilians remove their hats in respect. The battered and threadbare Colours to be found laid up in cathedrals and churches throughout the country bear witness both to acts of desperate courage and to the emotional bonds that unite soldiers thrown together in common trials and hardship.

It was necessary for soldiers to recognize their own Colours and for that reason they were 'trooped' slowly along the ranks in order to be seen at close quarters. 'Trooping the Colour', enacted each year on Horse Guards Parade to

Royal Standard of the Regiment: the Queen's Company Colour presented by Queen Elizabeth II in 1953 and still in use in 2005.

celebrate the sovereign's birthday, is a ceremony known over the world for its precision and grandeur, and stems directly from the original purpose. Indeed, battalions stationed abroad have often staged a similar parade, clad in a uniform suitable to their environment.

Though a number of variations have been made over the years, the present Colours of the Grenadier Guards are directly derived from those originally granted by Charles II to the regiments of Lord Wentworth and Colonel Russell in 1661. Before 1700 every company flew its own Colour, but the number was reduced and by 1751 each battalion had two only, the companies contenting themselves with small, unconsecrated flags or badges.

The Queen's Company Colour, the Royal Standard of the Regiment

The Colour of the Sovereign's Company is also the Royal Standard of the Regiment, often referred to as a State Colour. It is known as the Queen's (or King's) Company Colour and is considerably larger than the battalion Colours, measuring 5ft 10ins by 4ft 10ins, and with a pike of 10ft

Intricate work: detail for the Queen's Company Colour being prepared by skilful ladies at Hobson and Sons.

5ins. It requires real strength and dexterity to manage, especially in a wind when it can act as a sail and drag its ensign out of line. When lowering the Colour in salute, the ensign needs to use both hands, the left bearing on the pike behind his back in order to provide extra leverage and control. This Colour is carried on ceremonial duties only when the Queen herself is present. Where the 1st Battalion finds a guard of honour on such an occasion, the Queen's Company furnishes the guard and carries its Colour, except when it is at the same time on duty at St James's Palace and Buckingham Palace as the Queen's Guard. Where, however, an equivalent guard of honour has been found by another battalion, it has carried the Royal Standard.

The Queen's Company Colour is lowered only to the King or Queen, the Sovereign's consort and to visiting heads of state when the monarch is present. A new Colour is presented on the accession of a new sovereign.

Battalion Colours

Each regular battalion of infantry has a pair (or stand) of Colours, the Queen's Colour and the Regimental Colour. In most regiments the Queen's Colour is in the form of a Union Flag and the Regimental Colour of plain crimson silk, but in the Foot Guards the reverse is the case as a result of a special distinction laid down by the Duke of Cumberland in 1745. In 1859 the War Office made an attempt to unseat the distinction, but a protest to the Queen quickly removed the threat. There has been one exception to this rule. In recognition of its service during the First World War, and not long before it was disbanded, the 4th Battalion was presented with a single Colour in 1919. This was a Union Flag, issued as the King's Colour.

The three regular battalions of Grenadiers have

Highest point: the gilt silver pike top of the Queen's Company Colour.

each had their normal stand of two Colours. The 3rd Battalion was the last of the Regiment to carry Colours into battle, in the Crimea, and at Inkerman they were saved only after a desperate struggle. The Colours held by that battalion in 1960 were laid up when the 3rd Grenadiers went into suspended animation that year. The 2nd Battalion, however, though similarly

Four in line: the new Colours presented to the two battalions in 1992. *Roger Thompson*

suspended in 1994, is still embodied as the separate Nijmegen Company, which still carries the 2nd Battalion Colours, new ones having being most recently presented by the Queen in 2001. It is the Queen's Colour that is trooped in London, while elsewhere it is the Regimental Colour unless Her Majesty is present in person.

Colours, especially those of the Foot Guards which are constantly used on ceremonial occasions, become worn and frayed and need replacing, usually at intervals of ten to fifteen years. The presentation of new Colours is a major occasion in the life of the Regiment. So, too, is the laying up of old Colours, normally in places with which Grenadiers have a particular association and from where they recruit. Old Colours of the three battalions laid up since 1945 are to be found in cathedrals and churches of Manchester, Nottingham, Liverpool, Lincoln, Worcester, Derby, Ely, Westminster, Bristol and in the Guards Chapel and St Paul's Cathedral.

A long list of battle honours (correctly described as honorary distinctions): however, these honours, shown on the Queen's Colour of the 1st Battalion, do not include several battles, including Steenkirk and Fontenoy, in which the First Guards fought with great distinction. Where such battles were not counted as victories, honours were not allowed.

Company Badges and Camp Colours

When the regiments of Wentworth and Russell were formed, each contained twelve companies and to each company a Colour was granted by Royal Warrant. All of them were based first on the St George's Cross, and later the Union. Twenty-four royal badges, dating back to Edward III, were selected by Garter Principal King-at-Arms and one superimposed on each Colour. The senior companies in each regiment, however, were the King's, Colonel's, Lieutenant Colonel's and Major's, and their Colours were different from the others. They were known as Field Officers' Colours and seven of the eight were of white silk. On the amalgamation of the two regiments into a single one of twenty-four companies, all the Colours remained, except that there were now four Field Officers' Colours rather than eight.

In 1713 these four Field Officers' Colours were withdrawn for ceremonial use only and further Colours were issued to companies to restore the original total of twenty-four. When battalion Colours came into use the Field Officers' Colours became the King's (or Queen's) Company Colour (the Royal Standard of the Regiment) and the King's Colours of the three battalions – the Colonel's to the 1st, the Lieutenant Colonel's to the 2nd and the Major's to the 3rd Battalion. The Regimental Colours were simply a larger version of the earlier company Colours, taken in succession. In 1859 the emphasis was changed and Regimental Colours were described as bearing company badges, emblazoned in rotation.

There were still only twenty-four company badges in 1713 when the Regiment consisted of that number of battalion companies. The four grenadier companies, and from 1792 the light companies, were not issued with Colours. In 1854, however, the Regiment was established at thirty companies, all of the same kind, and the number of badges increased to thirty.

These company badges, numbered from one to thirty and originally used to mark lines in camp, still remain on small flags or camp colours (familiarly, though incorrectly, known as 'company colours'). With changes in organization they were eventually allotted to the 1st Battalion (1-8), 2nd Battalion (9-16), 3rd Battalion (17-24), 13th and 14th Companies at the Training Battalion and Guards Depot (25-26) and Regimental Headquarters (27-30). Within each battalion, the eight badges were given to each of the five companies, the Commanding Officer, Senior Major and Adjutant. The demise of the 2nd and 3rd Battalions caused further changes, but Inkerman Company (representing the 3rd Battalion) still flies No 20, and Nijmegen Company (the residue of the 2nd Battalion) No 12.

It is the custom for a retiring company commander, or other officer entitled to a badge,

Day to remember: Colours are decked with laurel wreaths on the anniversary of a battle honour.
Roger Scruton

Colours of the 1st & 2nd Battalions Grenadier Guards. Presented by Her Majesty The Queen, Colonel-in-Chief. 3rd May 1978. And The Thirty Company Badges of The Regiment

A fine display: the Colours presented in 1978 and the thirty company badges. *Christopher Collins*

to take away with him the camp colour under which he served, replacing it with a new one for his successor. Sometimes he is given it as a farewell present. The camp colours normally adorn the offices in the orderly room and 'company bunks' to which they apply.

Badges also used to be painted on small metal plates, mounted on the radiators of landrovers and taken into the field as a colourful and elegant mark of the close association between Grenadiers and the throne.

See Grenadier Guards (7)

Chapter Four

A GENERATION AT PEACE
1815-1854

The epoch-making battle at Waterloo in June 1815 was not quite the end of the campaign. The allied armies advanced into France, with a few minor engagements on the way, and took up residence in Paris, the two Grenadier battalions being quartered in the Bois de Boulogne and boosted by reinforcements sent from England to replace their heavy losses. On 22 July there was a grand review of the Prussian Guards, 13,000 strong, in the city before the emperors of Russia and Austria and several kings and princes from the German states and the Netherlands. The fine appearance of the Prussians caused a great stir, it having been conveniently forgotten that they had been worsted by the French. And Wellington certainly was not taken in. 'I can show you on Monday some men that can lick these fellows,' he observed.

In January 1816 the 2nd Battalion returned home, and immediately took the leading part in a great parade to lodge in Whitehall Chapel the two French standards with eagles taken at Waterloo. These trophies were placed in the middle of the Grenadier guard of honour and the eagles borne into the chapel by two sergeants, one Grenadier and one Coldstream. The 3rd Battalion had to wait almost three years longer. Leaving Paris, they were quartered for much of that time on the ramparts of Cambrai. The tedious garrison life was enlivened by large-scale manoeuvres in the autumn months and at last they sailed for England in November 1818. All those who had taken part in the campaign were given the Waterloo Medal, the first of its kind ever to be issued. It was a fitting award, as many in the army had served continuously under the Duke for ten long years.

Still a fairly modest bearskin, though a prominent plume: a private of the First or Grenadier Regiment in 1825. Exactly how soon after 1815 the whole regiment was fitted out with bearskin caps is uncertain.
Bryan Fosten

In 1820 King George III died after his long reign of sixty years. The Prince Regent came to the throne as George IV and all three battalions took part in the grand ceremonial of his coronation in July 1821. The three regimental majors (commanding battalions as colonels in the army) were promoted major general by the Coronation Brevet.[1] The new king delighted in fine and extravagant uniforms and tried all kinds of experiments on his troops, notably the Household Cavalry. His new regiment of Grenadiers began to adopt the uniform of scarlet tunic and bearskin cap, which in its essence was to remain for two hundred years, and to wear the grenade badge. The grenadier companies of the Coldstream and Third Guards continued to wear bearskins as before, with white plumes, and in 1831 the caps were granted to those regiments entire, thus bringing all three regiments of Foot Guards into line. The Coldstream chose to wear a red plume on the right-hand side and extraneous decoration on the bearskins of all three regiments was cut down to a more modest scale.

In 1827 the Duke of York died and was succeeded in the colonelcy of the Regiment by the Duke of Wellington, who himself died in 1852. The state funeral of the Great Duke was on a colossal scale. A guard of honour drawn from the 2nd Battalion was the first to be mounted on his body, which lay in state in Chelsea Hospital from 10 to 17 November. He was borne to St Paul's Cathedral on an immense funeral bier and in the procession every regiment in the Army was represented by three officers, three NCOs and six

---

[1] A major occasion of this kind was sometimes used as an opportunity to hand out special honours and promotions

73

Beneath the castle: the First Guards at Windsor in 1815.
Reginald Wymer

Staff and sash with
drumsticks: a drum
major of 1815-16.
Bryan Fosten

Pink-cheeked young
blade: an officer of
the age of elegance
in 1831. *Bryan Fosten*

On guard: Grenadiers
at Buckingham Palace
in 1820. *Reginald Wymer*

privates. All three Grenadier battalions took part in the ceremony, the flank companies of the 1st and 2nd Battalions being posted immediately outside the cathedral and the 3rd Battalion stationed in Trafalgar Square helping to control the vast crowds about Charing Cross. The new Colonel of the Regiment was Prince Albert, the Prince Consort.

Royal Guards and Security Duties

The primary role of the Regiment, to safeguard the person of the monarch and his family, was no light task in these years, for members of royalty had frequently been guilty of outrageous behaviour and had attracted serious hostility. Demonstrations and physical assault were not uncommon and considerable armed escorts were needed when the royal family travelled about.

Sometimes the attentions of royalty could be unwelcome. The Duke of York's younger brother the Duke of Clarence[2], a naval officer, once decided to inflict his skills on the army by a minute inspection of the Guards, horse and foot, and then 'had a musket brought to him, that he might show them the way to use it in some new sort of exercise that he wanted to introduce: in short, he gave a great deal of trouble and made a fool of himself'.[3]

During the reign of William IV (1830-1837) the Buckingham House detachment of the King's Guard was only a sergeant's guard, but when Queen Victoria took up residence there the guard was increased to one officer and forty men. It has always been, and still is, a detachment of the Queen's Guard based at St James's Palace.

An intriguing dispute occurred on 9 November 1841, when the future King Edward VII was born at 10.48 am. By tradition, the Captain of the Queen's Guard on the day when an heir to the throne was born was granted a brevet[4] majority, but at that precise moment the guards were changing and both commanders claimed promotion. Happily, the decision went in favour of Udney, the Grenadier Captain of the Old Guard.

There was a remarkable event when the 1st Battalion were drilling in Hyde Park in 1843, under their commanding officer, Colonel Robert Ellison, a veteran of Waterloo and lately in command of the 2nd Battalion in Canada.[5] He gave the order 'Present Arms' and then

---

[2] Later King William IV
[3] Holmes
[4] Brevet rank was a temporary promotion, though normally in advance of later confirmation
[5] Another example of the unsettling practice of moving an officer already commanding a battalion to a more 'senior' one when a vacancy arose

Wellington at the head of his Grenadiers in 1829: a flamboyant account which demonstrates the taste of the times. The Colonel is wearing the shako which can still be seen today; once, when he chose the bearskin, he fell off his horse. *Mark Charms*

suffered a heart attack and fell stone dead from his horse, his battalion paying the appropriate compliment over his body – on his own command.

It was a time of great political upheaval. Until a police force was established in 1829 it fell to the Army to maintain law and order. Even after that date troops were frequently called out to disperse crowds, protect property and provide escorts for bullion, prisoners and important visitors. Guards were placed on important public buildings and it was even necessary sometimes to protect theatres from the effects of rowdy behaviour. On one famous occasion, the Cato Street conspiracy, a serious plot to murder several members of the cabinet, it fell to a detachment of Grenadiers to be on duty at Newgate Gaol when the conspirators were executed. It was usual after hanging to cut off the heads of the victims. On this occasion the officers were eating breakfast with the governor of the gaol when a servant hurried in to borrow the largest carving knife so that the job could be tidily finished.

In 1826 the 2nd Battalion were called upon to deal with riots in Manchester and were commended for their orderly conduct during the disturbances. The duties of the army

even included fire-fighting and the Guards were commended by the Home Secretary for their part in trying to control the fire which destroyed the Houses of Parliament in 1834 and 'reduced that interesting old pile of buildings to ashes'.[6]

By Canal Boat to Dublin

The Brigade of Guards was first called upon for public duty in Dublin in 1821, initially to ensure the safety of the Lord Lieutenant, Marquess Wellesley[7], who was said to have accepted the scarcely popular post only under this condition. A long succession of battalions followed into the 1870s. Ireland still of course belonged to the Crown – the present republic would not come into being until the next century, and then only after serious convulsions.

The journey to Liverpool, the embarkation point for Dublin, was by canal boat and normally started in Paddington Basin. The boats were usually hired from Pickfords, whose craft were able to carry up to sixty men sitting on benches, each carrying his musket. Movement

[6] Hamilton
[7] Eldest brother of the Duke of Wellington

76

was continuous by day and night, with straw provided on which to sleep. The military boats had priority, especially in the one-way tunnels, and seven days was a good time.

The 3rd Grenadiers were the first to go, in December 1821, 650 officers and men with twenty women and two children, and were relieved by the 1st Battalion in July 1822. The 2nd Battalion took its turn in July 1825 and it fell to the 3rd Battalion again to make the last journey of this kind in August 1827. Thereafter the railways took over.

The garrison in Ireland was a mixed one and the subalterns had been called upon to take their share of duty with those of the other regiments. However, as captains in the army, they were excused by the intervention of the Duke of York, no doubt to the irritation of their fellows of the Line.

Muffled in Canada: a corporal well wrapped up in 1838. *Pierre Turner (from 'British Infantry Uniforms Since 1660' by Michael Barthorp – Blandford Press)*

The duties were humdrum enough, judging by the paucity of information about the time spent in Ireland. There was, however, an innovation in 1831 when 'orders were issued, shortly after its arrival there, that a certain number of men in every company should be instructed in the rudiments of Gunnery, and go through the repository course as practised at Woolwich, in order that every Battalion might have sufficient knowledge of Field Artillery practice to enable it to work its own guns in the field. A detachment of the Second Battalion Grenadier Guards was accordingly daily sent down to the Island Bridge Barracks, under a subaltern, to go through the requisite course, and considerable progress was made with the men during their stay in Dublin'.[8]

What subsequent use was made of this valuable training is not recorded, though the laudable experiment in widening the skills of Grenadiers was repeated in 1852 when parties of a similar size were detached to Chatham for a course of instruction in siege operations and the construction of field works.

Elegance also in the sergeants' mess: a gold sergeant of 1846. *Christopher Collins*

Improvements in the Military Life

As the standard of living rose, better arrangements were made for the regiments of Guards. Permanent barracks became more the rule than the exception, though it took time for messes to be established.

The five battalions of Foot Guards in London were stationed chiefly in the Tower of London, Wellington Barracks and other barracks near the National Gallery, in Portman Street and in Knightsbridge, which at the time were on the outskirts of London – the enormous expansion of the city was not to come until the second half of the century. The new Wellington Barracks was completed in 1834 in two parts (St George's and Wellington Barracks) and the barracks at the Tower built on the site of the old armoury, which suffered a destructive fire in 1841, several trophies taken by the First Guards from the French at Blenheim being destroyed.

Quarters were changed every six months. Detachments went from time to time to Windsor, Hampton Court, Winchester, and even Brighton when the King was in residence there. It was normal at the time for at least one battalion at a time to go out to a hutted camp at Chichester for fresh air and field training, and in 1853 the camp at Chobham was first established.

The Guards took more interest than most other regiments in the welfare of their men. Regimental schools had been started 1811, a regimental hospital was established in Rochester Row (reputed to be primarily for treating venereal disease) and married quarters followed. Wives and children had hitherto lived in barrack rooms, often separated from the men only by a blanket or curtain, a dreadful situation – 'though it was said that the arrangement had a very moderating effect on the language of the men'.[9] The first married quarters were established in 1852 as a hostel in Francis Street, just off the Vauxhall Bridge Road, on the initiative of a group of officers who raised the money for the project and were later bought out by the War Department when the need to accommodate families was at last recognized officially. The same committee of officers then

[8] Hamilton
[9] Paget

77

LIEUTENANT COLONEL
LESLIE 'BUFFER' JONES
1779-1839

Pugnacious
Commanding Officer
whose wild behaviour
led to enforced
resignation

Leslie Jones, known as the 'Buffer', is one of the few commanding officers of the early nineteenth century about whom a good deal is known – and for all the wrong reasons. As a young man he was expelled from school and spent some time at sea as a midshipman before joining the First Guards. He was a known Jacobin, sympathizing with the wilder element of the French Revolution, but attempts to throw him out of the Army failed. He served in the Netherlands and at Corunna, and was commandant in Brussels during the Waterloo campaign.

In July 1825 he was in command of the 2nd Battalion embarked in canal boats en route for Liverpool and thence for Dublin. After a row with some of the officers at the halfway point, he ordered his men to wait in their boats for five hours before the crews were ready, although they had already spent three days and nights aboard and needed time to recover. The following day he intervened in an altercation between the boatmen and broke his sword over the back of one of them. After a rough crossing to Dublin, Jones made his men stand on the dockside, in close column with their heavy equipment while it rained heavily; they then had to march for two hours before being dismissed to their quarters.

Six months later an inspecting officer reported unfavourably on Jones's 'violence, unmanly temper and conduct deviating from the general system of the Guards'. He was told by the Adjutant General to resign his commission, which he did immediately. Several of the battalion under punishment ordered by him were excused. He then became an active radical and a commercial printer, which enabled him to publish a colourful history of his disgraceful antics.

See Compton and Carr-Gomm

directed their efforts to improving the interior of the Guards Chapel, built in Wellington Barracks in 1838.

Smoking in those days was regarded as highly undesirable – indeed a vice because the fumes were thought to be intoxicating and it was supposed to encourage intemperate drinking – and was forbidden in barrack rooms until 1864, even then being limited to the hours between dinner and Tattoo. Officers were eventually permitted to smoke in the Guards Club, which had first been opened in 1810, but then only in a special room and on payment of a supplementary subscription. It was to be a century and a half later, in modern times, before smoking was again perceived to be unhealthy and obnoxious.

An Abortive Visit to Portugal

There were few excursions abroad in this period. The first was to Portugal, where six companies of the 1st Battalion went as part of a Guards brigade in 1826, to support the right of succession to the throne of the niece of the Princess Regent. Shortly afterwards the Duke of Wellington became Colonel and received a letter of congratulation from Sir Henry Bouverie, commanding in Portugal, which was fulsome in praise of 'your Grace's regiment'. 'It has never fallen to my lot,' he wrote, 'to have to do with a Battalion in a more perfect state of discipline; there has been little or no drunkenness, and they have made the two marches from Belem to Santarem, and from thence to this place [Villa Franca], notwithstanding the very heavy rain, without having had, at the end of the march, one of them absent or lagging in the rear'.[10] It was, however, an abortive and politically inept expedition, which came home in 1828 having seen no fighting.

Arctic Conditions in Canada (Map page 34)

An expedition to Canada was altogether a longer, more drawn-out and taxing affair, though again there turned out to be no fighting. Another Guards brigade, of the **2nd Battalion** (Col Turner Grant and later Col Robert Ellison) and 2nd Coldstream went out in 1838 to deal with a revolt by the French-speaking part of the population. Their general was Sir John Colborne, who had commanded the 52nd with such flair when they joined the First Guards in destroying the Imperial Guard at Waterloo.

The battalion carried out an operational deployment by the new-fangled railway train from Montreal to a few miles

[10] Hamilton

Queen and Consort: Victoria and Albert, Colonel-in-Chief and Colonel, dressed as field marshals as they ride out together on an inspection. *George Houseman Thomas*

inhabitants sternly, the Grenadiers were guilty of very few instances of ill-treatment or excess. Discipline was strict, cleanliness was insisted upon whatever the conditions and they marched with their greatcoats rolled in order to gain the benefit of the extra covering at the halt. It was a fine example of what could be achieved by close supervision and good morale. Colborne complimented the Guards on their record of sobriety: 'In a place where spirits were so cheap he had heard of no man being drunk on duty for upwards of ten months and during the first six months not a single man was court-martialled.'[11]

During the winter of 1840-41 the battalion was instructed by the Indians in the use of snow shoes, and a party of thirty was sent for several days into the forest, accompanied by some Indians, to practise the art of encamping or hutting in the snow. It was the earliest recorded version of the type of exercise that would take place in Norway a century and a half later. The union of upper and lower Canada was agreed, but a frontier dispute with the United States required the continued presence of British troops. It was not until September 1842, four and a half years after they had left, that the Grenadiers returned home.

Quite a number stayed, preferring to settle in Canada on advantageous terms offered as an indulgence in consequence of the good behaviour of the Guards brigade. They had indeed done well and the regimental historian did not exaggerate when he wrote: 'It is much to the credit of the Second Battalion Grenadier Guards that when there was so much temptation, so much facility to desert, and so much security after desertion, that in the course of four and a half years only seven men left their Colours, proving a faithfulness to duty and a noble esprit de corps, entitled to the highest admiration, and presenting an example which it is to be hoped will be followed by regimental posterity.'[12]

Principal sources: Hamilton, Whitworth (2), Paget

beyond La Prairie. The train, returning empty for a second load, ran off the line, probably as the result of sabotage. In order to reach their assembly point before dawn the men had then to make a severe night march through adhesive mud more than ankle-deep, resulting from continuous snow and rain. On another occasion, in similar dreadful conditions, a company attempted to make a route for the artillery horses by felling and laying down small trees, but the regulation axes and billhooks were so poor that the edges turned in a few minutes and they became utterly useless. The gunners were left to bivouac.

The rebels rarely chose to stand and fight, but a good deal of punitive action was taken against them along the south bank of the St Lawrence below Montreal, close to the American border. Troops were billeted on recalcitrant villages and the inhabitants compelled to provide food. The soldiers had been specifically ordered not to carry any rations with them, but to preserve order and discipline the meat and vegetables collected were put in charge of the Quartermaster and thence distributed to the men. In places houses were burnt down to bring the inhabitants to heel. Though they had to face great hardship while operating in temperatures 40° to 50° below freezing, and as a matter of policy treated the

---

[11] Hamilton
[12] Hamilton

BAND AND DRUMS

*M*usic has served from time immemorial to lift the spirits and fire the blood of soldiers. Many a long and weary march has been transformed by the sound of a band: the steady thud of the bass drum, the rattling counterbeat of the side drum, the clash of the cymbals and the familiar tunes on blaring brass and piping woodwind. In battle the side drum stirred the men into action and communicated orders and directions. Later the bugle, ringing out over the tumult, served the same purpose, and in camp marked out the day's routine.

The Music

In 1726 the first performance of George Frederick Handel's opera *Scipio* was given in London. He composed the noble slow march of that name for the First Guards and presented it to the Regiment before adding it to the score of his opera.

Two other marches peculiar to the Regiment are *The Duke of York's March* (slow), adopted in 1805 and *The Grenadier's March* (quick but can also be slow), but by far the most famous is the quick march *The British Grenadiers*. The most tone-deaf of Grenadiers, and indeed of the general public, can surely say, after the familiar formula, 'I only know two tunes: one is *The British Grenadiers* and the other isn't'. The origin of the march is obscure but it seems to have become common currency among grenadier companies of the Army in about 1780 and, with *The Grenadier's March*, was adopted by the First Guards when they became a regiment of grenadiers in 1815. One version of *The British Grenadiers*, evidently dated 1842, contains no fewer than twenty-seven verses, celebrating the deeds of all earlier grenadiers, not only those of the First Guards. But there is no doubt which regiment is meant in such verses (in the best Victorian idiom) as these:

For little boys and babies now,
In arms, the pretty dears,
Shall take our place in time to come,
And be the Grenadiers
And grown to manhood tall and strong,

All shapes and sizes: 18th century band and drums in action. *Christopher Collins*

Major discord: this print by Seccombe was published in 1880 in response to a new standing order for the Brigade of Guards which read, '515. Care will be taken so that Bands and Drums do not frighten horses, and to this end Side-drummers will beat pianissimo when necessary'.

Shall march with arms in hand,
The dauntless champions of their Queen,
And glorious native land.
So let shrill fifes and thundering drums,
Sweet music to our ears,
Strike up our warlike tune, the march
Of the British Grenadiers.
Then for our Queen and country dear,
We'll give three noble cheers;
In danger's hour they may rely
On the British Grenadiers.

The Regimental Band

In 1664 a musician by the name of Peter Vanhausen was engaged to instruct one man per company in the fife. The fruit of his labours is generally considered to mark the birth of the regimental band in 1665. Twenty years later, in January 1685, Charles II authorized the maintenance of twelve hautbois in the companies of the King's Regiment of Foot Guards in London. It was initially suggested that false names were added to the regimental roll to allow these musicians higher pay, though the accusation probably cannot be sustained. What is certain is that the King died of apoplexy a month later and that the bass drummer (time beater) wore a black mourning armband at his funeral. The armband was incorporated into the time beater's tunic until musicians' uniforms were fully standardized in 1974.

Most regiments tended to spend a good deal of money on their 'bands of music', which often included both professional musicians and serving soldiers. The Guards bands were in a privileged position, not only by association with the monarchy, but also because of the opportunities for lucrative private engagements in London. William IV, however, upset them by insisting that they play for him every night, thus depriving them of this extra income.

Instruments changed over the years. French horns appeared in 1725 and by 1794 there were one flute,

Beating it up: a drummers' practice room in the 1890s.

Time-beater in mourning: bass drummer of the 1920s with black armbands worked into his uniform in memory of Charles II.
Gary Gibbs Collection

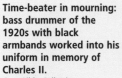

In full strength: Band and Drums of the present day step out in Wellington Barracks.

Hard hats: the Corps of Drums of the 2nd Battalion setting the pace during the General Strike of 1926.

Memorable musicians: Rodney Bashford OBE (right) became a lieutenant colonel and Senior Director of Music to the Guards Division; Karl Schauenburg, brought up in Holland to German parents, was dragooned into the Hitler Youth and actually awarded the Iron Cross, but became renowned for his loyalty to his adopted country over long years of outstanding and good-humoured service.

six clarinets, three bassoons, three horns, one trumpet, bass drum, cymbals and tambourine. It was to a similar baroque ensemble that Handel presented *Scipio*. Instruments such as the euphonium, flugelhorn and saxophone were introduced as they came to prominence in the wider musical world, until by 1859 the band existed in much the form seen today. In around the 1830s 'jingling johnnies' were

played by three black musicians leading the band in highly exotic dress. They were not thought in the end to contribute to the dignity of the proceedings and were quietly discarded.

The military role of the band has been a constant feature. It was not until the 1890s that the musicians were taken out of the battalions where they lived and worked with the regular soldiers and joined the staff of the regiment. They were to be 'drilled in their exercise and in case of actual service are to fall in with their companies completely armed and accoutred'. Military bandsmen were traditionally used as stretcher-bearers and today, when mobilized, the band operates with the medical services in a chemical decontamination role.

Today the band covers the whole range of state occasions: the Changing of the Guard, state visits, investitures, banquets, and massed with the four other bands of the Foot Guards on the Queen's Birthday Parade (Trooping the Colour) and the Remembrance Day parade at the Cenotaph. They are in constant demand for other public occasions at home and regularly undertake concert tours to huge audiences abroad. As well as the marching band, musicians form

Big brass: tubas on parade. *Roger Scruton*

different combinations as concert band, string quartets and chamber ensembles, dance band and big band, dinner trios and quartets, fanfare trumpet team and eighteenth century ensemble.

Until some time in the 19th Century the musicians numbered between twelve and nineteen, but by 1844 more had been added, and there were thirty-eight by 1848. By the end of the 1970s there was a fine total of sixty musicians in the band, though it has now been reduced to an operational strength of forty-nine, including a number of women. The musical standards are extremely high – several prominent players in major orchestras and ensembles cut their teeth in bearskin and tunic.

The band played in triumph in Paris in 1815 after Waterloo and in later wars visited service battalions in the field to entertain them when out of the line. On one occasion, in Italy in 1944, they diverted the visiting George VI in his bath, while a battle raged a few miles away.

Bandmasters, from 1914 named directors of music, were properly established in about 1780 and several became tremendous figures.

A visit to Sarajevo: stirring hearts in Bosnia-Herzegovina.

The first, Dan Godfrey, was followed by Albert Williams, awarded the degree of Doctor of Music at Oxford in the presence of his entire band, who had travelled to the occasion at their own expense. He served for twenty-five years and his successors, George Miller and Fred Harris, for twenty-one and eighteen years respectively.

The Corps of Drums

The earliest mention of instruments of music in the British Army comes from an order of 1622, which begins:

'DRUMS AND PHIFE'

'There is commonly two Drums to every Company, and one Phife to excite cheerfulness and alacrity in the Souldier; one drum to attend the Colours, another the Marchings and Troopings as occasion shall call them forth: they had neede be personable men and faithful, expert in Languages, and of good reputation.'

From the formation of the First Guards, drummers were included on the strength, the King's Company being allowed three and the remaining companies two each. In October 1662 a single fifer was added, and the position of drum major was created at one shilling and sixpence a day. When battalions became permanently established, each formed its own corps of drums. While the musicians of the band are professionals, drummers are professional soldiers who are also amateur musicians.

Drummers of old were rarely required to fight, but they were always in a conspicuous position. After beating the charge they carried their drums in front of them by the hoops, in what would seem a forlorn hope of some protection.

The bugle is used in barracks to sound the calls throughout the day, but is never used on parade, the side drum serving instead. Neither do side drummers perform tricks with their sticks, nor drum majors with their maces 'as is the custom in the Line' (as Regimental Standing Orders used to state, rather sniffily). While this may entertain the onlooker (especially the one who hopes to witness a mishap) it has never been regarded as a soldierly practice or in keeping with the stateliness of royal ceremonial.

Chapter Five

CRIMEAN AGONY
1854-1856

The war fought over the period of a year, in a remote peninsula of Russia to the north of the Black Sea, was foolish and quite unnecessary. But it burned deep into the memory of the British Army as one of great suffering, high gallantry, incompetence in command and scandalous deficiencies in organization. It brought about a complete overhaul in military management, most notably in the field of medicine where the astonishing abilities and ruthless energies of Florence Nightingale were to spark a revolution whose effects are still evident today.

In one respect, at least, it was a modern war. It was well reported, notably by William Russell, correspondent of *The Times*. The electric telegraph speeded the transmission of news and the earliest photographs from a theatre of war date from this time. Thus those at home became aware of what was happening in the Crimea in a way that was unthinkable forty years earlier, and at much greater speed. This, inevitably, stirred public outrage about the inept handling of affairs and encouraged the application of remedies.

For guardsmen it was the only war in which they fought impressively (though hardly comfortably) attired in tunic and bearskin cap. The first battle, on the Alma, was the only occasion where the three regiments of Guards – Grenadier, Coldstream and Scots Fusiliers, as they were then named – advanced together in one line against the enemy, the bearskin plumes indicating their position as they were designed to do. For Grenadiers there was a special significance: the historic battle of Inkerman, won by the heroic efforts of individual soldiers, was to leave behind it a name famous in the history of the Regiment.

The Preparation of an Unready Army
The war arose from a dispute between Imperial Russia

Crimea Medal and Turkish Crimea Medal: the former with unusually ornate clasps for Alma, Balaclava, Inkerman and Sebastopol.

and Ottoman Turkey, who had long been rivals. The Turks were threatened by the Russians and both British and French thought it necessary to give them support in order to maintain the balance of power in Europe and the Middle East. Thus was formed an unlikely alliance between the old enemies, Britain and France, with an enfeebled Muslim nation, against the Christian Tsar of Russia.

In time-honoured fashion the British army was very ill-prepared for such an adventure. For forty years of peace it had been living on the capital won at Waterloo. The government was loath to spend money on what they considered the remotest possibility of a new war. Even the great Duke of Wellington acted as a brake on improvement – his battles had been won by courage and good leadership, and surely these would not be wanting should a new challenge appear.

To be sure, the alarms from Russia did to some extent ruffle the still waters of military complacency. In 1852 the Great Duke, not long retired as Commander-in-Chief, died at the age of eighty-three. His successor, Lord Hardinge (a Grenadier) set in hand new permanent camps of instruction[1] and the issue of the new French Minié rifle, though with familiar perversity only the 1st and 2nd Grenadiers attended the camp. The 3rd Battalion, eventually sent to the Crimea, did not; nor did they all receive their new rifles and learn to use them until half-way to the theatre of war. Those in the other battalions were no doubt miffed at being left behind; they need not have troubled as many were to be on their way to the Crimea as reinforcements before a year was out, and scores of those to their graves also.

[1] The training areas at Aldershot, Ash, Pirbright and Chobham, acquired by the War Office on the recommendation of Grenadier officers and beloved of guardsmen ever since, date from this time

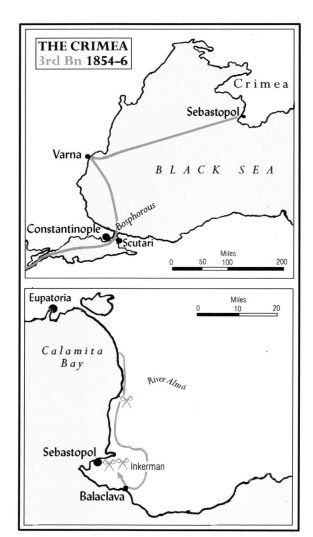

THE CRIMEA
3rd Bn 1854–6

Crimea

Sebastopol

Varna

BLACK SEA

Bosphorous

Constantinople

Scutari

Miles
0   50   100   200

Eupatoria

Miles
0   10   20

Calamita
Bay

River Alma

Sebastopol

Inkerman

Balaclava

Malta, Constantinople and Varna

On 22 February 1854 the **3rd Battalion**, having had three changes in commanding officer[2] in a single year but now under Colonel Thomas Wood and almost 1000 strong, marched through a cheering crowd to Waterloo station. They were placed in the Guards Brigade with the 1st Coldstream and 1st Scots Fusiliers and in early March arrived in Malta, where they threw away their old Brown Bess muskets and spent several weeks getting used to the vastly improved Minié. Because of its accuracy and thus effectiveness at greater ranges, training was given in the use of sights and judging distance. 'Their officers took them to broken ground on the shore where a man was placed every fifty yards. It was pointed out that at fifty yards, the features of a man and the buttons on his tunic could be clearly seen, whereas at 100 yards the buttons faded to form a continuous line; at 150 yards the buttons

were quite invisible and the face appeared like a whitish ball under the line of a cap.'[3]

In Malta they were joined by the Duke of Cambridge, commanding the 1st Division in which were the brigades of Guards (under Henry Bentinck) and Highlanders, and by Lord Raglan in command of the whole force. Many of the generals, including Raglan himself, were old men, and few survived the expedition. They would be hard put to it to call upon the experience of Wellington's campaigns forty years before and put it to active use, much less to endure the physical hardships they would soon encounter.

After some weeks at Scutari, looking across the Bosphorous toward Constantinople, the expedition moved up to Varna on the west coast of the Black Sea, to forestall a threatened Russian attack. There they were assaulted, not by Russians but by an epidemic of cholera. They attempted extensive field training in unsuitable equipment and in very hot weather. The men lost a lot of weight and began to wear beards. Captain Higginson, the Adjutant, wrote, 'We have been trying on the moustache agitation [up to then only the cavalry were allowed moustaches]. The Duke of Cambridge expressed his entire sympathy with the movement, so we set to work, and in about three weeks we [the officers] were curling and twisting away at the ends of our beards, until the men thought fit to follow our example.'[4] There were other hazards. Higginson told of the Sergeant Major catching some men buying quantities of 'raki' for a penny. He was furious and on his orders the wretched native peddler of the stuff 'was pegged down on his back and a half pint of the pernicious spirit poured down his throat'.[5]

To the great relief of the soldiers, Raglan was now directed to land in the Crimea, in order to take Sebastopol and prevent the hostile operations of the Russian fleet. The landing was made thirty miles north of the naval base on 14 September and, though still weakened by cholera, the army advanced confidently southwards. Early success was imperative as there was no transport in which to carry tents and other supplies, much less the wounded, and the men had to carry what possessions they could in a single rolled blanket.

[2] A mixture of unforeseen resignation and the practice of commanding officers being appointed to battalions according to their seniority as 'regimental majors'. Thus, when a change was made at the top, the commanding officers below moved up a battalion.
[3] Clark (2)
[4] Higginson
[5] Whitworth

In camp at Scutari: the enormous barracks where Florence Nightingale laboured is seen in the background and still stands today.

Victory on the Alma – 20 September 1854

The Russians had taken up defensive positions on the heights across the River Alma, and the allied armies of British, French and Turkish troops had to dislodge them by crossing the river and assaulting up a steep slope. The 1st Division was placed in reserve behind the Light Division, which forded the river under fire and climbed the slope towards the Russian masses on the ridge beyond. They did well and penetrated the grand redoubt below the crest, but were then counter-attacked by a large enemy force and hard put to hold on. The Duke of Cambridge's division was sent up in support, the Highlanders on the left and the Guards on the right in order of seniority – Grenadiers on the right, Coldstream on the left and Scots Fusiliers in the centre. Moving through a broken-up country of walled vineyards the 3rd Grenadiers became a little disarranged. Although the Scots Fusiliers had been ordered ahead before they were quite ready, Colonel Grosvenor Hood (now commanding) determined at all costs to restore the coherence of the Grenadier line; so he halted on the far bank of the river under cover from the plunging fire of the Russians, and dressed the battalion in two lines before ordering them forward up the fire-swept slope.[6]

By this time parties of the Light Division were being forced back down the hill by massive battalion columns of the enemy and the Scots Fusiliers had received a serious check. However, the Grenadiers pressed on steadily and took the Russians around the grand redoubt in the flank. The impetus was unstoppable. The two ranks of the line fired alternate volleys as they went, the rear rank over the heads of the front rank as they knelt momentarily to reload. The reply of the Russian muskets had little effect. Forty yards from the redoubt the line charged and with a great shout ran with the bayonet at the enemy masses. The Russians, threatened also by the Highlanders and

---

[6] This procedure was assisted, no doubt, by there being no fewer than nine former adjutants serving in the battalion

Divine service in the camp of the Guards at Scutari: Grenadiers are on the left and Coldstream on the right. *The Royal Archives © 2005 Her Majesty Queen Elizabeth II*

Crossing the Alma: Grenadiers advance towards the enemy on the high ground.
Richard Simkin

On the march: a Grenadier well-laden.
Gary Gibbs Collection

Well turned out for battle in tunic and bearskin: the smart appearance of this colour sergeant of 1854 at the outset of the campaign. *Bryan Fosten*

The Alma: getting in among the Russians. *19th century British school*

Getting practical: the dress of this corporal of 1855 is more down-to-earth. *Bob Marrion*

The Alma: Grenadiers move up the slope. *Reginald Wymer*

shot at in the flank by guns of the Royal Horse Artillery, were not used to the bayonet and did not wait to feel the effects of cold steel before pulling back down the rearward slope. The heights were taken.

The battalion had lost only eleven killed, but 180 were wounded and many of those subsequently died. No Grenadier present had ever been in action before, but they made a deep impression. A Russian general, taken prisoner, remarked that he had expected to fight brave men, but had met red devils.

One of the heroes of the battalion was the drummer boy Thomas Keep, who during the fighting collected up the rifles of casualties and went about tending the wounded, even managing to make a fire and brew tea for them. He was only fourteen years old, having joined the Regiment in 1849 at the age of nine, and when four foot four inches tall.

Balaclava and Inkerman

The advance continued; the armies dug trenches and settled into siege positions around the south and east of Sebastopol. Heavy artillery was brought up, with great difficulty and labour, and on 17 October opened up bombardment on the city. On the following day Colonel Hood, commanding a large covering party in the trenches, was struck by a grape-shot full in the chest and killed instantly.

A week later the Russians, hoping to disrupt the siege, issued from Sebastopol in force and made a vigorous advance on Balaclava. The 93rd Highlanders, directly defending the town, repelled a strong cavalry attack with great precision and thus prevented a disastrous breakthrough. The Guards battalions were brought up from the north in their support, following orders delivered cheerfully by the Duke of Cambridge's ADC to Bentinck in the following uncomplicated terms, 'There's a row going on down the plain of Balaclava and you fellows are wanted'. As it happened there was nothing further for the guardsmen to do.

It was the day of the cavalry. The Heavy Brigade charged the Russian cavalry in four times their strength and 'cut their way through and back most gloriously'. Then came the turn of the Light Brigade. By a sequence of misunderstanding, confusion and high temper, the 600 horsemen were launched down the North Valley directly at the Russian guns, which predictably tore them to pieces. It was an act of crass stupidity and high heroism, from which few escaped unscathed.

The campaign then stalled. Balaclava was safe, but the

PRIVATE

ALFRED ABLETT VC

DCM *1830-1877*

Victoria Cross
of the
Siege of Sebastopol,
who threw a
fizzing shell over
the parapet

*A*lfred Ablett was born at Weybread and became the first Suffolk man to win the Victoria Cross. He joined the Grenadiers in 1850 and fought at the Alma and Inkerman.

He was in the trenches in front of Sebastopol on 2 September 1855, just before the town fell. A working party of Grenadiers was moving explosives into a forward trench when an alert sentry spotted a high-trajectory shell heading straight for the trench, now packed with barrels of gunpowder. The sentry had just time to let out a desperate warning before the shell fell, the fuse burning. Everyone except Ablett dived for what little cover there was. He rushed to the smoking shell and succeeded in lifting it, but it was so hot that it slipped from his burning hands between his legs. He quickly turned and with the strength of desperation picked up the heavy object again and heaved it over the parapet, where it at once exploded. Ablett was thrown to the ground and covered with earth. Sergeant Baker, in charge of the working party, asked if he was hurt. 'No, but I have had a good shaking,' was the reply.

For his gallantry he was awarded the Victoria Cross and promoted corporal. The Commanding Officer gave him his own silk necktie, which had been made by Queen Victoria.

Ablett was also awarded the Distinguished Conduct Medal for his general conduct in the campaign and received a gratuity of £5. He was promoted sergeant on return to England.

He became a sergeant instructor of the 4th Volunteer Battalion of the Norfolk Regiment and served as a sergeant of police at the Millwall docks, having been recruited by Anthony Palmer VC. He lies buried at Weybread.

See Clark (2) (3)

Russians were left in control of the only good road to Sebastopol. This would cause great difficulties to the besieging troops, who thereafter would have to haul their supplies from Balaclava ten miles each way across country, usually in dreadful conditions. Only two weeks later came the Battle of Inkerman, which is described separately.

A Gruesome Winter in the Camp and Trenches

The siege continued and conditions worsened rapidly. On 14 November a terrific storm lashed the Crimean coast. Twenty-one ships were sunk and with them disappeared much of the army's food, clothing, equipment and comforts. Tents were destroyed by the hundred, leaving the men with almost no shelter. All the bearskin caps of the battalion, which had stood on posts or pegs outside the tents, were swept into a ravine a quarter of a mile off. As the snow, frost and icy winds swept in, the troops had to endure the grimmest hardships. Cholera and scurvy killed many and all suffered in varying degrees from frostbite or trench foot, caused by tight boots. Fresh meat and vegetables were almost entirely lacking.

William Russell of *The Times* wrote, 'It is now pouring rain – the skies are black as ink – the wind is howling over the staggering tents – the trenches are turned into dykes – in the tents the water is sometimes a foot deep – our men have not either warm or waterproof clothing – they are out for twelve hours at a time in the trenches – they are plunged into the inevitable miseries of a winter campaign – and not a soul seems to care for their comfort or even for their lives'.[7]

A little later he wrote, 'Why were they in tents? Where were the huts which had been sent out to them? The huts were on board ships in the harbour of Balaclava. Some of these huts were floating about the beach; others had been converted into firewood or used for stabling for officers' horses.'[8]

Even the French were unimpressed. One remarked, 'It seems to me that your soldiers are not looked after as they should be. They merit in your hands priceless care. If you have such soldiers you should look after them as you would your eyes'.[9]

At last the battalion was reinforced by a large draft from home. Guardsmen were employed constantly in working parties and protective duties in the trenches, enlivened by spasmodic gun and rifle fire, and night raids

[7] Clark (2)
[8] Springman
[9] Tipping

Standing by: Grenadiers await their turn for the fray. *Orlando Norie*

No further pretence to smartness: a battle now to survive as the freezing weather sets in. *Orlando Norie*

Pain shown in his eyes: Sergeant Dawson lost his arm at the Alma but was able to return to his family. He was seen by the Queen at Buckingham Palace on 20 February 1855. *The Royal Archives © 2005 Her Majesty Queen Elizabeth II*

Quick and courageous thinking: Alfred Ablett flings the fizzing shell over the parapet.

Lucky to survive: veterans on their way to recovery.

A tough posting: Sergeant William Powell commemorated 150 years later by a 57p stamp.

In the trenches: a small group keeping an eye on Sebastopol. *After Lord Harding*

with some bayonet fighting. In two months 129 wounded were added to the long list of sick. On one day in February 1855 the battalion, over 1200 strong, had 530 in hospital in Scutari and 30 elsewhere, 159 sick in camp, 92 on detached duty and fewer than 350 for active work in the trenches.

Eventually there was some improvement. In March the battalion moved into huts, their uniforms and boots were replaced and supplies actually appeared with some regularity. The weather warmed up, now sometimes being oppressively hot, and further large drafts appeared.

The Assaults on Sebastopol

The time had come for an attempt to bring the war to a conclusion. In June the French made a major assault on Sebastopol but it foundered and Raglan reluctantly ordered his own army forward in support. The operation was hasty and ill-judged, and proved very costly. The Guards, fortunately, were in reserve and not committed. The reverse was, however, the last straw for the hapless Commander-in-Chief, who died on 28 June, worn out by work and anxiety. 'He was succeeded by an excellent red-nosed old gentleman, General Simpson, whom nobody has ever heard of, and who took Sebastopol.'[10] Sir James Simpson, Raglan's chief of staff, had previously been an officer of the First Guards and had been wounded at Quatre Bras. In September the Russians evacuated the southern part of the town and, though peace was not made until the following March, hostilities were virtually over. 'Sebastopol', however, was awarded as a battle honour, alongside 'Alma', 'Balaclava' and 'Inkerman', to all those regiments employed in the siege.

Many months more were to pass before the battalion returned home. Another severe winter had to be endured, though the conditions were greatly improved and at least there was no fighting. Even senior officers found new amusements. Colonel Augustus Foley, now commanding the 3rd Grenadiers, 'with hammer and nails in hand, was often to be seen on the roof of a half-finished hut, setting a laudable example to others'.[11] At last, in June 1856, the battalion sailed for home, arriving in the following month.

The Cost to the Regiment

The Regiment, as well as the whole army, had paid a dreadful price. No fewer than 2458 Grenadiers had served in the campaign, not far short of the entire regimental

Chaos and destruction: the interior of the captured Redan, 1855. *The Royal Archives © 2005 Her Majesty Queen Elizabeth II*

strength before the war. Of these 150 were killed in action or died of wounds; 750 died of disease, mostly of cholera, and a further 138 were invalided. Almost all of those remaining were at one time or another sick, often desperately sick, and there were times when companies could muster only a handful of men fit for duty. In accordance with the priorities of the day, however, the officers were much better looked after than the men. Battle and disease together accounted for only eight dead.

The Medical Disaster and Florence Nightingale

The most enduring legacy of the war was the work of Florence Nightingale. An enormous number of soldiers, including hundreds of Grenadiers, passed through her hands, and that any of them survived at all was largely her doing.

'In these surroundings, those who had been long inured to scenes of human suffering – surgeons with a world-wide knowledge of agonies, soldiers familiar with fields of carnage, missionaries with remembrances of famine and of plague – yet found a depth of horror which they had never known before. There were moments, there were places, in the Barrack Hospital of Scutari, where the strongest hand was struck with trembling, and the boldest eye would turn away its gaze.'[12]

---

[10] Strachey (1). This was not quite true. During the battle Simpson, 'suffering from some illness, just sat in a trench, with his nose and eyes just facing the cold and dust, and his cloak drawn over his head to protect him against both'. (Lindsay (2))
[11] Hamilton
[12] Strachey (1)

Inkerman – The Soldiers' Battle
5 November 1854

The desperate battle at Inkerman on 5 November 1854 was the most crucial and the most bitter of the war. It was fought in fog at close quarters. No leadership above company level was noticed, even had it been possible. Its outcome depended entirely on the gallantry and endurance of the soldiers, fighting individually or in small groups. If the battle had been lost, capitulation or, at the very best, a fighting evacuation would probably have followed.

The British army, which was not deployed in any recognizable defensive position, was taken by surprise in the early misty morning by the advance of enormous Russian masses who themselves lost direction in their advance against the heights of Inkerman. Their object was to penetrate and outflank the British right in a decisive stroke that would break the siege.

Prince Edward's Company on the Picquet Line

The 3rd Battalion, commanded by Colonel Edward Birch Reynardson, was some 450 strong, and three of the eight weak companies were detached forward, either on picquet duty or relieving picquets. The night had been wet and the weapons of the picquets were damp and largely ineffective. When the firing was first heard No 1 Company, led by Prince Edward of Saxe Weimar, was out to relieve a picquet and thus happily with dry weapons. They saw a Russian column moving up the side of the ravine towards them. By taking skirmishing order they were able to direct a fire on the column which had an effect out of all proportion to its numbers and managed to divert it towards the 2nd Division's position. This company held its isolated position all day and was not able at any stage to join the rest of the battalion.

The Fight in the Sandbag Battery

As soon as the direction of the Russian attack was clear the Guards Brigade was ordered to move forward half-right 700 yards beyond the 2nd Division camp to the Sandbag Battery. This was an emplacement for two guns (though without guns at the time) with two embrasures

A titanic struggle: Grenadiers and Russians at the Sandbag Battery. *Victorian chromolithograph*

A desperate mêlée: another representation of the tremendous battle, which could well have resulted in an inglorious end to the war. *Victorian lithograph*

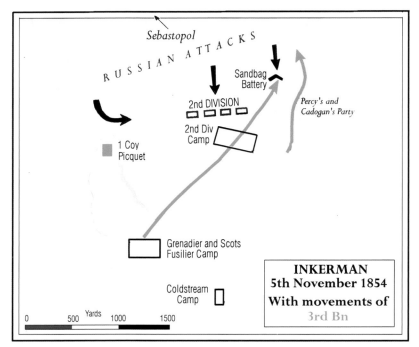

in a nine-foot-high wall of sandbags, set up to rake the Russian posts above Sebastopol. A small picquet of the 55th Regiment was originally in the battery but had been chased out. It was retaken by the 41st, but they in turn were driven off by the Russian Tarutine Regiment. The main body of the 3rd Grenadiers, consisting of five companies, led the new counter-attack force over rough country strewn with boulders and thickly set with scrub. The battalion, carrying its Colours into battle, charged into the battery with a cheer and sent the grey-coated, flat-capped Russians reeling back to the head of the ravine. But they had withdrawn only a hundred yards and, recovering themselves, came back once more. For four hours attack and counter-attack succeeded each other. Each time they were cleared away the Russians, fortified by a good dose of spirits, came back yelling and shouting through the scrub. Sergeant Major John Algar was killed in one of the forward rushes as he climbed the parapet. Standing on the growing pile of bodies in the battery, the men rose above the parapet.

The two other companies (Nos 4 and 7) that had started the day in the picquet line now joined the battalion, having returned to camp on the way to exchange damp and useless weapons for dry. Troops from other regiments, caught up in the action, rallied on the Grenadier Colours. The Russians disliked the bayonet, which they were hardly taught to use

themselves, and time and again wilted before the practice made by the guardsmen. (Sergeant Minor, who examined his greatcoat after the battle and found in it ten holes made by bayonet or shot, remarked that it was difficult to run a bayonet through a Russian greatcoat, so he worked on their faces and necks[13]). Nor apparently had the Russians ever been taught to break into a charge and their ponderous methods were overwhelmed by agile, aggressive parties acting in twos and threes and led by officers and NCOs.

Private James Bancroft of No 3 Company was amazed, while fighting for his life, to be reprimanded by Sergeant Major Algar:

'We were driven out of the battery, and had to retreat; but charged and retook it, and then a desperate fight took place on each side of the battery. I was beside Captain Burnaby and saw him lift his sword and kill a Russian. I then followed him; he asked us how many would do so; we were about six or seven. We drove the enemy, and kept them beyond the battery for some time; when I jumped over it, I was attacked immediately. I bayoneted the first Russian in the chest; he fell dead. I was then stabbed in the mouth with great force, which caused me to stagger back a few paces, where I shot this second Russian, and thereupon ran a third one through, and brought him to the ground, A fourth and fifth Russian then came at me, and ran me through the right side. I fell, but managed to rise and run one of them through, and brought him down. I killed him, or either stunned him by kicking him, whilst I was engaging my bayonet with another. Serjeant-Major Algar called out to me not to kick the man that was down, but not being dead, he was very troublesome to my legs; in fact, I was fighting the other over his body. I returned to the battery, and spat out my teeth in my hand. I found two only.'[14]

Another Grenadier of the same company, Private John Morris, recalled:

'We charged up to the battery. Most of our pieces would not go off, the damp had got into them during the

[13] Clark (2)
[14] Burnaby

PRIVATE
ANTHONY PALMER VC
1819-1892

Victoria Cross
of Inkerman
whose later life was
almost as crammed
with incident

GENERAL
Sir GEORGE HIGGINSON
GCB GCVO *1826-1927*

Adjutant in the
Crimea,
survivor of the
Sandbag Battery,
centenarian,
'Father of the Guards'

*A*nthony Palmer was born at Brereton, Congleton, Cheshire, and enlisted as a Grenadier in 1838.

He was one of those who followed Sir Charles Russell into the Sandbag Battery and at one point saved Russell's life. He was also one of the small group that fought its way out through the encircling Russians and thereby saved the Colours. He was promoted corporal on parade the morning after the battle (the first of three attempts - he was reduced to private regularly).

He later became a captain in the 3rd Essex Volunteer Regiment and head constable of Millwall docks police (see Ablett VC). Both were surprising appointments as he was better known for escapades that were much less reputable. He was fond of his drink, which got him into all sorts of trouble. He carried on his body a tattooed 'D' for desertion after being absent without leave following a drunken spree. Legends grew up around this colourful character. He is supposed to have stolen the officers' mess silver and sold it for drink, and is said also to have sold his sentry box while on guard outside Buckingham Palace. Neither misdemeanour, unfortunately, is supported in his service records.

He also managed to receive two Victoria Crosses for the same act of gallantry. He lost the first, probably in a pub brawl. It was an indication of the popularity of this old soldier rogue that the officers of the Regiment petitioned Queen Victoria for a replacement and paid for it. Naturally the original turned up in due course, so there are now two crosses to mark his bravery.

His grave was discovered at Heywood, Greater Manchester, in 1992 and a plaque erected.

See Clark (3)

*G*eorge Higginson was a towering figure in Victorian times and beyond, living to the tremendous age of 101 and being known as the 'Father of the Guards'. He joined the Regiment in 1845, to be greeted by the Quartermaster, who had been his father's colour sergeant at Corunna.

Being both able and industrious, he was soon Adjutant. For several years he virtually ran the 3rd Battalion, his commanding officers dropping in now and then to pursue their hobby. In the Crimea he was present at every major action and played a notable part in saving the Colours at Inkerman. He was immortalized as the mounted figure in Lady Butler's famous painting *The Roll Call*. He served the rest of the campaign as a brigade major and adapted himself well to the grim winter conditions, keeping his feet warm on an 18 lb shot heated on the fire. His mother at home proved equally practical. He sent her his bearskin cap, peppered with Russian bullet holes, expecting her to display it reverently in a glass case. Not a bit of it: she sliced off the end and turned it into a muff.

Higginson returned home to be re-introduced swiftly to *proper* soldiering and sent on guard as subaltern of the Buckingham Palace detachment. However, he rose rapidly, commanding the 2nd Battalion from 1870 to 1877 and progressing to senior commands at the Horse Guards and the Tower of London.

On his centenary the Regiment marched through his home town of Marlow and he visited the 1st Battalion at Windsor. There the youngest drummer was told off to present him with a basket of roses. 'Take them away, boy,' growled the old warrior with a curl to his lip, 'and give them to your girlfriend.'

See Higginson, Garrett

GENERAL

Lord HENRY PERCY VC

KCB *1817-1877*

Victoria Cross
of Inkerman
who was
twice wounded and
became a General

he Hon Henry Percy (later to be Lord Henry) was a captain and lieutenant-colonel commanding a company of the 3rd Battalion in the Crimea. He served throughout the war and was present at all the major battles, being twice wounded.

Obtaining his commission in the Regiment in 1836, he went to Canada during the insurrection in 1838 and remained there until 1842.

At Inkerman, 'at a moment when the Guards were at some distance from the Sandbag Battery' he 'charged singly into the battery, followed immediately by the Guards; the embrasures of the battery, as also the parapet, were held by the Russians, who put up a most severe fire of musketry.' He then 'found himself, with many men of various regiments who had charged too far, nearly surrounded by the Russians and without ammunition, but by his knowledge of the ground, though wounded, he extricated these men, and, passing under a heavy fire from the Russians then in the Sandbag Battery, brought them safe to where ammunition was to be obtained, thereby saving some fifty men, and enabling them to renew the combat. He received the approval of HRH the Duke of Cambridge for this action on the spot.' It was a fine achievement of leadership, in the mist and in difficult country, and under conditions of extreme danger.

He commanded the parade in Hyde Park on 26 June 1857 at which Queen Victoria presented the first Victoria Crosses, including his own and those of the other three Grenadiers. Later he commanded the 1st Battalion in Dublin, where he supervised the military education of the Prince of Wales, and then in Canada in 1861. He subsequently became a member of parliament and was promoted full general two months before his death.

See Percy

LIEUTENANT COLONEL

Sir CHARLES RUSSELL Bt VC

1826-1883

Victoria Cross
of Inkerman,
won for his
stirring leadership
in the
Sandbag Battery

ir Charles Russell, a small slight man, joined the Regiment in 1848 through the influence of the Duke of Wellington, a well-recognized route in those times.

He served throughout the Crimean campaign. As lieutenant and captain (though apparently not, as according to Hamilton, of No 8 Company) he won the Victoria Cross for his part in the desperate action in the Sandbag Battery at Inkerman.

At one point in the fight, where fortune was swinging to and fro, a number of guardsmen shouted, 'If any officer will lead us, we will charge them.' Sir Charles immediately responded, jumping into the embrasure waving his revolver and shouting, 'Come on my lads, who will follow me?' A group of Grenadiers at once did so. He went forward and fired his revolver at a Russian who barred his way; it misfired but at the second attempt he killed the man. He was then aware of being touched on the shoulder from behind. It was Private Palmer, who said to him, 'Sir, you were near done for.' 'Oh no,' replied Sir Charles, 'he was some way from me.' Palmer replied, 'His bayonet was all but into you when I clouted him on the head.' Looking round, Russell saw another Russian on the ground and realized that Palmer had spoken no less than the truth.

He then continued with Percy beyond the battery and in the mist was for a time separated from the rest of his company with a few men.

Russell was promoted brevet-major and, like Percy, was also given French and Turkish decorations. He retired in 1868 as a lieutenant colonel, having already become MP for Berkshire in 1865, and died unmarried in 1883.

There is a stained-glass window to his memory in All Saints Church, Swallowfield.

The Roll Call: one of several variations on Lady Butler's celebrated painting added deep snow for further effect. George Higginson, the mounted Adjutant, though not yet thirty, already looks the centenarian he eventually became. *Elizabeth Thompson*

night ... I was close on the right when we reached the battery, and then began a terrible fight at it. We threw stones, for our ammunition was nearly all gone. The last shot I fired I killed a Russian; I hit him through the head. I then was wounded in the testicle and fell; the pain I suffered was great. Captain Burnaby ... asked me what was the matter with me. I told him, and he said I was not to mind, that it would get better soon, and to get under cover; but the battery was very low on the right.'[15]

At one point Quartermaster Sergeant Hill, knowing that most of the men had gone into action without food since the previous night, made his appearance in the battery, with some refreshments on his shoulders, regardless of the firing all around him. The historian, who was himself present at the time, recorded with some understatement 'and his thoughtfulness was thoroughly appreciated'.[16]

Percy's and Cadogan's Companies

Meanwhile an attack by the 4th Division was developing on the right, close to the battery, and so promising did it seem that some of the Grenadier companies moved along with it, in particular No 3 Company and parts of Nos 2, 5 and 8, all under Colonels Percy and Cadogan. They pushed along quite some way before finding themselves threatened by more Russians descending on them from high ground to their left. Out of ammunition, it took all the skill and courage of those two officers to bring the survivors back by a covered route through the undergrowth, whence eventually they found their way out, not knowing the fate of those left in the battery.

The Fight to Save the Colours

Meanwhile, in the battery, the centre companies and the headquarters were holding on. A Russian penetration between the left of the Guards Brigade and the 2nd Division caused the Scots Fusiliers and Coldstream to move to the left to seal the gap. This left Colonel Reynardson with a band of about a hundred Grenadiers momentarily isolated. As the battle raged the Colours

[15] Burnaby
[16] Hamilton

Coming back: the second charge of the Guards at Inkerman. *W Simpson*

Clouting him on the head: Russell, busily engaged, saved from a Russian bayonet by Palmer. Both won the Victoria Cross. *Louis Desanges*

were passed from hand to hand – privates, sergeants and officers in turn holding them aloft. Eventually, left with little ammunition, the small force broke out and fought their way back inch by inch. Corporal Isaac Archer of No 3 Company described the action in graphic terms:

'Seeing the Colours surrounded we made to them. This was a struggle. I saw Sergeant Mann with the Colours. Likewise I saw Private Morris there. We closed about the Queen's Colour but two Russian columns coming up on either side of the battery were closing upon us and would have seized it had not a few of us made a desperate resistance. We were not more than could have been covered by a sheet. We kept close together. Captain Burnaby was the officer with us but there were men of the Coldstream and the Line. He told us to keep close together and charge and as these two Russian columns were about fifteen yards from us we dashed through the few Russians who were between us and knocking them out of the way met the column. The blow was a desperate one. Some of us hardly were loaded. Step by step we prevented their advance until we nearly all fell and they, eager upon the Colours, pushed on. But it was too late to gain them. The Colours had had time to regain the English lines and the French had come up.'

The re-appearance of the Colours, safe in the hands of two officers, Turner and Verschoyle, brought final relief to the Duke of Cambridge. 'Ah,' he exclaimed, moved almost to tears, 'the Colours are saved.' The battalion had been the only one to carry Colours into battle that day and it was the last occasion on which it was ever done. Captain Higginson, the Adjutant, wrote:

'The mere possibility of the Colours of the First Regiment of our Sovereign's Guards being laid as a trophy at the feet of the Czar had to be faced, and I believe that a prayer went up from all of us that such dishonour might be averted at all costs. Certainly the grave faces and resolute attitude of our Grenadiers made me realize that there was no exaggeration in the language used by Sir William Napier in his well-known description of the behaviour of the 1500 British soldiers, all who remained to stand triumphant on the fatal hill of Albuera – "None knows with what majesty the British soldier fights". ... The tattered fragments of the Colours have found their final resting place on the walls of the Guards Chapel. I feel confident that none of my readers is so cynical as to smile if I admit that I never enter that treasure-house of memorials, so dear to every member of the Brigade of Guards, and feel able to gaze without emotion on the Colours which served as our rallying point on the dark upland of Inkerman.'[17]

The whole Guards Brigade had fought with great distinction. The Grenadiers had lost 101 killed and 124 wounded, half the battalion strength, and won three Victoria Crosses. They had fired 19,000 rounds, twice as many as at the Alma. 'Now I understand Waterloo,' remarked a French officer to a guardsman.

Principal Sources: Clark (2), Fraser(1), Hamilton, Higginson, Lindsay (2), Peget, Whitworth (2

---

[17] Higginson

'If this keeps up we could well become the Regimental Christmas Card.' A century later it was possible to draw a lighter side even out of so dreadful a battle. *Philip Wright*

THE DRUMMER

*E*very drummer must be competent on the bugle (though never described as 'bugler' or indeed 'guardsman') and able to sound the correct calls to order. He also plays either flute or drum, on which he has to master some thirty marches. In modern times, however, he is also as skilful and as highly trained a soldier as any guardsman and often serves in specialist roles.

Drummers were always trouble, and are still the first to be blamed when 'drama' occurs in a battalion. This undoubtedly stems from the early days when they enlisted as boys. Queens' Regulations of 1859 stated:

'No boy is to be received into the service for the purpose of being trained as a trumpeter, drummer or bugler, who does not, from his make and stature, offer the fairest hopes of growth ... and no boy is eligible for enlistment under the age of fourteen years, except under very special circumstances.'

The beat of drum: drummer in marching order 1918.
Christopher Morley

Prize picture: Drummer Ted Bolan at Chelsea Barracks in June 1937, waiting to beat Stand to Arms before Trooping the Colour. The photograph won first prize in the military section of Kodak's photo of the year competition and was widely used both by Kodak and for recruiting.

Even in the 1930s boys would enlist at sixteen. Though those days are long past, few of them, even when grizzled old drum majors, ever quite shake off their youthful spirits and their appetite for a lark. 'Look at that drummer,' a bystander once observed, 'even his feet are in an insubordinate position.'

They have both sauce and style. It was reported that, shortly after Princess Elizabeth became Colonel in 1942, she was taken to a soldiers' dance of some kind, very closely chaperoned of course and with all her dancing partners carefully lined up and instructed. All this fell into ruin when a young drummer (of about her

Trooping the Colour the lone figure of a single drummer peels off from the Massed Bands and Drums to place himself on the right of the Escort for the Colour. The sharp taps of his *Drummer's Call* then breaks the silence on the enormous stage of Horse Guards Parade and the proud drummer returns to his place.

The drummer elevated to **Drum Major** takes on a highly conspicuous post. In early years he had to be able to converse in foreign languages when parleying

Drum Major of great style and influence: Tom Cornall was one of the most renowned of the post-war years.

age) appeared boldly from across the floor, came straight up to her and asked her to dance. She accepted graciously, they had a delightful turn around the floor, he brought her back and dismissed himself with perfect courtesy. No doubt he picked up a bob or two from his comrades; it is hard to believe that there wasn't something on it – but what *style*!

Drummers have sometimes been looked down on with disdain by the professional musicians of the regimental band, though, as one of them unwisely retorted to his chivvying drum major, 'We can't all be effing Mozart'. They do however have moments of pure glory. On

At a high pitch: fifer of 1750. *Pierre Turner (from 'British Infantry Uniforms Since 1660' by Michael Barthorp – Orion Publishing Group)*

Household Drummer to the Monarch: Drum Major in State Dress. His fine apron is secured by a grenade clasp.

The Present, the Blow, the Withdraw: a typically cheeky commentary on the drummer. *Andrew Fergusson-Cuninghame*

with the enemy, and was thus the official interpreter. In the days of flogging it was his duty to supervise the administration of the lash by one of his drummers and he had to ensure that 'no cat has more than nine tails'. On active service that barbaric instrument was carried in a fife case.

At some point 'Drum Major' was superseded by 'Sergeant Drummer', but the original appointment was restored in 1928. As a Household Drummer to the monarch he wears State Dress on State occasions. He is responsible for the Colours of the battalion and sees that they are decked with a laurel wreath on the anniversaries of certain battles.

'Drummy' constantly reminds his drummers that they are the shop window of the battalion and himself takes the most prominent position, leading the entire regimental band and corps of drums on parade and directing them with his mace.

Drummers and drum majors have risen to the highest ranks in the Regiment and their fierce pride in their colourful trade lasts a lifetime. Retired drummers regularly meet up to share a pint or two, blow the cobwebs from their instruments and revisit past glories.

Wearing the Fleur-de-Lys: Lance Corporal Wayne Jennings at Windsor in 2005. At the funeral of Charles II, the arms of England and of France were incorporated on the mourning band. It is to commemorate this that the Fleur-de-Lys is worked in braid on drummers' tunics in every regiment of the Foot Guards. *Roger Scruton*

Chapter Six

APEX OF EMPIRE
1856-1914

Service at Home

After the searing experience of the Crimea the Regiment settled down, with a large infusion of new men, into a regime very similar to that which prevailed before the war. In 1860 the two hundredth anniversary of the Regiment was celebrated, the date having being postponed from 1856 because of the Crimean War. The Prince Consort, Colonel of the Regiment, gave a stirring speech, in which he recalled famous victories of the past and remarked that 'the same discipline which has made the Regiment ever ready and terrible in war has enabled it to pass long periods of peace in the midst of all the temptation of a luxurious metropolis without loss of vigour and energy'.[1] The sergeants celebrated with a fine dinner in the Crystal Palace.

The Queen continued to show great interest in and affection for her Grenadiers. In 1864 she visited the 1st Battalion in Chelsea Barracks on its return from Canada, inspecting the battalion itself, 'as well as the men's barrack rooms, kitchens, messes etc'. In 1882 she sent the officers of the 2nd Battalion a piece of cake from the christening of the Duke of Connaught's son. 'Her Majesty is sorry she could not send a larger piece,' read the accompanying letter. In 1888 Trooping the Colour was performed before her at Windsor, by the same battalion and two squadrons of the 1st Life Guards. It was evidently the first time she had ever witnessed the ceremony, which did not take its present form until King Edward VII's reign and was not even rehearsed in full.

In 1856 a new appointment was authorized to oversee the Foot Guards: Major General, Commanding the Brigade of Guards. The incumbent was also responsible for the Home District (later named London District) and had his headquarters alongside the Commander-in-Chief in Horse Guards. Up to 1897 only the Grenadiers found three battalions, but in that year the Coldstream and Scots Guards also raised a third (though the 3rd Scots were removed eleven years later). The ups and downs of battalions and constant changes in strength, which became so familiar in later years, had already long been a feature of military life.

In 1856 also the Household Brigade Cricket Club was given permission to adopt the royal racing colours of blue, red, blue for their tie. These colours were later adopted for the whole body of Household troops, horse and foot. A few years later, in 1862, an unofficial journal, now named the *Guards Magazine*, was launched. At first much of the content was devoted to the sporting diversions of the officers, but as the years wore on far better notice was taken of the rank and file.

---

[1] Hamilton

Standing by: a rare photograph from 1855 of the Buckingham Palace detachment preparing for duty.

Anticipation at Windsor: a small party waits for the next move.

Hairy axemen: pioneers of the 1st Battalion in Dublin 1864.

An enthusiastic salute for mother: to the modern eye the Prince of Wales still does not seem to have absorbed his instruction, though perhaps saluting with both hand and sword was acceptable at the time, especially to Her Majesty.
Victorian music cover

On the square, in a square: the defensive formation was still practised at the turn of the century.

On the rope: the 2nd Battalion tug-of-war team, army champions in 1894 and 1895, with their mascot Private Sausage.

Taking it easy: battalion staff of the 2nd Battalion in Dublin 1871.

FIELD MARSHAL

HRH GEORGE, Duke of CAMBRIDGE
KG KP GCB GCH GCMG *1819-1904*

Reactionary
Commander-in-Chief
for thirty-nine years
and Colonel
of the Regiment
for forty-three

Georgia, Duke of Cambridge, grandson of George III, first cousin to Queen Victoria and exactly her age, was Commander-in-Chief of the Army from 1856 until 1895 and Colonel of the Regiment from 1861 until his death.

He had become Colonel of the Scots Fusilier Guards in 1852 and at the outset of the Crimean War was given command of the 1st Division, containing the brigades of Guards and Highlanders. These he led at the Alma and at Inkerman, where at one point he personally took command of the Guards. Though slow and cautious, he was certainly brave. In the dreadful conditions he was in some ways hardly better off than his men. When a surgeon of the Scots Fusilier Guards complained to his servant that his shirt was full of lice, the servant replied, 'The Duke of Cambridge is covered with them, sir'.

His long reign at the Horse Guards as Commander-in-Chief did little for military progress. Where any was made at all, it was usually in the face of his opposition, and he fought the reformers, Wolseley and Cardwell, with as much zeal as he had the Russians. For half a century he obstructed change, fearing that traditional military virtues would be undermined.

He was deeply attached to his army, however, and had its interests very much at heart. His soldiers were devoted to 'old Garge, God bless him'. But he did himself no favours, attracting ridicule and some rude nicknames, by staying on so long in the job. There was general relief when at last, in 1895, the Queen persuaded her reluctant cousin to stand down.

See St Aubyn

FIELD MARSHAL

HRH ARTHUR, Duke of CONNAUGHT
KG KT KP GCB GCSI GCMG GCIE GCVO GBE VD TD *1850-1942*

Dedicated and much
honoured soldier
who was
Colonel of the
Regiment for
thirty-eight years

Arthur, Duke of Connaught and Strathearn, held a full house of orders of chivalry: Knight of the Garter, the Thistle and St Patrick, and Knight Grand Cross of the Bath, the Star of India, St Michael and St George, the Indian Empire, the Victorian Order and the British Empire.

This might not seem so hard to manage when Queen Victoria is your mother and you her third and favourite son, but in fact he was a dedicated and competent soldier, entering the Army in 1868 and qualifying for every step in promotion. He was particularly well known for his leadership of the Guards Brigade in Wolseley's short and brilliantly successful campaign of 1882 in Egypt.

For a time it seemed that he might even succeed the Duke of Cambridge at the head of the Army. As it was, he held the chief command in Ireland and in 1904 was appointed Inspector General in preference to the veteran Lord Roberts, causing 'the little C-in-C to leave the W.O. for good in a devil of a temper'. In 1907 Connaught was persuaded to accept an experimental command in the Mediterranean, but felt himself to be as useful as 'a fifth wheel on a coach' and resigned in disgust. He became Governor General of Canada.

In 1904 he was appointed Colonel of the Regiment, two years after receiving his field marshal's baton, being succeeded on his death by the sixteen-year-old Princess Elizabeth. He built and lived at Bagshot Park and issued out from time to time to visit his Grenadiers. When almost ninety he attended an exercise, surveying the action from a Daimler fitted with a violent electric heater, which almost asphyxiated a luckless officer invited to join him for ten minutes.

LIEUTENANT GENERAL

Sir FREDERICK HAMILTON
KCB *1815-1898*

Veteran of the
Sandbag Battery,
Progressive Soldier,
Historian of the
Regiment

*F*rederick William Hamilton served as a page of honour to two kings, George IV and William IV, before being commissioned ensign in the Regiment in 1831. His early service was all at home, but in 1854 he went to the Crimea with the 3rd Battalion. He fought at the Alma and Balaclava and played a notable part at Inkerman, where he was one of several heroic Grenadiers in the desperate struggle for the Sandbag Battery. A senior regimental officer by the end of the war, he was awarded the CB for his services.

In his later years he proved equally useful and industrious. In 1860 he was military attaché in Berlin at a delicate time when Prussia was in dispute with Denmark and negotiations were proceeding for the marriage of the Prince of Wales to the Danish Princess Alexandra. He made strong contributions to military progress, especially in education and training, including a more scientific system of gymnastics. He commanded the forces in Scotland and later the Brigade of Guards.

But he will be best remembered by Grenadiers for his magisterial history of the Regiment, published in three fat volumes (in the best Victorian tradition) in 1874, with several maps and a number of portraits. It was an enormous work that required prodigious research. Finding in the regimental orderly room no documents at all that shed light on the first seventy years from 1656, he was compelled to raid countless libraries, government archives and private records. The appendices to his work cover details of every description: establishments, with scales of pay; battalion stations; nominal rolls of officers, including quartermasters and surgeons; and the Crimean casualty lists. It was a wonderful legacy.

See Hamilton

Reform, Improvement, Entertainment

Conditions improved steadily. Between 1865 and 1870 new barracks were built at Chelsea and Windsor and a new camp set up at Shorncliffe. The Foot Guards' quarters at St John's Wood and Portman Square in London were given up. Accommodation for families began to appear as a normal practice. Quarters were still changed continuously, at least once a year and often more frequently, the entire battalion normally taking to the road to march from one station to the other and being admired by spectators along the way.

Education also improved slowly, and it was high time, as sixty per cent of the soldiery were illiterate at the beginning of the period. Discipline became more humane, though it was not until 1871 that flogging was abolished. Deserters were still harshly treated, being branded 'D' on the arm with a tattooing iron. And the ordinary death rate was remarkably high by the standards of today. Regimental records reveal that between 1859 and 1879 no fewer than 390 serving Grenadiers died. By comparison with the rest of the country the rate was probably quite low, for at least soldiers were reasonably fed and a lot of other people were not. Most of the deaths were attributed to consumption (tuberculosis), fever and heart disease, although a surprising number were due to drowning, a curious fact until it is remembered that the Thames embankments were not yet built. Other unfortunates fell dead on parade, on a march, and one even at his post outside Buckingham Palace; one is recorded to have succumbed to 'disease of the heart accelerated by drink and excitement' and a few died in the dreadful-sounding Cold Bath Fields Prison.

By the major Army reforms of 1870, introduced by the Secretary of State for War, Sir Edward Cardwell, pay and terms of service were improved.[2] 'Pay was improved by the granting of good conduct pay but it was only a penny a day after three years, and sixpence after twenty-eight years. Basic pay was the traditional 'shilling a day' (5p). An extra penny was given for being in the Foot Guards, but it was subject to such stoppages for cleaning materials, haircuts, laundry and barrack damages that the men saw little of it. It was not until 1890 that the private soldier had officially to receive a minimum of twopence a day in cash, enough then for a pint of beer. A guardsman could however, supplement those meagre rates in various ways.

---

[2] This was also the time when infantry regiments of the Line were given county titles rather than numbers

A battalion all in white jackets: how they kept them clean, especially when handling rifles, is hard to imagine.

A bloody fatigue: meat distribution in 1891.

Slouch hats and silver: the 2nd Battalion shooting team with its trophy in 1902.

A final lodging: Waterloo Colours marched into the Guards Chapel.

Plain and simple: the essentials of kit layout in the early 1900s were much the same well after the Second World War.

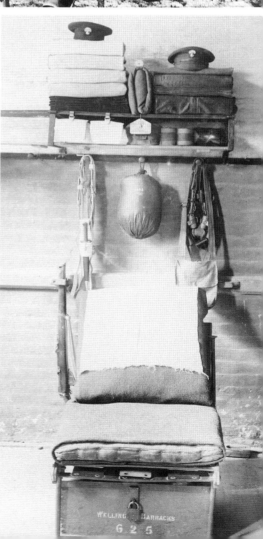

If lucky enough to be on Guard on a Royal birthday or other Royal occasion, he received an extra day's pay. Ninepence a day could be earned for acting as a 'guinea pig' in a drill squad for Volunteer officers under instruction, while some fatigues at the Royal Army Clothing Depot at Pimlico were paid for. A rarer duty was to act as an 'extra' at Covent Garden or Drury Lane Theatre, a custom dating back at least to the late eighteenth century when the rate was ninepence per performance or sixpence for a rehearsal. It is said that the practice was given Royal assent by Queen Victoria when she noted with disapproval the highly unmilitary bearing of some of the so-called soldiers in the chorus at a Royal Command Performance of *Aida*.[3]

In 1877 the Guards Depot was moved from Warley to the barracks at Caterham, where it was to remain for eighty-two years before moving to Pirbright, which itself had been adopted in 1882 as a site for field training and musketry.[4]

Before the days of radio, much less television, barrack entertainments played an important part. *A Brigade of Guards Magazine* report of 1888 described a typical concert: 'The Grenadier Guards Minstrel Troupe (under the direction of Captain F C Ricardo) began its second season at Chelsea Barracks on Tuesday 20, and Thursday 22 December. The first part consisted of the usual songs and choruses, and commenced with an overture admirably arranged by Mr Dan Godfrey, jun, introducing selections from old Ethiopian songs with vocal parts and choruses, and giving excellent opportunities for the free use of the bones and tambourines. The second part included a cornet solo by Musician Key, and song and dance by Corporal Atkinson and clog dancing by Privates Mayor, Dee, Stewart and Goatley, and Drummers Kimber and Phillips. The clog dancers were exceptionally good, and the effect was much added to by the lovely dresses in which Captain Ricardo had clothed them.'

The Reserve Regiment, New Organization

In 1900, as the demands of the South African war increased, the Irish Guards were formed (with a considerable Grenadier component) and, for a few short years, the Royal Guards Reserve Regiment, along with nine reserve regiments of infantry of the Line and four of cavalry. 'This Regiment was composed of three companies

[3] Paget
[4] A resounding term that long survived the disappearance of muskets

LIEUTENANT GENERAL
PHILIP SMITH
CB *1837-1894*

Philanthropic General who was largely responsible for the beauty of the Guards Chapel

*P*hilip, the first of a number of Grenadiers later to be known as Abel Smith, joined the Regiment in 1855, missing the Crimean campaign by a short distance. Quickly proving to be a capable and enthusiastic officer, he took command of the 2nd Battalion in 1881 and led it with distinction in the Egyptian campaign of the following year, being awarded the CB after the battle of Tel-el-Kebir. After serving on the staff in Canada and Gibraltar he commanded a brigade in Aldershot and chaired the committee that recommended the introduction of the Lee-Enfield rifle to the Army. Promoted major general in 1889 he was appointed to the command of the 'Home District', as the London District was then known. Three years later he was advanced to lieutenant general on retirement (not then uncommon), but he was already in ill health and died of paralysis in 1894.

He left an important legacy. An engaging and God-fearing bachelor, endowed with the robust Victorian virtues of churchmanship and public service, he seems to have been a favourite uncle to everyone, not least to his soldiers, in whose welfare he was closely interested. He took the lead in improving the Guards Chapel, built in 1838. After his death a subscription was raised to complete the semi-dome and several hundred NCOs and privates added their pennies to the pot. The semi-dome was almost all that remained after the bombing of the chapel in June 1944 with heavy loss of life, and remains in the restored building.

Butterfield's chapel at the Guards Depot in Caterham was also largely the result of his efforts and a great deal of his own money. It survives, fortunately, though now deconsecrated and used as a leisure centre. Jolly uncle though he was, he can hardly have enjoyed seeing his pews turned out to make way for skateboard ramps.

of Grenadiers, possibly the same number of Coldstreamers and two of Scots Guards, dressed in their regimental uniforms. There was a Corps of Drums, Majors, Captains, one Lieutenant and no Ensigns. The Battalion, for that is what it was, was brigaded with the 3rd Coldstream and 3rd Scots Guards for training, went to Pirbright for musketry, was inspected by the Major General in the normal way and carried out the public duties. It formed the eighth guard on the Birthday Parade of 1900, being described as 'formed of the pick of flank company men of the Brigade, all in the prime of life, and each with the Egyptian Medal and the Khedive's Star. The way they clean their buff and put on their equipment would form an instructive lesson to some of their young comrades in the Brigade ... as to marching past ... opinion seems to give the palm to them.'[5]

Further reforms followed the chastening lessons of South Africa. Lord Haldane, Secretary of State for War from 1907 to 1912, was largely responsible. A General Staff was created and, as the German threat became more alarming, an expeditionary force was formed, including two Guards brigades. Individual responsibility was encouraged and a more professional approach taken to soldiering. In 1913 changes were also made in organization. In the old battalion there had been first ten companies, and later eight, in which the senior NCO was a colour sergeant. This was now changed to four companies, each up to 250 men at full strength. The new warrant rank of company sergeant major was created to take this large body in hand. In the 1st Battalion the new King's Company was formed of the two flank companies, the old King's Company and No 8.

It was still necessary sometimes to deal with strikes and industrial unrest. All three battalions were deployed in sensitive parts of London in 1911. 'The dress for these duties was Service Dress, with Bearskin Caps, the latter in order to protect the head against missiles.'[6]

The Victorian Officers' Life

In 1858 a new Military University (later to be the Staff College) was set up for the officers, though received with little enthusiasm. It was to be many decades before an officer was well thought of by his peers for abandoning regimental life, even temporarily, for the purpose of studying his profession more closely. Military qualities could best be acquired by pleasant activities in extended periods of leave: courage and an eye for country in the

hunting field, skill at arms in pursuit of the pheasant and grouse, and the respect due to his class by success in society. It was a glittering life in a time of ostentation and elegance; officers attended state occasions and entertainments in uniform and were much admired. The Grenadiers were in fact rather less elitist than was often imagined. William Napier had complained that the army of his day (the early nineteenth century) wilted under 'the cool shade of the aristocracy'. The accusation was firmly rebutted by the Earl of Malmesbury in 1855, who made a detailed study of the Army List and found that only one sixth of officers in the Grenadiers – 'a regiment particularly charged with guarding the throne of an ancient monarchy' – had a blood connection with the peerage.[7]

Grenadier generals were extraordinarily plentiful. Honorary promotion after retirement accounted for a good many, but in 1877 there were no fewer than twenty-two on the active list, of whom seven were lieutenant generals and twelve full generals – and that not counting royal ones.

Cardwell abolished the purchase of commissions and double rank. The trade in commissions had been much abused earlier in the century. Great sums of money were involved, the regulation price for a company of the Foot Guards being almost £5000[8], which demand ... might inflate to as much as £9000. Double rank, a privilege enjoyed by the Household troops for over two centuries, was well past its time, though this did not prevent an officer opening a speech with, 'Gentlemen of the Guards, Friends of the Artillery, and you Blokes of the Line' and, then as now, 'The Army is very proud of the Guards regiments, but a Guards officer slipping on a banana skin would be regarded as a highly satisfactory sight by members of other units'.[9] The last officer to hold double rank was believed to be a Grenadier, Captain and Lieutenant Colonel Parry Bonham, who died in 1945 at the age of ninety-three.[10]

There was no doubt, however, that officers, as in any good regiment, were expected to be gentlemen. The regimental historian, writing in 1870, while fully in sympathy with the need for the professional education of

[5] Gow
[6] Grenadier Guards (1)
[7] Holmes
[8] Worth almost £300,000 in 2005
[9] Warner
[10] Paget

Honoured by the City: hemmed in by enthusiastic crowds, the 3rd Battalion in 1909 exercises its right to march through the City of London with Colours flying, drums beating and bayonets fixed. The privilege was extended to the other battalions in 1915 and later similar privileges were conferred by the cities of Manchester and Worcester.

Pros and cons of great height: the satisfaction of getting the better of a Coldstream drummer is modified when you cannot see out of your sentry box.

On the road: still smartly turned out, though in forage caps and with leather gaiters to spare the trousers.

Mass effect: the 1st Battalion in close column (top) and the three battalions together, in Hyde Park 1913.

officers, feared that it might be thought to set aside 'noblesse oblige'. 'We may rest assured,' he wrote, 'that the soldier in his hour of need and danger will ever be more ready to follow the officer and gentleman whose education, position in life and accident of birth, point out to be his natural leader ... than the man who, by dint of study and brainwork, has raised himself (much to his own credit, certainly) from the plough or the anvil, to rule without discrimination, and with a rod of iron, those who were born to be his superiors.'[11]

Training for War

Training was still firmly based on drill, which governed both the handling of weapons and the manoeuvring of bodies of men. This was very largely in the hands of the Adjutant, Sergeant Major, drill sergeants and NCOs, who ruled the square, the daily routine, the endless fatigues and the cleaning of kit. Company officers, except where there were specific duties, carried out a bare minimum of parades and inspections. The senior officers, certainly the Commanding Officer, would often appear only long enough to drink a glass of port in the middle of the morning, administer justice at noon and eat a good lunch.[12]

Occasionally there were more demanding times. One officer complained that 'my first season's dancing was severely interrupted by 1st Guards Brigade manoeuvres, held as far afield as Hyde Park. The start line was the road, now known as Park Lane ... My battalion happily was held in brigade reserve in the area of Apsley House ... The Scots Guards advanced with their left flank resting upon the Serpentine. The Coldstream, in their traditional station, advanced in good order along the opposite shore. Imagine my consternation when about four in the afternoon I was awoken by the *Officers' Call* from the vicinity of Kensington Palace, followed by the *Double*. We

Lively times in the ring: seen by *The Penny Illustrated Paper* of (appropriately enough) Boxing Day 1896.

were of course in full tunic order, large packs and bearskin caps. Fit as I was from my social life it proved a severe test of my youthful stamina. My servant never fully recovered from his exertions. My endeavours were well rewarded. We were addressed by the Commander-in-Chief, the Duke of Cambridge. "The rank and file," he said, "did their duty. The non-commissioned officers were magnificent. *It was the commanding officers who were to blame*".'[13]

There were periods in camp, usually in the summer months, but sometimes in the winter also. From 1878 reservists were recalled for training. Shooting was taken very seriously, especially in later years after the Boers had demonstrated so painfully how well it could be done. The introduction of the new Lee Metford magazine rifle in 1890, and the lighter Lee Enfield in 1906, was an enormous improvement on the old

Filling up: Grenadiers take on water at a halt on the downs near Newbury.

---

[11] Hamilton

[12] This habit died remarkably hard. As late as the 1950s, an enquirer rang to speak to an officer after lunch, without success. After several attempts the exasperated caller demanded to know whether this officer worked in the afternoons. 'Oh no,' came the candid reply. 'He doesn't work in the mornings. He doesn't *come in* in the afternoons.'

[13] Dalrymple-White

weapons, and shooting became highly competitive, the officers playing their part on equal terms. Marksmen received extra pay and those who excelled and won the prizes were held in high esteem.

Horse-drawn transport[14] integral to the battalion establishment began to appear, and bright, well educated men were selected as signallers, to be introduced to the mysteries of the semaphore and heliograph. Later there were field telephones, but radio communication was still far in the future.

Sport of all kinds was closely associated with skill at arms and much encouraged. As facilities improved, athletics, football, swimming and bayonet fencing were popular. Boxing had obvious attractions when individual strength and endurance were so highly prized. The periodic tournaments attracted huge interest and excitement, and no doubt a good deal of money changed hands in quiet corners of the barrack room and mess. A regular system of gymnastics was introduced, partly as the result of an investigation made into the system of the French army by Colonel Hamilton, a Grenadier, and a medical officer. Earlier, the Duke of Wellington had directed that exercises of this kind should be hidden from public view, in order not to offend delicate Victorian sensibilities.

The result of all these activities within a battalion was to produce a highly disciplined body of men, fit and strong, able to march long distances and to shoot straight and fast. 1914 was to call upon these qualities in the most dramatic way.

Dublin – the Heir to the Throne on the Square

Visits to Ireland continued into the 1880s, though no longer by canal. Nothing of great interest resulted, other than an engaging royal attachment. Edward, Prince of Wales, was being brought up by his serious-minded parents with stultifying strictness. Her Majesty and the Prince Consort took the greatest pains to see that the young prince, who was generous and good-natured but not in the least suited to intellectual activities, was kept too busy at his studies to enjoy himself. When he reached the age of seventeen his father drew up a great document outlining the responsibilities of manhood, especially one destined to kingship, on reading which the young man burst into tears. A Grenadier, Colonel Robert Bruce, later

[14] It is a delightful example of the endurance of terminology that 'MT' for 'Mechanical Transport' should still be used in the twenty-first century, as if the hearer might be misled into thinking that the hoofed variety was meant.

LIEUTENANT

DAN GODFREY
1831-1896

Bandmaster for forty years who brought military music to a wide public for the first time

*D*an Godfrey came from a family of bandmasters. His father Charles served the Coldstream in that capacity for over forty years and was succeeded by his son Fred. Another son, Charles, filled the same post in the Scots Guards. Between them they served the entire Brigade of Guards of their time.

Dan himself studied at the Royal Academy of Music and played flute solos in Julien's Orchestra, one of the best known of its day. In 1856, at the age of twenty-five, he was appointed to the Band of the Grenadier Guards, where he then emulated his father by serving for forty years. He composed several pieces of music, including *The Guards, Hilda* and *Mabel* waltzes.

In 1872 he took his band to Boston, where it was received with great enthusiasm by the American public. Although it was almost a century since the American colonies had been lost in humiliating circumstances, this was the first time since then that a British uniform had been seen in the country and indeed the first time a British military band had been allowed to entertain the public abroad at all. Permission was granted only after a stiff debate in Parliament and perhaps it helped that the German Grenadier Band had also been invited.

Godfrey also exposed his talents, and those of his musicians, to a wider public at home. He introduced strings, bass and saxophone to the instrumentation and his concerts in Hyde Park brought military music of the highest quality to ever-increasing audiences. He was a great favourite of Queen Victoria, who clearly was well amused by his performance, and it was she who decided that he should be specially rewarded on her Golden Jubilee of 1887. Thus Bandmaster Godfrey became Lieutenant Godfrey, the first commissioned bandmaster in the Army.

promoted major general, was appointed his governor and armed with further voluminous instructions.

The Prince was pressed through a crash course at both Oxford and Cambridge universities, where he was allowed no contact with ordinary undergraduates. He pleaded incessantly for a period of attachment to his father's regiment, and though Bruce had misgivings, well knowing the habits of military men, an arrangement was at last arrived at. Another great memorandum was drawn up by the Prince Consort and countersigned by the Duke of Cambridge and the young man himself.

In July 1861, at nineteen years old, he joined the 1st Battalion at the Curragh camp outside Dublin, dressed in the uniform of a staff colonel. His father had directed that he should 'learn the duties of every grade, from ensign upwards' and, contriving to earn promotion every fortnight, should 'with some exertion, arrive in the ten weeks before him, at the command of a battalion' and also be made competent to manoeuvre a brigade in the field. His instructors were the Commanding Officer Colonel Hon Henry Percy VC, Sergeant Major Baker and Drill Sergeant Haylock but, approaching the end of August, these talented gentlemen had to confess that the programme was rather more demanding than even they could achieve. Before being invited to perform the duties of a subaltern in front of his parents and the Commander-in-Chief, the Prince pleaded in vain to be allowed to command a company, but Percy replied, 'You are too imperfect in your drill, sir. Your word of command is indistinct. I will *not* try to make the Duke of Cambridge think you are more advanced than you are'. The Queen thoroughly approved of Percy's robust approach and on 11 September the Prince was glad to report to her that he had been allowed to manoeuvre a brigade 'with expert assistance'.

And in another, highly irregular, respect his brother officers had managed to enlarge his experience. It came to light several weeks later that they had smuggled a young actress, Nellie Clifden, into the Prince's quarters, so at last, it can easily be believed, he was allowed some of the enjoyment so long denied him.

As the years went on, he never lost his desire for soldiering or his affection for his Grenadiers. He was mortified when prevented from joining the Egyptian expedition of 1882, in which his brother the Duke of Connaught, whom he much admired, had a brigade command. 'He had been stung by French and German caricatures depicting him as a field-marshal whose experience of war was limited to the annual battle of flowers on the French Riviera, and by an uncouth and untrue taunt – attributed to Bismarck – that his love of uniforms was matched only by his fear of powder; but his fervent offer of service was rejected by the Cabinet.'[15]

Death of the Great Queen Empress

It was only shortly after the Dublin episode that the Prince Consort unexpectedly died, to the inexpressible grief of the Queen, who never fully recovered from the blow. The Duke of Cambridge succeeded him as Colonel. Queen Victoria herself was to survive another forty years, dying at Osborne in the Isle of Wight on 22 January 1901. By chance the 1st Battalion, and thus the Queen's Company, was at home, the other two battalions both being in South Africa. For nine days and nights a vigil was kept by the Queen's Company at Osborne. Each guardsman was 6ft 2in tall and most wore the medals won at Omdurman. On 2 February the coffin was brought to London by train and the funeral procession wound its way through immense crowds to Paddington and thence to Windsor. There Grenadiers lifted the coffin from the train to the gun carriage, but later in the procession the horses broke their traces and their place was taken by bluejackets from the guard of honour, establishing a tradition that has been followed ever since.[16] A further vigil of thirty-six hours took place in St George's Chapel, and the Queen's Company led the family procession to her interment in the mausoleum at Frogmore. On 9 February Edward VII gave awards to those who had been on duty and signified his wish that the company should henceforward be named the King's Company. Only nine years later came the turn of the King himself, and his son succeeded him as George V .

---

[15] Magnus. The Cabinet's view was understandable. Only a few years earlier the French Prince Imperial, heir to the exiled Emperor Napoleon III, had been killed in Zululand while fighting under Lord Chelmsford

[16] A Grenadier, Sir Frederick 'Fritz' Ponsonby, later to write the First World War history of the Regiment, was in charge. The crisis in the procession caused chaos and a furious row (conducted in whispers) between the sailors and the gunner officers, while 'poor Fritz was driven nearly mad with embarrassment'. (*JSAHR*, Spring 2003 and Ponsonby (2))

Service Abroad

'As rare as a guardsman's sweat in India' was the saying of the military in Victorian times. Indeed, Her Majesty did not like to see her guardsmen abroad, other than to engage in a serious campaign, so battalions of Foot Guards were never seen among the great number of British infantry stationed in the Indian Empire, facing the great Mutiny of 1857 or engaged in the numerous frontier campaigns. However, the period did encompass three campaigns in Egypt and the Sudan, and a long war in South Africa, all of which are covered in the following chapter.[17] And there were a few excursions to other parts.

Canada (Map page 34), Gibraltar and Ashanti

Another visit to **Canada** took place in December 1861. Civil war had erupted in the United States and a military presence was required over the border. The **1st Battalion** (Col Hon Henry Percy VC and Col Edward Wynyard), which had returned from Dublin in October and prepared itself for this new role in a couple of months, sailed in an uncomfortably crowded transport. The Grenadiers were evidently so accommodating to other men of the force occupying the precious space that they were known as the 'Lambs'. After a long journey they arrived in the depths of winter at St John in New Brunswick and then, clad in buffalo skins and moccasins, drove 300 miles by sleigh to Rivière-du-Loup on the St

Lawrence, before eventually moving on to Montreal. Owing to the size of the men, only six were allotted to each sleigh. They were given strict instructions to beware of the activities of 'crimps', tricksters who tried to induce them to desert, but, 'during the first six months but one man, a ranting Methodist, and a disgrace to his corps, succumbed to the machinations of these pests of society'.[18] In the event nothing very much occurred, but it was almost four years before they returned home.

In 1897 it was decided that a battalion of Guards should help regiments of the Line in an overseas garrison role and accordingly the 1st Battalion went that year to **Gibraltar**. They were refused permission to take bearskin caps. The following year they were relieved by the 2nd Battalion in order to go to the Sudan.

In 1895 a small expedition was sent to **Ashanti** on the west coast of Africa. This contained a composite body of Guards to which the 2nd Battalion contributed an officer, a sergeant, a corporal and fifteen privates, and the Coldstream and Scots Guards a similar number. The force made a trying march 145 miles from the coast to Kumasi,

---

[17] The Zulu wars in Africa did not come the way of the Regiment. However, it was a former Grenadier officer, Frederic Thesiger, Lord Chelmsford, who commanded the 1879 expedition in which occurred one of the greatest disasters of British military history, Isandlwana. Part of his force was caught unprepared and overwhelmed by great numbers of Zulus. The dead are thought to have numbered 1357, of which 599 were from the 24th Foot. Thesiger had joined the Grenadiers in the Crimea in 1855, but, seeing no immediate prospect of action, soon transferred to a Line regiment in India. His personal responsibility for the disaster is still argued about.
[18] Hamilton

Snowshoe in Canada: a varied group of the Sergeants' Mess in 1863.

and quickly overawed a feeble opposition. King Prembeh, a notorious slaver who had had the gall to raid the neighbouring British colony of the Gold Coast, was deposed. Though most of them had been sick, the little Grenadier contingent returned home complete, with the Ashanti Star and a gratuity (for a private £1.10s).[19]

Bermuda – Condemned to a Holiday in the Sun

On 7 July 1890 a dreadful thing happened. The regimental diary records: 'The most deplorable event that ever occurred in the Regiment took place in the **2nd Battalion** (Lt Col Crichton Maitland) at Wellington Barracks. A marching order parade having been ordered at 8.30, the officers and NCOs paraded as usual but when the fall-in sounded only one or two of the men answered to it. The bulk of the battalion remained in their barrack rooms until turned down [sic] by the officers. There was also considerable hissing when the Commanding Officer entered the barrack gate. The battalion mounted the public duties as usual.'

An investigation was mounted by the Commander-in-Chief, the Duke of Cambridge, and a Court of Inquiry sat for several days interviewing witnesses. On 18 July a District Court Martial was held to try the senior private soldier in each of the six companies concerned (two of the eight were stationed outside Wellington Barracks). The six privates were sentenced to between 18 months and two years IHL[20], and one of them was also discharged. Col Maitland declined to resign and even wrote to the newspapers to say so. He was, however, superceded by Lt Col Herbert Eaton on 20 July and placed on half-pay. The Adjutant, Lt Murray, resigned his appointment, but the C-in-C permitted him to keep his commission. The press had a wonderful time, the affair being widely reported, and with undisguised relish.

But already on 18 July orders had been received that the battalion was to be held in readiness for immediate foreign service and the following day it was known that

Into sunny exile: the 2nd Battalion embark for Bermuda to serve their sentence.

the destination would be Bermuda. On the 21st the C-in-C addressed the officers and NCOs, berating them for the disgrace that had fallen on the Regiment. A day later they embarked at Gravesend and sailed to Spithead where the wives and families embarked. On the 23rd they sailed again, arriving in Bermuda on 5 August.

On 26 July the Duke of Cambridge reviewed the other battalions then in London (1st Grenadiers, 1st Coldstream and 2nd Scots Guards) in Hyde Park. He expressed his admiration for the physique and drill of a magnificent body of men and then 'warned them in an impressive speech against the wickedness of listening to the pernicious doctrines of unscrupulous agitators who, it was supposed, had worked such ruin amongst the men of the 2nd Battalion'.

The battalion stayed in Bermuda until 19 September 1891, having occupied themselves happily enough, especially (dare one say it) the sergeants' mess. The graves of six of them can still be found at St George's and Boaz – one died by choking on a cherry stone and another by diving into two feet of water. It is hard in modern times to imagine that a year in such a balmy spot would be considered a punishment and indeed the incident in London had been hardly worth the name of mutiny. But the disgrace was keenly felt and subsequent regimental histories chose not to mention it.

It was, however, a salutary lesson that deserved to be remembered, nor was it the only time it had to be learned by a battalion of the Foot Guards. Whatever the standing, prestige and reputation of a fine regiment, it has always been a mistake for the management to take discipline and good order for granted and to lose touch with feelings in the barrack room.

Principal sources: Hamilton, Whitworth (2), Paget, Magnus

---

[19] McInnes and Fraser. £1.10s (£1.50p) would be worth about £100 in 2005
[20] Imprisonment with Hard Labour. The regime for this punishment was harsh, but extra food was allowed in the form of a pint of gruel for supper and an ounce of cheese on Sundays

THE OFFICERS

he style of officer ranks and appointments in the Grenadiers have a number of peculiarities that often mystify others in the Army, never mind those unversed in military matters, and call for some explanation.

The Colonel-in-Chief is invariably the monarch.

The Colonel[1] of the Regiment was a crucial figure in the early days when his personal responsibility for the safety of the sovereign was of paramount importance. The post was a huge prize and greatly coveted. A directive of 1669 stated that:

... the Colonel of the Regiment of his Majesty's Foot (1st Foot Guards) shall be looked upon and obeyed as a General Officer in the Field ... to command both Horse and Foot accordingly ...

The Colonel was thus the most senior officer in the army after the Lord General and he led his men in battle. In 1681 Henry Fitzroy, Duke of Grafton, bought the colonelcy from John Russell for £5,100, an enormous sum in those days. He also commanded the 2nd Company. The pre-eminent position of the First Guards was also demonstrated by several subsequent colonels being promoted from a previous colonelcy in the Coldstream or Scots Guards.

In many cases the Colonel virtually owned his regiment,[2] though this was much less so for the Sovereign's Guards. Generals were not paid above

An impressive sight: a bewigged officer of 1686. *Bob Marrion*

A superior pose: an officer of the First Guards in 1808. *T Woolnoth*

their regimental rank unless in a field command or governorship, so often a colonelcy was the only means of receiving some recompense in peacetime. Since the mid-18th century the Colonel of the First Guards has been most often a member of the royal family.

As the colonelcy became a less active and more honorary post, it was the **Lieutenant Colonel** 'taking the place' of the colonel, who became the executive commander of the Regiment. In the early days he commanded the 3rd Company and when battalions were firmly established he commanded the 1st Battalion. It was not until 1759 that his role was confined to the overall command of the entire Regiment. In the days of double rank he was often a general officer and

A more practical turnout: in the Crimea 1854. *Bob Marrion*

---

[1] From the Latin *colonna (a column)*
[2] As recently as the 1950s a cavalry colonel was reported to have said to his superior, who had been sharp with one of his soldiers, 'Brigadier, if you talk to my men like that I'll take my regiment out of your brigade'

Time for tennis: officers on duty at Wimbledon in 1888.

Away to the trenches: an officer in marching order 1915. Walking sticks made little impression on the enemy and were usually abandoned. *Christopher Morley*

Smart in battledress: an armoured officer of 1944. Battledress was introduced as a loose and baggy ensemble with trousers braced up almost to the armpits and the 'blouse' able to accommodate any amount of stowage. In due course tailoring and pressing made suits more elegant. They were worn well into the 1960s. *Courtesy Bryan Fosten – The Pompadour Gallery*

Keeping covered: at given times, hats may still be worn in an officers' mess of the Household Division. The custom, though ascribed to various fantastic origins, is in fact nothing more than a continuation of the practice of wearing hats indoors which was common almost into the twentieth century. *Roger Scruton*

which of course they had hardly ever exercised in practice. The senior of the regimental majors commanded the 1st Battalion and the junior the 3rd, which often meant an unsettling shifting around every time a change was made, so in 1864 the practice was abolished. From about 1837, moreover, two further field officers had been established in all three battalions, each to command a 'wing' of four companies. They also held the rank of colonel in the Army and were known as the 'Senior and Junior Mounted Officers' or 'the Senior and Junior Major'. When, late in the 19th century, a second-in-command of the battalion was introduced, he was sometimes known informally as the Senior Major. The title was used rather erratically thereafter and it was not until the 1950s that it settled permanently on the appointment, where it remains today as solidly as if prescribed by Charles II himself. Such is the inscrutable effect of regimental fashion.

The Captain[3], always now a major in rank, is a title that belongs exclusively to the Captain of the Queen's (or King's) Company. **A Subaltern Officer** is a lieutenant or second lieutenant, the first being known as a **Subaltern** and the second as an **Ensign**. The officer appointments in a Guard on parade are invariably described as captain, subaltern and ensign (whatever their actual rank) the ensign carrying the Colour. Within barracks the orderly officer for the day is known as the **Picquet Officer** (formally 'Officer of the Inlying Picquet', as the barrack guard used to be named).

Newly arrived young officers with the temerity to possess a triple-barrelled surname are in danger of being entered on the picquet officers' list once for each name and thus three times as frequently as their comrades.

later he was permanently established as a full colonel. During the two world wars in particular his was a heavy burden, with responsibility for the manning of several battalions and with an operational role in the London District. He also appointed senior warrant officers and quartermasters.

In 1989 all manning responsibilities were assumed by the Ministry of Defence and the duties of the Lieutenant Colonel were confined to the interests of the regimental family itself, the post becoming part-time and open to a senior serving or retired officer. He still interviews aspiring officers and influences the subsequent careers of those who meet the approval of his piercing eye and win a commission. He is supported by the Regimental Council, which is chaired by the Colonel.

The lieutenant colonel commanding a battalion is always known as the **Commanding Officer** (never 'CO'). His second-in-command is, in Grenadier language, the **Senior Major**. Originally the Regiment had a single major, commanding the 4th Company. Later the command of battalions (first the 2nd and 3rd, and from 1759 all three) was entrusted to regimental majors. Under the system of double rank they held the Army rank of full colonel and occasionally were even generals. In 1803 both they and the lieutenant colonel were relieved from command of their own companies,

---

[3] From the Latin *caput* (a head)

Chapter Seven

NORTH AFRICA, SOUTH AFRICA
1882-1902

Egypt and the Sudan 1882-1898

A Brilliant Victory at Tel el Kebir 1882

In 1875 Britain bought a large interest in the recently constructed Suez Canal. It was of enormous significance, providing a much shorter route to her empire of India than round the cape of South Africa, and would be fought over several times in later wars. Britain, with France, exercised strong influence over the Egyptians and was determined to preserve peace there. When, therefore, a Colonel Arabi led an insurrection demanding 'Egypt for the Egyptians' and massacred 150 Europeans, the British government took immediate steps to help the Egyptian Khedive to suppress him.

In 1882 an expedition was sent out under General Sir Garnet Wolseley. It contained a brigade of Guards commanded by the Duke of Connaught, son of Queen Victoria and later to be Colonel of the Grenadiers. In the brigade was the **2nd Battalion** (Col Philip Smith), warned for duty when in Cork, and clothed for the desert in scarlet serge jackets, blue tweed trousers with a red stripe and pith helmets.

The effect of improved small arms on battlefield tactics in the desert led Wolseley to favour night marches and assaults, and accordingly he decided upon an ambitious plan. On 13 September he advanced upon Arabi's fortified camp at Tel el Kebir, sixty miles from Cairo. He employed an eight-mile night march, navigated by the stars, followed by a dawn attack against the enemy, who were in twice his strength and behind walls four miles long. The battalion deployed on the right of its brigade in two parts: the first half-battalion having two companies

Egypt Medal 1882-89 and Khedive's Star: the colours of the Egypt Medal represent the Blue and White Nile.

up and two in support, and the remaining half-battalion of four companies being in reserve in depth. The plan worked perfectly. The enemy, thousands of well-disciplined fellahin in white uniforms and red tarbooshes, who had manned the ramparts all night but never seriously expected an attack to be made in the dark, were taken completely by surprise and the battle was over in thirty-five minutes. Wolseley's two divisions poured over the ramparts, his cavalry followed up and two days later he entered Cairo. It was a fine demonstration of British military prowess and made a deep impression.

The Guards up the Nile on Camels 1884

By 1884 the action had moved south into the Sudan, against a quite different enemy. General Gordon was locked up in Khartoum, besieged by the Mahdi and his fanatical Dervish horde. The whole of the country, nominally a province of Egypt, was in open revolt. Again the British government sent out Wolseley, this time to rescue Gordon and other Europeans with him, before abandoning the province altogether.

Wolseley's army included a novel force: the **Guards Camel Regiment**. It was formed of detachments from the three regiments of Foot Guards, alongside the Heavy Camel Regiment taken from the Household Cavalry and cavalry of the Line, and despite the initial objections of the Duke of Cambridge, the Commander-in-Chief, who 'condemned the idea of camels in particular, as being "unsound, and distasteful to regiments, officers and men".' The soldiers were all in

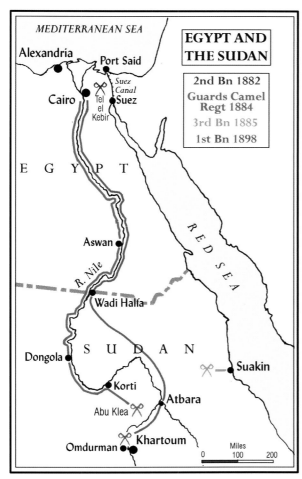

MEDITERRANEAN SEA

EGYPT AND THE SUDAN

2nd Bn 1882
Guards Camel Regt 1884
3rd Bn 1885
1st Bn 1898

Khartoum could be established through Atbara, and a railway built, by which a suitable force could later be brought up to recapture the city.

A force of 12,000 men was raised for the expedition, under the command of Lieutenant General Sir Gerald Graham VC. One of the three brigades was to be of Guards and the **3rd Battalion** (Lt Col Hon William Home) joined it. The battalion was at Windsor at the time and, being warned for duty on 10 February, underwent ten days of frantic activity. Both the Commanding Officer (whom Home replaced) and the Quartermaster were found to be unfit for the tropics, and drafts were pulled in from the other battalions. The final establishment was thirty officers and 1128 soldiers, formed into the usual eight companies. Fifty men with two officers were equipped and embarked as mounted infantry and everyone drew new Martini-Henry rifles. The defaulter sheets were not taken. It was recalled how the battalion had (conveniently, perhaps) lost all of theirs in the Crimea.

The battalion sailed from Gravesend on 20 February 1885 and encamped at Suakin on arrival. Their tents were double-pole Indian (double thickness) holding about sixteen men. Outposts, 300 to 500 yards out, were attacked nightly by enemy skirmishers, but the only casualty in the brigade was a Scots guardsman who went sleep-walking beyond his lines and, failing to answer a challenge on his return, was duly bayoneted through the heart by one of his comrades.

An advance in full force began on 20 March and the enemy were driven from a forward position. However, the cavalry had difficulty in the broken country and retired at one point. Then, as the *Daily Telegraph* correspondent reported: 'The enemy starting forward in close pursuit of the retiring Cavalry, rounded the hill and there, all at once, came upon the Guards Brigade drawn up in square. With a yell they went straight at it without hesitation, but in face of the withering fire which met them, they never succeeded in getting nearer than 15 to 20 yards of the line of Bayonets. Nothing could surpass the steadiness of the Guards, they fired as coolly as on a field day. I even heard them quietly joking along the ranks up to the moment of the charge.'

The force was then ordered to retire on a newly made defensive position (zariba) and the artillery, ambulance

khaki, in fact a nondescript grey colour or 'a sort of cafe-au-lait shade' which had not appealed to Queen Victoria as being suitable for her Household troops.[1]

The expedition advanced up the Nile under Sir Herbert Stewart, cutting south across a loop in the river from Korti and beating off a fierce and alarming enemy attack at **Abu Klea**, but they found on arriving in sight of Khartoum on 28 January 1885 that it had fallen to the Dervishes just two days before and that Gordon was dead. Wolseley withdrew and went into summer quarters back in Egypt. Of the 135 Grenadiers taking part, four had been killed and eleven wounded.

Suakin 1885 – A Trying Expedition

But Gordon had attained heroic status at home and public opinion demanded revenge. The government therefore decided to send an expedition to Suakin, a port of the Red Sea, with a view to crushing Osman Digna, one of the Mahdi's principal lieutenants whose home was there. It was also hoped that a shorter overland route to

---

[1] Paget

121

Goodbye: Grenadiers entrain for the war. *After George Harcourt*

Still in red jackets: a foot patrol in the Sudan. *Orlando Norie*

Hot and motley: a scruffy group of officers on the Suakin campaign.

Into khaki: the Grenadier on the left is dressed for his camel. *Bob Marrion*

SUDAN – 1884/85

DESERT COLUMN
GUARDS CAMEL   SUAKIN

and transport took their place within the Guards square, which was in the rearguard. They were constantly harassed by the enemy and by the time they reached the zariba were much exhausted, having been out in the heat of the sun for nine hours. The 3rd Grenadiers had had three casualties though, because of their position in the square, for much of the time they had been unable to fire without hitting their comrades.

During the next few days the time was occupied in sending convoys with water from Suakin to the zariba. This was particularly exhausting work, which fell mostly to the Guards, and it was not uncommon for the men to be at it for sixteen hours out of the twenty-four. Meanwhile the zariba was becoming thoroughly unpleasant owing to the stench from the putrefying corpses of Arabs and camels surrounding it. The smell was declared to be detectable from Suakin itself, seven miles away.

Not having succeeded in finding the elusive Osman, and sickness increasing in the force, Graham withdrew to Suakin, where the battalion managed to find some amusement in the form of horseracing and cricket. There was, however, some final work for the Grenadier mounted infantry detachment, which on 5 May, with the Bengal Lancers and Camel Corps, attacked a body of the enemy in the hills, killing some fifty of them and taking off several hundred head of cattle. Corporal Locke, of the detachment, was severely wounded by the last shot fired in the battle, which also proved for the Guards to be the last action of the campaign. The next day orders were received to return home, which they did with relief, eventually arriving at Portsmouth on 10 September. Their ship, the *Orontes*, nearly turned turtle in drawing up to the wharf. They had lost twenty-three men, while 136 were invalided home. It had been a much less glorious affair than that of 1882.[2]

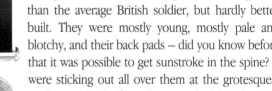

Queen's Sudan and Khedive's Sudan medals. The colours of the first represent the desert and the Sudanese nation, divided by the thin red line of British forces, those of the second the Nile running through the sands of the desert.

Omdurman 1898 – an Imperial Massacre

At last, thirteen years later, came the final reckoning in Sudan. Sir Herbert Kitchener was appointed Sirdar (commander) and with ruthless efficiency he planned the destruction of the Khalifa, successor to the Mahdi, and his vast army of Dervishes. After long preparation Kitchener assembled his force in Egypt and the **1st Battalion** (Col Villiers Hatton), then in Gibraltar, sailed to Alexandria to join it. It was the first time since Blenheim that a single battalion of Foot Guards had been deployed for a major campaign. Arriving at Atbara on 6 August, after a dreadfully cramped journey on the recently built railway, they made an impression on one witness that was less flattering than they might have hoped, though it rings true enough.

'Emerging from the roofed trucks they were less impressive [than on the barrack square]. Of course it was the worst possible moment to see them .... Falling in beside the train they were certainly taller than the average British soldier, but hardly better built. They were mostly young, mostly pale and blotchy, and their back pads – did you know before that it was possible to get sunstroke in the spine? – were sticking out all over them at the grotesquest angles .... The half-battalion marched limply. Only remember that they had hardly stretched their legs since they embarked at Gibraltar three weeks before. The wonder was that they could march at all.'[3]

The Dervishes, though armed with spears and swords (and a few firearms), were formidable enemies, savage, fanatical, desperately brave, and heedless of their own lives. Just allow them to get in close and their numbers could well prove overwhelming. But this Kitchener was determined to prevent. He would keep his formations tight and lure the enemy into running straight into the overwhelming firepower of his rifles, machine-guns and artillery – which they obligingly did. His infantrymen did not even bother to lie down for cover against the small number of Dervishes with firearms, and a few casualties were thereby sustained. They stood shoulder to shoulder, the front rank kneeling and the rear rank standing, firing volleys, just as redcoats had fought at Waterloo. It was the last time that anything of the kind was to be seen on the battlefield – indeed, only a year later the Boers, in a dramatic reversal of fortune, were to give the British a heavy dose of their own medicine.

Arrived at Omdurman, Kitchener formed his army in a tight defensive arc, the river at his back. On the right of

---

[2] *Principal source: Craster (2)*
[3] Steevens

123

Up river: a large Nile boat accompanied by smaller ones.

Eye to the glass: spotting the Dervish.

Private, Grenadier Guards, 1897.

Striding out: a private on the march in 1897. Much of his equipment is still white. *Player's Cigarettes*

Omdurman 1898.

At close quarters: a romantic view of the action. In fact the Dervishes came nothing like so near in the face of the British and Egyptian fire.
Faulkner's Celebrated Cigarettes

Rest while you can: awaiting the Dervish.

Here they come: a distant cloud of dust announces the approach of the enemy. The first volley was fired at the astonishing range of 2,700 yards.

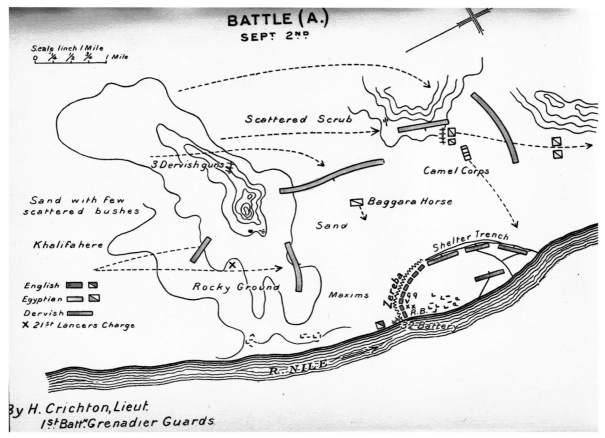

BATTLE (A.)
SEPT 2ND

Scale 1inch 1 Mile
0 ¼ ½ ¾ 1 Mile

Scattered Scrub

3 Dervish guns

Camel Corps

Sand with few
scattered bushes

Baggara Horse

Khalifa here

Sand

Shelter Trench

Zereba

Rocky Ground

Maxims

R.B.

English
Egyptian
Dervish
X 21st Lancers Charge

32 Battery

R. NILE

By H. Crichton, Lieut.
1st Batt. Grenadier Guards

Green swarms: the map drawn for the Commanding Officer's report shows the 'English' (blithely ignoring the presence of Scottish battalions) in red, Egyptians in blue and the Dervish masses in green.

the 2nd Infantry Brigade the Battalion formed line with six companies forward, the Queen's and No 8 Company being slightly in rear on either flank. The battalion's single Maxim gun was placed on the left. They were ready.[4]

'... at 6.30 am, the Dervishes appeared in sight with a roar like the sea. Their numbers seemed enormous, they overlapped our left flank, and appeared eight or ten deep. They came both sides S. and N. of the hill and at first with innumerable standards came at a great pace towards us. The guns opened fire with great result .... The Battalion was ordered to open fire, and the first volley was fired at 2,700 yards[5] – the range being obtained from 32nd Field Battery. Before this the camels had all been sent close to the river. Boxes of ammunition were unloaded from the mules for each company in the firing line [six] and placed immediately behind the company .... We had a beautiful field of fire .... As the Dervishes came over the ridge one of the men was heard to say: "I don't care how b..... far I march to see a sight like this". Our firing line began with section volleys at 6.40 am. The fire discipline was superb. The sights were continually

lowered as the Dervishes got nearer, and I never heard better volleys at field firing... Standards, which were grouped in large squares, rocked and fell like sinking ships... There were two or three narrow escapes. One man had his bayonet shot in two, and another had a bullet in his ammunition pouch.'[6]

Sergeant Harris had mixed emotions: 'Our fire was terrible: the artillery, maxims and rifles making a terrible hell of it for the Dervishes. It was a wonderful sight and never to be forgotten.'[7]

Half an hour later the British followed up. 'We then marched across the plain and our orders were, "If any man sees a Dervish who is wounded making grimaces he will at once bayonet him".'[8] There was just one near

[4] Ziegler writes of a messy and inglorious scuffle in front of the line, at an early point in the battle, which he asserts involved a Dervish and 'one of the Sirdar's ADCs, Lt Smith of the Grenadiers.' Not so. The Grenadier Wilfrid Abel Smith was in charge of battalion transport and quietly looking after the mules in rear. It was Smyth of the Queen's Bays who got the better of the Dervish. He was awarded the Victoria Cross
[5] An enormous range, though apparently effective against the dense mass of Dervishes
[6] Hatton
[7] Harris
[8] Higgins (AH)

A dreadful massacre: a few of the thousands of bodies on the battlefield. No measures were taken to help the wounded.

disaster when the 21st Lancers, moving forward on reconnaissance, were lured into a charge on a large force of the enemy, suddenly encountered. They were fortunate to cut their way out with twenty-one dead and sixty-five wounded. But by 11.30 the battle was over and at 4 pm the Grenadier battalion led the division in triumph into Omdurman, having sustained four men wounded altogether.

'Officers from all regiments had been sent out to count the dead on the battlefield. G Legh was in command. Strong escorts were taken, and the ground divided into sections. The number – twice counted – was declared to be 10,800, of which 5,000 were of the Dervish *first* attack.'[9]

The cost was higher than the fighting implied, as some twenty-nine men died of enteric fever, contracted in Egypt. Fortunately no further lives were lost, for on starting home by river boat a week later a severe storm arose and three boats, containing all kinds of equipment and stores, and all the regimental loot, foundered. On 6 October they tied up at Southampton.

Colonel Hatton, who incidentally was the last commanding officer to have held double rank, was awarded the CB, five officers the DSO and five NCOs the DCM. There was one final accolade back in Wellington Barracks: 'The rifles were very carefully inspected by Government Viewers soon after arrival, and only one barrel showed any signs of want of care. The viewers said that they had seen many rifles from abroad, but that they could declare that the rifles of this Battalion were in a much better state than those of many Battalions who had never left England. Every single action was filled with a fine powdery sand, but no springs were broken, and there was no action which did not work freely.'[10]

[9] Hatton
[10] Hatton

The homecoming: Grenadiers, some with spears strapped to their rifles, return to barracks through admiring crowds.

The Boer War 1899-1902

A Very Different Kind of Enemy

Only a year after the simple and bloody surgical operation of Omdurman was to follow a war of an entirely different kind, which was to send shock waves through the nation and the army. The war in South Africa arose from a collision between British imperial ambitions and the independent spirit of the Boers (Dutch farmers). It turned out to be far more nasty and protracted than either side had anticipated.

The Boers had been the first settlers in the Cape, but the British began to occupy it in strength in 1820, and in 1843 also annexed Natal as a colony. From 1834 the Boers, unwilling to submit, took off across the Orange River in the 'Great Trek' and founded the Orange Free State, later crossing the Vaal River also and establishing the Transvaal. These two Boer republics might have been ignored had not diamonds been discovered at Kimberley and gold in the Witwatersrand, close to Johannesburg. Britain's deep interests in the mines fed tensions and the two sides lived together in an uneasy peace, punctuated by periodic armed clashes.[11]

Queen's South Africa and King's South Africa medals: the Boer War spanned the last years of Victoria and the first of Edward VII.

War broke out in October 1899 when the Boers, led by President Kruger of the Transvaal, made incursions into the British colonies, laying siege to Mafeking, Kimberley and, in November, to Ladysmith. The Boers were to prove a proud and formidable enemy, fierce in their religion, determined, knowing their way around the veldt (grassy, bushy, thinly-forested country), and highly skilled as marksmen and horsemen. This was more than enough, at least in the early stages, to compensate for their scruffiness and ill-discipline. Organized in 'commandos',[12] they were a very different enemy to the Dervishes who had been so easily despatched only a year before.

The British responded with an expeditionary force under General Sir Redvers Buller, who earlier had won a Victoria Cross in Zululand. He led a relieving force into Natal while his subordinate, Lord Methuen, prepared to recover Kimberley and Mafeking from Cape Colony.

The **3rd Battalion** (Lt Col Eyre Crabbe) was to spend the entire war in South Africa. The adventure started in a strange fashion. The battalion had arrived in Gibraltar on 27 September 1899 to take over from the 2nd Battalion, which embarked immediately in the same ship. During the night a message was received ordering the 'battalion' to stand fast pending orders for South Africa. For some hours it was unclear which was meant, but at last it was stated to be the 3rd Battalion and the 2nd duly returned to England.

On 15 November the battalion disembarked at Cape Town and moved at once by rail to the Orange River station to join the 2nd Coldstream and 1st Scots Guards in the 1st, or Guards, Brigade in Methuen's command. There was little time to get fit but route marching quickly followed, part of the programme being a night march in extended order across broken country. The result was far from satisfactory but gave warning of difficulties ahead, particularly of the effect upon compasses of the iron-stone boulders that littered the veldt.

Methuen was in no doubt that the new enemy would be very different to that previously encountered in imperial wars and, before the very first encounter with the Boers, ordered brass and buttons to be obscured and distinguishing equipment to be removed. This was not universally popular. 'I believe they will be making us dye our whiskers khaki colour next,' grumbled a sergeant. Officers were told to remove their swords and Sam Browne belts and march equipped like the men. Most carried rifles, though some were content with walking sticks. Methuen himself set the tone, declaring that he looked 'like a second-class conductor in a khaki coat with no mark of rank on it and a Boer hat and in Norwegian slippers'. Water was too precious to waste on washing and shaving. A Guards colonel wrote: 'We are all dirty and hairy and look great ruffians.'[13] But Methuen was full of confidence

---

[11] One of these was the infamous 'Jameson Raid' of December 1895, a reckless and disastrous attempt to overthrow the Transvaal government. A principal lieutenant of Dr Jameson was Harry White, a wild adventurer who earlier had been a Grenadier officer. After some months imprisonment for his pains, he bounced back to win a DSO with the Rhodesian Volunteer Force and become Mayor of Bulawayo. His medals are held by the Regiment

[12] A form later adopted by the Royal Marines

[13] Baring Pemberton

A rock or a hard place: a group of Grenadiers in confident pose. The officer on the right still has his sword but no doubt got rid of it when the fun started.

Aboard the troopship: it is not known whether this group is going to South Africa or returning. The smart white plumes show up well on the two seated figures.

Two queues: crossing the Vilje river (right) and lining up for rations (above).

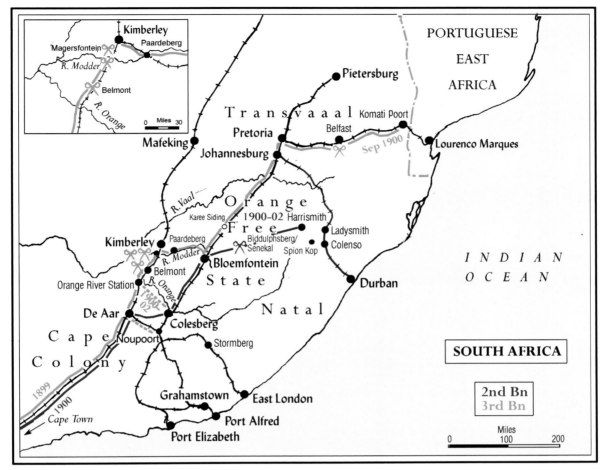

in his two brigades of guardsmen and infantry of the Line, especially as the Boers were reported to have an aversion to cold steel. He was, however, very weak in cavalry and nervous of breaking away from the line of the railway to make encircling movements.

Belmont – Success at a Price

The general's purpose was a quick relief of the besieged Kimberley and accordingly his force set off along the railway. The first resistance was encountered at **Belmont**. Though successful, it was the most costly battle of the war for the 3rd Grenadiers. The only map available was on a scale of 1 inch to 1 mile. It was supplemented by an inaccurate and misleading sketch prepared by divisional intelligence on the basis of a long-range view (close reconnaissance, in the face of the deadly Mauser, was too dangerous). The Guards Brigade was ordered to take the hills on which the Boers were established, the Scots and Grenadiers first attacking Gun Hill in the early morning, followed by a Coldstream assault on Middle Hill (or Grenadier Hill as it came to be known). There seemed every reason to suppose that this would be another Tel el Kebir. Despite having to hack down the railway fence with axes (nobody had thought to supply wire-cutters), the approach and advance went smoothly and by 3.50 am it seemed that the Boers had left their positions. Not so; the ridge ahead suddenly burst into flame, like a hundred gas lamps instantly lit, as the attackers came under modern rifle fire for the first time.

The brigade found itself at the base of a long and steep line of kopjes (low hills) lined from end to end by the enemy. Gun Hill was speedily taken by the Scots and half a company of Grenadiers, but the objective was very much smaller than the sketch had indicated and seriously enfiladed from Middle or Grenadier Hill. This, a steep kopje of iron-stone boulders, had to be cleared at all speed. In only fifteen minutes the Grenadiers did so, though the cost was heavy, thirty-six being killed outright or dying later and 114 being wounded. The Scots Guards had been more fortunate as they had been nearer to their adversaries, and many bullets sped harmlessly overhead.

CAPTAIN

FRANK COOKE

MBE DCM *1875-1948*

Gallant NCO and Sergeant Major who fought at Biddulphsberg and was back in uniform at sixty-six

rank Alexander Cooke, who liked to be known as 'Alec', transferred into the Grenadiers from the Gloucestershire Regiment in 1892. He joined the 2nd Battalion and rose within it to the rank of sergeant. A keen sportsman and gymnast, and an excellent shot who often represented the Army at Bisley, he was also a PT and signals instructor.

In March 1900 he went to South Africa with the battalion and was severely wounded two months later in the action at Biddulphsberg. He returned to England but in April 1902 went out again to see the end of the war, returning six months later.

In 1905 he was promoted colour sergeant and posted to the permanent staff of the 4th Volunteer Bn, East Surrey Regiment, later to become the 23rd County of London Battalion, the London Regiment (Territorial Force). Here he rose to be acting Sergeant Major in 1910.

In March 1915 he was sent to France as a Grenadier and in May was awarded the DCM 'for conspicuous gallantry and ability at Givenchy, in organizing the despatch of ammunition supplies to a captured German trench and continuing his work after being stunned by the explosion of a shell. He showed the greatest bravery and coolness under very dangerous conditions'.

Having completed more than twenty-three years service he left the Regiment in November 1915 and was awarded a pension of 3s 5d and 6d for the DCM – a total of 3s 11d per day for life. He went to the Office of Works, where he was responsible for security of government buildings ranging from No 10 Downing Street to Stonehenge, and was made MBE for organizing the public stands for the coronation of King George VI in 1937. In 1940, at sixty-six, he was back in uniform as a captain in the Home Guard.

LIEUTENANT COLONEL

WILLIAM GARTON

1860-1929

Quartermaster of distinction who had enlisted at twelve and was Sergeant Major at thirty

illiam Garton was born in Dublin, the son of Sgt George Garton, a veteran of the Crimea who was stationed there with the 3rd Battalion. It was hardly surprising that young George enlisted as a boy. He was only twelve, which seems an extraordinary age, but his brother had been only ten when he joined and in those days boys under sixteen could be taken into the Army as short as 5ft 1in if they were 'well made' and 'long in the fork', and were usually employed as drummers.

Garton developed fast, becoming a corporal at nineteen and a colour sergeant at twenty-two. In 1885 he went out to the Suakin campaign as Drill Sergeant and was mentioned in despatches, a singular honour at a time when awards such as DCM or MM had not yet been instituted. He was appointed Sergeant Major of the 3rd Battalion in 1890, at the age of thirty, and in 1897 was commissioned Quartermaster of the 2nd Battalion, with whom he served with distinction in South Africa and was again mentioned in despatches.

In 1910 Captain Garton retired and joined the staff of the Sergeant-at-Arms in the House of Commons. In 1913 he was appointed Hon Secretary of the recently formed Grenadier Guards Comrades Association, but when war was declared in 1914 he was not to be left out. He joined the 1st Life Guards and served with them at the First Battle of Ypres before returning home as Quartermaster of the Blues Reserve Regiment. He eventually retired in 1917, having been the first Quartermaster of the Household Brigade to be promoted lieutenant colonel. He lost both his sons in the war, fighting with other regiments, and thereafter gave himself unsparingly to his Comrades Association.

See Webb-Carter (2)

Boers surprised on a kopje at Belmont: a visit by Grenadiers.

An expensive assault: Grenadier Hill, Belmont.

The Grenadiers, however, who were a little off line because of compass inaccuracy, were some 350 yards away when fire was opened and a much easier target. Most of the casualties were incurred in doubling forward into the protection of dead ground. But they pressed on.

'We pushed up by degrees, firing steadily as our heaving chests and modicum of wind would allow after crawling and clambering from stone to stone – companies in a grand tangle – till at last we stood on the top and saw the Boers bolting.'[14]

On arrival they gave three cheers for the Queen. The brigade on the left also made progress after a stiff fight, the Coldstream moved up on the right and the Boers called it a day, mounting their ponies and trotting off the battlefield. They were in fact in no great hurry. As Methuen had no horse artillery and his cavalry were exhausted, he

had nothing with which to pursue them. It was still only 7.30 in the morning. The feared marksmanship of the Boers had been overcome by a fine display of British dash and the general's confidence seemed fully justified. But it was only the beginning of the story.

Pinned Down on the Modder River

A few days later the advance continued to the next Boer position on the Modder River. Here the enemy demonstrated with great clarity what he was capable of. The ground in front of the river was flat and green, quite unlike the rocky slopes of the kopjes, and offered by daylight an uninterrupted field of fire of over 2000 yards. The Boers were entrenched in a staggered arrangement well forward of a tree line, which was the only reference suitable for artillery. They were invisible and they used smokeless powder. They had painted white marks on rocks in front of them to indicate range.

Imagining the enemy to be nothing more than a rearguard, Methuen decided on a frontal approach. Again, his maps and sketches were badly at fault and the whole line of the river unclear. The battalions approached in line down a long gradual forward slope and at about 1200 yards came under a hail of fire from rifles and a pom-pom gun. The air became 'absolutely alive with bullets' and everyone fell flat on the ground except those serving the Scots Guards machine gun, all of whom in a few minutes were dead or wounded. The fire was devastatingly accurate. Merely to show a helmet or a hand drew fire.

The Grenadiers and the other guardsmen were there for eight hours, noses pressed to the ground, hungry and thirsty in the scorching heat and tormented by ants. Several, desperate for water, were shot as they tried to crawl back. Ammunition was brought up with the greatest

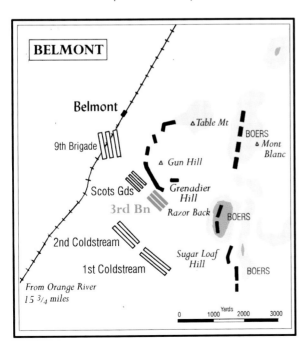

[14] Baring Pemberton

The air alive with bullets: at the Modder River the Grenadiers lay pinned down for eight hours, unable to respond to the devastating accuracy of the Boer shooting.

difficulty. The only soldiers who suffered more were the kilted Highlanders. Painful blisters rose behind their knees and when at last they got up, they were barely able to move.

Eventually progress was made on the left of the line, though by nightfall nobody knew whether the battle had been won or not. Fifty-six Grenadiers had been killed or wounded. Daylight, however, revealed that the Boers had at last abandoned their position. It was a victory, but at heavy cost. It had introduced the British soldier to the terrors of an invisible enemy who, using smokeless powder, rained lead upon him with uncanny accuracy and upon whom he could not retaliate.

'Black Week' and the Campaign of Roberts

A little north of the Modder river was the hill of **Magersfontein**, and here on 11 December the next battle was fought. It was disastrous, the Highland Brigade suffering severely and being altogether thrown back. The Guards were in reserve and the 3rd Grenadiers had little to do other than to cover the withdrawal back to the Modder 'in the coolest fashion imaginable, four lines of companies retiring in daylight through each other by half companies alternately with impressive deliberation'.[15] They suffered only one killed[16] and three wounded. The Commanding Officer of the Coldstream was hit in the ankle. 'Outer, low right,' he observed.

As if this was not enough, two other disastrous battles were fought in the same week, Colenso in Natal and Stormberg in Cape Colony. It was called 'Black Week' and

the nation was appalled both by the casualties and the humiliation visited upon them by these uncouth and undisciplined Boers, who in January inflicted yet another stunning defeat at Spion Kop in Natal. Stern action was necessary. Methuen was relieved. Field Marshal Lord Roberts of Kandahar VC, the greatest soldier of his time,

[15] Whitworth (2)
[16] This was LCpl William Cooksey of No 8 Company. His grave was mistakenly opened by a farmer in 1980 and a number of interesting items recovered

General salute: a Grenadier of the 3rd Battalion presents to Roberts as he enters Pretoria in triumph. The battalion was due to escort him home after his victorious campaign, but after all was needed for another two years of campaigning.

132

Line upon line: the advance on Diamond Hill, on the way to Belfast, seen from a high vantage point.

In a wide open space: the Guards camp at Bloemfontein.

was despatched with large reinforcements and Lord Kitchener as his chief of staff, to sort out the mess. And so, in quick time, he did.

Kimberley and Ladysmith were relieved in February 1900, and Mafeking in May. The main towns were taken in succession: in March Bloemfontein, in May Johannesburg, in June Pretoria. The Boer general, Cronje, surrendered at Paardeberg in February. He and 4000 men were placed in the charge of the 3rd Battalion, who escorted them back in a vast protected square, Cronje himself, rather strangely 'being received with a Guard of Honour furnished by the Coldstream Guards'.[17] Thanks to the efficiency of supply under Quartermaster May, all the prisoners were fed in a period of three-quarters of an hour and then housed in the luxury of tents in the pouring rain while their escort was lying in the open.

The battalion then made a forced march east to join Roberts's main force, covering forty-one miles in twenty hours in great heat, and were the first infantry to enter Bloemfontein. A little distance north of the town, at Karee Siding, Lt Col Crabbe, with three other officers and an orderly, made an unwise and impetuous attack on a small party of Boers. The enemy were stronger and better posted than expected and the whole party was wounded and captured, one officer being killed. The Boers, however, treated them well after removing their arms and saddlery.

Thereafter there was little more serious work to do than to join the victorious procession to Johannesburg and Pretoria, with one or two small engagements on the

[17] Russell

133

GRENADIER GUARDS.
Ordeal of Fire at Biddulph'sberg.

The 2nd Battalion at Biddulphsberg: controlling companies in the long grass of the veldt proved very difficult. *After Richard Eaton Woodville*

Hot tin roof: thousands of these blockhouses were built, mostly along the railway lines, and manned by small parties such as this.

A courageous rescue: those who carried wounded out of the inferno of Biddulphsberg were refused awards as they had had to lay down their weapons in the process. *J R Beadle*

The wagon bridge at Colesberg: two companies of the 3rd Battalion guarded this bridge to prevent movement by De Wet.

way. In August they set off east with the division, securing the railway all the way to the border of Portuguese East Africa at Komati Poort, which was occupied unopposed on 24 September. On the way there was a sharp engagement at **Belfast**, which cost a single casualty.

The same month they left by rail to return to Pretoria. The engines were not always equal to the task and at one point the train had to be shoved up the inclines. By early November they were back at Bloemfontein. The war seemed to be over and the victorious Roberts was preparing to return home escorted by the Grenadier battalion. It was not to be. They were to stay in South Africa for almost two more years.

The Agony of Biddulphsberg

In March 1900 came the turn of the **2nd Battalion** (Lt Col Francis Lloyd) to join the campaign. They sailed from England in March and, moving up from Cape Town, found themselves on 23 April close to Bloemfontein, where by chance the 3rd Battalion were out on an excursion before the victorious move north. On that day the two battalions came within eight miles of each other. For the rest of the war they were never to be anything like so close again.

On 29 May the 2nd Grenadiers were on the move east of Bloemfontein when ordered to take a Boer gun which was holding up the advance at Biddulphsberg, near Senekal. It was to be the most harrowing experience of the campaign. The battalion was in the usual formation of column of companies, the eight companies (each over a hundred strong) deployed in all over an enormous frontage of over a thousand yards. While such dispersion clearly had advantages against the highly accurate long-range shooting of the Boers, the difficulties of control were soon to become apparent. When committed to the open the order was given to turn half-right to gain the shelter of what was thought to be a lightly occupied kopje, from which the assault on the gun position could then be made.

Lt Col Lloyd rode forward to guide the change, but the Boers in unexpected strength suddenly opened a heavy fire from concealed rifle pits on the kopje and he fell wounded from his horse. Down on the ground, in the long grass of the veldt, visibility was nil and the noise terrific, and a bush fire soon broke out. The companies who had received the order to change direction attempted to carry the kopje in short rushes by alternate half-companies, and continued thus for some 300 yards until casualties among the officers caused loss of control. The smoke and fire added to the confusion. The leading company appeared to have been almost wiped out and the momentum lost was never regained.

Worse still, the constantly changing wind fanned the flames this way and that and then began to surge towards the place where most of the wounded were lying. After two and a half hours in this growing inferno of bullets and flame it was clear that no further progress was possible but that the smoke might be used to cover a withdrawal. The order was passed, but over the hugely extended line many did not receive it. Several, indeed, had fallen asleep in the great heat and awoke to find themselves prisoners. One was these was Private Harry Malle:

'Our fire was directed near the guns. We could not see a soul. I emptied my pouches. I got a smack in the head. I turned on my back and lay still. About an hour afterwards another went in the left side of my head and out at the neck. Just after, two more crashed through, one in my shoulder and out at my back and the other two through both thighs. I had my wits for the whole of the time. I took off my equipment and rolled coat. Put them at my head for shelter. That saved my life. The coat got riddled and the mess tin shattered. I lay altogether 5 hours under a tremendous fire. I heard the order 'retire' and saw what few was left slowly fall back in good order. As soon as they were gone, I heard a crackling and a roaring. "My God," I said, "We have now got to be burned to death." The veldt had got afire. I was soon on the long line of wounded and dying. An awful sight. I rose to my feet and dragged myself through it somehow. Just got through and dropped down. My face was much burned.

The Boers came out of their trenches and helped us. They acted like Christians. One got me water, unrolled my coat and a dead man's next to me and wrapped me up with both. The Boer to the wounded is a true-hearted being, though he smashed a lot of us with explosive and soft-nosed bullets. Altogether I have got 10 wounds and severely burned. I am in hospital at Senekal. The church is made into a hospital.'[18]

Lt Quilter and a few men from No 1 Company were determined to rescue who they could and, putting down their weapons, plunged into the smoke and flames, returning with a number of wounded. For this

---

[18] Malle

135

LIEUTENANT GENERAL
Sir FRANCIS LLOYD
GCVO KCB DSO *1853-1926*

Wartime Major
General at Horse
Guards with much
distinguished service
in Africa

*F*rancis Lloyd first joined the 33rd (later the Duke of Wellington's Regiment) but after a few months transferred to the Grenadiers in 1874.

In 1885, having obtained his captaincy, he served as signalling officer to the Guards Brigade in the Suakin expedition, being mentioned in despatches after the Battle of Hasheen. In 1898 he was again in Egypt as second-in-command of the 1st Battalion. Moving with them to the Sudan, he was awarded the DSO after Omdurman. Shortly afterwards he was for a third time in action in Africa, commanding the 2nd Battalion against the Boers. At the Battle of Biddulphsberg, struggling to control his battalion in the difficult conditions, he was seriously wounded. His men suffered heavily from the flames of the burning veldt.

From 1904 to 1908 he commanded the 1st Guards Brigade and the following year became GOC of the new Welsh Division of the Territorial Army. This was followed by command of the London District. Here he remained after war had broken out in 1914. Although by then over sixty, he might have expected a major field command in the rapidly expanding army, but he cheerfully accepted a lesser role in London.

It was, however, no sinecure, and in February 1915 he had a sharp exchange with Lord Kitchener, Secretary of State for War: *Kitchener (very abruptly)*, 'You have got to raise a regiment of Welsh Guards.' *Lloyd*, 'Sir, there are a great many difficulties in the way which I would like to point out first.' *Kitchener (very rudely)*, 'If you do not like to do it someone else will.' *Lloyd*, 'Sir, when do you want them?' *Kitchener*, 'Immediately.' *Lloyd*, 'Very well, sir; they shall go on Guard on St David's Day.' Three weeks later, largely composed of former Grenadiers, they did.

courageous action they were recommended for awards, but were refused on the strictly correct, though ungenerous, grounds that they had laid down their arms in the process. The total losses in this agonizing battle were 148, of whom almost fifty were killed or burned to death.

The battalion then moved on by stages to the area of Harrismith, near the border of Natal Colony, from where they continued operations.

Kitchener's War on the Veldt

Roberts, having evidently concluded the business, returned home victorious, leaving Kitchener behind to do such clearing up as might be necessary. There turned out to be a great deal as many of the Boers were not prepared to submit. They preferred to fight a guerrilla war, living off the land with no base camps, defensive positions or lines of communication and set about making raids on the railways and into the Cape Colony and Natal. Kitchener's reply to this was a ruthless one. He would round up the livestock and destroy the farms which gave assistance to the commandos. He would dominate the railway lines by means of strong points, block houses, barbed wire and armoured trains and hunt down the guerrillas with mobile columns, launching great drives to pin the enemy commandos against the fortified lines and force their surrender. The trains themselves were treated like ships. They carried guns and searchlights; Kitchener's staff travelled in one called His Majesty's Train *Cobra*, commanded by an 'admiral'.[19]

Worse still, as the months rolled on and progress proved to be painfully slow, he decided to remove the women and children from their homes and concentrate them into camps along the railway lines. It was thus the British who first used 'concentration' camps. There was no intention to mistreat their occupants, much less to exterminate them as the Nazis were later to do, but, equally, very little attention was paid to their welfare. Medical arrangements were grossly inadequate. The result was a dreadful death toll, which certainly in the end broke the spirit of the commandos, but also provoked outrage at home and in the wider world. It was a shameful and inglorious affair.

[19] Pakenham

The Work of the Battalions

The Grenadier battalions in the field saw little or nothing of the camps, though their job was to conduct sweeps and punitive expeditions and round up the unfortunate civilians. Mobile operations were conducted in columns. There were some eighty of them altogether, mixed forces of infantry, cavalry, mounted infantry of every quality and some artillery. The Household Cavalry had returned home in November 1900 and so 'the Foot Guards stepped somewhat smugly into the breach and formed two Guards mounted infantry companies'.[20]

The work of guarding the static lines took great numbers of men and inevitably occupied most of the guardsmen for much of the time. Thus, Grenadiers went hither and thither, by companies and half-companies, under now this command and now that, guarding parties building blockhouses and then manning them, and undertaking every kind of protective and escort work.

By May 1902 there were over 8000 of these concrete and tin blockhouses (costing £16 each to build) covering 3700 miles and guarded by over 65,000 white and native troops. They were connected by barbed wire and within rifle range of each other. The blockhouse duties were horribly tedious, though:

'Boredom was the enemy Tommy knew best ... They planted petunias in bully-beef tins; they chalked up the usual facetious names ... and they wrote letters home, tens of thousands of them, stiff-upper-lip letters for the most part, to be collected by the weekly mail wagon. There was little to gossip about on the telephone that connected every blockhouse to its neighbours. But there were pets to look after: dogs, goats, pigs, even lizards. There were the convoy's visits. And just occasionally, a whirlwind in the night, a summer storm rattling the tin-cans on the trip-wires so that they rang like a xylophone, and, setting off a fusillade of shots into the darkness, there was a visit from a party of guerrillas.'[21]

The **2nd Battalion** remained in the general area of Harrismith, whence they conducted operations of this kind, ranging as far as Senekal to the west and Ladysmith to the east, being sniped at and harassed from time to time. Losses were slight, though wear and tear was considerable and there were incidents recognizable to soldiers in any age:

'July 28th – Marched at 9 am towards Fouriesburg, the Battalion having been sent for by General Rundle on the 25th; but unfortunately the native runner got drunk and was therefore three days late... November 26th – Marched at 7 am. Reached Brindisi at 10 am. The men in rags. None of the expected clothing had arrived ...

December 14th – No 1 ... saw either a baboon or a Boer watching them – were uncertain which!'[22]

They ended up manning blockhouses covering some eighty miles of railway, and it was at one of these that the Boer General De Wet gave himself up in April 1902, just before the war was finally concluded. It was not until September that they embarked at Durban for home, where they arrived on 8 October.

The **3rd Battalion** had a rather more varied time in the south. In October 1900 they took up a defensive line along the Orange River to prevent incursions into the Cape Colony, and from March 1901 manned blockhouses along the railway further south. In December 1900 two companies joined a column under Col Herbert, and over five months covered 1500 miles in pursuit of Boer raiding parties. In the same month Lt Col Crabbe took out a similar column which was out for three months on a similar mission. Predictably, over a vast country, the Boers proved hard to catch. And, because some used dum-dum bullets, engagements could be vicious. Private Higgins recorded:

'Most of our fellows who have been wounded have been struck by poisoned bullets. Started our march back to Bloemfontein. Every farmhouse we passed (if the owners were not loyal) was burned to the ground and all the cattle looted. Ten Boers were seen trying to escape from a farmhouse and two were shot, the others got away. Still looting and burning farms on our way back.'[23]

The battalion eventually returned home at the same time as the 2nd Grenadiers, though sailing from Cape Town.

The Scale and Cost of the War

Some 450,000 imperial, colonial and native soldiers served in this war, against a Boer population of some 90,000, of whom 7000 died, as well as perhaps 20,000 in the concentration camps. Over 400,000 horses, mules and donkeys were 'expended'. Disease and wounds claimed 22,000 British troops. Enteric fever alone cost the 3rd Battalion sixty-seven out of eighty-seven dead from all causes. It seemed to have been preventable, however. Before going abroad, 'officers, drummers and as many men as could be induced to have the operation were inoculated'[24] and, though some of those so treated did contract enteric, none died as a result.

---

[20] Paget
[21] Pakenham
[22] Lloyd
[23] Higgins (Harold)
[24] Russell

THE QUARTERMASTER

he origins of the Quartermaster are to be found as far back as the sixteenth century. The early term 'harbinger' came from the Dutch 'herberg' and was itself a corruption of the French 'auberge', a lodging place where bed and board could be obtained for payment. Long before proper barracks were established, it was thus his responsibility to arrange the quarters for the men.

The hapless Quartermaster seems to have been treated as a kind of escape-pipe for all work too arduous or distasteful to others and in about 1680 the duty of 'provost martial' was thrust upon him, thereby in effect making him Adjutant also. In the early days the appointment, though well regarded, was not a commissioned one.

They had other tribulations. Mr Payne, acting Quartermaster of the 1st Battalion, was subjected to a

Three famous quartermasters between the wars (from left): Majors Randolph Beard MBE DCM MM MSM, Johnnie Walker MBE RVM and Joseph Paterson.

regimental enquiry in 1813 when the Colours of the 3rd Battalion, being taken out to Spain in his charge, were lost. They had been packed in a box along with some of his own possessions (2 pair of drawers, 2 cotton night caps etc) and the box had disappeared. There is no record of any very dreadful punishment having being awarded him.

It was in Napoleonic times that the appointment seemed to take something like the form familiar in later years. Robert Colquhoun, who enlisted in 1787, rose through the ranks to be Sergeant Major for five years and then Quartermaster for over twenty-three. In Victorian days it became regular procedure for sergeant majors to be promoted into the post, and its standing grew correspondingly. He had to supply all the material needs of his battalion, food, clothing, ammunition and fuel, and in operations a high degree of improvisation was often needed.

If the Sergeant Major is the father of his battalion, the Quartermaster is the grandfather. A member of both the officers' and sergeants' messes, his influence spreads over every part of the battalion and his advice

At the Tower of London in 1931: Harry Wood (left) hands over his duties as Quartermaster of the 2nd Battalion to 'Tubby' Aston. Wood had made a name sniping in the trenches and won a DCM. In 1940 a crane was used to hoist Aston on board a ship at Dunkirk. The captain told him that if left in the water he would constitute a danger to shipping.

Notable quartermasters since 1945: (from left) Majors George Hackett MBE, Lou Drouet MBE, Bill Nash MVO MBE and Fred Clutton MBE MM RVM.

is often called upon by both Commanding Officer and Sergeant Major.

The quartermaster commission has always been highly prized, the letters (QM) after the rank commanding high respect. The Ministry of Defence, however, decided to name this type of commission 'LE' for 'Late Entry', a singularly unfortunate term for those (especially, it must be said, Grenadiers) who have spent some twenty years of devoted service never being less than five minutes early for anything. The term 'Commissioned Warrant Officer' is a more elegant substitute.

Over the last few decades rank has been pitched at a more appropriate level. Where quartermasters were commissioned as lieutenant and rarely rose above captain, it is now possible to become a lieutenant colonel. Indeed, in 2004 there were no fewer than four Grenadiers serving in this high rank, an extraordinary achievement for a single-battalion regiment.

It was from about the 1970s that the Army began to take a more robust view of the value of commissioning more warrant officers, who had acquired vast experience and

Cocked hat: Captain Peter Dunkerley in distinctive quartermasters' headgear.

who otherwise, at the age of only forty or so, could expect their talents to be lost both to their regiment and to the armed forces as a whole. These have taken on new responsibilities, as technical quartermasters, transport officers, training officers, families and welfare officers, and sometimes the command of Headquarter Company. In ceremonial dress most of them are entitled to a distinctive cocked hat.

The Household Division Quartermasters, Directors of Music and Riding Masters Association, composed entirely of commissioned warrant officers, forms a highly distinguished body which dines together annually.

Principal source: Lewis

A quartet of lieutenant colonels: four quartermasters at the same time in the highest possible rank. Seen at Sandhurst in February 2005 are (from left): Andrew Phasey BEM, Steve Tuck BEM, Rick Kitchen MBE and Paul Harris MBE.

139

Chapter Eight

THE GREAT WAR – TO END ALL WARS 1914-1918

Seen from our viewpoint in the early 21st Century the war that broke out in August 1914 remains almost impossible to comprehend in its scale, its futility and its cost. Over four full years millions of men slugged it out along a line of trenches that stretched hundreds of miles along the Western Front. For the infantry soldiers it was generally a life (all too often a short one) of hardship, misery and danger; of toiling up to the front line, there to endure constant bombardment before toiling back into rest or reserve; of vicious trench raids and hair-raising patrols; of titanic offensives, often lasting for weeks, in which battalions were reduced to skeletons in the course of making derisory gains in worthless acres of swamp and filth.

1914-15 Star, British War Medal 1914-20, Victory Medal: known as Pip, Squeak and Wilfred after popular cartoon characters. The first was issued in two versions, for 1914 alone and for 1914-15, and all 2,500,000 recipients were regulars or volunteers. The other two were given to everyone who served in the war.

It was the 'Great War'. Nothing like it had ever been imagined, much less experienced. By the time the exhausted combatants had left the ring, it was described as the 'War to End All Wars' since a repeat seemed inconceivable. But only twenty-one years later there was another, though of rather a different nature, and the dreadful years of 1914 to 1918 were given the dismal description of 'The *First* World War'.

When the great conflict began Britain had not been at war in Europe for the whole century since Waterloo and even then only a tiny proportion of her manhood had taken part. The new war made unprecedented demands on the nation, drawing in almost every man of military age and consuming enormous resources. And those years are still not so far away. A very few veterans are still alive; the fathers of many of us now living were there and the grandfathers of a great number. The losses are still almost impossible to take in. Three-quarters of a million British were killed. It is as if all the young men of our present population, aged from eighteen to twenty-five, were to be taken out on to Salisbury Plain and cut down by artillery and machine guns. A third would be killed and the rest wounded, many with painful and crippling injuries that would endure for the rest of their lives. The loss is all too visible today on memorials in every town and village.

How can it have been allowed? And once it had started, and the casualty lists lengthened relentlessly, how can it have been accepted, and for so long? It emerged from a spirit of rampant nationalism, in which the continental empires of Germany, Austria-Hungary, Russia and Turkey, and the republic of France, rattled their sabres at each other and the British (on the whole) strove to maintain the balance. Germany, in particular, under Kaiser Wilhelm II, a grandson of Queen Victoria, was in a boisterous mood. Born as a single nation only in 1870, by invading and defeating France in only six weeks, she formed an enormous military machine, which she was perfectly prepared to use again for the same purpose, and would relish the opportunity. Her soldiers toasted '*der tag*', the day when new glory would visit their arms. France, determined not to be humiliated again, also raised huge armies.

But none of the great powers had any conception of the nature of the tiger whose tail they were twisting so blithely. Had they done so, they might perhaps have held back. For no longer was war in Europe to be won by

GENERAL
GEORGE, Lord JEFFREYS
KCB KCVO CMG *1878-1960*

Fierce and
redoubtable
Commanding Officer
and General, Colonel
of the Regiment

George Jeffreys, descended from the brother of the notorious 17th century judge, was known as 'Ma', after a lady of that name who kept a naughty house in Kensington in the 1890s. Perhaps she was more disciplinary than motherly, for certainly he was, and sometimes 'Ma' was taken for 'Martinet'.

Jeffreys joined the Regiment in 1898 and served at Omdurman and in South Africa. In 1914 he was commanding the Guards Depot when sent to be second-in-command of the 2nd Battalion, which he led for much of the retreat from Mons, the Marne and the Aisne. He took over command in 1915 and remained on the Western Front for the rest of the war, except for a period in 1916 when recovering from severe wounds. By 1918 he was a major-general, commanding the 19th Division.

He was GOC London District at the time of the General Strike and later GOC-in-C Southern Command in India. On retirement he became MP for Petersfield. In 1952 he was created a baron and appointed Colonel of the Regiment, the first outside the royal family since the Duke of Wellington. The distinction was richly deserved, for he had been a superlative regimental officer whose dauntless spirit had been frequently proved in the most desperate dangers and difficulties.

A fierce and austere man, with a dry sense of humour and an eagle eye for detail, he might in some respects have been happier remaining in the nineteenth century. He objected to the young regiments of Irish and Welsh Guards being ranked with the original trinity of Grenadiers, Coldstream and Scots, and even in the 1950s would demonstrate the merits of Victorian drill and warn officers not to drink gin, 'a housemaid's drink', as possibly he had discovered from 'Ma' herself.

See Craster

LANCE CORPORAL
WILFRED FULLER VC
1893-1947

Victoria Cross of
the 1st Battalion
bombing party at
Neuve Chapelle,
March 1915

Wilfred Dolby Fuller was born in East Kirkby, Nottinghamshire, in July 1893 and worked at Mansfield colliery before enlisting as a Grenadier in December 1914.

He won his Victoria Cross as a lance corporal in the 1st Battalion, where he was one of the bombing party specially assembled under Captain WE Nicol, who himself won a DSO at Neuve Chapelle. At that time each brigade formed a company of 150 bomb-throwers, specially trained in the difficult and dangerous art of handling these new weapons. At the time they were at an experimental stage and there were many varieties. They were called 'bombs' and thrown by 'bombers'. Later in 1915 an attempt was made by the army in general to adopt the name of 'grenadier' to that purpose, but after a frosty dispute the King decreed that the title of 'Grenadier' should be confined to his First Regiment of Foot Guards.

Fuller's citation reads, 'For most conspicuous bravery at Neuve Chapelle on the 12th March 1915. Seeing a party of the enemy attempting to escape along a communication trench, he ran towards them and killed the leading man with a bomb; the remainder (nearly fifty), finding no means of evading his bombs, surrendered to him. Lance Corporal Fuller was quite alone at the time'.

He received his Victoria Cross from King George V at Buckingham Palace on 4 June 1915 and in September was also decorated by the King at Sheffield with the Russian Order of St George.

He was discharged in October 1916 as medically unfit and joined the Somerset police, but ill health forced him to resign. He died at Frome in Somerset on 22 November 1947 and lies buried in the churchyard of Christchurch there.

His Victoria Cross is held in the Guards Museum.

PRIVATE

EDWARD BARBER VC
1893-1915

Victoria Cross of the 1st Battalion bombing at Neuve Chapelle, but killed three days later

*E*dward Barber was born in Tring, Hertfordshire, in June 1893 and enlisted in the Regiment in October 1911.

With Lance Corporal Fuller, he was a member of the bombing party of the 1st Battalion and won his Victoria Cross in very similar circumstances. The battle was very difficult and entangled. It was easy to get lost in the labyrinth of trenches, both friendly and enemy, and hard to distinguish objectives in the smoke and confusion. But the whole line watched with admiration as the Germans were pursued by Captain Nicol and his bombers.

Barber's citation reads, 'For most conspicuous bravery on the 12th March 1915 at Neuve Chapelle. He ran speedily in front of the Grenade Company to which he belonged and threw bombs on the enemy with such effect that a very great number of them at once surrendered. When the grenade party reached Private Barber they found him quite alone and unsupported, with the enemy surrendering all about him'.

He had in fact advanced by himself down one of the enemy communication trenches with a bag of bombs. When a sniper's bullet struck them he threw them away and they exploded. Gathering up a fresh supply from a dead man, he rushed along, throwing them with deadly effect. He continued his advance until shot by a sniper and was responsible for taking over a hundred prisoners.

Only three days later he was killed in action. His name is on the memorial in the cemetery at Le Touret in France.

His mother received his Victoria Cross from King George V at Buckingham Palace on 16 November 1916. The decoration, together with his other medals, is in the regimental collection.

LANCE SERGEANTS

PERCY WARWICK AM
1885 – date of death not known

WILLIAM MEREDITH AM
dates not known

William Meredith

Winners of the Albert Medal for bravery while instructing in grenade throwing

*T*he Albert Medal, said to have been designed by Prince Albert, was established by Queen Victoria in 1866. It was initially intended to recognize gallantry in saving life at sea, but in 1877 the scope was broadened to the 'many heroic acts performed on land and sea by those who endanger their lives in saving or endeavouring to save the lives of others'. King George V subsequently approved the use of the letters AM after the names of the recipients. In 1971 the award was discontinued and surviving holders were invited to exchange them for the George Cross, which had been instituted by King George VI in 1940.

The award was twice given to Grenadiers who showed great courage and presence of mind while supervising grenade practice. In September 1915 Percy Warwick picked up a 'bomb' which had been dropped under the legs of several men by a nervous thrower and flung it out of the trench to safety.

In November 1916 William Meredith was instructing in the firing of rifle grenades when one failed to discharge properly and fell back into the projector on the rifle with the fuse ignited. Meredith threw himself in front of the man holding the rifle and attempted to remove the grenade, but it exploded, blowing off three fingers of his right hand and wounding him elsewhere. The guardsman was only slightly hurt.

What became of Warwick is not known, but Meredith was one of those invited to accept a George Cross in 1971. But he was not impressed. Thank you very much, he said, but his Albert Medal had been given by the King's own hand, and that was the one he would keep.

movement, manoeuvre and the spirited assault. The defensive power of machine guns, artillery and barbed wire was to command the battlefield, and it was not until a later war that aircraft and armour were to restore the balance. In the modern way of thinking, of course, someone must have been to blame and the odium has fallen, predictably enough, on the generals. But, until late in the war, none of the military leaders, on either side, were able to find a way out because the rules had altogether changed and not one of them had the least experience in it. Even Allenby, who took Palestine from the Turks in a fine campaign of manoeuvre, had been as stuck on the Western Front as anyone else. The British leaders, Field Marshals French and Haig, were cavalrymen and the day of their arm was well over. They launched offensives on a huge scale and, of course, the next one, bigger and better than the last, would always be the decider. It never was. Plain endurance was to govern the outcome and the British simply refused to give in. Even late in the war, when its horrors were all too evident, young men were disguising their age in order to join up, desperate not to be left out. The side that could stick it out would win, and so, eventually, it did.

The whole war was fought on a wider canvas, in Russia, Italy, Turkey and the Middle East, but Grenadiers were engaged only against the Germans in France and Flanders. The regimental history[1] records the four years in a thousand pages of a depressingly familiar litany: the great offensives, enormous, long-drawn-out, and hideous in their human toll; the long periods in and out of the trenches in different parts of the line; the variety of French and Belgian place-names, once pastoral and in many cases beautiful, but now just labels to yet more dreadful spots on that ravaged landscape.

It is a mark of those times that the history was written entirely for the officers. The arrival, departure and fate of every single one are recorded. The periodic lists for each battalion do not even mention the Sergeant Major, and soldiers are named only when performing some outstanding feat. The author even regretted that he could not write at greater length – in order to say more about individual officers. But that simply reflected the strict social order of that era. The soldiers expected to be led by a courageous officer class and they were.[2] They expected to do as they were told and they did. The horror of their circumstances was far beyond them, or anyone else, to understand. But there they were and there they would do their duty while hoping to survive. They were hardly

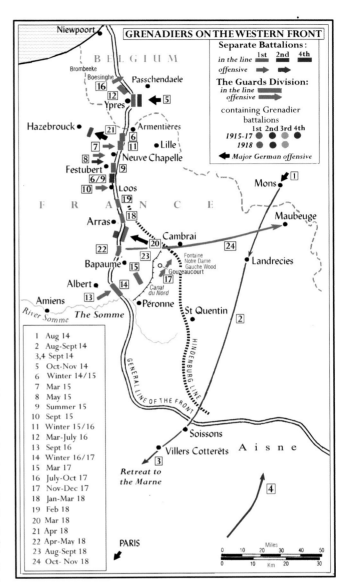

conscious of anything except their immediate surroundings and their comrades. As Rudyard Kipling put it, 'A man may join for King and Country, but he goes over the top for the honour of his own platoon, company and battalion'.[3]

The BEF, Mons, the Marne and the Aisne

The fuse for war was lit by a pistol shot in Sarajevo, in Bosnia-Herzegovina, by which the Austrian Archduke Franz Ferdinand was assassinated. The explosive train at once lit up and one declaration of war followed another

[1] Ponsonby (1)
[2] It is all the more remarkable that the Chief of the Imperial General Staff from December 1915 had once been a cavalry ranker. Sir William (Wully) Robertson remained thoroughly down to earth. 'It's no good pissing and farting at these 'ere Germans,' he said
[3] Kipling

The COURSE of the WAR
for the FOUR SERVICE BATTALIONS of GRENADIERS

The Wider War			Periods in Theatres of War in Bold Colours			
Details	Year	Month	1st Bn	2nd Bn	3rd Bn	4th Bn
			20th Bde	4th Gds Bde		
Germany invades Russia	1914	Aug		MONS		
		Sep		MARNE/AISNE		
		Oct	1st YPRES	1st YPRES		
		Nov				
		Dec				
	1915	Jan				
		Feb				
		Mar	NEUVE			
Gallipoli landings		Apr	CHAPELLE			
		May	FESTUBERT	FESTUBERT		
		Jun				
		Jul				Raised
Guards Division formed		Aug	3rd Gds Bde	1st Gds Bde	2nd Gds Bde	3rd Gds Bde
		Sep	LOOS	LOOS	LOOS	LOOS
		Oct				
		Nov				
Gallipoli evacuated		Dec				
	1916	Jan				
French defence of Verdun		Feb				
		Mar				
		Apr				
		May				
Naval battle of Jutland		Jun				
		Jul				
		Aug				
Italians defeated at Caporetto by Austro-Germans		Sep	SOMME	SOMME	SOMME	SOMME
		Oct				
		Nov			3rd Gds Bde	
		Dec				
	1917	Jan				
Russian Revolution		Feb				
		Mar				
USA enters the war		Apr				
		May				
French mutinies		Jun			2nd Gds Bde	
		Jul	3rd YPRES	3rd YPRES	3rd YPRES	3rd YPRES
		Aug	(Passchendaele)	(Passchendaele)	(Passchendaele)	(Passchendaele)
		Sep				
		Oct				
Allenby takes Jerusalem from the Turks		Nov	CAMBRAI	CAMBRAI	CAMBRAI	CAMBRAI
		Dec				
	1918	Jan				4th Gds Bde
		Feb				
		Mar	ARRAS	ARRAS	ARRAS	
		Apr				HAZEBROUCK
		May				
		Jun				
		Jul				
		Aug	HINDENBURG	HINDENBURG	HINDENBURG	
		Sep	LINE	LINE	LINE	
		Oct				
Armistice		Nov				
		Dec	Cologne	Cologne	Cologne	Cologne
	1919	Jan				Disbanded Feb 1919
		Feb				

A poignant picture: few of those shown in this 1914 shot are likely to have survived.

until by August 1914 most of the nations of Europe were in arms.

The opening weeks were the only ones of the war to see manoeuvre on a large scale. A massive German force of eighty-seven divisions descended upon France. The French deployed sixty-two divisions in defence, but were steadily pressed back. The German army of von Kluck violated the neutrality of Belgium and swept down from the north. The British Expeditionary Force, of only six infantry divisions and one cavalry, passed over to France and moved up to Mons to meet the threat. In German eyes it was a derisory effort – a contemptible little army, they called it. They reckoned without its quality, however, and the 'Old Contemptibles' thereafter adopted the insult with pride.

The regular battalions of Foot Guards numbered nine.[4] Of these a few were always unallotted to field formations and two happened at the time to be Grenadier battalions. Thus the BEF contained only the **2nd Battalion** (Lt Col Noel Corry), with the 2nd and 3rd Coldstream and 1st Irish in 4th (Guards) Brigade (Brig Gen Robert Scott-Kerr, a Grenadier).[5] This brigade, in the 2nd Division, was thrown straight into a blocking position at Mons, but the French had given way on the right flank

and it became necessary to pull back before even a shot had been fired.

There followed the long **Retreat from Mons**, an operation of the most taxing and dispiriting kind to which British arms were unhappily prone at the outset of a campaign (it had happened at Corunna in 1809 and would happen again at Dunkirk in 1940). From 24 August to 5 September, for thirteen weary and frustrating days and in stifling heat, they trudged 216 miles along cobbled roads which tore their boots to shreds, stopping only for a brief rest or to be set immediately to digging defences which were as quickly abandoned when further retreat

Off to war: a Grenadier battalion in Chelsea barracks ready to go in 1914.

[4] Three Grenadier, three Coldstream, two Scots, one Irish
[5] Brigades then contained four battalions each, some 1000 strong in four rifle companies

Knocked to pieces: Grenadiers in the ruins of an enemy position.

'One of the proudest moments of my existence': this silver figure was given by the 18th Bengal Lancers who fought so bravely as infantry alongside the 2nd Battalion at Gauche Wood.

A beautiful landscape: St Christ on the Somme gives an indication of some normality in a countryside which was to be shattered by war. *G.C.S.*

Walking wounded: a Grenadier is helped on his way by a comrade and a German prisoner.

A third award for gallantry: John Rhodes winning his Victoria Cross. *Sean Bolan*

The GRENADIER GUARDS are "holding their own"

Holding their own: the pains of parting.

Commanding officers and brigadiers over long periods (from left): 'Copper' Seymour, Charles Corkran, 'Boy' Brooke and 'Crawley' de Crespigny.

was ordered. Only twice did the Grenadiers have a chance to stand and fight. In the small town of **Landrecies** they supported the 3rd Coldstream in a stiff fight, in the dark, to block a strong enemy force and slow down the pursuit. Further south, at **Villers-Cotterêts**, there was a second, much more costly encounter. During this difficult rearguard action in thick woodland it was extremely hard to communicate the fast-changing situation, or pass orders to deal with it. The Germans lost heavily, especially to the battalion's machine guns, employed here for the first time in the war, but they were in great numbers and came to close quarters. In the confusion, two whole platoons failed to receive the order to retire. Though fighting with great courage, they were cut off and destroyed, every man being killed or wounded. The battalion suffered 164 casualties in all.

'We started tramping it again, and we were dead beat, and didn't we look gems, some of us with half our equipment missing. We had no washing kit, razor or mess tin, in fact, we had hardly anything but our fighting material, and when we did get a drop of tea or stew, we had to use jam tins or any pot we could pick up.'[6]

On 5 September the sadly tattered, unshaven, footsore body of men went into billets at Fontenay-Trésigny, east of Paris. But fortune was now to turn. The ambitious German advance, aimed at Paris itself, was over-extended and had run out of steam. The French gathered a new Sixth Army, which was rushed up to a critical point in a fleet of Parisian taxicabs and threw the enemy back. The rest of the Allied armies joined in and the German masses were checked short of the capital. The army then forged forward to turn the tables on their assailants. It was the

'miracle of the **Marne**', an exhilarating moment after the agony and frustration of the long retreat. The 2nd Grenadiers crossed that river, in a fast-moving and muddled fight, and suffered forty casualties.

The BEF advanced further to the **River Aisne**. The battalion crossed the river on 14 September and pressed the enemy back in a confused battle.

'The next day we had another good time, as we advanced up the River Aisne, and got more credit. We crossed the river and advanced up the hill. The Germans were in a good position. The Connaught Rangers were in front of us, and we got orders to reinforce them at the double, as the Germans were in large force, and the Connaughts were being hard pressed. We doubled across a ploughed field, and we did have it hot. The bullets and shells came over in swarms, and I thought it was all over for us. We lay down expecting to be knocked over, but we stuck it, and wasn't it a battle that day! Heavy losses on both sides; it was a terrible time, fighting like cats all day. Towards night it became a real battlefield, a large barn being on fire, as well as some houses. When our company mustered together that night, a shell dropped in our midst killing six and wounding forty; it was terrible.'[7]

In this fighting a young private named Parsons distinguished himself by taking charge of a dozen lost soldiers from another battalion and commanding them for the rest of the battle. He was promoted corporal on the field and mentioned in despatches, but tragically was killed in October.

---

[6] Carter
[7] Carter

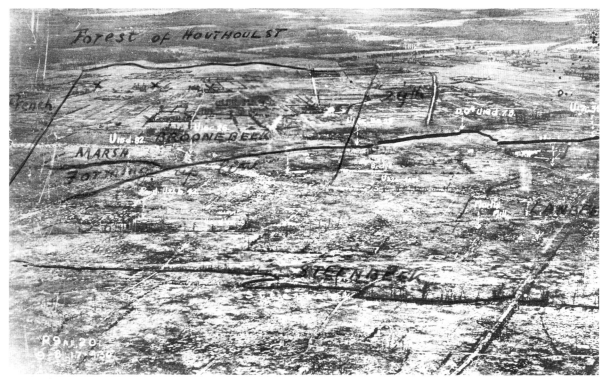

Marked for attention: an air photograph of 9 October 1917 showing Broembeek in the Ypres sector. The Guards Division sector is indicated and enemy strongpoints by crosses. A note below states: 'all were splendidly smashed by our artillery' but the effect, combined with the dreadful weather, was to turn the ground into a quagmire through which it was almost impossible to move and in which it was not difficult to drown.

Here the front stabilized, and settled into the long lines of trenches that were to stretch for several hundred miles from Switzerland to the English Channel and for the most part to be very little changed for four years.

The Decimation of the Regular Battalions – Ypres, Neuve Chapelle and Festubert

But the line was not complete. At the northern end the Germans made a great effort to take the Channel ports and it fell to the BEF to prevent them. The Belgians, though supported by the French, fell under the German steamroller and, despite some heroic resistance, were unable to do much to stem its advance. As the antagonists raced to outflank one another to the north, the struggle came to focus on the ancient Flemish city of **Ypres**. In October the **2nd Battalion** (Lt Col Wilfrid Abel Smith) moved rapidly up with 4th (Guards) Brigade (now under a new Grenadier brigadier, the Earl of Cavan) and was soon thrown into the line. It was here also that the **1st Battalion** (Lt Col Max Earle) came out in the 20th Brigade to play its part. The 7th Division had been sent out in an attempt to save Antwerp, though the opportunity for doing so was soon lost. After much

marching and counter-marching deep into Belgium, in the course of which it passed through the Grenadiers' founding city of Bruges, the battalion was pulled back to Ypres to join in the desperate defensive battle that followed (and is described separately).

In December 1914 the two shattered battalions were withdrawn and reconstituted with large drafts, including many men from the 3rd Battalion, still in London. The rest of the winter that followed was spent in and out of the trenches between Ypres and Loos, the 1st Battalion being north of Neuve Chapelle and the 2nd Battalion in the area of Festubert. The conditions were freezing cold and very bad.

In the warmer and drier conditions of early spring an attempt was made to break through the German line in a number of places. The **1st Battalion** (Lt Col Lawrence Fisher-Rowe) was launched into an ill-judged attack at **Neuve Chapelle** in March. It was very costly, 341 being killed and wounded (including the Commanding Officer killed) for a very small gain in ground. It was here that the first Grenadier Victoria Crosses of the war were won by the bombing exploits of LCpl Fuller and Pte Barber.

In May a similar attempt was made at **Festubert**. Both the **1st Battalion** (Lt Col Charles Corkran) and **2nd**

GENERAL
Sir ANDREW THORNE
KCB CMG DSO and 2 Bars *1885-1970*

Valiant Commanding
Officer and General
who well knew
the mind of
Adolf Hitler

SERGEANT
JOHN RHODES VC
DCM and Bar *1891-1917*

Victoria Cross of the
3rd Battalion on
the Broembeek who
had already twice
won the DCM

Andrew Thorne, otherwise know as 'Bulgy', was commissioned into the Grenadiers in 1904 and joined the 3rd Battalion. He went to war in 1914 in the headquarters of 1st Guards Brigade (which contained no Grenadier battalion) and later served in the headquarters of the Guards Division.

In September 1916, a day before his thirty-first birthday, he took command of the 3rd Battalion, which had just emerged from a heavy battle on the Somme. He led it with great distinction at 3rd Ypres, Cambrai and Arras, and a month before the end of the war was given command of a brigade.

After the war he rose steadily. He was military attaché in Berlin from 1932 to 1935, at the crucial time of Hitler's coming to power. Corporal Hitler had won an Iron Cross while serving as a runner opposite 1st Guards Brigade at Gheluvelt in front of Ypres and, discovering Thorne's own part in the battle, had a long private conversation with him about it. The Führer held him in high regard.

But Thorne had no illusions about Hitler's intentions and was not surprised by the outbreak of war again in 1939. He commanded a division in the Dunkirk campaign and then the corps in the south-east of England before being appointed GOC-in-C Scotland. He was well conscious of his own abilities and was disappointed not to be given an army overseas. However, he oversaw the liberation of Norway, taking the surrender of 300,000 men. It has been suggested that the Scottish appointment was a deliberate attempt to mislead Hitler into expecting the Second Front in 1944 to open under his leadership through Norway rather than France.

An exceptionally fit and active man, even when a full general he used to stop his staff car so that he could run up a hill alongside it.

See Lindsay (Donald)

John Rhodes won the greatest distinction for bravery of any Grenadier of the war save only Lord Gort himself. Born in 1891 in Packmoor, North Staffordshire, he joined the 3rd Battalion at the age of nineteen.

Both his DCMs were won with the 2nd Battalion in the area of Festubert. On 18 May 1915 he led a patrol forward and crept so close to the enemy trenches that he gained valuable information. On returning to his own trench he discovered that wounded men were lying out in No Man's Land in full view of the enemy and twice ran out to rescue them. A few months later, on 6 August, a forward trench was blown in. Rhodes, now a lance corporal, went up, although under sharp fire, and coolly dug out the men entombed, continuing to dig even when shot in the right shoulder, thus saving several lives. Wounded a second time, he returned home, where he married.

In October 1917 he was back as an acting sergeant with the 3rd Battalion in the Ypres Salient, commanding a Lewis-gun section. In the assault on the Broembeek his company had been beaten back by a nest of machine guns firing from pill-boxes. A further attack seemed futile and the artillery put down a barrage on the pill-boxes that left the ground a 'churned-up mass of high explosives'. Rhodes saw three Germans escape from one of the pill-boxes and, despite the still-bursting shells, ran forward quite alone to the enemy positions. He emerged from the pill-boxes a few seconds later with nine prisoners, including a forward observation officer who had been controlling the fire of his battery, and drove them back to his lines.

He was killed on 27 November, the day after it was announced that he had been awarded the Victoria Cross.

CAPTAIN
GEORGE PATON VC
MC *1895-1917*

Victoria Cross of the
4th Battalion at
Gonnelieu, Cambrai,
December 1917

George Henry Tatham Paton was born in Argyllshire, the son of William Paton, Deputy Chairman and Managing Director of Bryant and May, the famous match manufacturers. He joined the Regiment in January 1916 and was promoted acting captain in June 1917. In August 1917 he won the Military Cross.

On 1 December he won a posthumous Victoria Cross for his action at Gonnelieu, in the Cambrai battle, while commanding No 4 Company. The citation reads: 'For most conspicuous bravery and self-sacrifice. When a unit on his left was driven back, thus leaving his flank in the air and his company practically surrounded, he fearlessly exposed himself to readjust the line, walking up and down within fifty yards of the enemy under a withering fire. He personally removed several wounded men and was the last to leave the village. Later he again readjusted the line, exposing himself regardless of all danger the whole time, and when the enemy four times counter-attacked he sprang each time upon the parapet, deliberately risking his life, and being eventually mortally wounded, in order to stimulate his command. After the enemy had broken through on his left, he again mounted the parapet, and with a few men – who were inspired by his great example – forced them once more to withdraw, thereby undoubtedly saving the left flank.' He was killed in action.

His commanding officer, Lord Gort VC, wrote of him, 'His loss was a great personal grief to me, as he was extremely popular with everyone, both officers and men; always cheerful in difficulties, and, above all, an officer who had a wonderful natural aptitude for soldiering which I am confident would have carried him a long way had he been spared to develop it.'

PRIVATE
EDGAR HOLMES VC
1895-1918

Victoria Cross of the
2nd Battalion at
Cattenières, just a
month before the
Armistice

William Edgar Holmes won his Victoria Cross on 9 October 1918, in almost the last major action of the war fought by his battalion.

His citation reads: 'Pte Holmes carried in two men under the most intense fire and, while he was attending to a third case, he was severely wounded. In spite of this, he continued to carry wounded, and was shortly afterwards again wounded, with fatal results. By his self-sacrifice and disregard of danger he was the means of saving the lives of several of his comrades.'

His loss just before the end of the war was especially tragic, for he had served from the outset and so far had survived everything thrown at him. He marched on the retreat from Mons and later, in the Ypres Salient, was so badly frost-bitten that two of his toes had to be amputated. Returning to France in 1915, he was twice wounded before his final acts of gallantry.

A letter written to his family by two Grenadiers in the platoon illustrates the scale of the tragedy. They had lost a friend who for four years must have seen his platoon torn to pieces time and again. The part he must have played in helping and encouraging a constant flow of new men can well be imagined. 'In your loss,' they wrote, 'it will be a great comfort to you to know that Edgar died the bravest of deaths whilst trying to save a wounded comrade. His loss to us will be very great, as we have always been close comrades for the last four years. He was always the life and soul of our platoon.'

Holmes, a Gloucestershire man born at Wood Stanway, is remembered by an oak seat in the churchyard at Didbrook, made from timber cut from the Stanway estate where he had worked before becoming a Grenadier.

Wiped off the map: another hapless village before and after a bombardment.

Battalion (Lt Col Wilfrid Abel Smith) took part and, though still in different brigades, were at one point alongside each other in the line. 'The attack was ordered off the map and no general or staff officer came to look at the ground,' complained Major George Jeffreys, who took over the 2nd Battalion when the Commanding Officer was mortally wounded. It was another fruitless and expensive battle.

These two actions, on top of the carnage of Ypres, completed the ruin of the original regular battalions. Very few of their original members remained and inevitably the war now moved into a higher gear.

The Guards Division and Loos 1915

In the summer of 1914 volunteers poured into the recruiting offices, anxious not to miss the war that would be 'over by Christmas'. In order to succeed, many pretended they were older than they were. One recalled his mother's reaction: 'You come home in uniform and I'll break your neck,' she said. But he succeeded and found himself 'in a hut in the charge of two trained soldiers who played cards, drank beer and broke wind. They told us that the smell of the battlefield would compare unfavourably'.[8] In 1915 Lord Kitchener, Secretary of State for War, called for more. 'Your country needs you' was the message under the compelling image and pointing finger of his famous poster and two and a half million volunteers were to respond by the spring of 1916. In the course of this more battalions of Foot Guards were also raised, including a fourth of Grenadiers.[9]

In September the Guards Division was formed, though in the face of many misgivings. It seemed all too probable that the single division might receive such a mauling that the distinctive qualities of the Guards would

be obliterated. Many would also have preferred to see separate Guards brigades leavening other divisions of the army. However, Kitchener was anxious for an elite formation that would act as a model and example to the rest. He insisted and it was done. The twelve battalions were divided between three brigades (another suggestion that the four of Grenadiers should be brigaded together was happily dropped) and thus they fought for the next two and half years. They were:

1st Guards Brigade – **2nd Grenadiers**,
  2nd Coldstream, 3rd Coldstream, 1st Irish.
2nd Guards Brigade – **3rd Grenadiers**,
  1st Coldstream, 1st Scots, 2nd Irish.
3rd Guards Brigade – **1st Grenadiers**,
  4th Grenadiers, 2nd Scots, 1st Welsh.
The 4th Coldstream was divisional pioneer
  battalion and there were the usual supporting
  arms and services.

The division, whose first commander was the Grenadier Earl of Cavan, adopted the 'Ever Open Eye' for its emblem.

In February 1915 the Welsh Guards had been formed, again at the personal insistence of Kitchener. South Wales having been a Grenadier recruiting area, 639 Grenadiers transferred, forming the largest component of the new regiment.[10]

Compared to regiments of the line, many of which, especially from the industrial cities, formed twenty

---

[8] Scott
[9] The reserve battalion, formerly the 4th, now became the 5th
[10] Many still remained as Grenadiers. 'When we were in trenches very close to the Hun, I was doing my rounds at night when I suddenly thought I heard German being spoken. In some trepidation, I drew my revolver and crept around the traverse to find out what was going on. To my great relief, it was men of my own company speaking Welsh.' (Westmacott)

Deep cover: another German position knocked out. On the whole their dugouts were deeper and more solidly built than those of the Allies.

battalions or more, the expansion of the Foot Guards was in fact extremely small.[11] But a premium was placed on more thorough training and, although the composition of each battalion was virtually to be renewed three or four times during the war, it proved possible to instil and preserve the special qualities of the guardsman. And this despite the often unpromising raw material.

'It was often supposed that the Brigade of Guards was made up of picked men, but in fact their height was the only standard applied. When recruiting was brisk the height standard was raised, when it was slack it was lowered. I saw some of the recruits when they enlisted: they were often weedy and narrow-chested, but after only a few weeks of plentiful food, hard exercise and drill, they were almost unrecognizable. They were new men.'[12]

The baptism of fire of the Guards Division came at **Loos** in September 1915. It was the biggest offensive so far, but it started in dismal fashion. The preparations were insufficient, the first wave of the assault was held up and new, totally inexperienced 'Kitchener' divisions, only just arrived in France, were thrown in as a reserve, much too late. Predictably they were broken in pieces and hurled

back. The Guards Division was ordered up to make a new attempt.

'Next morning we were at half-an-hour's notice to move and spent a most jumpy morning, expecting to move off at any moment. Waiting to "pop the parapet" is one of the richer sensations of warfare, and perhaps the most trying of the lot.'[13]

The **1st Battalion** (Lt Col Gerald Trotter) and **2nd Battalion** (Lt Col George Jeffreys) were in reserve and, though shelled, were little engaged. The **3rd Battalion** (Lt Col Noel Corry[14]) advanced over the earlier third line German defences, which they were astonished to find dug twenty to thirty feet down in the chalk. They then joined the 1st Scots in a difficult assault on a heavily defended point, from which they then had to withdraw after being almost surrounded. They hung on in a retired position for two days before being relieved, having suffered 229 casualties. To the **4th Battalion** (Lt Col Claude Hamilton) fell the hardest work. Their objective,

---

[11] In the Second World War the Grenadiers formed six battalions rather than four
[12] Chandos (1)
[13] Fryer
[14] He returned to a command after having been relieved of the 2nd Battalion for withdrawing prematurely at Mons, a charge that eventually was not sustained.

FIELD MARSHAL
JOHN VEREKER,
Viscount GORT VC
GCB CBE DSO and 2 Bars MVO MC *1886-1946*

Victoria Cross of 1918,
Chief of the Imperial
General Staff,
Commander-in-Chief
British Expeditionary
Force

ord Gort achieved the astonishing count of five decorations for gallantry. Only thirty-two when he took command of a battalion, he was promoted from brigadier to full general in the space of three years in the 1930s and appointed head of the Army. He led the BEF to France in 1939 and in May 1940 took the crucial decision, against the express wishes of the British war cabinet and the French high command, to withdraw to Dunkirk, thereby saving the greater part of his force.

Gort went to war in 1914 on the staff of the 2nd Division, in which the 2nd Grenadiers were serving, and took part in the retreat from Mons (though in rather more comfort than the soldiers) and First Ypres. After a short time at the headquarters of the First Army, he became brigade major of 4th (Guards) Brigade under Lord Cavan and continued in a similar role after the Guards Division was formed in August 1915.

During the Great War relations between front-line soldiers and the headquarter staffs were often frigid. Staff officers (all then wearing red tabs on their collars) were not always seen in the trenches as often as they should have been. 'Like flowers', remarked one veteran, 'they come out only in good weather'. This, however, was not Gort's way. He disliked being in a safe or sedentary position and took every opportunity to visit the front line.

After a frustrating year at General HQ, Gort was given command of the 4th Grenadiers in April 1917. He led them with great distinction in the offensive

battles of Third Ypres and Cambrai, being wounded on each occasion.

In 1918 he took over the 1st Battalion to face the Ludendorff offensive and then to turn the tables in the final offensive of the war. This enabled him to display his talent in more open warfare. Showing leadership and bravery of the highest order, he led the attack on Premy Ridge, by the Canal du Nord, constantly exposing himself to fire. Though twice wounded, he forced himself on and would not be evacuated until the success signals had gone up. 'The sight of this dauntless man, with his square figure, clipped moustache, fair windswept hair, cap tilted over his left ear and blood-soaked bandages, leaping into action, stirred our hearts and impelled us to efforts we thought were beyond our powers.' He was awarded the Victoria Cross.

After the war 'Fat Boy', as he was inaccurately nicknamed, always retained his youthful zest and interest in the practical concerns of the soldier in the field. His friends accused him of sleeping on concrete, which was hosed down every night.

He commanded the Regiment from 1930 to 1932. Five years later he was appointed CIGS by Hore-Belisha, the reforming new Secretary of State. Although by then he was not unduly young, peacetime generals were on the whole well stricken in years and it was an astonishing elevation over the heads of many more senior contenders, which inevitably provoked jealousy.

On war breaking out again in 1939, he was appointed to command the BEF. It was a poisoned chalice. The decision he took to withdraw to Dunkirk in 1940 was suicidal to his own prospects, but he preserved the army, thereby enabling it to pursue the fight against Germany in North Africa and Italy, and to return to Normandy four years later to finish the job.

Back in England he became Inspector General to the Forces before being appointed in succession Governor of Gibraltar, Governor of Malta during the last few months of its heroic resistance, and High Commissioner for Palestine and Transjordan. By then he was a sick man. Only a few months after leaving Jerusalem cancer was diagnosed and on 31 March 1946 he died.

His Chief Secretary in Palestine pronounced this verdict: 'He was the finest man I ever served. Like Gideon, he was a mighty man of valour.'

See Colville, Cliff

Well loaded-up for another march: a lance corporal in 1918. *Christopher Morley*

1916 in the northern part of the Ypres Salient. 'We first started wearing the steel helmet at this time, and very heavy and uncomfortable it felt at first.'[15] And it was by no means peaceful. In one period of two days the 2nd Battalion lost no fewer than 150 men from artillery and trench mortar bombardments, sniping and bombing raids.

But there was a surprising break.

'We could scarcely believe our luck when cattle trucks transported us all the way to the coast and deposited us at Calais – just a wave's length from home, but with no ferry running at the moment. Greatly daring, we encamped on a sandy plateau at Beaumaris in a snowstorm and dense fog. But, oh, the tang of salt spray and the scent of seaweed.'[16]

The enormous number of men required in France and Flanders alone (it was to reach some two million, in five great armies) could no longer be supplied by volunteers and in the spring of 1916 conscription was introduced, yielding by the end of the war a further two and a half million men.

In August the Guards Division moved south to join the major offensive on the **Somme** (described separately). After the battle it settled into yet another winter along the line gained. In order to ease the continuous process of relief and rest the division was reorganized into two large brigades. 2nd Guards Brigade was temporarily suspended until reconstituted in July 1917 for the next round of offensives.

1917 – Third Ypres and Cambrai

In March 1917 the full effect of the 1916 gains on the Somme was recognized by the Germans, who pulled back on the southern part of the British front for several miles, settling into formidable defences prepared along the Hindenburg Line. The Guards Division was able therefore to advance its line on the Somme.

with the 1st Welsh, was Hill 70. A lodgement was duly made, but casualties were so heavy that the guardsmen had to be withdrawn. The battalion was split in two; the Commanding Officer, who was gassed, was unable to pass on critical orders; the enemy artillery and machine-gun fire was unrelenting; the din, confusion and smoke extreme; the small bodies that succeeded in making real progress were soon isolated; it was difficult for anyone to see where anyone else really was. It was a pattern to be tragically repeated, time and time again, in the fighting on the Western Front. The battalion was eventually relieved after suffering 353 casualties.

September 1915 to July 1916 and the Somme

The winter that followed was spent in and out of the line north of Neuve Chapelle, and from March to July

---

[15] Fryer
[16] Cliff

On the mend: this group is probably from the 5th (Reserve) Battalion at Chelsea convalescing from wounds and no doubt expecting to return to the front.

Happy to be out of it: German prisoners taken by Grenadiers show signs of relief.

REGIMENTAL SERGEANT MAJOR
ARTHUR 'IVO' HILL
MC DCM RVM *1876-1969*

Gallant Drill Sergeant and Sergeant Major, Yeoman of the Body Guard for 38 years

*A*rthur Munns Hill, always known as Ivo, acquired in his long service fifteen decorations and medals, one of the most impressive collections in the possession of the Regiment.

Hill, from Ware in Hertfordshire, enlisted at the London Recruiting Depot (on the site of the present Home Office, next to Wellington Barracks) in January 1895 and was sent to the 3rd Battalion at the Tower of London. In 1898 he was already a lance sergeant and in November 1901 embarked for the war in South Africa, returning a year later. In 1904 he was a member of the bearer party for the Duke of Cambridge, Colonel of the Regiment.

In 1913 he moved to the 2nd Battalion as Drill Sergeant and in the following year took part in the fighting in the retreat from Mons, the Marne and the Aisne. On the Aisne he 'behaved with the utmost gallantry and owing to the lack of officers he commanded a platoon of various regiments which eventually grew to 250 strong.' However, during the action he was severely wounded by shrapnel in the chest. His gallantry was rewarded by the Military Cross, instituted at the end of 1914.

In 1915 he returned to his beloved 3rd Battalion as Sergeant Major and remained there till 1920. He distinguished himself in reviving his battalion on several occasions when battered by the heavy toll of the fighting and was awarded the DCM.

After the war he worked for the British Legion, though suffering from ill health. In 1924 he became a 'Yeoman in Ordinary' of the King's Body Guard of the Yeomen of the Guard. He served through two coronations and for thirty-eight years until 1964, wearing the short 'George V' beard which was required of all yeomen when he joined. He took to the grave the shrapnel from his 1914 wound.

See Webb-Carter (1)

The French had been close to outright mutiny after the failure of a new offensive and, to support his ally, Haig made preparations for another major effort in the summer. This was to be **3rd Ypres** (the second battle having been fought in 1915 when the Guards were further south) a long-drawn-out affair in atrocious conditions. The battle is often known as **Passchendaele**, after a town in the sector where the weather conditions and losses were at their most appalling, and which, with the Somme, came to represent the most senseless and agonizing example of the waste and futility of the war.

The Guards Division moved up to the north of Ypres and fought its way for four miles over a front of some 1,500 yards. It took three months. After an initial advance from **Boesinghe** in July of an unprecedented two and a half miles, rain fell and the battlefield became a quagmire. The battle was bogged down before a further offensive to cross the **Broembeek** was launched in October. It was a major struggle to survive in the morass, never mind the attentions of the enemy. Men had to stand up to their knees in water. The only way to ensure warmth was to dig a new trench at dawn and dusk every day, and 48 hours in them was considered the limit of endurance.

'The approach to the ridge was a desolate swamp, over which brooded an evil menacing atmosphere that seemed to defy encroachment. Far more treacherous than the visible surface defences with which we were familiar, such as barbed wire; deep devouring mud spread deadly traps in all directions. We splashed and slithered, and dragged our feet from the pull of an invisible enemy determined to suck us into its depths. Every few steps someone would slide and stumble and, weighed down by rifle and equipment, rapidly sink into the squelching mess. Those nearest grabbed his arms, struggled against being themselves engulfed and, if humanly possible, dragged him out. When helpers floundered in as well and doubled the task, it became hopeless. All the straining efforts failed, the swamp swallowed its screaming victims, and we had to be ordered to plod on dejectedly and fight this relentless enemy as stubbornly as we did those we could see.'[17]

The casualties from the fighting were modest by the standards of the war, between twenty-five and forty percent, the **2nd Battalion** (Lt Col Claude de Crespigny,

---

[17] Cliff

An astonishing collection: the medals of Ivo Hill.

later Lt Col Guy Rasch) coming off worst. The other battalions were commanded as follows: **1st Battalion** (Lt Col Mark Makgill-Crichton-Maitland), **3rd Battalion** (Lt Col Andrew Thorne), **4th Battalion** (Lt Col Viscount Gort). In the Broembeek battle, and subsequently at Cambrai and Arras, all three brigades were commanded by Grenadiers (Seymour, de Crespigny and Sergison-Brooke).

Hardly was the long slog of Ypres over than the Guards were ordered south to assault the Hindenburg Line south-west of **Cambrai**. Here tanks were to be used en masse for the first time. On 20 November the army launched a surprise attack, without the usual preliminary bombardment. It succeeded, but a key position was not taken. Despite the protests of the divisional commander, 2nd Guards Brigade was given the task of taking **Fontaine Nòtre Dame** at very short notice and without time for the most basic preparation. The artillery was not coordinated and no tanks appeared. And, unknown to them, the Germans had prepared their own attack and had plenty of reserves. The objectives were gained, but the Germans counter-attacked and the battle raged all day. The brigade was eventually forced to withdraw, having suffered badly.

Three days later came the main German counter-offensive. In a matter of hours they had advanced three miles.

'We then witnessed a most extraordinary sight – an army in retreat, and a British one at that! There were men scurrying along in great disarray – including many in pyjamas and overcoats.'[18]

At **Gouzeaucourt** the enemy were checked by 1st Guards Brigade, while 3rd Guards Brigade regained the St Quentin Ridge to the east. The **2nd Battalion** (Lt Col Guy Rasch) was directed to take **Gauche Wood**. Despite the absence of the promised tanks, the companies pressed on and were soon fighting hand-to-hand in the wood. The position was consolidated and two counter-attacks were beaten off. This was followed by heavy shelling and in the

confusion the battalion became intermixed with the neighbouring dismounted regiment of Indian Army cavalry, the 18th Bengal Lancers.[19] They agreed to combine their efforts and a lasting bond was formed between the two regiments. A Bengali said, 'One of the proudest moments of my existence has been lying alongside and defending the same trench as these fellows'.

1918 – The War Almost Lost and At Last Won

Early in 1918 the strain on manpower was such that brigades were reduced from four battalions to three. The **4th Battalion** (Lt Col William Pilcher) went into a new 4th Guards Brigade, which was taken out of the Guards Division.[20] Its first tour in the line, north of Arras, saw the notable repulse by twelve Grenadiers of a picked force of sixty Germans, who made an elaborate and well-rehearsed raid to secure positive identification of what they believed to be a battalion of guardsmen. They were right, but they took no prisoners and the quality of their opponents was borne in upon them by more decisive and painful means.

Circumstances overall had moved in favour of the enemy and in March and April the war was very nearly lost. The Russian Revolution in 1917 and the subsequent collapse of their war effort had released a million and a half German troops from the eastern front. The Americans, who had come into the war in 1917, were not yet in France. This time it was the Germans who made a last enormous effort to break the allied line, hoping to fall upon the British with such force that they would have to pull out and leave France to her fate. The experience of early years had much improved their tactics and the Ludendorff offensive very nearly succeeded. In March the Guards Division at **Arras** came under heavy attack and

---

[18] Westmacott
[19] Now the 19th Lancers of Pakistan
[20] It was also at this time that the **Guards Machine Gun Regiment** was formed, principally from the Household Cavalry, who had relinquished their horses. Before that, each Guards Brigade had its own machine-gun company

was forced to withdraw a few miles to conform to the general line which had been forced well back on the Somme. As it happened 4th Guards Brigade, in its new division, was fighting alongside. But another assault came further north in April. It made deep inroads and penetrated almost as far as **Hazebrouck**. The division containing 4th Guards Brigade was sent to stem the flood and it was here that the **4th Battalion** found its finest hour. Its desperate defensive battle (described separately) prevented a breakthrough that threatened to be disastrous. It was the last major action for that battalion, which remained recovering and in reserve for the rest of the war.

As on the Marne four years before, the German bolt was shot, and it was now the turn of the Allies to finish the job. American troops arrived in large numbers and were able to make a deep impression in a part of the French sector.[21] In August the Guards Division was launched south of Arras as part of a general advance and fought its way across the **Canal du Nord**, on the **Hindenburg Line**. This, at last, was more fluid warfare and it was well practised by the Grenadiers remaining in the division – the **1st Battalion** (Lt Col Viscount Gort), **2nd Battalion** (Lt Col Guy Rasch) and **3rd Battalion** (Lt Col Viscount Lascelles). Though their strength was often well below that established, the enormous casualties of the early great battles were not sustained. But new hazards appeared as the enemy was pressed back.

'The Germans had done a lot of mining; there were continual explosions going on: also booby traps were plentiful; an expert sapper used to go round the billets looking for bombs under the pianos, or traps concealed in the rooms. We luckily never got caught by one of these.'[22]

The Armistice and the Return Home

Eventually the division captured Maubeuge, through which the 2nd Battalion had passed on the retreat from Mons. There, on 11 November, the armistice was declared.

The war was over at last. The Guards Division, including again the battalions of 4th Guards Brigade, moved into Germany to occupy Cologne. In January 1919 the Colours were taken out to the battalions, a special Union Colour being presented to the 4th Battalion by the Prince of Wales. In February they all returned home and

in March the entire division marched past the King at Buckingham Palace and into the City of London, followed by great crowds of demobilized guardsmen, including the wounded. The 4th Battalion was disbanded the same month.

The Cost, the Numbers and the Awards

The war had cost the Regiment 4,711 dead and 7,181 wounded (of which officers counted 203 and 242 respectively). Over 25,000 had passed through the Reserve Battalion (4th and later 5th Grenadiers). Many awards had been made for gallantry and distinguished service, though in the familiar fashion they had been rationed, and were deserved by a far greater number than ever received them.[23]

The Grenadier Family in Support

The war called forth a tremendous effort of support from home. Under the direction of Colonel Sir Henry Streatfeild, the Lieutenant Colonel of the Regiment for most of the period, committees and funds were set up to provide comforts for the men abroad, to support the bereaved families and the wounded, and to help prisoners of war, of whom, fortunately, there were not many. One prisoner, who wanted to tell his friends what his conditions were really like, got a postcard through the German censor by simply writing '1 Corinthians iv. 11'. The verse reads: 'Even unto this present hour we both hunger, and thirst, and are naked, and are buffeted, and have no certain dwelling-place.' All this work was largely carried out by the womenfolk of Grenadiers.

The 'Guardsman'

From the earliest years to the present day members of the Foot Guards, both officers and men, have taken pride in being known as 'guardsmen'. However, on 22 November 1918, just eleven days after the Armistice, the King decreed that a private[24] of the Guards would henceforward carry the formal title of 'Guardsman' as 'a mark of His Majesty's appreciation and pride of the splendid services rendered by the Brigade of Guards during the war'.

---

[21] and, some of them, to announce that they had won the war all on their own
[22] Fryer
[23] Grenadier decorations for gallantry are summarized in Annex B
[24] The rank of 'private', strange for an occupation that attracts little privacy, comes from the Latin *privatus*, indicating a person deprived of status and of responsibility for anyone but himself

Two Victoria Crosses together: George Paton (second from left) and Thomas Pryce (second from right) in this group of officers in 1917. The day after this photograph was taken the officer on the right (possibly Captain Fanshawe) was alone in the shelter and was killed when a shell landed on it.

The qualities required of a guardsman were never in such demand, or subjected to such strain, as over these long and cruel four years. Never 'has higher courage or greater determination ever been demanded and shown'.[25] 'But perhaps their most important contribution was the development and dissemination of the Guards way of doing things. It was all-embracing; it took for granted leadership of the highest order, discipline and gallantry at all levels. It also extended to matters such as leaving trenches always better than they were found, smartness whatever the conditions, the maintenance of morale, meticulous administration and a care for one's men that transcended every self-interest.'[26] Raymond Asquith, Grenadier son of the Prime Minister and killed on the Somme, wrote: 'No troops can be first-rate unless they are punished for small faults and get their meals with regularity. The Canadians are frequently famished and never rebuked, whereas the Brigade of Guards are gorged and damned the whole time.'[27]

The Grenadiers had made a greater mark. Four service battalions had been in the field for most of the war. The first battalion of Welsh Guards was largely raised by Grenadiers. No fewer than 372 Grenadiers were promoted from the ranks to take commissions, almost all in other regiments where they infused the values and standards of guardsmen. Many won distinction.

The historian of the Guards Division concluded:
'Remember, then, whichever way the balance doth decline,
If God is in His Heaven, and the Guards are in the line, All's Well'.[28]

[25] Fraser (1)
[26] Paget
[27] Asquith
[28] Headlam, Paget

First Ypres 1914 – A Desperate Defence

The first battle of Ypres ('Wipers' to hundreds of thousands of British soldiers) lasted for four desperate weeks, from 19 October to 20 November, mostly over the higher ground to the east of the town. There was a good deal of woodland which, battered to pieces in ensuing months, did not survive long. Despite pouring huge numbers of troops into the assault, the Germans failed to force their way through and the scene was set for four years of further gruelling struggle in the Salient.

It was hoped at first to use Ypres as a base for offensive operations against the 'cooks and waiters' that one general expected the German Army to consist of. It was clear soon enough that much more serious work was in prospect. By 23 October the 7th Division was strung out over a line of seven miles, with every man in the trenches, braced for an assault by several German divisions. Communication was difficult and unreliable, made by messenger or runner (a dangerous job) and where possible by telephone, though lines were frequently cut by gunfire.

The **1st Battalion** (Lt Col Max Earle) in the 20th Brigade (Brig-Gen Harold Ruggles-Brise, a Grenadier), was first seriously engaged on 24 October.[29] No 4 Company carried out a successful counter-attack in the area of Polygon Wood, but had heavy losses. On 26 October, in the Kruiseik salient,

'a terrific shelling of our trenches began early in the morning, and reached such a pitch that the men counted as many as sixty rounds a minute on each small trench. The whole of the enemy's artillery fire was concentrated on Kruiseik. Gallantly our men held on, in spite of the fact that again and again, the shells blew in the trenches and buried half a dozen men at a time, all of whom had to be dug out with shovels. Some of them had as many as three feet of earth on top of them, and many were suffocated before they could be rescued.'[30]

The King's Company were cut off and had to fight

---

[29] Other than at Omdurman, by any measure a one-sided affair, the battalion had not been in action since the Peninsula just a century before
[30] Ponsonby (1)

An ancient and once a proud city: Ypres from the air in 1916.

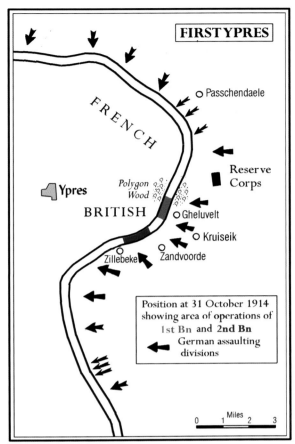

FIRST YPRES

FRENCH

Passchendaele

Reserve Corps

Ypres

Polygon Wood

BRITISH

Gheluvelt

Kruiseik

Zillebeke

Zandvoorde

Position at 31 October 1914 showing area of operations of **1st Bn** and **2nd Bn** German assaulting divisions

0 1 2 3 Miles

FIELD MARSHAL

FREDERICK LAMBART, Earl of CAVAN

KP GCB GCMG GCVO GBE *1865-1946*

Commander of 4th Guards Brigade and the Guards Division, Chief of the Imperial General Staff

*I*t was the view of another field marshal, Sir Henry Wilson, that Lord Cavan 'doesn't see very far, but what he does see he sees very clear'. It was by no means a bad verdict, for nothing could have been more important than clarity of vision, particularly in the desperate days of 1914. And, after all, Cavan, who as Viscount Kilcoursie had joined the Grenadiers in 1885 and served with the 2nd Battalion in South Africa, had never been ambitious beyond a command in his own regiment.

In September 1914 he took command of 4th (Guards) Brigade, which he led in his calm and unruffled fashion in the dreadful, exhausting days of First Ypres and later at Festubert.

In September 1915 he was appointed the first commander of the new Guards Division, though he did not approve of the concept. He was especially horrified to hear that it was planned to put all four Grenadier battalions in a single brigade and managed to persuade Kitchener against the idea. He also refused to allow the division to be put into another assault on the Somme in November 1916, saying, 'No one who has not visited the trenches can know the extent of exhaustion to which the men are reduced'.

He was subsequently promoted to command of a corps, first in France and then on the Italian front. In 1922 he became head of the army as CIGS, where he remained for four years. It was an unrewarding post, at a lean time for the Army. He also became Colonel of the Irish Guards.

He was nicknamed 'Fatty', another example of the schoolboy style that Grenadiers rejoiced to give their most illustrious officers – and for no very obvious reason as he was trim and spare.

See Chandos, Ball

their way back, but the order did not reach two platoons, who were overwhelmed.

In the mists of early morning on 29 October, 'standing to' in hastily dug individual trenches east of Gheluvelt, the Grenadiers saw great masses of German infantry moving behind their left rear, and were simultaneously attacked in front. They withdrew, refaced with part of the battalion and manned a ditch as well as support trenches dug behind them. The Germans attacked in mass formation and fell by the hundred before the sustained and accurate British rifle fire. The Grenadiers launched two counter-attacks with the bayonet across open ground to clear the enemy from a lodgement they had gained. Eventually, the battalion withdrew to some brickyards and were able to reorganize. There were only 100 men under four officers and a few NCOs, though others dribbling in later from where the confusion of the battle had detached them made the number up to 250.

Rest was almost impossible and new orders were constantly received and new marches made in preparation for yet another deployment. Once more, on 31 October, the most critical day of the whole battle, they

Commanding officers were little safer than their men: **Wilfrid Abel Smith** (left) survived Ypres, only to die at Festubert a few months later. **Max Earle** was wounded and taken prisoner. His successor in the 1st Battalion, **Lawrence Fisher-Rowe**, was killed at Neuve Chapelle.

were sent forward to plug another gap in the line and, once more, shredded by gunfire, they beat off further dense masses of the enemy. On 7 November, now withdrawn into billets and reorganized into a single King's Company, they recovered themselves with an hour's steady drill.

The experience of the **2nd Battalion** (Lt Col Wilfrid Abel Smith) in 4th (Guards) Brigade (Brig-Gen the Earl of Cavan, a Grenadier), 2nd Division, was very similar, and equally desperate. Moved to one brigade and division after another as the occasion demanded, they went in to plug hole after hole. First they joined in the early attempts to make ground under severe artillery fire, but progress proved impossible though German counter-attacks were successfully resisted. On 30 October the battalion, then in reserve, was called up to make a counter-attack to restore, and then hold, a broken part of the line. Over the following two days, well dug into slit trenches, they were subjected to the most gruelling bombardment and enfilade fire of the worst description. The brigadier, Lord Cavan, told them, 'The situation is extremely critical. You are to hold your ground at all costs. Sir Douglas Haig relies on the Grenadiers to save the First Corps and possibly the Army'. And hold they did, until relieved.

But there was no rest, as they went back time and again, marching hither and thither, digging and holding new positions, and putting in counter-attacks. No 1 Company was practically wiped out. The platoon of Sgt Thomas was down to three men, he himself having been twice buried by shells and had three rifles broken in his hand. The Commanding Officer wrote:

'One of the saddest days of my life. I have lost over 300 men in this wood, and we have been at it for ten days, day and night. I am now waiting (10 pm) for a relief that is coming. I really do not think that even this battalion could stand another twenty-four hours of it. The men have been wonderful. Many are buried by the shells, and I have no idea how many I have lost today. But I am sad tonight, and must write no more.

[Nov 13] Still having a poor time. I got away from my wood only to get to a worse place after but four hours rest. For two days we had perfect misery, wandering about all night wet to the skin, and finally fetched up in a horrible place where we can get no water or anything. I haven't had a wash of any sort or description for three days. It rains on and off continually. We are close to the Germans so can show no lights except in our dugouts, and the mud is awful. I can only describe our condition as being weary beyond words, and I really cannot read the papers, which give such rosy accounts of our so-called progress anymore.'[31]

'The line that stood between the British Empire and ruin was composed of tired, haggard and unshaven men, unwashed, plastered with mud, clad in little more than rags, but they had their rifles and bayonets and plenty of ammunition,' Lord Cavan wrote. 'No words can describe what the devotion of the men and the officers has been under the trials of dirt, squalor, cold, sleeplessness and perpetual strain of the last three weeks.'

Not until 19 November, now in freezing cold weather, was the battalion finally relieved. Over the last month they had lost 478, half their strength.

Fifteen Rounds a Minute

The guardsmen were highly skilled in their shooting and trained to fire fifteen aimed rounds per minute. So devastating was the effect that the enemy were convinced that they were facing machine guns, though at the time each battalion had only two on establishment. On 15 November one company alone of the 2nd Battalion fired 24,000 rounds. The enemy were sometimes in such numbers, and so close (often less than a hundred yards away), that the difficulty was to shoot them quickly enough.

Principal Sources: Ponsonby (1), Craster (1), Jeffreys (1)

---

[31] Smith, Wilfrid Abel

Misery and Anguish in the Trenches

Life in the Trenches

'The water was always knee-deep and in some places waist-deep and the enemy trenches were only 25 yards away. Men were constantly getting stuck and it could take four hours to extract them. One relief took six hours to complete. The water made the communication trenches impassable and accounted for more men than the enemy's bullets. It ate away the parapet, rotted the men's clothing, rusted and jammed the rifles, retarded the food supply, and generally made the life of the men in the trenches hideous; but in spite of all this discomfort the men remained cheerful and in good spirits ... The gruesome task of removing the dead was effected by floating the bodies down the communication trenches.'[32]

'We remained on the Somme during the whole of the 1916/17 winter ... We lost many men from trench foot. After Xmas heavy snow and severe frost took over. We were but a short distance from the Germans but the conditions were so vile that for several weeks no shots were fired. The only way we could get a drink of tea was by melting some ice in a mess tin and putting it over a candle wrapped in four-by-two. I have hated candles ever since that time.'[33]

'Although provided with gum-boots, we lived and worked in mud, even cleaning our mess tins with the stuff.

Twenty-four hours on sentry-go, one on and two off, alternated with twenty-four hours of digging, three on and three off. Lest we should luxuriate in such conditions, a Corps memorandum was circulated laying down that the natural desire of the troops to have a quiet time in the trenches must be discouraged in every possible way. So we splashed about shovelling mud and debris into sandbags to build up our defences, which the Jerries delighted in demolishing by shell-fire as soon as the job was done. With friend and foe cooperating in ensuring that we should not enjoy a quiet time, there was no danger of us lacking employment or reclining in leisured ease.

'Nevertheless, whoever invented sandbags deserves a permanent monument. Stuffed with mud and rubbish, they formed as sound a bulwark as was conceivable in the circumstances; tied round our legs, they protected our puttees; fitted over steel helmets, they obliterated the give-away shine; draped over our shoulders, they kept out some of the rain and kept in some of the warmth; and, most important of all, they carried our rations. I shall always, whenever I see a sandbag, treat it with the greatest respect.

---

[32] Ponsonby (1)
[33] Arrowsmith

Zigzag lines: forward, support and communication trenches near Neuve Chapelle, pockmarked with shell holes.

THE RIGHT HONOURABLE
Sir WINSTON CHURCHILL
KG OM CH PC *1874-1965*

Supernumerary Major
in the trenches,
Prime Minister
and War Leader

'*I* think I ought to tell you that we were not at all consulted in the matter of your coming to join us.' With such encouraging words was Major Churchill greeted by his commanding officer, George Jeffreys, on arriving in the 2nd Battalion trenches in November 1915.

Churchill, then forty years old, was in disgrace. As First Lord of the Admiralty he had been the moving force behind the disastrous Gallipoli campaign and had now lost his post. But, a direct descendant of the great Duke of Marlborough, he was a soldier at heart and indeed boasted a lively military record in India, the Sudan (where he had charged at Omdurman with the 21st Lancers) and South Africa. He came at once to France in urgent pursuit of a brigade command, but was diverted to a first-rate battalion for instruction in trench warfare.

Despite his unpromising welcome, followed by an exhausting tramp around the battalion trenches which put him in bed for almost a day, it was not long before his indomitable energy and enthusiasm reasserted themselves and he quickly won the admiration and respect of his colleagues. And his hosts, in turn, made an enduring impression on him. 'The discipline of this battalion is very strict,' he wrote, 'but the results are good. The spirit is admirable... A total indifference to death or casualties prevails. What has to be done is done, and the losses accepted without fuss or comment.'

After only two weeks he left to take command of the 6th Royal Scots Fusiliers, and a few months later was back at home in a new ministerial post.

In 1940, twenty-five years later and just at retiring age, he became the great wartime leader and, as many have judged him, the greatest Briton of all time.

Grenadiers of the 2nd Battalion bore him to his funeral in 1965.

'Nothing less than a battlefield as normally imagined was this Ypres scene. A chaos of rat-infested debris, human and material, in a sea of green and yellow mud pock-marked with shell-holes overflowing with slime, and crossed by irregular lines of muck heaps, once trenches, now burial mounds on which rotted the bloated bodies of horses and men. Hanging over the whole area, so all-pervading as to be almost visible as a mist, was the foul stench of death, presiding, penetrating, permanent and horribly inescapable.'[34]

'The trench mortar teams were roundly cursed by the men in the trenches when along they would bring their trench mortar, set it up, fire a dozen shells into the German line and then rush away to a place of safety, and the men in the trenches would take the full and inevitable return fire from the annoyed Germans.'[35]

Under Bombardment

'Everything was quite quiet until midnight and then suddenly a terrific bombardment started: I, in common with everyone else, just crouched at the bottom of the trench and hoped. Shells of every size seemed to follow one another, and burst in front of the parapet, behind us, and all around us. The din was terrific. Bits of the trench fell in and shell splinters went with a thud into the side of the trench. I know I was literally shivering with fright, and I noticed that we all spoke in quivering and husky tones, quite unlike our usual voices.'[36]

[Ypres 1916] 'I shall never forget Sanctuary Wood if I live to the age of Methuselah. It was mid-summer, and light for nineteen out of the twenty-four hours: thus for nineteen hours per day one couldn't move a muscle, but just lay in the bottom of the trench, getting shelled by 5.9 shells which traversed the trench at intervals.... The trench was stuffed full of men, and we were all sitting in each other's laps. I luckily found myself next to the company wag, one Tonge, whose wit became more intense as the situation grew worse: men like him were invaluable at times like these.'[37]

The Gas Attacks

'The Boche have begun to use a new kind of gas, called mustard gas, which makes horrible burns and affects the eyes. They fire it in shells, and have been

---

[34] Cliff
[35] Calvert
[36] Lawrence
[37] Fryer

Ready to dive in: some comfort could be had in the open air, but overhead cover is close at hand.

simply drenching all the back areas with it. As it is a very heavy gas it sinks into the bottom of every trench and dugout and is very difficult to get rid of .... The other night on fatigue we had to wear our masks for three hours, and as it is difficult to see anything in a mask we lost our way, were shelled, and got mixed up with another fatigue party. There was a fearful mess so I took off my helmet so as to be able to sort things out and find my bearings again; the result was that I got a dose of gas and was very sick, and had bad eyes the next day.'[38]

An artillery officer wrote: 'Sleeping as only an eighteen-year-old can, I was awakened by a shake of the shoulder. Peering out into the near black darkness, I made out a huge figure scratching his ear and saying, "Beg leave to speak, sir". I grunted, and he continued, "Colonel's compliments, sir, there is a gas attack. You, sir, being a Gunner officer, have probably forgotten your gas mask. Here is one".'[39]

On Sentry Duty

'It was on lonely sentry duty that my spirits sometimes sank to their lowest depths. One saw, and smelt, and sensed nothing but slime, stench, debris, hopeless misery, the agony of broken bodies and broken hearts,

the senseless waste of youth quenched, suffering of the spirit deep and bitter.'[40]

'On sentry at night, when facing the German line, we placed a piece of fat bacon (not eatable) on the bayonet end and when a rat came we fired, hoping to kill it and also hit a German.'[41]

'Dawn came up slightly earlier than usual and he [the lisping officer] noticed that a sentry, whose duty it was to keep watch over the top at night, had lowered his head. "Thergeant, that man should be looking over the top," he exclaimed. The boy heard and obeyed, a shot rang out and he fell dead. "Thergeant, put another man on there," ordered the Captain and passed on. In those few seconds some family at home suffered a terrible bereavement. A young life had been snuffed out. Fierce anger and resentment seized me, standing at attention nearby. With a tremendous effort I remained silent, but I have never found it in my heart to forgive [him], though his long and gallant service in the fighting line earned admiration.'[42]

[38] Lawrence
[39] Lawrence
[40] Cliff
[41] Calvert
[42] Cliff

A brief respite: this shallow trench was either temporary or in the early stages of construction.

No Man's Land and Trench Raids

'The terrible tragedies that went on daily between the two firing lines gave some idea of the barbarous cruelty of the Germans. Men who were wounded in any attack or raid were forced to lie out between the lines, often in great agony, but whenever any of our stretcher-bearers attempted to reach them they were promptly shot at by the Germans. To show the vitality possessed by some human beings, cases occurred of men being left out wounded and without food or drink four or five days, conscious all the time that if they moved the Germans would shoot or throw bombs at them. At night German raiding parties would be sent out to bayonet any of the wounded still living, and would feel these unfortunate men's hands to see if they were stiff and cold. If any doubt existed, the bayonet would settle the question. In spite of this, men often managed to crawl back just alive, and were quickly resuscitated by their comrades.'[43]

'Ten Grenadiers under a kid went across by night to the German Trench which they found largely deserted or waterlogged.... They fell upon a picket of Germans, beat the brains out of two of them with clubs and dragged a third home triumphantly as a prisoner. The young officer by accident let off his pistol & shot one of his own Grenadiers dead: but the others kept this secret and pretended it was done by the enemy – do likewise. The

scene in the little dugout when the prisoner was brought in surrounded by these terrific warriors, in jerkins and steel helmets with their bloody clubs in hand – looking pictures of ruthless war – was one to stay in the memory. *C'est tres bon.'*[44]

'We reached a section opposite Big Willie with orders for Number 1 Company to make a bombing attack on the Redoubt to regain chunks the Germans had taken from those preceding us. Before dawn the next morning we clambered over the parapet carrying in hands and pockets and sandbags an early type of Mills bomb about which we knew very little. Leaping into a crumbling concrete maze, in an instant we learned what war – at least this war – was about. Machine guns rattled, bullets were sprayed at us from both flanks and men fell like skittles in a bowling alley. On all sides grey caps bobbed up – the first Germans we had seen and only a few yards away. Hastily pulling out the pins of our bombs and ignoring the regulation five-second delay, we lobbed them inexpertly at the bobbing heads – too hastily, for back they came, blowing several men into lumps of bleeding flesh. Quickly learning the bitter lesson, we held our bombs seconds longer, whereupon from just around

[43] Ponsonby (1)
[44] Ball, quoting letter from Winston Churchill

166

the corner the Jerries hurled their own missiles, trying to bomb their way towards us, but one after another being knocked out or being buried alive by trench mortars fired from behind us. We had been living up to our title of Grenadiers – or dying messily if we were unlucky – and earning the right to wear the brass grenade as our cap badge. But it was a high price to pay.'[45]

Relief and Supply

'On a modern battlefield lines of wooden "duckboards" run like arteries across the trackless waste towards the front. Up the arteries flow fresh men, new blood, human forms complete; food to support life, ammunition to destroy it. Down the arteries flow ghosts of what yesterday were men, with tissues torn, and muscles rent; gibbering prisoners and men who have been spared to be shattered another day.'[46]

'It has now been raining for about twelve hours, the mud is beginning to get troublesome and the sides of the trenches to slip down. What with the mud and the rain and the constant shelling just in front of us, I don't think I have ever seen a more hopeless aspect. When it was dark, we all got into the trench and lined up in the order we were to lead into the front line. Each platoon had its own guide, who was to lead them to their own section of the trench. The water and rations for the day were very late in coming up, so that we had no time to let the men fill their water bottles but just gave them a petrol can to each section, which they had to take turns to carry.

'You may not know that all the water you get in the trenches is carried up in petrol cans, real petrol cans still tasting of that precious spirit. It is extraordinary how flavour clings to those cans, literally for weeks and months, and the result is that tea, coffee and cocoa have a flavour peculiar to themselves in the trenches.

'The men, exhausted by their toil up the hill, began to straggle, and getting a few yards to right or left lost touch, and then the wholesale dropping of the heavy water cans began. The zip of a few machine-gun bullets finished many of the inexperienced, who simply dropped in a heap and said, 'Me 'eart's broke' and refused to move. When we were close up to the front line we seemed to be clear of shells and with infinite trouble and great delay we collected the stragglers. My platoon was taken by the guide to the wrong piece of line, so we had to scramble

---

[45] Cliff
[46] Chapman

Tender care: a wounded man prepared for evacuation. The dangerous, lurching journey to a dressing station was usually more painful than the moment of being hit, and often long weeks and months of agony lay ahead.

along asking which was No 4 platoon (the one we had to relieve). We found it at last, in a very narrow and absolutely straight piece of trench about 150 yards to 200 long, with a dugout at one end. We were completely cut off from the rest of the company and our line had of course to be very thinly held.

'On going round the line I found both our Lewis guns had jammed, several of the men were absolutely exhausted, one badly hit in the stomach and what was worse no one had any water at all ... Further, many of the men had dropped their rations ... and the only thing that arrived intact was the rum ration, this of course for thirsty and hungry men was so strong that it went straight to their heads and made them drowsy.

'The dugout was beastly and smelt most terrible; it had the stale smell of filthy mud, peculiar to all dugouts, and a little extra special as well. I don't know for certain what it was, but as half a stale Boche fell out of the wall during the night, I might guess.'[47]

A Phlegmatic Attitude to Loss

'When his commanding officer [Wilfrid Abel Smith] was killed at Festubert, he [George Jeffreys] showed no emotion: "After seven months in the closest intimacy with a man whom he liked, you might have thought that that man's death by a bullet which passed though his own coat would have shaken him. Not at all".'[48]

'Three men crouched in a trench. Two were cooking; some conversation was in progress. The third man sat by their side and took no part. He seemed by his attitude to be thinking deeply, immersed in the solution to a problem. His face was turned away. The attitude was of puzzled thought. The Intelligence Officer made enquiries as to how they had fared. Two of the men looked up; they gave him a friendly smile and told him all they knew. The other sat with his head bent, still studying that inscrutable problem. The Intelligence Officer noticed with a start the colour of his ears, how wax-like in appearance; then he knew in a flash – the man was dead. His comrades did not even explain the fact. They seemed to realize that the figure by their side no longer counted, that there was nothing dreadful in the husk that sat there and still seemed one of them.'[49]

Undeterred from Duty

In March 1917 a shell fell among the King's Company, wounding CSM Bradbury and three sergeants. Bradbury, with both legs blown off, was being carried back on a stretcher and asked to speak to the Adjutant who, expecting from the dying man some personal request or last wish, bent down to hear it. 'You won't forget, sir,' said Bradbury, 'the battalion has to find a fatigue party of a hundred men tomorrow early.'[50]

Historic Rivalries Kept Alive

There was no reason to abandon the normal civilities of life. On one famous occasion two parties of the Guards Division met head-on in a dark and narrow communication trench. The following exchange took place between the conducting NCOs:

'Make way!'

'Make way!'

'Make way for Captain Sir Walter Barttelot, 2nd Battalion Coldstream Guards. Make way!'

'Make way for Major Lord Henry Seymour, 1st Battalion Grenadier Guards. That beats you on all counts. Make way!'

Out of the Line

To restore an impression of normality and re-assert standards, there were regular drill parades. This did not suit everyone. One complained, 'I would far rather be shelled for an hour than drilled for an hour'.[51]

'We have a parson attached to us now – a Cambridge don – who wanted to hold a service in our battalion mess room, but the walls have been so thickly papered with French pictures of naked women he had to confess the site inappropriate for any holy purpose.'[52]

'The next night we marched back to billets. We were very tired, and when we regained the road were marching at less than two miles an hour when a staff car nearly scattered my two rear ranks. I pretended I did not know that there was a senior officer inside and let fly with a good stream of oaths and abuse. A voice said, "I am Major Gathorne-Hardy" (a Grenadier[53]) "and from your language you must be from our 2nd Battalion." "Sir!" '

'The winter of 1916-17 was the coldest and bleakest that I ever remember. Even the back areas, where we rested in support, were a sea of mud, and even when resting we were under canvas. The horse lines at Carnoy

[47] Lawrence
[48] Chandos (2), Ball
[49] Chapman
[50] Ponsonby (1)
[51] Asquith
[52] Asquith
[53] Later General Sir Francis Gathorne-Hardy, an alarming officer who, when commanding at Aldershot after the war, was known as 'Stop me and buy one', after the ice-cream man

'For wounded – teacake free at any hour': so reads the notice beneath the Divisional Soldiers' Club sign. The Ever Open Eye of the Guards Division can be seen on the right.

were so deep in mud that 'horse-drawn sledges had to be used to get forage from the road to the horses'. It nearly always blew, and the razor-like wind brought scuds of snow through the camps, and set the canvas billowing and flapping with a noise like cannon-fire.'[54]

'The French people in the village are all old men and women, there seem to be no males above 17 or under 50. I live with the Mayor, who is very old and fat, and owns more cows, more dogs, a bigger house and a bigger muck heap in the centre of his yard and bigger stinks than anyone else in the village ... When your soldier relative comes home on leave he must not do any work, he must not sit in the house, he must dress himself up in full uniform and medals and walk slowly up and down the street in the mud in order that all the village may look at him. The village is proud of its soldiers and considers them common property.'[55]

[54] Chandos (1)
[55] Lawrence

Above left: In he goes: a rare moment of fun while out of harm's way.

Above right: Navvy work: road-building while out of the line.

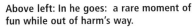

Living like a King: or at least like the Grenadier Prince of Wales (circled), about to sample field scoff. He persistently agitated to be sent into the trenches with a battalion, insisting that he had several spare brothers to take his place on the throne should he be killed, but it was not allowed.

The Somme Offensive 1916

From February to June 1916 the Germans launched massive attacks against the key French fortress of Verdun. In its defence the French sustained their greatest losses – 460,000 men. It therefore fell to the British to ease the pressure by launching a new offensive further north, on the Somme. This also was to prove one of the most painful episodes of the war. The battle lasted for four and a half months.

The German positions were extremely strong. 'First came a network of trenches, well provided with bomb–proof shelters and protected in front by wire entanglements, many of which were in two belts forty yards broad and built of iron stakes, interlaced with barbed wire, often as thick as a man's finger. Behind these lines the enemy's strongholds had been reinforced with every device of military ingenuity – woods and villages turned into fortresses, cellars filled with machine guns and trench mortars, dug-outs connected by elaborate passages ... the whole line was as nearly impregnable as Nature, art and the unstinted labour of close on two years could make it.'[56]

On 1 July, after a bombardment of seven days, the first divisions went over the top. By that evening they had suffered 60,000 casualties, 'the greatest loss and slaughter in the whole history of the British Army'.

The Guards Division, in XIV Corps under Lord Cavan, was in the Ypres Salient in July, but in August it moved south to take a turn on the Somme. As usual the **2nd Battalion** (Lt Col Claude de Crespigny) was in 1st Guards Brigade, the **3rd Battalion** (Lt Col Bertram Sergison-Brooke, later Lt Col Andrew Thorne) in 2nd Guards Brigade, and the **1st Battalion** (Lt Col Mark Makgill-Crichton-Maitland) and **4th Battalion** (Lt Col Lord Henry Seymour) together in 3rd Guards Brigade (now under a

---

[56] Ponsonby (1)

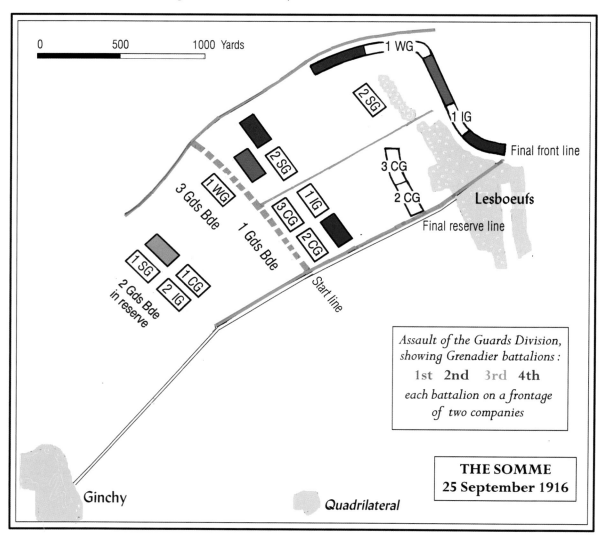

Assault of the Guards Division, showing Grenadier battalions:
1st 2nd 3rd 4th
each battalion on a frontage of two companies

THE SOMME
25 September 1916

Grenadier, Brig Gen Charles Corkran). Each brigade was supported by its own separate machine-gun company.

A little sharpening up was required: 'We are going to have battalion leap-frog to take the stiffness out of the men. The last few days marching after so much standing around in the trenches have left them all very stiff and weary, but the leap-frog should put them all right.'[57] Mobile communications, as usual, hardly existed, though carrier pigeons were used – with mixed success. One infantry brigade headquarters anxiously awaiting news at last received a pigeon and tore the message from its leg in a fever of anticipation. It read: 'I am absolutely fed up with carrying this bloody bird around France.'[58] It was not unknown for commanders to cut their own wire before a major attack in order to prevent interference from higher headquarters.

Ginchy – 15-16 September 1916

The first battle was fought at Ginchy, supported for the first time by that new invention, the tank.[59] There were just ten of them, their main purpose being to subdue enemy machine-gun fire. The start line having been cleared out by 3rd Guards Brigade by moonlight, the main attack, led by the 1st and 2nd Guards Brigades,[60] began at 0620 on 15 September behind a creeping barrage.

It was soon largely chaotic. The objective lines, neatly marked on the map, would have been hard enough to detect on that shattered ground on a peaceful summer day. In the noise and smoke and confusion it was almost impossible. The lines of assaulting troops, just as neatly marked, quickly became broken and detached, and easily lost direction where there was no firm feature to follow. Very soon it was a matter of small groups, under their officers and NCOs, tackling the enemy where they found him and pressing on, with great determination, against the obstacles, while protecting themselves as best they could against the withering machine-gun and artillery fire. Thus, eventually, the first two objectives were taken. 'I have only a blurred image of slaughter,' wrote a Grenadier, 'I saw about ten Germans writhing like trout in a creel at the bottom of a shell hole and our fellows firing at them from the hip. One or two red bayonets.'[61]

[57] Lindsay (Donald)
[58] Montgomery
[59] So named in development to preserve secrecy. Moved around under tarpaulins, these bulbous creatures appeared to be water or fuel tanks
[60] For the first time in their history, the three Coldstream battalions attacked together in line
[61] Chandos (2)

A fierce struggle on the Somme: No 3 Company of the 1st Battalion under Captain Napoleon Vaughan were in a very precarious position and almost surrounded, but held their trenches with rifles, Lewis guns and grenades, killing over 100 of the enemy and taking twenty prisoners. Vaughan won a DSO. Lance Sergeant T G Whitaker, who organized and led the bombing parties with great skill, won a DCM and promotion, but was killed only two weeks later.

But the divisions on the flanks failed to keep pace and the Guards were soon isolated, suffering particularly from the 'Quadrilateral' strongpoint. The tanks were late in appearing and little use when they did. On the second day the 3rd Guards Brigade took the third objective, but being by then totally unsupported had to pull back to the second, where the division suffered twenty-four hours of constant bombardment before being relieved.

Rest and Reinforcement

Ten days of respite followed, during which the battalions were reinforced by new drafts. At this point in the war these were more plentiful in the Guards than in other regiments and the men were well trained. By this time also it was the practice to leave out of battle enough experienced officers and senior ranks to absorb the new arrivals and prepare them quickly for the next operation.

Lesboeufs – 25 September 1916

The second major assault was made on Lesboeufs. This time the 1st and 3rd Guards Brigades took the lead. The 2nd Battalion was on the extreme right of the division and the 4th Battalion on the extreme left. It was necessary to cut through three lines of barbed wire in the

open and take the enemy trenches by bomb and bayonet. The advance then pushed on by way of a sunken road into the shattered village of Lesboeufs. The 1st Battalion moved through and captured the final objective. The Germans were seen withdrawing over open country, their line penetrated at last. It was one of the most successful attacks of the war, but once again circumstances beyond the control of the division limited the use made of it, and the offensive ground to a halt. The 3rd Battalion was in reserve and not engaged.

In the two battles the battalions each suffered between forty and fifty percent casualties and a higher proportion of officers.

A Nasty Fatigue

'On the 27th my company had the unpleasant job of burying the dead ... lying out in the open in front of Ginchy ... the weather was hot, and they had been lying out twelve days, and were almost all turned jet black: we buried that morning 200 men, rather more Germans than English: it was a nasty fatigue, and I won't dwell more on it.'[62]

Principal Sources: Ponsonby (1), Headlam

---

[62] Fryer

Hazebrouck, April 1918 – Backs to the Wall

The Ludendorff offensive of 1918 had been prepared for several months. The tactics were based on a study of the successes and failures of the antagonists over the previous years. A great concentrated artillery barrage was followed by a creeping barrage behind which lightly armed storm troopers would advance, using every opportunity to penetrate the line and isolate parts that resisted for the later attention of orthodox infantry. The most threatening thrust on the north of the allied line came on 9 April, down the valley of the River Lys. It broke into the line at Armentières, south of Ypres, and penetrated as far as Merville, fifteen miles south-east of Hazebrouck, where the Germans paused to sample the delights of the massive quartermasters' stores. North of Merville a gap developed, opening the way to Hazebrouck itself and thence to the sea. An Australian division, being moved up by train to fill it, was some days away.

The only formation immediately available to help was the new 4th Guards Brigade, containing the **4th Grenadiers** (Lt Col William Pilcher), the 3rd Coldstream and 2nd Irish Guards.[63] These battalions were in billets at Tinques, some twenty miles to the south-west. Buses were arranged to take them to the front, but they were some twelve hours late and the night of 10/11 April was spent waiting by the roadside. Then for twelve hours, terribly cramped and with no opportunity for real rest, they jolted along roads crowded with refugees and retreating troops. They were ordered to hold a position between the two main roads that head north from Merville. The country was perfectly flat, with no natural defensive features other than a few farm buildings.

'Fight On to the End'

It was on 11 April that Field Marshal Haig issued his dramatic Order of the Day: 'To All Ranks of the British Army in France.... There is no course open to us but to fight it out.... With our backs to the wall and believing in the justice of our cause, each one of us must fight on to the end.'

On the morning of 12 April 4th Guards Brigade was ordered to move forward from a temporary position. It ran into heavy opposition, though No 2 Company under Capt Pryce made good headway by the use of skilful

tactics. The battalion was then heavily battered by repeated assaults, though the enemy suffered even more: in some places heaps of bodies were piled up in front of the trenches. But it was necessary to take up a new line. The remaining men, already exhausted after two nights without sleep, took all the night of 12/13 April to achieve this. Numbers were now so reduced that the frontage was only about one man for ten yards, in the form of a series of pits each containing four or five men and in many cases separated from each other by a considerable distance. Ammunition was short and that brought up with difficulty. The Grenadiers and Coldstream were in the front line, supported by the Irish and, rather further back, by the Australians, who now were beginning to arrive. The 12th King's Own Yorkshire Light Infantry had also been allotted to the brigade and took up positions to the north of La Couronne, on the left of the Grenadiers. The brigade was virtually the only fighting force in position between the Germans and the sea.

---

[63] Commanded by Harold Alexander, later to be a field marshal

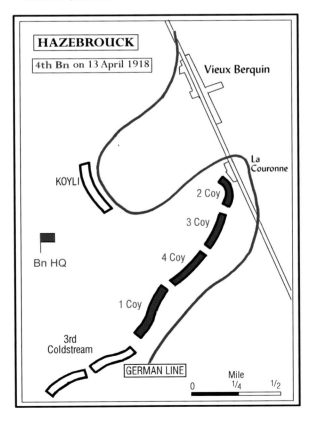

173

CAPTAIN
THOMAS PRYCE VC
MC and Bar *1886-1918*

Victoria Cross of the
4th Battalion at
Hazebrouck, already
twice winner of the
Military Cross

Thomas Tannatt Pryce was commissioned into the Gloucestershire Regiment in October 1915. He won his first Military Cross for his leadership of a highly successful trench raid in November, and the Bar for commanding the leading platoon in one of the earliest assaults on the Somme in July 1916. Shortly afterwards he transferred to the Grenadiers and joined the 4th Battalion.

He won a posthumous Victoria Cross for his leading part in the desperate defence at La Couronne, in front of Hazebrouck, on 11 April 1918. Having already been in heavy fighting, his company was reduced to thirty or forty men. His left flank was surrounded, but four times they beat off the enemy, who were supported by three field guns firing at close range over open sights. By the evening they were down to eighteen men and every round of ammunition had been fired. The enemy were baffled by the strength of opposition and supposed the numbers to be much greater. Seeing a new attack being prepared, Pryce led his small party in a fierce bayonet charge which took the Germans completely aback. They did not fire for fear of hitting their own men, now in rear of the Grenadier position, and retired. Pryce took his men back to their trenches, but the weakness of his force had now been exposed and the Germans made another attempt. Once more the Grenadiers charged. They were last seen in a fierce hand-to-hand struggle with great numbers of enemy.

This small force had held up a full battalion and had thus delayed the advance of an entire division. It undoubtedly stopped the penetration of the British line at the most crucial point of the battle, which, if lost, could well have altered the course of the war itself. The army commander wrote, 'There was no finer stand made in the history of the British Army'.

Under cover of the morning fog on 13 April the Germans worked machine guns up close to the front line. Continuous attacks were made on the line all morning, but were repulsed. Such was the enemy frustration that they brought up field guns to fire at short range over open sights. The KOYLI threw back four attacks before being literally blown out of their trenches and forced back through Vieux Berquin. Lt Col Alexander sent forward a company of the 2nd Irish to cover the Grenadiers, thus exposed, but they were caught in the open and only six of them returned. The remains of No 2 Company, under Capt Pryce, were in the most forward position, where they were eventually cut off and their fate sealed. Only one man returned.

But the crucial delay had allowed the Australians to take up their position. Thus the army, even possibly the war itself, was saved. The Germans, who had launched 106 divisions and 6000 guns against the British armies, did not get through. The offensive had run out of steam.

It was, however, the end of the brigade as a fighting force. The 4th Battalion, which had started in a depleted state, less than 600 strong, lost 519. There was no more heroic fighting by Grenadiers in the whole war.

Principal Sources: Ponsonby (1), Headlam, Blades

Leader of Hazebrouck: it fell to 'Pilch' Pilcher to command the 4th Battalion in one of the most critical moments of the war.

THE SERGEANT MAJOR

The Regimental Sergeant Major is by definition a formidable figure, the senior soldier of a battalion. Like a good father he is always ready to discipline and correct his military family, but also (though it may not be so obvious to his NCOs and guardsmen) he takes pride in them and defends their interests. In the Foot Guards he is always known as the 'Sergeant Major', never the 'RSM' as elsewhere in the Army. He is addressed by the officers as 'Sarnt Major', not 'Mister', and nobody else ever fails to call him 'Sir', while standing very strictly to attention. In the field he is in charge of the security of battalion headquarters and often also sees to the supply of ammunition.

A hard high collar: a sergeant major of the early Victorian era. The superimposing of the Royal Arms on the four chevrons, the 'big badge', appears to date from about 1830. *Late 19th century British school*

In the 16th century the full title of the Serjeant Major was in fact Serjeant Major General, one of the highest ranking officers of the Army. It was later applied to the 'major' of each regiment, and a warrant signed by Charles II in Brussels in 1660 was addressed to Colonel Wheeler as 'Serjeant-Major of our Regiment of Guards'.

One of the first references to a non-commissioned sergeant major can be found in a letter of 1724. Although the senior sergeant of the battalion, and ranking as a colour sergeant, his role was relatively modest. In 1777 he was described as:

'a person who has discovered an early genius of discipline ... ready at his pen, and expert at making out details and rosters etc.'[1]

Pacestick and sword: Sergeant Major Richard Dorney at Wellington Barracks. *Sean Bolan*

He had indeed to be literate – by no means a universal military accomplishment, even well into the twentieth century. A sergeant major of a Line regiment recorded how his clerical skills saw him promoted to this elevated rank, which brought him in close contact with the whole of 'the epaulet gentry, whose profound and surprising ignorance I discovered in a twinkling'.[2]

Sergeant majors (together with quartermaster sergeants and armourer sergeants) were established in the First Foot Guards in 1802, wearing a distinctive badge of four chevrons. However, it was not until 1859, after the Crimean War, that they were firmly shown in the dominant role that has since been most characteristic of them. They were made warrant officers in 1881 and in 1915 the Sergeant Major became Warrant Officer Class 1.

It is thus only since late Victorian times that the archetypal sergeant major, of fierce expression, short temper and booming voice, is fully recognizable, his reputation coloured by the experience of countless conscripts who passed under his eye during the two world wars and the subsequent years of National Service. In 1929 proposals were made for *Brightening the Army*. Under *Fewer and*

---

[1] Alford (2)
[2] Holmes

Three great sergeant majors (from left): It was said that Arthur Brand MVO MBE was never seen to smile, but he made an indelible impression on legions of wartime officer cadets passing through the officer cadet training unit at Sandhurst; Tom Taylor MVO MBE was for twelve years Garrison Sergeant Major at Horse Guards and expert in major ceremonial events; over ten years as Academy Sergeant Major, Ray Huggins MBE also attained great distinction at Sandhurst, a fine training ground for warrant officers as well as officer cadets.

Friendlier Sergeant Majors it was suggested that the proportion of these gentlemen to a battalion was altogether too high and that they should attend a special school of instruction where they would be taught to break into a quick smile, both by numbers and judging the time.[3] The proposition fell on deaf ears, of course, but in fact this reputation was often undeserved. Many found that it was more often the Drill Sergeant who showed no compassion to guardsmen, NCOs or ensigns – until he was promoted to Sergeant Major, at which point he would again revert to being a human being.

The Sergeant Major comes in a number of variations: the Band Sergeant Major, the Garrison Sergeant Major at Horse Guards, the Superintending Clerk at Regimental Headquarters (in former years), and, at the RMA Sandhurst, College Sergeant Majors and the Academy Sergeant Major, the senior of his kind in the Army. More often than not these senior warrant officers are later commissioned.

[3] *Household Brigade Magazine*, Autumn 1929

On Horse Guards Parade: the Sergeant Major takes the Colour from the colour party before delivering it to the Ensign to be trooped. It is the only occasion on which he draws his sword on parade. *Christopher Collins*

A double-breasted tunic with easier collar: the model of tunic worn by this sergeant major of 1856 lasted only a single year before being changed to the familiar single-breasted style. He is also the possessor of a very fine bearskin cap.

Chapter Nine

A SHORT INTERMISSION
1919-1939

The First World War had been 'the war to end all wars'. Nobody could have imagined that it was only the first half of a match that would resume a mere twenty years later. The Prime Minister, David Lloyd George, had promised his soldiers a 'home fit for heroes', but the reality was very different. Despite the lure of the jazz age and a frenetic indulgence in entertainment, the postwar years were grim ones for the country, with high unemployment and industrial unrest. They saw the General Strike of 1926 and the Wall Street crash. The Welfare State was still thirty years away and unemployment meant serious hardship.

For the military the immediate result of returning to peacetime conditions was that familiar after any major war: reduction, retrenchment and an attempt to return to former ways of soldiering. The extra wartime battalions of Foot Guards, including the 4th Grenadiers, were disbanded and there was even a proposal to abolish the Irish and Welsh Guards, the Welsh to be reduced to a single company absorbed into a Grenadier battalion (the reorganizations and reductions of the twentieth and early twenty-first centuries were nothing new). In the event, and in response to a loud outcry, these measures were not pursued and the Grenadiers returned to their historic establishment of three battalions and, for the most part, to their previous round of stations in England. The wartime Guards brigades were disbanded (though reconstituted for service in Turkey and Egypt) and the battalions of Foot Guards returned to the general oversight of HQ Brigade of Guards.

There was a six-month coal strike in 1921, when reservists were actually called up to bring battalions up to strength, installations had to be protected and men stood by in case of trouble. The General Strike of 1926 was more serious and prolonged, and they were similarly employed, particularly in protecting the docks and carrying out convoy duties. The north-east part of London came under the command of the Lieutenant Colonel, operating from Hackney police station.

Ceremonial duties continued as before. Home service clothing was back in general use in February 1921 and in July King George V presented new Colours to all battalions of the Brigade of Guards. In 1924 Regimental Headquarters moved from Buckingham Gate to Wellington Barracks, where, with an interval of exile in the late 1970s and early 1980s when the barracks were rebuilt, it has been ever since.

The death and funeral of George V in January 1936 and the proclamation of his successor Edward VIII were followed by the drama of the new king's abdication in

Impressions of the Trooping 1920: an unusual black and white study. No doubt Winston Churchill recalls his time with the Grenadiers as he doffs his hat.

Horse-drawn cookers on manoeuvres: still too early for mechanical transport in 1926.

Helmets in Hyde Park: guardsmen move out during the General Strike of 1926.

Wiring a bus: a Grenadier with fixed bayonet stands by while a bus is protected against boarders.

Veteran sergeant: khaki with white pouches for a gold sergeant in 1922 as men in guard order are inspected behind him.
Christopher Morley

December, the proclamation and subsequent coronation of George VI. The two battalions of the Regiment serving at home were closely concerned in the accompanying ceremonial.

A regular event was the Royal Tournament at Olympia. In 1920 the King's Company, with the Corps of Drums, performed as a grenadier company of the First Guards in

1793. To taps of the drum they performed with firelocks of the day 'a mere forty motions – twenty-one to load and nineteen to fire' where they 'considerably frightened most of the audience. Unfortunately, the authorities would not allow all the firelocks to be discharged at once, for fear of bringing the glass out of the roof on to the heads of spectators, if the explosion was too big. Hence only a few were loaded for each performance; this somewhat detracted from the general effect. The only accidents recorded were a man in the audience who received a wad in his face, and a performer who sat on his own bayonet.'[1]

There were some changes in battalion organization, a headquarter company and a Vickers machine-gun platoon being established in 1920 and a machine-gun company in 1928.

The Frustrations of Home Service

The service chiefs had been told in 1919 that there was no need to plan for a major war for at least ten years. This 'ten-year rule' was extended annually until as late as 1932, so major improvements were impossible to achieve. Economy dominated and in the financial crisis of 1931 pay was actually reduced. Everything was lacking in quality and quantity: equipment, ammunition and transport. There was barely enough ammunition for range work, though shooting was taken very seriously and a good shot was rewarded by higher pay. There was very little blank. Machine guns were represented by wooden rattles, anti-tank guns by green and white flags,

---

[1] *Household Brigade Magazine*, February 1921

Stand Easy: an interpretation by Bateman in 1926. The tiny figure on the gate is the only one unable to avail himself of the respite.

Marching and shooting: a platoon competing in the Evelyn Wood competition in 1928.

Early acquaintance: a fuzzy photograph of the young Princess Elizabeth acknowledging a salute at Windsor.

Under a Nazi flag: a bizarre episode in 1936 when Grenadiers bore the coffin of the German ambassador. The onlookers above join in with Nazi salutes.

and tanks by trucks marked with a large 'T' or by bicycles carrying cardboard outlines. From 1936 there were a few, very necessary, improvements in the form of the Bren light machine gun and the 3-inch mortar. It was not until 1938, when war was perilously close, that even units of the expeditionary force were given motor transport to replace their horses and radio began to arrive in the company headquarters. Even then 'during one exercise Sid [Dowland]'s company was actually charged by a troop of the Household Cavalry complete with snorting horses and drawn sabres. The whole episode was reminiscent of Waterloo and the guardsmen thought it was ridiculous. There was unfortunately one casualty during the manoeuvres when a guardsman was hit on the head by a wooden 3-inch mortar. The poor fellow was never allowed to forget the incident.'[2]

And all this even from the late 1930s, when it became evident that the Nazis had clear ambitions on their neighbours and that Germany was rearming on an alarming scale. Despite the restrictions on weapons and troop numbers imposed on them by the victors of 1918, the Germans had found ingenious ways round. They were said to have designed a pram which, however assembled, always came out as a machine gun.

The whole pace of life, not least of promotion, slowed to a walk. In days of widespread unemployment nothing was so important as security in a job. The main beneficiaries were quartermasters and sergeant majors. It

A recruit's view (left to right): 'Sgt xxx showing 'em how at Caterham. The first man I saw in Chelsea Barracks – Gdsm Browndoff in elegant canvas. My first impression of the Guards scarlet.'

is extraordinary to think that the 3rd Battalion had only two quartermasters in twenty-four years. George Wall filled the post for thirteen years from 1915 to 1928 and his successor Randolph Beard for eleven, having already served seven as Sergeant Major. Frank Speller was Quartermaster of the 1st Battalion for twelve years.[3] Five years was a modest term for both quartermasters and sergeant majors, and this of course put a heavy brake on promotion.

---

[2] Dorney
[3] By the rigid social rule of the day none of these, of course, qualified for membership of the First Guards Club (the dining club for 'proper' officers), which was not opened until much later to those commissioned from the ranks, however long and glittering their service

Greatcoat and cape: the correct folding of these articles for parade required patience, skill and considerable violence. Nimble-fingered drummers were often expert at it and their services could command fat fees from ham-fisted guardsmen. Here a company is inspected by King Edward VIII in 1936, during his short-lived reign. He is followed by the Duke of Connaught.

LIEUTENANT GENERAL

BERNARD, Lord FREYBERG VC

GCMG KCB KBE DSO and 2 Bars MC *1889-1963*

Valiant New Zealander who was chased by the Drill Sergeant and almost swam the Channel

ernard Freyberg was a New Zealander who won great renown in the First World War. At Gallipoli he won his first DSO in the Dardanelles, swimming ashore alone at night to light distracting flares. On the Western Front he added two bars to the decoration (the second in the last five minutes of the war), the Military Cross, and in December 1917 the Victoria Cross for his gallant leadership of the Hood Battalion (Royal Naval Division) on the Somme. He was said to bear on his body some thirty scars and gashes from his numerous wounds.

Becoming a Grenadier after the war, he appeared at the Tower of London, to be put at once on the square. Even the Drill Sergeant might have been a little overawed at the prospect of chasing about this highly decorated brevet lieutenant colonel of twenty-nine, though his student readily admitted that drill was not his strong point.

He quickly moved on to the Staff College and thence to duty with the 1st Battalion. Here he made his name on exercise at Pirbright, defeating the umpires and staff of London District by leading his advance guard along the railway line and through the tunnel under Emperor's Hill, thereby taking the enemy in rear and ruining the carefully planned scheme of the Major General. Trains rushing by in the darkness inches from the face held no terrors for Bernard Freyberg. In August 1925, wounds and all, he tried to swim the Channel but failed to beat the turn of the tide by a mere 500 yards.

In the Second World War his fighting reputation was further enhanced and he was again wounded. He became Commander-in-Chief of the New Zealand forces and after the war Governor General of his native country.

See Freyberg

Sir FREDERICK BURROWS

GCSI GCIE *1887-1973*

Railwayman, Quartermaster Sergeant, Trade Unionist, Governor of Bengal

rederick Burrows was born in Bollow, Westbury-on-Severn, Gloucestershire, and became a railway porter at Ross-on-Wye and then a goods checker at the wayside halt of Backney. A large, fine-looking man, he enlisted in the Grenadiers on a three-year engagement and then spent nine further years on the reserve. Called up for the First World War, he was for three years almost continually with the 4th Battalion, rising to the rank of company sergeant major. Towards the end of the war he was appointed RQMS of the 1st Battalion.

He returned to the railway at Ross and for sixteen years was secretary of the local branch of the National Union of Railworkers. In 1938 he was elected to the executive and three years later became president of the union. Once his term was up he would have returned to checking beet into the trucks at Backney, but he had caught the eye of Winston Churchill (himself a Grenadier for a short time), who was impressed by his tact, moderation and the good sense he showed in pay negotiations.

After the war Clement Attlee became Prime Minister. He also had admired Burrows's work and before he knew where he was this 'former parcels clerk' had been appointed Governor of Bengal at a time of acute racial tension when the partition of India and Pakistan was imminent. Burrows cheerfully recognized how widely his background differed from that of other exalted servants of the Empire by telling them that when they were *huntin' and shootin'* he had been *shuntin' and hootin'*.

The job was no easy one. The aftermath of inter-racial violence on the streets reminded him of the Somme. But his straight and sensible dealing won the confidence of both the Hindu and Muslim leaders and the two viceroys, Wavell and Mountbatten, and he returned to his little cottage at Ross covered in honour.

Lining the route: a smartly attired guardsman stands out (even in black and white) in a khaki crowd before the coronation of George VI in 1937.

The Officer's Life

Nor were the regimental officers unaffected. Periods of command were very seldom less than four years and promotion within any regiment depended, as in the old days, on vacancies arising. The regiments of Guards were in fact comparatively fortunate because many officers had private means[4] and an occupation to go to – tending the family acres or the family business – and the turnover was distinctly higher than in regiments of the Line. There it was not uncommon to find gnarled old subalterns well into their thirties, anxiously waiting for an even older captain to suffer a nasty disease or a fatal accident – or perhaps to expire from sheer ennui.[5]

The life of officers of the Guards was not so very far removed from that led by their Victorian fathers. Certainly the Adjutant had to work, and was paid extra for it, but for most of the others the military life was humdrum, idle, undemanding – and highly enjoyable. Their energies were largely consumed in the company of brother officers, hunting, shooting and fishing, and enjoying a variety of clubs supplied for their amusement. Quite apart from the familiar cricket and golf, the Household Brigade had the Yacht Club, the Boat Club (at Maidenhead) and even the Flying Club, in which many incipient pilots won their licenses. All these could easily be reached by rail from London, Windsor or Aldershot. Not every officer, by any means, owned a car and if investing in one was advised to choose a model tall enough to accommodate a top hat. Dress remained very

formal and a white tie and tail coat were still required for the opera.

Opportunities to develop in the military art, or even to exercise in the field with any hint of realism, were woefully short. Adventurous training was still far in the future and it was hard for a young officer to get to know his men in any but the most formal circumstances of public duties. By the same token such tactical training as there was gave NCOs no real scope for testing and developing powers of leadership.

For what it was worth, in those bleak years, Grenadiers were prominent in high places. Both the Earl of Cavan and Viscount Gort VC became field marshals at the head of the Army. Several wartime commanding officers reached general rank, Corkran, Jeffreys and Sergison-Brooke all becoming the Major General at Horse Guards. Sir Charles Fergusson, Sir Francis Davies, Sir George Jeffreys and Sir Francis Gathorne-Hardy became full generals and Sir Sidney Clive a lieutenant general.

The Guardsman's Viewpoint

The guardsmen, on limited engagements, hung on grimly to their jobs and hoped for an extension. Gdsm J I Burke, of the 3rd Battalion, spoke for many when he wrote:

---

[4] That said, the expense of ordinary mess life was often less than that in other regiments, especially the cavalry. An officer's expenditure was largely in his own hands and not dictated by extravagant formalities

[5] Field Marshal Sir Francis Festing, a Rifleman and father of two Grenadiers, was still a subaltern at thirty-three. Hostilities coming to his assistance, however, he was commanding a division in Burma only a few years later

Home call: Queen Elizabeth visits the married quarter of Sergeant Major Fred Turner, whose children are well lined up and sized, but not quite all standing to attention.

Olympic Gold: David Cecil, Lord Burghley, later to be Marquess of Exeter, won the 400 metres hurdles in the 1928 Olympics in Amsterdam. He was a Grenadier from 1927 to 1929.

On his bike: a fine study of Guardsman Wakefield of the 1st Battalion in 1938. *Lance Cattermole*

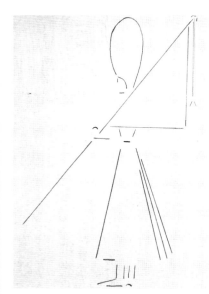

Economical ensign: a wonderfully effective drawing of an ensign in greatcoat order carrying his Colour. *Colette Cregan*

A sprained ankle? Lance Sergeant Henderson will sort you out. *Lance Cattermole*

'I joined His Majesty's Army for exactly the same reason that others join – because I was out of employment and "fed up" with eating the food that other members of the family were paying for.... For eighteen long weeks I was "put through" it, but I do admit that when I left the Depot I felt healthier and happier than I had done for a long time. Army training is thorough, perhaps hard, on some learners, but everyone starts at the bottom here, just as a civilian has to in his job. There is nothing unreasonable expected and nobody is expected to do anything beyond their ability. But the Army way of doing a job is to do it thoroughly, and that is how men are taught.... I joined my battalion, and in time made many friends and, I admit, many mistakes. As time went on I realized that all I had to do was what I was told, and in doing so I made good headway. In November of 1933 I went to Egypt – something that I would never have done if I had not enlisted. I liked my life out there very much and saw for myself the places that I had only heard about when I was at school.

My health was and is very good. The Army has given me a cheerful outlook on life that was missing when I was unemployed. A soldier knows that every Friday will see him with some money to spend. He knows that his meals are regular and that his bed is always comfortable. He can make friends, and good friends too. Such things as dances, books, entertainments and all forms of amusement are provided. The facilities for every kind of sport are a living part of the Army. How do those attractions compare with the prospects of those men who know no home but public parks or the Embankment?'[6]

Records from the Diaries

The First Guards Club handbooks of the time give some flavour of a life largely devoted to drill, sport and chores:

30 April 1923. From this date troops of the Brigade of Guards in London and Windsor wear Home Service Clothing[7] on all occasions when walking out.

16 October 1926. HRH the Colonel unveiled the Guards Division Memorial [on Horse Guards]. 2,400 old Grenadiers attended, and marched from Chelsea Barracks. 1,565 of them were entertained to dinner after the ceremony.

2 May 1927. The 3rd Battalion moved from the Tower to Chelsea Barracks, and exercised *en route* the privilege of the Regiment[8] to march through the City with fixed bayonets, beating drums and flying Colours. The Band of the Regiment accompanied the Battalion.

24 January 1928. The Lieutenant Colonel inspected the 1st Battalion in winter training.

31 January 1928. The Guards Sub-Depot at Warley closed and the Guards Depot temporarily transferred to Canterbury.

1 March 1928. Reorganization of Battalions into three Rifle Companies and one Machine Gun Company effected this day.

31 October 1928. Household Brigade Swimming Championships at St George's Baths... The 1st Battalion won the Tug-of-War... The 2nd Battalion was second in the Sergeants' Race... Lieut-Colonel Freyberg won the Plunging.

22 April 1929. In the Limber Driving and 30 Yards Range Competition, held at the Small Arms School, Netheravon, open to any number per unit of four-horsed limbers, three teams entered from the 2nd Battalion. No 1 Team was 1st; No 2 Team was 2nd; No 3 Team missed third place by one point.

16 May 1929. To commemorate his 35th anniversary as Colonel of the Regiment, Field Marshal His Royal Highness the Duke of Connaught and Strathearn, KG etc, inspected the three Battalions of the Regiment on Horse Guards Parade.

11 September 1929. The 1st Battalion Football XI defeated Slough Postal District by 3 goals to 1.

13 November 1929. The 3rd Battalion defeated Chelmsford Wednesday in a football match by 8 goals to 1.

6 March 1930. The height standard for the Regiment was decreased from 5 ft 11 ins to 5 ft 10 ins, with a view to increasing the influx of recruits.[9]

23 July 1930. At the Household Brigade Regatta held at Maidenhead [competitions for Battalion Fours, Double Punting, Double Sculling, Double Canadian Canoe Race, Single Punting Handicap, Single Punting, and Punting Race]. The Regiment thus won every race except the Double Sculling, in which they secured 2nd and 3rd places.

25 August 1930. The 1st Battalion commenced divisional training. Two exercises were held. During the second

---

[6] *Household Brigade Magazine*, Spring 1937
[7] Scarlet tunic, though with a forage cap rather than bearskin when walking out
[8] Formerly a privilege of the 3rd Battalion alone, it was extended to the whole regiment in October 1915
[9] This in spite of the *Household Brigade Magazine* of February 1921, which had observed, 'For some time past we have advocated an increase in the standard of height for recruits. Our case is somewhat strengthened by a recent occurrence when the Sergeant of the Guard mislaid one of the Guard, and after a protracted search found the little fellow, fast asleep, curled up inside a ration tin'

Leaving with relief: the 2nd Battalion march out after a less than enjoyable time in Constantinople.

exercise the order of dress was Service dress, shirt sleeves. Sun blinds were worn. The temperature on the second day reached 94° in the shade.

11 September 1931. The War Office issued a letter, on the grounds of economy restricting recruiting for the Regiment to six recruits per week until 31st March 1932. The Mess Allowance for the King's Guard was reduced from £2,500 to £1,100 by Army Order 163.

21 September 1931. A Conference on Economy was held by the Lieutenant Colonels of the Brigade.

1 August 1932. The Memorial to the Missing on the Somme during the Great War, 1914-1918, erected at Thiepval, was unveiled by HRH the Prince of Wales. This memorial bears the names of 568 Grenadiers.

18 January 1933. The 2nd Battalion Bayonet fencing team defeated the 2nd Bn London Regiment by 10 fights to 6.

2 February 1933. The boys of the 1st Battalion won the Household Brigade Enlisted Boys Boxing Championships. The boys of the 2nd Battalion were second.

27 June 1934. The Cecil Outing took place in the form of a trip to Worthing by rail; 25 adults and 27 children attended.

Constantinople 1922-23 – Not to be Repeated

Turkey, having sided with Germany during the war, was subject to peace terms which included occupation of part of the country. An international force, of British, Italian and French troops, was stationed around Constantinople (since named Istanbul) to be ready to intervene between Turks and Greeks at Chanak nearby. By September 1922 1st Guards Brigade, including the

2nd Battalion (Lt Col Hon Edward Colston)[10] was present in the city. An incipient crisis blew over and the battalion settled into the normal life of an overseas garrison before returning home in October 1923.

There was little for the Grenadiers to record other than the novelty of a Middle Eastern country, last visited by their ancestors on the way to untold horrors in the Crimea. In days when few travelled outside their own country widely or often, the novelty was considerable – though not always welcome. The citizens and the soldiers annoyed each other by their different habits. QMS H Allitt complained of the night watchman, who 'combines with his duties the post of town crier, and taps the drum instead of ringing a bell to draw the attention of the faithful during Ramazan.[11] He acquaints the native population when there is a fire, assists in calling up the reserves for the Army, and makes himself a d---- nuisance when you want to go to sleep'.[12] The Turks were equally put out: 'Communication received by the OC --- Battalion --- Guards: "The residents near the Barracks would be much obliged if you would stop such frequent use of the bugle, as it is very disturbing for many who wish to rest in the early part of the morning."'[13]

The international force left the city in October 1923, with some ceremony, without any trouble and to the relief of all parties. And once they were safely out of the way the radical papers made the most of it. 'Tashkishla

---

[10] Later Lord Roundway
[11] Ramadan
[12] *Household Brigade Magazine*, Winter 1922/23
[13] *Household Brigade Magazine*, Winter 1922/23

Barracks were handed over to the Turkish authorities in a very dirty and deteriorated state', complained one of them. It was felt to be a particularly insulting remark from such as them, who had never been known to win prizes for cleanliness, to such as Grenadiers.

It was left to a Coldstreamer to write the last word, which surely would have been echoed by his comrades of the 2nd Grenadiers:

So if when I die I'm sent for a spell
To some place where stained souls are made clean
and well,
Pray to Peter and Mary to send me to Hell,
But not back to Constantinople.[14]

Egypt – Cairo and Alexandria (Map page 271)

Between 1928 and 1939 Cairo and Alexandria became regular stations for Guards battalions in the resident Guards brigade and all three Grenadier battalions took their turn: the **1st Battalion** (Lt Col Jack Hughes) from November 1930 to November 1932, the **3rd Battalion** (Lt Col William Pilcher and later Lt Col Charles Britten) from November 1933 to March 1936, and the **2nd Battalion** (Lt Col Frederick Browning) from March 1936 to December 1937. They took their families with them and later received considerable drafts from other battalions to replace men discharged to the reserve.

Kasr-el-Nil (Nile Barracks) in Cairo was one of the barracks. 'These bug-ridden odiferous buildings had long since been condemned as unfit for human habitation, but they had to be occupied nevertheless. Each successive battalion, having battled with flies, lice, shite-hawks, heat and hopeless hygiene, tried to leave the crumbling place slightly better than they found it.'[15] The work consisted of guards, normal training and some large-scale exercises. A King's Birthday Parade was held each year. The diaries record:

15 November 1930. The 1st Battalion embarked in the HT *Somersetshire* at Southampton. ... Approximately 150 officers and other ranks of the Regiment, both past and present, journeyed to Southampton to see the Battalion depart. The Band of the Regiment played selections of music until the ship sailed. The War Office refused railway warrants for the Band. The journey was therefore paid out of regimental funds.

3 February 1931. The 1st Battalion was inspected at Cairo by Brigadier WGS Dobbie CB CMG DSO.[16]

31 March 1931. Fifteen men who had previously served in the Regiment (5 in each battalion) and are now members

---

[14] *Household Brigade Magazine*, Autumn 1923
[15] Paget
[16] Like Gordon of Khartoum Sir William Dobbie, as he became, was a Sapper general who fought with a sword in one hand and a bible in the other. He had already put down disturbances in Palestine, though they said he would never have time to impose a lasting solution: 'the Arabs won't fight on Friday, or the Jews on Saturday, or Dobbie on Sunday.' Later he led the heroic defence of Malta before being succeeded by the Grenadier Lord Gort VC, who brought with him the George Cross awarded to the gallant island

Under the pyramids: the 1st Battalion in camp.

Testing the gradient: by 1936, even in Egypt, vehicles were becoming more plentiful.

Fit to serve a pharaoh:
Corporal Spragg in
immaculate order.
Lance Cattermole

CPL. E. SPRAGG.
3ʀᴅ BN. GRENADIER GUARDS
1953

Desert halt: time for refreshment.

of the Palestine Police, recently dined with the Officers of the 1st Battalion in Jerusalem. [The Guards battalion in Cairo made an annual visit to Palestine. There were several sporting events and sight-seeing, while the Palestine Police fished for recruits.]

31 July 1931. The 1st Battalion held an Angling Competition in barracks at selected points along the River Nile... The result of the competition was judged by weight and much amusement was caused when No 3 Company caught 26 fish and were beaten by No 2 (MG) Company, who caught only 3 fish and 2 eels.

30 July 1932. The King's Company practised emplaning in Vickers Victoria bombing machines at No 216 Squadron, RAF, Heliopolis.

26 August 1932. Brigadier JC Browne, CMG, DSO, in presenting the prizes (five cups and fifty-one medals) stated that the 1st Battalion had exploded the myth which said that no unit stationed in Egypt could possibly win the Command Swimming Championship until after their second year in the country.

14 April 1934. The 3rd Battalion furnished a guard of honour ... on the occasion of the departure of the GOC British Troops in Egypt... An escort of one warrant officer and three other ranks accompanied him to Port Said.

30 May 1934. No 2 Company, 3rd Battalion, carried out a practice run with the Armoured Train stationed at Kasr-el-Nil Barracks.

December 1934. Their [the new draft] first experience was to proceed to Mena Camp for Battalion training. ... Although the schemes are varied, how we miss the barns, the hedges and the roads, and sigh for the Chobham Ridges. There are ridges on the desert and some hills have familiar English names, but only distance counts here. It is unfortunate for a company if the cooker gets lost in the darkness. ... A couple of sandstorms played havoc with the camp, and a touch of food poisoning played havoc with members of the Sergeants' Mess and caused a lot of trouble but had no serious results... Whilst at camp a Gymkhana was held on 15th December in the shadow of the Pyramids [there were races for horses, camels, mules and donkeys] ... The starter also had to act as shepherd to the wayward camels

Smartly dressed for Egypt: a gold sergeant well fitted out for the heat. *Pierre Turner (from 'British Infantry Uniforms Since 1660' by Michael Barthorp – Orion Publishing Group)*

and a GS wagon made a good substitute for the Royal Box.

Summer 1936. Training proceeds on pretty much the same lines as in England, though under different conditions. Individual training is well ahead; three Companies and a recruit party have already visited our local Pirbright Camp for musketry. This Camp, situated on the edge of the desert, about twelve miles from our barracks, lays alongside an Egyptian Army Barracks[17], whose range we use, and differs largely from Pirbright in the complete absence of rain.

Winter 1936. At the invitation of the High Commissioner, Drum Major Tankard was asked to blow a trumpet which had been recovered from Tut-ank-Amen's tomb and which was over 3,000 years old. The trumpet was a straight pipe 2 ft 6 ins long, opened out at one end and with a narrow mouthpiece. The Governor of the Museum said that the result was the best effort he had heard. The Drum Major agreed that it was an effort.

January 1937. On the last day of January the Battalion became mechanized, the vehicles being brought from Cairo by our newly trained drivers.

22 February 1937. During Canal Brigade Training, the 2nd Battalion repulsed a heavy tank attack on Point 271 near Iweibid Station. In honour of this, Point 271 is to be named Grenadier Hill.

Spring 1937. An interesting event during Easter was the visit of the German cruiser *Emden*. A football match was arranged [the Grenadiers won 3-1] and visits to the ship were welcomed. ... The Germans proved themselves experts in the art of entertaining and thoroughly enjoyed themselves during their return visits to our barracks, the Sergeants' Mess and institutes resounding to the tunes of the old German drinking songs. ... Summer is practically upon us. Bathing commenced on Good Friday and by the end of March we were back in our summer dress. Summer routine, during the afternoons of which the Battalion, or the larger part of it, foregathers on the beach, came into effect early in April, and we are now

[17] There were some dealings with the Egyptian Army. 'We kept their ammunition in a cell in our guardroom and allowed them two rounds a year for practice' (Britten). On one occasion a party of generals had to be escorted to the top of a sand dune to observe an exercise. They never made it, a result (it was said) of promotion being based on girth and ballast

looking forward to and hope to make the best of our second season in this not-too-bad station.

The Looming War

Thus were preparations made for a new contest with Germany. There was a serious scare in 1938, just a year before hostilities broke out. Working parties of guardsmen dug trenches in Hyde Park and loaded anti-aircraft shells from the Hyde Park magazine on to lorries to feed the various gun sites. The scare passed, but mercifully it both exposed the true nature of the Nazi menace and allowed more time for preparation. Equipment, especially transport, began to arrive in proper quantities and the pace of training was stepped up. Reservists were drawn in for their annual two weeks' training. One officer was Bill Sidney, later to win the Victoria Cross at Anzio who, being a chartered accountant, was condemned to spend the entire fortnight auditing the battalion accounts.

An officer of the 1st Battalion wrote years later:

'I have often given much thought to how prepared and well trained the battalion was to fight the German Army. Our morale, discipline and confidence were excellent. We did not know or realize the efficiency of the German Army, well supported as it was by its Air Force. Our tactical training was fair but we had had no experience of firing live ammunition on exercises, nor had we any cooperation with artillery and tanks. After four years in London we were not physically very fit, nor were many of the reservists. Our various training exercises had not been long enough and we had had little opportunity to experience what it feels like to be really tired. This was something we learnt for the first time from the 16th May 1940 when the order was received to retire from Louvain. Nor had we much opportunity to train from September 1939 to May 1940. Most of the battalion's time and energy was spent in fortifying the frontier. However, during the retreat to Dunkirk this lack of real physical fitness, total exhaustion and very little sleep was compensated by confidence in our divisional commander [Montgomery], high morale and first-class discipline.'[18]

---

[18] Wigram (2)

Warm work in Alex: the King's Birthday Parade on Sporting Club ground, Alexandria.

WARRANT AND NON-COMMISSIONED OFFICERS

The strength of a regiment resides very largely in its warrant officers, sergeants and corporals. While leadership and direction is supplied in the first place by the officers, the fabric, the engine room, the true essence of a regiment, is to be found in the Sergeants' Mess (never, in Foot Guards battalions, 'Warrant Officers' and Sergeants' Mess'). It was the Duke of Wellington himself who declared:

'The Guards are superior to the Line ... from the goodness of the non-commissioned officers. They do, in fact, all that the commissioned officers of the Line are expected to do – and don't do.'

He admitted that:

'they regularly get drunk once a day – by eight in the evening – and go to bed soon after, but then they always take care to do first whatever they are bid.'

Within these ranks there are a number of peculiarities common to the Foot Guards, and others that the Grenadiers claim as their own. The enduring comradeship of the Sergeants' Mess is marked by the **Sergeants' (Past and Present) Club**, which since its inaugural dinner in November 1899 has gathered every year (except in wartime) to celebrate and renew friendships.

The Warrant Officers

Beneath the dominant **Sergeant Major** (described elsewhere) in a battalion come the **Regimental Quartermaster Sergeants**. There used to be only one of these, the right-hand man to the Quartermaster, but later the rank was often held by the senior clerk in the orderly room and in modern times another was established to deal with the increasingly technical nature of 20th century soldiering. They are never spoken of, as elsewhere in the Army, as 'RQMS' or 'RQ'. Grenadiers do not care to abbreviate in speech by using initials and can rattle out 'Kormarsarnt' in a fraction of the time it takes anyone else to say 'RQ'.

Then come the **Drill Sergeants**, of whom there are two in a battalion. They, of course, supervise the drill, but they also adopt active roles in the field for which their earlier experience as warrant officers makes them particularly suitable. Armed with sword and pacestick, they are often more alarming than the Sergeant Major himself, and usually are on the way to stepping into his boots. It is their special pleasure, and sometimes pain, to chase junior officers about the square, a procedure that gives comfort and entertainment to the ordinary guardsman. From time to time it falls to them to instruct the band. One, not well versed in musical matters, was appalled to see a large musician carrying a flute alongside a much smaller one burdened with a tuba. 'You horrible great

At Hougoumont: sergeant of a light company on the battlefield of Waterloo. *Brian Fosten*

Well garnished with gold: this early Victorian colour sergeant, Richard Tidman, even has a gold cap band. *Late 19th century British school*

Hanging the brick: a less formal prelude to a long period of Christmas revels in the sergeants' mess.

Colours. In 1813 he was established as the senior rank in each company, when there were eight or ten to a battalion. He now operates in many specialized roles, but is still to be found in each company as the company quartermaster sergeant, where he is known as the **Pay Sergeant**, or familiarly as the 'Pay Bloke'.

---

[1] Sergeant came from the Latin *servire* (to serve) and corporal from *corpus* (a body)

idle man,' was his outraged remark to the hapless flautist, 'Change over!' The effect on the subsequent performance is not recorded.

The remaining warrant officers are the **Company Sergeant Majors**, who are addressed as such even though some now work in specialized roles, such as signals and transport, rather than having charge of a company. The rank was established only in 1913, when the eight companies in a battalion were reduced to four large ones, each of 250 men at full strength. Company sergeant majors are never known as 'sergeant major', but, again at speed, as 'cumpsamajor'.

Sergeants and Corporals[1]

The non-commissioned officers (again, written as 'NCOs' but pronounced 'noncmissofrs') are the sergeants and corporals. The senior is the **Colour Sergeant**, whose original role was to protect the

Well turned out for a good party: NCOs of No 2 Company, 1st Battalion, in festive mood.

This strange Grenadier expression has hung on, for no well understood reason, from the days when he was responsible for pay in addition to his main duty of feeding, equipping and supplying his men.

Next is the **Sergeant**, known as the **Gold Sergeant** after the gold chevrons on his tunic. Like the warrant officers and colour sergeants he wears a red sash, a superior type of grenade and heavier brass on his forage cap to distinguish him from the **Lance Sergeant,** who wears white chevrons. Lance rank was originally given as a temporary unpaid promotion and first appeared in the Regiment after the Crimean War. In the First World War one corporal in each platoon was made lance sergeant to assist the platoon sergeant. Today every corporal, though paid in that rank, is automatically made a lance sergeant. This curious procedure, which applies only to the Foot Guards, carries echoes of the double rank given to officers in earlier days, and is not always appreciated elsewhere in the Army. But it results in a large sergeants' mess, reinforcing the strength of that crucial institution. Not only does the lance sergeant enjoy enhanced status, but he is able to draw on the experience of the most senior ranks by social contact at an early stage.

Sergeants may still wish to take advice offered in 1787:

'As by your appointment to the halberd, you are probably at the summit of your preferment (unless you have a pretty wife, sister or daughter) you may now begin to take a little ease and relax from that rigid discipline you observed when corporal. Into whatever company you are admitted you must be careful to impress everyone with an idea of your own consequence and to make people believe that serjeants are the only useful and intelligent men in the corps.'[2]

Three memorable veterans of the sergeants' mess: Sid Dowland BEM (above) fought with several different battalions and special forces, and escaped from a prisoner-of-war camp; 'Uncle Tom' Yardley BEM served with distinction for thirteen years as Officers' Mess Steward on Queen's Guard; Arthur Evans was one of large numbers of Grenadiers who joined the police forces, and became a chief superintendent.

Corporals awaiting elevation to the sergeants' mess were still occasionally to be found in a battalion until soon after the Second World War, but now appear only as **Lance Corporals**. The rank of lance corporal[3] came permanently into use in later Victorian times, but, unlike others of the Army who wear one chevron, those of the Foot Guards wear two. Grenadiers have long been brought up to believe that Queen Victoria, looking out of her window one day, saw a lance corporal wearing a single chevron, decided that it looked insufficiently impressive for her Foot Guards and ordered that two should be worn instead. The story has not been substantiated, though it seems perfectly probable, and there is evidently photographic evidence[4] from about 1882 that a single chevron was once worn.

Sir!

Warrant officers and colour sergeants are addressed as 'Sir' by NCOs and guardsmen and a Grenadier of any rank always acknowledges an order with the word 'Sir'. The use of this simple rule has been expanded into something both more universal and more subtle. In the words of one regimental historian, 'From their innate sense of loyalty and discipline they recognize every intonation of the expression "Sir" except the languid.'[5] The meaning, which depends on inflexion, tone of voice, volume, facial expression (within limits) and even the position of the feet, is frequently incomprehensible to those outside the Regiment.

[2] See 'Advice'
[3] It also had roots in the 'chosen man', a superior private, peculiar to the Rifles, who acted as deputy for a corporal and wore a white armband
[4] Dawnay
[5] Whitworth (2)

Chapter Ten

HITLER'S WAR
1939-1945

The Old Enemy, a New Kind of War

Those who had endured the horror and loss of the First World War can hardly have imagined that another would follow only twenty years later. But so it was, and it would be a war of new dimensions and new horrors. No longer was the conflict to be confined to the fighting forces, with huge armies slugging it out along entrenched lines. This was to be a war of space and movement, the bombing of cities, the deliberate extermination of millions and the displacement of millions more. At times it was more dangerous for the families in British cities than for their men fighting overseas. In the Far East the fanaticism and cruelty of the Japanese had also to be faced and overcome.

1939-45 Star, Defence Medal, War Medal 1939-45: the colours of the first represent the Royal Navy, the Army and the RAF, and those of the second the 'green and pleasant land', black stripes for the blackout and orange for fire-bombing. George VI had a close hand in the design of the medal ribbons.

Grenadiers, as in the First War, were to be pitted against the German enemy alone,[1] but this time fighting in the deserts of North Africa and the mountains of Italy, as well as in the familiar country of north-west Europe where they were to achieve conspicuous success in tanks as well as on foot. At the outbreak of war Hitler's promised 'Thousand Year Reich' had run for six years and would last for only six more. Three of these years would see the whole of the continent, including European Russia, overwhelmed or shrugged aside. The tide would then turn and the loathsome Nazi regime finally collapse in the cataclysm of 1945.

In fighting qualities the British and Germans were well matched, sharing many of the same qualities of courage, doggedness and resourcefulness. The front-line soldier of the Reich was, on the whole, honourable and civilized, respecting his British enemies and treating prisoners

properly. It was left to second-line troops, men of little worth and mean motive, to oppress, enslave and exterminate the conquered peoples. Hitler, indeed, had never wanted to go to war with the British at all. He regarded us as natural allies. He saw and admired, especially in our huge Indian possessions, evidence of a British master race of the kind he aspired to for his Aryans and hoped that Britain would not impede his dominating the landmass of Europe if left alone to rule her own empire by sea. The British people, however, were not taken in. We determined to thwart his evil ambitions and incurred his special wrath for so doing.

Mobilization, the BEF and the Phoney War

War was declared on 3 September 1939 and the three regular battalions immediately drew in their reservists and prepared for operations. The **1st Battalion** (Lt Col John Prescott) and **2nd Battalion** (Lt Col George Cornish, later Lt Col John Lloyd) mobilized at Pirbright in 7th Guards Brigade, and the **3rd Battalion** (Lt Col Sir John Aird, later Maj Allan Adair) at Aldershot in 1st Guards Brigade. Their divisional commanders were, respectively, Montgomery and Alexander, both to become field marshals and towering figures later in the war. All three battalions formed part of the British Expeditionary Force and were in France before the end of the month. They moved up to the Franco-Belgian frontier, 7th Guards

---

[1] Germany's Italian allies also fought in North Africa, but were not encountered by Grenadiers

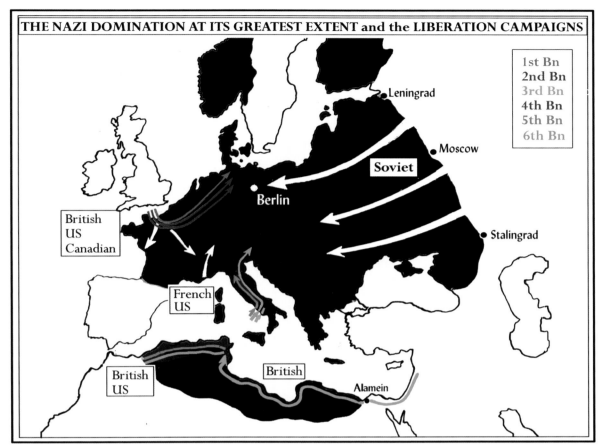

Brigade being east of Lille and 1st Guards Brigade fifteen miles to the south-east.

Then, for seven long months, nothing happened. The Germans were not ready to move during what was said to be the hardest winter for a century. It was known as the 'Phoney War' or the '*sitzkrieg*'. For two weeks in February 1940, however, the 3rd Battalion was moved to part of the French Maginot Line, east of Metz, where the first patrols were sent out and the first Grenadier casualties suffered.

Dunkirk and the Defence of Britain

On 10 May 1940 the Germans launched their blitzkrieg on neutral Holland and Belgium, and thence by the side door into France (the campaign is described separately). The three battalions were evacuated from Dunkirk and returned to England. France fell and it was to be four long years before Grenadiers set foot in the country again.

The immediate concern was invasion, which seemed at the time to be inevitable. The south of England was put into a state of defence, the 1st and 2nd Battalions being stationed at Littlehampton and Arundel in Sussex, and later as a mobile reserve at Stow-on-the-Wold in Gloucestershire. Pillboxes, of which many can still be seen today, were constructed in large numbers. However, the massive air attacks which Hitler launched as a preliminary to invasion, and which he regarded as essential to success, were brilliantly thwarted by the RAF in the autumn of 1940. It was justly called the Battle of Britain and, though the possibility of invasion remained until the summer of 1941, the threat was virtually removed.

It was clear, at this time, that the war was likely to run for several years. Hitler was rampaging through Europe and, in his attempt to starve Britain into submission, his U-boats were causing serious loss to shipping bringing supplies across the Atlantic. In 1940 he also opened the blitz on British cities, especially London, of which the most horrifying result for guardsmen was to be the destruction of the Guards Chapel by a flying bomb on 18 June 1944, with the death of 121 worshippers.

New Battalions and the Adoption of Armour

In the general expansion of the Army three new

The COURSE of the WAR
for the SIX SERVICE BATTALIONS of GRENADIERS

The Wider War			Periods in Theatres of War in Bold Colours					
Details	Year	Month	1st Bn	2nd Bn	3rd Bn	4th Bn	5th Bn	6th Bn
			7th Gds Bde		1st Gds Bde			
Germany invades Poland, war declared	1939	Sep	To France	To France	To France			
		Oct						
Battle of the Atlantic begins		Nov						
		Dec						
	1940	Jan						
		Feb						
		Mar						
		Apr						
Germany invades Belgium		May	DUNKIRK campaign	DUNKIRK campaign	DUNKIRK campaign			
Fall of France		Jun						
		Jul						
		Aug						
Battle of Britain		Sep						
Height of London Blitz		Oct				Raised		
		Nov						
		Dec						
	1941	Jan						
		Feb						
		Mar						
		Apr						
		May						
Germany invades Russia (Operation Barbarossa)		Jun	Guards Armoured Division 5th Gds Armoured Bde			5th Gds Tank Bde		
		Jul						
		Aug						
		Sep						
		Oct					Raised	Raised
		Nov						
Pearl Harbour, America enters the war		Dec						
	1942	Jan						
Japanese conquests in the Far East		Feb						
		Mar			1st Gds Bde		24th Gds Bde	201st Gds Bde
		Apr						
		May						
		Jun						
		Jul						
American offensive in the Pacific begins		Aug						
		Sep						Syria
El Alamein		Oct			Tunisia			
		Nov						
		Dec						
German surrender at Stalingrad	1943	Jan						
		Feb			DJEBEL MANSOUR		Tunisia	Tunisia
		Mar						MARETH
		Apr					MEDJEZ el BAB	
Germans and Italians surrender in Tunisia		May						
		Jun						
Allies invade Sicily		Jul						
		Aug						Italy
Italians surrender, but Germans continue to fight in Italy		Sep						SALERNO
		Oct						CAMINO
		Nov					Italy	
		Dec						
	1944	Jan			Italy		ANZIO	Garigliano
		Feb			Garigliano CASSINO			
		Mar						
		Apr						Home
		May	NW Europe	NW Europe		NW Europe		
Normandy invasion (Operation Overlord)		Jun	NORMANDY	NORMANDY		NORMANDY		
		Jul						
Reconquest of Burma begins		Aug	(P-a-Marcq NIJMEGEN Heesch	(P-a-Marcq NIJMEGEN Heesch	GOTHIC LINE Battaglia	Tilburg Meijel	GOTHIC LINE Sole	
		Sep	(	(				
		Oct	(	(				
		Nov						
		Dec						Disbanded
	1945	Jan						
		Feb						
		Mar	RHINE	RHINE	River Po	RHINE	Home	
		Apr					Disbanded	
Victory in Europe		May						
		Jun	Farewell to Armour		Austria	Kiel		
		Jul	Occupation of Germany	Occupation of Germany		Disbanded		
Japan surrenders after atom bombs on Hiroshima and Nagasaki		Aug			Home			

An endless column: large numbers of men went for training to Windsor, where they are seen here filling the Long Walk.

Grenadier battalions were raised, the 4th in October 1940 and the 5th and 6th in October 1941.[2] All six battalions were to be supplied with reinforcements by the Training Battalion at Windsor, through which 15,000 men and 750 officers were to pass during the war. At the same time the fortunes of the Regiment were to be divided into two distinct parts.

The first followed the formation of the Guards Armoured Division[3] in June 1941, in preparation for the eventual liberation of France and the rest of occupied Europe. The decision was reached after much discussion about the suitability of guardsmen in such a role. It was said that they would be too tall for tanks and that their qualities as infantry soldiers would be wasted. However, the decision was taken and, in the light of subsequent events, never regretted. The 1st Battalion became motorized infantry and the 2nd Battalion were equipped with tanks, the two battalions being together in 5th Guards Armoured Brigade. The 4th Battalion started as infantry, but were then given tanks and fought with 6th Guards Tank Brigade, an independent formation separate from the Guards Armoured Division.

The second strand was quite different and concerned the other three battalions, which were to be prepared for earlier activity in other theatres of war. The 3rd Battalion, which had gone to Louth in Lincolnshire on return from Dunkirk, then moved to Scotland to train in combined operations. These included projected assault landings on various shores from Norway to North Africa, none of which in the event took place. The 5th Battalion, soon after being raised, also moved to Scotland and prepared for a similar role, with similar results. The 6th Battalion,

formed at Caterham in Surrey, was earmarked for special purposes and would be the first of the six to be sent overseas, in June 1942 and a few months before the battle of El Alamein.

It was during these years that the battalions inevitably became more youthful. In peacetime promotion was slow (though not so slow as in the rest of the Army) and it was rare to find a commanding officer or sergeant major who was not comfortably past his fortieth birthday. Now, however, younger, fitter and more active men came to prominence in command of battalions, companies (and squadrons of tanks) and as warrant officers. Sergeants were frequently in their early twenties and a large number of guardsmen went into battle still in their teens.

HRH Princess Elizabeth Becomes Colonel

April 1941 saw an event of great and lasting significance. The Duke of Connaught, who had been Colonel of the Regiment since 1904, died at the age of 91 and the inspired suggestion was made that the young Princess Elizabeth should be invited to succeed him. This she did, to the great delight and satisfaction of 'her' Grenadiers, as they then became. She reviewed detachments of all six battalions at Windsor Castle on 21 April 1942, her sixteenth birthday. The Royal Family refused to move to greater safety than their subjects, and it fell to a company of the Training Battalion to provide them with close protection at the castle throughout the war.

[2] The Foot Guards raised twenty-one battalions in all: the Grenadiers six, Coldstream six (of which five saw action), the Scots, Irish and Welsh three apiece
[3] The division adopted the 'Ever Open Eye' sign used by the Guards Division in the Great War, though in an altered form designed by the Welsh Guards artist, Rex Whistler

Bayonet and ring: training to stick one in the enemy.

Ready for gas attack: Recruit Borthwick with respirator on his chest. The threat of gas was very real and even small children carried masks in a little cardboard box.
Lance Cattermole

Under Churchill's eye: the great war leader visits the 3rd Battalion in Scotland.

Early mechanization: motor cycles and Bren gun carriers on the road.

Under the Blitz: in this war the civil population were often in as much danger as the fighting men. Here Grenadiers march through a bombed London street.

The Wider War – Turning of the Tide

The campaign in Egypt and Libya, in which Grenadiers were not engaged, had been grinding on with mixed results ever since 1940. The Suez Canal was the last major prize coveted by Hitler in the Mediterranean, but he had finally been denied it at the crucial battle of El Alamein in October 1942, where Rommel was roundly defeated by Montgomery's Eighth Army and began the long retreat to Tunisia. The end of 1942 was also to prove the time when the fortunes of Germany began to turn in the east. Hitler's conquests had reached their greatest extent, and in Russia he had bitten off more than he could chew. The enormous Barbarossa invasion of June 1941, while bringing instant results, had been ground down by heroic Russian resistance and the severe winter weather. His army besieging Stalingrad was forced to surrender in February 1943 and thereafter, though momentous battles were to follow, it was retreat all the way to Berlin.

The Allies had also been strengthened immeasurably by the entry of America into the war, first against the Japanese in the Pacific following the surprise attack on Pearl Harbour in Hawaii in December 1941, and then against Germany. The Battle of the Atlantic had brought the U-boat menace under control. Food, armaments and materiel of all kinds were beginning to pour across the

ocean in great quantities and many thousands of fighting men were soon to follow.

The Campaign in Tunisia (Map page 221)

The **6th Battalion** (Lt Col Archer Clive) sailed from Liverpool in June 1942, making a long journey round the African continent as the Mediterranean route to the Middle East was still hotly disputed by the Germans. They spent three weeks at Durban on the way, and eventually arrived with 201st Guards Brigade (Brig Julian Gascoigne, a Grenadier) in northern Syria, where they embarked on a tour of one thousand miles to show the British flag. It was not until February 1943 that they were called upon to join the Eighth Army, which by then had driven their opponents right along the North African coast to Tunisia. In March they fought at **Mareth** (described separately) what was probably the most severe and costly battle in which Grenadiers were engaged during the whole war.

In the meantime the **3rd Battalion** (Lt Col Algernon Heber Percy) had already been fighting. Sailing from Scotland with 1st Guards Brigade, they joined Anderson's First Army in Algiers in November 1942, moved into Tunisia from the west and in February 1943 fought the most violent of their North African battles at **Djebel Mansour**, attempting, at considerable cost, to dislodge

Notable Grenadiers: three who gave fine service in the war and later became public figures, (from left): Sir Edward Ford made an eminent career in the Royal Household (where many other Grenadiers have served); Marmaduke, Lord Hussey, though gravely wounded and crippled at Anzio, became chairman of the BBC; Brian Johnston, who won an MC, was widely known for his broadcasting and cricket commentaries.

the enemy from one of the wild and rocky hills. The brigade was known as 'The Plumbers', being called upon time and again, and at the shortest notice, to plug the leaks as the Germans attempted to break out from their encircled position. But stopped they were, and pursued over the **Kasserine Pass** towards Tunis.

The **5th Battalion** (Lt Col George Gordon Lennox) had sailed to Algiers with 24th Guards Brigade (Brig Richard Colvin, a Grenadier). In April 1943 they were installed on Grenadier Hill, near **Medjez el Bab**, when called upon for their major effort. Their objectives formed part of **The Bou**, hills that had to be approached over an open plain of cornfields by daylight. The Germans were in great strength and entrenched, and defensive fire, especially from mortars and machine guns, was unrelenting. But the hill was taken, and then held for eight days under continual fire. The losses were very severe: 60 killed and over 200 wounded, and only three of the sixteen officers in the rifle companies who were engaged from the start emerged unharmed at the end of the battle. The 1st Irish Guards, in the same brigade, fought with exceptional gallantry – the battle was marked down as one of the most severe in their history.

The end of the campaign came with the junction of the First Army with the Eighth and, in May, the fall of Tunis. The German army was crowded into Cape Bon peninsula but hopes of a Dunkirk of their own were to be dashed. It was triumph on the grandest and most complete scale and, in the words of one of the German commanders, it was no disgrace to surrender to the Grenadier Guards, 'the finest troops in the British Army'. And that despite appearances: 'Along the road came

several thousand German troops, smartly turned out, in columns led by officers, all singing their wonderful marching songs. They were the famous 90th Light Division [the opponents of Mareth], fortunately now disarmed, but their bearing showed no sign that they had been defeated. Beside them, how shabby we looked.'[4]

The Campaign in Italy (Map page 221)

The three battalions remained for several months in different parts of North Africa making preparations for the next phase of the war. This was to be the invasion of Italy, the first step in the liberation of Europe, by the Eighth Army and the American Fifth Army.

The **6th Battalion** (Lt Col William Kingsmill), in the Fifth Army, was again the first to go. In September 1943 the leading brigades had landed unopposed at **Salerno**, 201 Guards Brigade moved through them to enlarge the beachhead and the whole force then began the long slog up the boot of Italy. In November it fell to the battalion to endure another severe trial at **Monte Camino**. This mountain formed part of the enemy's winter line and was strongly defended, but the battalion's objective was taken

[4] Bowley

Taking the fight to the enemy: a Grenadier in battle order.
Christopher Morley

MAJOR GENERAL
Sir ALLAN ADAIR Bt
GCVO CB DSO MC and Bar DL JP *1897-1988*

Command of the 3rd
Battalion and the
Guards Armoured
Division, Colonel of
the Regiment

Allan Adair was without question the best known and most loved Grenadier of his time.

Allan Henry Shafto Adair, sixth Baronet of Ballymena, Co Antrim, was born on 3rd November 1897. Commissioned into the Regiment in 1916, he went to France just after the Battle of the Somme. He served in the 3rd Battalion through the last two years of the terrible struggle of the First World War: 1917, the year of frustration and slaughter, the year of Passchendaele and 1918, the year of near defeat in March and final triumph in November. In 1917 he broke his shoulder, fortuitously, for by the time he rejoined his battalion only four officers with whom he served earlier were still there, most of the others having been killed or seriously wounded. He himself was lucky to survive, being hit by machine-gun fire only a week before the armistice. But his military skill and courage were well established – he twice won the Military Cross.

Between the wars he served entirely with the Regiment, including a happy three years in Egypt, save a single staff appointment at Horse Guards, which, however, proved a strenuous time, as it was during the General Strike of 1926.

In May 1940 he was teaching at Sandhurst when summoned to take command of the 3rd Battalion in Belgium, at the critical time of the German invasion. He reached it in a taxi driven by a French prize-fighter. His battalion saw the hardest fighting that fell to any Grenadier battalion during the retreat to Dunkirk and he was awarded the DSO for 'conspicuous courage and coolness under fire that were an inspiration to his battalion'.

Back at home Adair commanded, in succession, 30th and 6th Guards Brigades before being appointed to command the Guards Armoured Division. He trained it in England and then led it with conspicuous success throughout the fighting in Europe: the breakout from Normandy, the liberation of Brussels, the advance towards Arnhem and the capture of the Nijmegen bridge, the crossing of the Rhine, and eventually to Cuxhaven on the Elbe estuary. The race to Brussels was launched by his famous order 'My intention is to advance and liberate Brussels', adding (with a grin) 'and that is a grand intention'.

To have commanded the division so successfully and for so long under so exacting a commander as Montgomery was something of a *tour de force* for an officer who had not passed through the staff college and knew very little about tanks until late in his career. But Monty had no doubts about his subordinate and told the Guards Armoured Division in June 1945, 'He never failed me and he never failed you. He gave of his best that the division might do well in battle... You owe him more than you can ever repay'.

General Allan (as he was universally known) was very conscious of the price that was paid for victory and after the war frequently visited the graves of the dead. His own son Desmond was lost at Monte Camino with the 6th Battalion and for many months his fate was uncertain.

He retired a few years after the war, but continued to give of himself unstintingly. He was President of the Grenadier Guards Association from 1947 to 1961, and from 1960 to 1975 Colonel of the Regiment. He took on much other work, and in it all attained distinction.

It was General Sir David Fraser who best described the 'constant, diamond-like quality' of his character, the consideration and courtesy that overlaid his steely will, and his natural authority. 'He took a man's hand, looked very directly into his eyes, spoke a few words, kindly, lightly, gently, and one knew that for that man the day was a little brighter, the battle a little more worthwhile, the pain, where there had been pain, a little less.'

See Adair

Infantry and tanks: Grenadiers mastered the combined roles with conspicuous success.

with little loss. However, as was so often the case, the Germans were determined to regain what they had lost and struck back with great violence. The conditions were appalling. For four days intense cold, a tearing wind and constant mortaring deprived the Grenadiers of any chance of sleep. For three days they had no food other than emergency ration packs. It took five hours, with eight men to each stretcher, to bring down the wounded and many died of exposure. On the last day the Germans redoubled their efforts, but again were driven off. Relieved at the last moment, their ammunition almost gone, only 263 of the 483 Grenadiers who had gone up the hill came back down, completely exhausted, frostbitten and almost starved.

The battalion did not survive such treatment. In March 1944 it was taken out of the line, some of its number moving to the 5th Battalion and the remainder returning home. In December, covered with honour, it was finally disbanded.

The **5th Battalion** (Lt Col 'Geordie' Gordon Lennox) landed at Taranto in November 1943 and spent two months at rest before embarking near Naples as part of the **Anzio** assault force. (The subsequent battle is described separately.)

Returning to Naples in March 1944, in a seriously depleted state, the battalion took on reinforcements and prepared to resume the advance through Italy. For the next ten months they operated roughly parallel to the 3rd

Battalion, though under different command. There was no great battle, but a succession of small actions. There was constant movement, one line of hills after another to cross or circumvent, danger always around the corner, orders received and countermanded, the constant strain of the uncertain and the draining away of strength in minor skirmishes. It was a war for the infantryman, the skilful patrol and the sharp eye, but it was wearing on the nerves and exhausting on the frame.

North of Florence and stretching across the peninsula, the Germans had constructed the **Gothic Line**, which they supposed impregnable. It was not. In September 1944 the Allied armies penetrated it by a great operation in which the Grenadier battalions took no major part. But all was not over. Fierce fighting was required by the 5th Grenadiers in the northern Appenines, their last battle being fought on **Monte Sole**.

In the meantime the **3rd Battalion** (Lt Cols Algernon Heber Percy, John Goschen and John Nelson in succession) had arrived from North Africa in February 1944 and held positions on the hills north of the **Garigliano River**. In March came the occupation of **Cassino**. This town, with the monastery on the top of the mountain, had become a symbol of the fierce fighting in Italy. The 3rd Battalion's turn in the rubble and cellars of the town came at a quiet time between two great offensives. It was an eerie existence, cut off for a fortnight at a time in cramped conditions, but it was relatively safe.

More dangerous was the role carried out by the reserve companies, whose porters had to carry up supplies in heavy rucksacks, over the pitted roads and twisted wrecks of bridges, and under fire.

The subsequent advance followed the same relentless pattern as that of the 5th Battalion, up to and beyond the **Gothic Line**, though there were occasional moments of exhilaration as Italians poured out to greet their liberators. And there were more trying times still in the dreadful weather. The battalion endured appalling hardship on **Monte Battaglia** (Battle Mountain), lying under shellfire among the corpses of American and German soldiers and supplied by men and mules along a single track, knee deep in glutinous mud.

In February 1945 both battalions were withdrawn for rest. The longest-serving veterans were collected into the 5th Battalion and sent home (the battalion being formally disbanded in May), and the later enlistments into the 3rd Grenadiers. It was left to that battalion to finish the business. It led the Eighth Army across the **River Po**, a highly risky operation accomplished by good fortune at a spot where the enemy was unprepared, and crossing the Austrian frontier on VE Day, 8 May 1945. Victory in Europe was complete.

The Invasion of Normandy (Map page 232)

The three battalions at home had been waiting impatiently for their moment to arrive, though constantly training and improving their preparations. The Russians, under serious pressure in the east, had urged the Allies to launch the Second Front in the west in 1943, but they were not ready for such a huge undertaking. The south of England became a vast encampment containing hundreds of thousands of British and American troops and supplies and equipment of every kind. On 6 June 1944, D Day, the invasion of Normandy began. It was by far the largest amphibious operation in history.

The **1st Battalion** (Lt Col Edward Goulburn) and **2nd Battalion** (Lt Col Rodney Moore) in the Guards Armoured Division landed in France at the end of June and in July were ordered to break out of the bridgehead south-east of Caen. At dawn on 18 July a thousand Lancaster bombers pounded the suburbs of the city and several hundred guns then took up the bombardment. But the German anti-tank defences in the village of **Cagny** were formidable and advantage lay with them. The division lost fifty-seven tanks and the attack stalled.

Early in August a further attempt was made to the south of Caen. It was desperate fighting in the bocage country, with narrow lanes, steep banks and thick hedges, which was extremely difficult for tanks. North and east of **Vire** the fighting was particularly stiff and some serious losses were incurred.

It was at this point that the **4th Battalion** (Lt Col John Davies[5]), which had landed in France later in July and already had supported the 15th Scottish Division in a successful assault at **Caumont,** found itself fighting close to the other Grenadier battalions.

---

[5] HRH Davies

Air raid precautions: trenches dug at Victoria Barracks, Windsor.

Grenadier commandos: Churchill ordered the raising of commandos in May 1940. They were recruited from across the army. No 8 Commando included this Grenadier troop, which fought in Tobruk in 1941 before being succeeded by new forces such as the SAS. It was the beginning of a long tradition of Grenadiers serving as parachutists and in Special Forces.

'My Grenadiers': a cheer from representatives of every battalion parade at Windsor Castle on 21 April 1942, the sixteenth birthday of their new Colonel. It was the beginning of a long and momentous association.

Khaki berets and blue berets: the 1st and 2nd Battalions celebrate with a victory parade.

The new Colonel: HRH Princess Elizabeth in 1942, at the age of sixteen. *Cecil Beaton*

BRIGADIER
ALGERNON HEBER PERCY
DSO and Bar *1904-1961*

Imaginative and
gallant Commanding
Officer of the
3rd Battalion in
North Africa and Italy

Algy Heber Percy arrived to command the 3rd Battalion in Perth in September 1942. Almost two and a half years after the evacuation from Dunkirk, it was a difficult time. The battalion had been earmarked for combined operations, a whole series of which had been planned and prepared for, though none in the event had come off. There were to have been, at various times, commando-type raids on Sicily, Italy, Norway, the Channel Islands, Boulogne and North Africa. All this maintained the spirit of the battalion at a high state of expectation and gave them a distinct status in the eyes of the Regiment and indeed the Army. But in every case they were doomed to disappointment.

The new Commanding Officer, though slight in stature, was a man of tireless energy and imagination, always thinking up new schemes for the instruction and entertainment of his men and, in the eyes of one observer, displaying the spirit and enthusiasm more usually seen in an eager young subaltern. Unimpeded by the weary demands of administration (which he entrusted to other hands) he raised his battalion to a pitch of excellence which caused one senior commander to judge them the best trained in the Army. Their time came in November 1942 when 1st Guards Brigade landed in North Africa. In February 1943 they fought their most severe battle at Djebel Mansour, and in May, after a series of testing operations, the campaign was won.

In February 1944 the 3rd Grenadiers landed at Naples and took up positions on the Garigliano before moving up to Cassino. At this point Heber Percy was promoted to lead the 12th Infantry Brigade, where he won a bar to the DSO already awarded for his gallant work as Commanding Officer. He was given two further brigade commands before retiring in 1954.

LIEUTENANT COLONEL
ARTHUR SPRATLEY
MBE MM *1910-1978*

Drummer,
Sergeant Major,
Quartermaster,
General Secretary,
Military Knight

AJ Spratley became a Grenadier in 1926 as a sixteen-year-old drummer. He was destined to be a memorable follower of that colourful and sometimes troublesome occupation. One day, at Windsor Castle, he was collecting laurel leaves to adorn the Colour on a battle honour day when he encountered none other than the King, George V, who took it upon himself to choose the leaves. Back at the guardroom the Drill Sergeant put His Majesty's selection in bad order and the drummer in the book for offering so rich an excuse.

By 1939 Spratley had risen in the 3rd Battalion to the strange rank of WO3 or platoon sergeant major (PSM), a short-lived army measure to alleviate the scarcity of officers to command platoons. He saw action in the Dunkirk campaign and at one stage, being a fine athlete, ran seventeen miles to recover a left-behind anti-tank rifle and then catch up his companions.

As the Regiment expanded he rose rapidly and in 1944 became Sergeant Major of the 4th Battalion. He fought with it in his Churchill tank (well named 'Windsor') from Normandy to the Baltic and was awarded the Military Medal. In the sergeants' mess he would give an impressive rendering of *Drifting and Dreaming,* which became the theme song of the battalion.

After the war he was Sergeant Major of the 1st Battalion for three years before being commissioned Quartermaster to his old 3rd Battalion and later progressing to the Guards Depot and to Sandhurst as a lieutenant colonel.

After retirement he was for ten years a most active and popular General Secretary of the Grenadier Guards Association and spent his last years as a Military Knight of Windsor.

The Liberation of France, Belgium and Holland (Map page 232)

The pressure by the Allied armies continued relentlessly and at last the defence gave way, the Germans racing back to the Seine crossings while the Grenadiers were able to rest and reorganize. The two months of hard fighting in the Normandy bridgehead had paid off. The Germans, badly battered and also under heavy pressure on the Russian front, cut their losses and pulled out of France altogether. Paris was liberated and there followed an advance of extraordinary speed as the Allied armies swept across the great open spaces of France. It fell to the Guards Armoured Division to liberate **Brussels** on 3 September, the fifth anniversary of the declaration of war, after the longest advance achieved in a single day by any division during the war. By now the **1st** and **2nd Battalions** were operating hand in glove as the Grenadier Group. Crossing in a matter of hours the battlefields of the First War where so many Grenadiers lay buried, they raced across the Belgian border and entered the city to a tumultuous welcome. They were a short head behind the faster Cromwell tanks of the Welsh Guards Group, having met a serious check at **Pont-à-Marcq**, where the enemy, well placed and entrenched, chose to make an attempt to stem the tide. They were driven out by the King's Company on foot, supported by No 2 Squadron of the 2nd Battalion in their tanks, after a heavy fight and serious losses. It was a classic example of the cooperation between infantry and tanks for which the division became so renowned. Even Montgomery, commanding the Allied army group and no natural admirer of guardsmen, conceded that no other division could do it so well.

They were to stay in Brussels for a single night, and then pushed on to Louvain, close to their opening positions in May 1940, to poise on the Dutch border for their most famous exploit – Operation *Market Garden* and the capture of the **Nijmegen** bridge (described separately). The battle was immediately followed by a bitter encounter further south at **Heesch**, where the Germans had attempted to cut the Nijmegen corridor. It took three days to turn them out and more casualties were incurred than at Nijmegen.

The tragic disaster at Arnhem and the failure of *Market Garden* condemned the Grenadier battalions to a winter in the freezing cold and mud of the Low Countries, in preparation for the final assault into the German homeland. Much of the time was spent in a counter-attack role, as it was at this time that the German army launched its final desperate offensive in the Ardennes, which, however was checked and thrown back.

The **4th Battalion** in the meantime had moved up to Holland and over the winter months conducted a series of operations, several of them difficult and dangerous, in support of other divisions clearing the eastern part of the country of enemy. **Tilburg** was liberated and there was a hard fight at **Meijel**.

The Drive into Germany (Map page 233)

The last stage of the campaign opened with the crossing of the **Rhine** on 24 March 1945. The war had only six weeks to run, but the Germans were now defending their homeland and some fanatical resistance was yet to be encountered. The Guards Armoured Division crossed the river at Rees. The going was stiff and the **1st Battalion** (Lt Col Patrick Lort-Phillips), and **2nd Battalion**, still operating together as the Grenadier Group, had a hard struggle at **Bentheim**, just short of the River Ems. Once across the river, however, resistance faded and the battalions advanced steadily to the Elbe, though the going was often difficult. At the end of April they were ordered to liberate the concentration camp at **Sandbostel**, where typhus was reported to be causing three hundred deaths a day. Though it proved to be their last battle of the war, the approach to the camp was fiercely contested and a full-scale assault was necessary. The camp was an appalling place that revealed the full horror and brutality of Nazi rule. It was a worthy last objective of a war, costly as it was, to rid the world of so evil a regime.

The **4th Battalion** (Lt Col Lord Tryon) had taken their Churchill tanks across the Rhine and, placed under command of the British 6th Airborne Division, raced on to the Ems with their paratroopers. Resistance was relatively slight and the advance continued across the Elbe and up to Kiel on the Baltic. In the last stages progress was constantly impeded, not this time by hostile fire but by hordes of surrendering enemy.

Berlin fell to the Russians, who met their British and American allies on the Elbe. Montgomery took the German surrender on 3 May 1945. Hitler, in the last stage of desperation in his bunker, committed suicide. The Thousand Year Reich had lasted just twelve years. It was Victory in Europe, though won only with prodigious effort and heavy cost.[6]

Principal Sources: Forbes (2), Nicolson (1),(2)

---

[6] Grenadier decorations for gallantry are summarized in Annex B

Dunkirk – Retreat and Deliverance

On 10 May 1940 the Germans launched their *blitzkrieg* (lightning war) on Holland and Belgium. The campaign was to last only three weeks and end with the merciful deliverance of most of the British Expeditionary Force from Dunkirk.

The BEF, under the command of the Grenadier Lord Gort, had already deployed to meet the assault, which was not unexpected. Under a well-rehearsed plan the three Grenadier battalions in 1st and 7th Guards Brigades moved across the Belgian frontier and into positions near Louvain. On their way they met streams of refugees. Old men were pushing their wives and household goods in wheelbarrows; mothers, with babies slung from their shoulders, trudged wearily through the dust; small farm-carts, crammed with twenty people apiece, fought for a place among the luxury cars of the well-to-do and the convoys of Allied troops and lorries moving in the opposite direction. Many German agents were among them and Fifth Column activities were everywhere – arrows would be painted on buildings and scythed out of the long grass to indicate targets to the Luftwaffe, which met no opposition and was very active by day and night.

The Long Retreat and the River Lines

On 12 May news came that the French line had collapsed at Sedan and the Grenadiers were compelled to pull back west of Brussels before firing a shot. It was a long and taxing withdrawal, almost all on foot as there was little transport. Arriving in a new position, often after a march of twenty miles, the battalions would immediately start constructing new trenches and then be ordered further back again.

At last, on the **River Escaut** (Scheldt) the **3rd Battalion** (Maj Allan Adair) were able to get to grips with the enemy. On the morning of 21 May, shortly before dawn, the Germans launched a sudden and very violent attack on the river line and succeeded in crossing between the Grenadiers and the neighbouring 2nd Coldstream. They were well hidden by rye, standing high in the fields. The reserve company was at once ordered to counter-attack. It came under heavy machine-gun fire and, though suffering many casualties, succeeded through two spectacularly courageous actions. In the first, the Bren-gun carriers of the carrier platoon were launched across the bullet-swept ground as if tanks, and silenced the machine guns on the left with grenades. The second action was that of LCpl Harry Nicholls, who won the first Victoria Cross to be awarded to a soldier during the war. The enemy withdrew back across the river, but the cost to the battalion had been very severe, almost two hundred casualties.

The retreat continued and still the 1st and 2nd Battalions were not engaged, but a week later the **3rd Battalion** were ordered to support another division by regaining a line on the **Ypres-Comines Canal**. The two leading companies fought desperately alongside men of

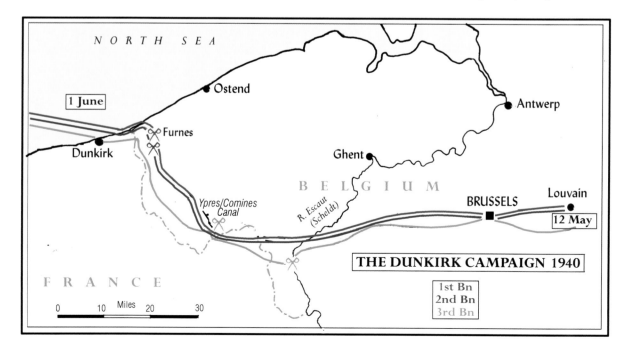

LANCE CORPORAL
HARRY NICHOLLS VC
1915-1975

Champion Boxer,
Victoria Cross
of the River Escaut,
whose decoration
was twice presented

Harry Nicholls, of the 3rd Battalion, won the first Victoria Cross of the Second World War to go to a non-commissioned officer or soldier.

A Nottingham man and one of a family of thirteen, Nicholls enlisted in 1936 and soon distinguished himself as a boxer, becoming both the British Army and Imperial Services Heavyweight Champion.

On 21 May 1940 LCpl Nicholls was commanding a section in the right-forward platoon of his company when ordered to counter-attack. At the very start of the advance he was wounded in the arm by shrapnel, but continued to lead his section forward. As the company came over a small ridge, the enemy opened heavy machine-gun fire at short range.

Realizing the danger to his company, he immediately seized a Bren gun and dashed forward, firing from the hip. He succeeded in silencing the machine gun, and then two others, in spite of being again severely wounded. He then went up on to a higher piece of ground and engaged the German infantry massed behind, causing many casualties, and continuing to fire until he had no ammunition left. He was wounded at least four times in all, but absolutely refused to give up.

Harry Nicholls was reported to have been killed in action and in August 1940 his widow received his Victoria Cross from King George VI. It was not until many months later that he was discovered alive and in a prisoner-of-war camp. He was repatriated in May 1945, returned to Nottingham to a hero's welcome and was himself presented with his Victoria Cross by the King.

It is believed that this is the only time a Victoria Cross has been presented twice.

See Sarkar

LIEUTENANT COLONEL
FRED TURNER
OBE DCM *1898-1968*

DCM of 1918,
Sergeant Major,
Quartermaster,
Association General
Secretary

George Frederick Godwin Turner enlisted in November 1915. In the last weeks of 1918, just before the war drew to a close, he won the Distinguished Conduct Medal during the battle of the Canal du Nord. As a corporal of the 2nd Battalion he maintained communication between his battalion and company headquarters under conditions of the utmost difficulty and danger.

A champion shot and water polo player, he was a company sergeant major within five years and in 1934 became Sergeant Major of the Guards Depot, quickly moving on to the same post in the 3rd Battalion, and in 1939 becoming its Quartermaster. Here he would instruct the young officers that 'no gentleman consents to serve beyond the range of a medium gun'. He saw his battalion through the exhausting and desperate days of the Dunkirk campaign, still using his rifle. Over twenty-one miles of the retreat he was said to have fired twenty-one shots and accounted for twenty-one enemy. He went on to serve in the headquarters of First Army in North Africa, where in May 1943 he celebrated victory there with the three Grenadier battalions in the theatre. Moving on to the Second Army he was promoted to lieutenant colonel. As well as the MBE, advanced in 1944 to OBE, he was awarded the *Croix de Guerre* with Gilt Star.

'Fwed', as he was known from his endearing lisp ('Stwike your wifles with more delibewation, and move with more alacwity the non-commissioned officers'), was a towering character who inspired both awe and great affection, working tirelessly as General Secretary of the Grenadier Guards Assocation.

He ended a life of exceptional service as a Military Knight of Windsor. His funeral in St George's Chapel drew one of the greatest gatherings of Grenadiers ever remembered.

The highest award: Harry Nicholls winning his Victoria Cross. *David Rowlands*

the Black Watch to clear the Germans from the west bank of the canal and eventually the position was consolidated and held by the battalion over the following day, though they were constantly attacked and without food. Eventually ordered to withdraw, they did so with difficulty. Approaching the coast, dog-tired, they were suddenly ordered to march to attention as they passed the immaculate figure of their greatly admired divisional commander, Harold Alexander. His composure and confidence lifted their spirits immeasurably.

Furnes and the Embarkation

By 29 May much of the British force of over 330,000 men had been evacuated, though most of the equipment had to be abandoned. But on the left flank the Belgians were about to surrender, and on the right the French were unable to stem the German advance. In a fog of weariness and uncertainty 7th Guards Brigade was ordered to hold the perimeter at the town of **Furnes**. The **1st Battalion** (Lt Col John Prescott) took up

2nd Battalion commander: 'Jackie' Lloyd, with two other officers, fell to a single German sniper in the streets of Furnes.

positions, as did the **2nd Battalion**, whose Commanding Officer (Lt Col John Lloyd) and two company commanders[7] were killed in the streets by a single sniper. The situation was critical. Under continuous bombardment, and without artillery support of their own (the ammunition having been used up and guns destroyed) every section was barricaded into a cellar with orders to live and fight there and to come out only to evacuate the wounded and collect rations.

On 1 June came the time for the final withdrawal to the beaches. Passing La Panne, where thousands of men, in a solid mass about five miles long and a hundred yards wide, were still waiting to embark, the two battalions were able to embark in small parties by the end of the day. The remains of the **3rd Battalion** were evacuated from the Dunkirk mole. It was an extraordinary deliverance.

Principal Source: Forbes (2)

---

[7] One was Captain Christopher Jeffreys, son of General Lord Jeffreys

The Experience of Dunkirk

Getting Started – An Early Visit by Monty

'I was the first man sacked by Monty three hours after the war had started. The day war was declared Monty as commander of the 3rd Division came at once to inspect the 2nd Grenadiers. He reached my platoon at five past two. "How long," he asked my platoon sergeant, "have you been in charge of this platoon?" "Since ten minutes to two, sir," replied Sgt Hamilton. "What were you before that?" "Fourteen years sergeants' mess cook, sir." I was summoned before the Commanding Officer. "The general did not think much of your choice of platoon sergeant. Besides, he said you stuttered. He told me not to take you to war." My hopes rose. "Don't worry, Ivor," he went on. "I know you a lot better than the general." He did too. Sgt Hamilton got a DCM and I didn't stay sacked.'[8]

Emergency Care of Weapons

[3rd Grenadiers, May 1940] 'I was a Bren gunner [in the Carrier Platoon] and my driver Bob Pearce took me to a farmhouse on the right. I went to a low window and started firing at the German occupants. I fired until my gun over-heated. I only had one barrel and had to keep it firing somehow. I took the gun to a pump in the yard and pumped some water on to it. I don't know what my Depot musketry instructor would have said to that, but it cooled the gun. I went into the farmhouse kitchen, grabbed a handful of fat I found there and smeared this all over the action. I put my foot on the cocking handle and cleared the action. Then I slapped another magazine on and it fired like the clappers throughout the night.'[9]

An Exhausting March

'The march continued throughout the night and still no-one knew the ultimate destination. Men grew listless and spoke very little, automatically marching in step as they had been trained so well to do. Occasionally a guardsman would weave off to a flank, half asleep or suffering from dehydration. His weapons and ammunition would then be distributed among his comrades, who would steer him by his elbows in the required direction. No-one was allowed to fall out, or be left behind.'[10]

A Test of Endurance and High Morale

'During the night the 3rd Battalion had covered twenty miles which he [the Commanding Officer] described as "perhaps the most trying march of all", in single file, through stifling dust and along roads which were choked with British and French vehicles. On arrival they had begun to dig positions along the River Lys, only to be told to pack up and withdraw to Dunkirk. This news, depressing as it was, at least promised them some relief from the strain of endless marching and fighting. Then came the second message. Divorced from their own familiar brigade and division – whom they were not to see again until they re-assembled in England – without even the time to snatch some food, the battalion now had a further nine miles to march before they reached their start line, and from there it was a three-mile advance over unknown country to attack an enemy whose strength and exact positions were likewise unknown. It was a test of endurance and high morale to which the guardsmen responded splendidly. An outside observer later wrote: "The Grenadiers seemed fresh and in good spirits ... it was a lovely evening with a glorious sunset, and the guardsmen marched away towards the line as if they were on parade at home." And another wrote: "They seemed to be carrying out a model attack. It was a fine and inspiring sight, and I shall never forget it".'[11]

Eminent quartermasters: Bernard Pratt (above) was wounded by fifth columnists in Belgium when Sergeant Major of the 2nd Battalion, but went on to be Quartermaster of the 6th Battalion and rose to lieutenant colonel; Archie Douglas was decorated for his fine work in the Dunkirk evacuation.

The Beaches of Dunkirk

'We stayed at Furnes for approximately two days and at midnight of the second day we were told to prepare to

---

[8] Crosthwaite (2). Major Ivor Crosthwaite, an outstanding squadron commander of the 4th Battalion, won a DSO himself
[9] Felstead
[10] Pritchard
[11] Forbes (2)

move, wrap our feet in blankets to prevent the sound of marching feet and go to the beaches. It was every man for himself but we kept together and at dawn marched on to the beaches – after coming through a route strewn with vehicles, abandoned and broken up so as to be of no use to the Germans. The sight that greeted us was unbelievable, ships waiting in the distance, many half sunk and all sizes. It wasn't long before the shelling and bombing started. There were four of us still together and we scrambled for safety in slit trenches in the dunes. We survived and decided to make our way towards Dunkirk, a mass of smoke and flames in the far distance. By about four o'clock in the afternoon we came to one of the moles where a destroyer, the *Worcester,* lay waiting. The mole had been badly bombed but we managed to get across and aboard and lay on the deck. It wasn't long before we left, thinking we were on our way and safe, but the German Stukas spotted us and dropped their bombs, just missing the main part of the ship, but many aboard were hit by flying shrapnel. When the bombers disappeared we helped the wounded as best we could (our first aid kits had long since been used) and eventually arrived in Dover.'[12]

Rescued by the *Salamander*

'On the 1st of June 1940 I was an eighteen-year-old Grenadier helping to defend the final perimeter of the Dunkirk evacuation beaches. My "mate" was nearly forty, a reservist who had been recalled to the Colours in 1939. One of the local innkeepers had recently referred to us as *pere et fils*, father and son. The German air force dropped a confetti of yellow leaflets informing us that we were surrounded and should surrender – they made good toilet paper.

'It was a dark night when we pulled out, but about 2 am the moon came out and we could see the final crossroads. RSM Cyril Sheather stood checking and counting how many had reached the beach. We never saw him again [he was killed shortly afterwards]. As the light improved and the tide came in, two destroyers appeared offshore. Spirits rose among the sand dunes. Sadly, though, before the destroyers could take on their full quota of troops one suffered a direct hit from the German bombardment and, in full view of our disbelieving eyes, sank within minutes. The second one was hit to starboard blowing a large hole through her plates. She managed to stay afloat and crept slowly away

with the troops on board up to their knees in water on the port side.

'A corporal and myself swam out and salvaged a Carley float, which held four of us. We tried to row out to the nearest ship and were given a tow by a lifeboat full of Scottish troops to the nearest minesweeper, the *Salamander*. Oh, that wonderful *Salamander*, one funnel, one gun and one hope – to get home. As the morning wore on we continued to cruise along the beach, hoisting on board anyone who made it to the netting slung over the sides. The 4.5 kept banging away, helped by several Bren guns carried on board by the troops. Fully loaded at last, we turned towards the open sea and headed for the White Cliffs and home.'[13]

Another Eventful Evacuation

'I had been towed out 800 yards in my underpants – none too warm at five in the morning – behind a collapsible boat to a destroyer, had with another man rowed back a string of a dozen boats to the beach – very, very hard work – had been sunk by a Messerschmitt 30 yards short of the destroyer, gone into Dunkirk harbour, been hit by dive bombers twice in ten minutes on two separate destroyers, collected a splinter in the head, passed out and woke up stark naked on Dover quay, glad to be home.'[14]

An Extraordinary Welcome Home

'I thought the reception amazing because, for one thing, we rather had our tails between our legs. We thought here we are, a bedraggled defeated army, but we were welcomed in a typically British style. We were welcomed as heroes at the stations outside Dover. We stopped at one, called Sellindge I remember, where there were a lot of lovely WVS women – all with packets of cigarettes, hot coffee, chocolate (Mars bars or whatever, you know), giving it to us as if we were heroes returning, and the train had to stop for all that to happen and then we went on.'[15]

---

[12] Crowe
[13] Fletcher
[14] Crosthwaite (1)
[15] Ford

Mareth – the Greatest Tragedy

The Battle of the Horseshoe (Mareth Line) on 16 and 17 March 1943 was one of such intensity, involving such hardship and loss, that it can scarcely be matched with any other battle in which Grenadiers were engaged in the whole war. It was won, and then lost again, in the course of a single moonlit night.

The **6th Battalion** (Lt Col Archer Clive) had waited nine months since leaving home in June 1942 and their travels had brought them to the Mareth Line, where the Germans hoped to check the relentless advance of the Eighth Army along the coast of North Africa.

The Seeds of Disaster

201st Guards Brigade were to capture a ring, or 'horseshoe' of low hills, held as an outpost just south of the German line and protected by a deep dry watercourse, the Wadi Zess. The attack was to be carried out 'quietly' by moonlight, the three rifle companies taking the objectives and then being reinforced by the support group with heavy weapons (No 2 Company) in order to meet the expected counter-attack. Resistance was expected to be light. 'This is going to be a good party,' said Montgomery.

Alas, it was not to be. Unknown to the brigade, an officer of the divisional artillery, carrying a map with details of the opening barrage, had been captured before the attack was launched. Having obtained this information, the enemy laid mines in profusion; furthermore, they were not weak, as their troops were some of the best in the Afrika Corps. Thus the seeds of disaster were sown before the Grenadiers even left their assembly area.

Advancing Through the Minefields

The three companies advanced over the Wadi Zess and began to move up the hill towards the German

The Mareth Cross: a striking representation of its original position among Grenadier graves on the moonlit battlefield.
Sean Bolan

The Mareth Cross today: wreaths laid at the cross by the Guards Museum in Wellington Barracks on Regimental Remembrance Day.

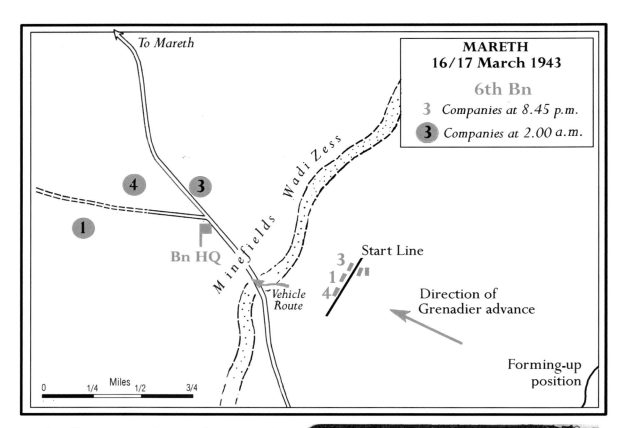

To Mareth

MARETH
16/17 March 1943

6th Bn

3 *Companies at 8.45 p.m.*

3 *Companies at 2.00 a.m.*

Wadi Zess

4

3

1

Bn HQ

Minefields

Vehicle Route

3
1
4

Start Line

Direction of
Grenadier advance

Forming-up
position

Miles
0   1/4   1/2   3/4

trenches. The enemy machine-gun fire was mostly passing harmlessly overhead and it was a little time before the Grenadiers realized that the numerous explosions which wrenched the ground and tore at their lower limbs were caused not by mortar fire but by mines – shrapnel mines, the Italian box mines, heavy Teller mines. Men began to fall on every side, but the survivors did not pause, knowing that the danger could only be lessened by coming to grips with the enemy. Filled with fury and determination, they stormed up to the enemy line to find the Germans lying terrified at the bottom of their entrenchments.

A Desperate Defence

All the objectives had been taken, but at terrible cost. No 4 Company had suffered seventy-five percent casualties; they had only two Bren guns working and little ammunition. No 1 Company mustered only thirty-five men. The companies were isolated from each other and communications were working only fitfully. And, in their usual fashion, the Germans were quick to recover. Strong pockets of infantry, which had been momentarily stunned by

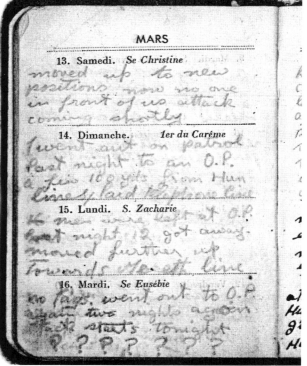

'Attack starts tonight ? ?': the ominous entry made by Lance Sergeant John Leese on the eve of the Mareth battle. The diary had been given him as a Christmas present by the Free French forces.

the bombardment and bypassed by the Grenadier advance, now began to raise their heads, shoot into the rear of the positions, block the approaches to them and burst upon the depleted platoons with showers of grenades. All, however, were repelled.

Carnage at the Wadi Crossing

All depended on the arrival of support, but this had to come over the wadi, where the situation was, if anything, more desperate still. It proved extremely difficult for the carriers to find a way out. Ten were blown up by mines in the wadi bed itself and, before a route was found, heavy losses had been incurred. Casualties in the support group were now even greater than those in the assault companies. The wadi was under the direct fire of ten or twelve machine guns and a blazing lorry illuminated the whole area, focusing German mortar fire on the few vehicles that remained.

The Withdrawal, and the Cost

Just before dawn it became clear that, without support, the forward positions could not be held. Already the objectives taken by the 3rd Coldstream on the left had been lost and that flank opened. The order for withdrawal was therefore given. To achieve this was no easy task. Communications were still bad. No 1 Company never received the order at all and of the other two companies only a handful returned after bitter close-quarter fighting. Many positions were simply overwhelmed and the shattered battalion was back where it had started sixteen hours earlier.

The losses were dreadful: 77 (including 14 officers) killed, 93 wounded and 109 taken prisoner. But it should be added that the Germans came to consider the Horseshoe as the key to the defence of the whole Mareth Line. British intelligence had initially underestimated the enemy strength but, far worse, and unknown to 201st Guards Brigade, surprise, a vital element for the night attack, had been lost. That the 6th Battalion, in its first battle, had actually gained and held its objectives for so long, under such conditions, was truly extraordinary.

Principal Sources: Nicolson,(1), though modified by later accounts. Forbes (Nigel, Lord)

The Anzio Beachhead

By the end of 1943 the progress of the allied armies fighting their way up the Italian peninsula was painfully slow. The purpose of the landings at Anzio in January 1944 was to break the deadlock by outflanking the Germans and achieving a swift advance on Rome. In the event the breakout from the beachhead was fatally delayed and five months of bitter fighting were to ensue before the aims of this great expedition were realized.

It fell to the **5th Battalion** (Lt Col 'Geordie' Gordon Lennox, later Lt Col Charles Huntington) to play their part in the defence of the bridgehead over a period of six weeks, but it was in the early days after the landing that their contribution was truly critical and that the second Grenadier Victoria Cross of the war was won.

The Landing and Exploitation

24th Guards Brigade embarked at Castellammare, south of Naples, as part of the invasion force of three divisions, and landed at Anzio virtually unopposed. It had been expected that swift exploitation would follow, but the elderly American corps commander[16] decided instead to spend a few days consolidating his forces and bringing ashore his heavy equipment. He reckoned without the

Scene of ferocious fighting: the gully at Anzio.

ability of the Germans, displayed so often during the war, to recover from an initial setback and strike back swiftly. At Anzio they wasted no time in doing so.

On 25 January the battalion took the village of Carroceto and 'The Factory' (in fact a Fascist agricultural settlement named Aprilia, ten miles inland) after a stiff fight. Here they remained for a week while, as it turned out, the enemy were pouring great numbers into preparations for a major counter-attack on the beachhead.

---

[16] General Lucas, who said shortly before the landing, 'I never commanded troops in action before and it's going to be a mighty interesting experience'. (Taylor)

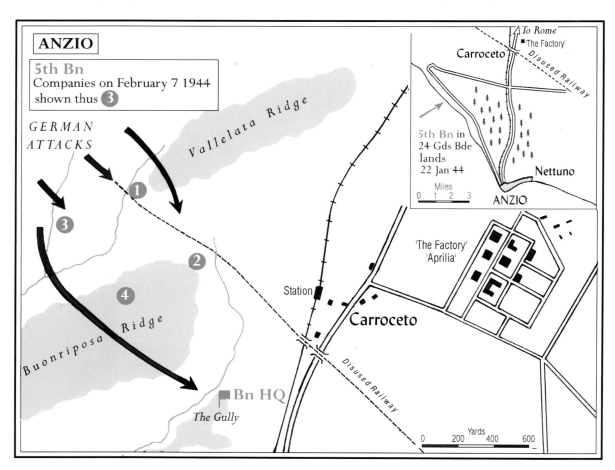

LIEUTENANT GENERAL
Sir GEORGE GORDON LENNOX
KBE CB CVO DSO *1908-1988*

Command of the 5th Battalion in North Africa and Italy, Command of the Regiment

'Geordie' Gordon Lennox was one of a long family line to be a Grenadier. His father, Lord Bernard Gordon Lennox, was killed at Ypres in 1914 and he also lost his mother when the Guards Chapel was bombed in June 1944. His two sons, Bernard and David, and two grandsons, followed him into the Regiment.

He won the King's Medal at Sandhurst and it fell to him, at the age of thirty-five, to take command of the 5th Battalion in Tunisia, which he then led with great skill in the fiercely contested Battle of the Bou in April 1943. He was to remain with it for two years, save for a short period when recovering from a wound received at Anzio. In that battle he commanded his battalion for many hours from a stretcher, a radio set by his side. While under his direction the battalion never lost even a platoon position or failed in an attack.

His men recognized the certainty of his leadership, his ability to read a battle and his fearlessness. He set exacting standards and his look of disapproval was to be avoided, but he instilled great confidence in the 5th Grenadiers, which suffered greater casualties than any other battalion of the Regiment.

After the war he commanded the 2nd Battalion in Germany and in 1951 his Regiment, before being appointed in turn to 1st Guards Brigade in Egypt, the 3rd Division and RMA Sandhurst .

As a lieutenant general he became Director General of Military Training and then GOC Scottish Command.

He was also Colonel of the Gordon Highlanders until succeeded by the Prince of Wales thirteen years later.

THE RIGHT HONOURABLE
WILLIAM SIDNEY, Viscount De L'ISLE VC
KG GCMG GCVO PC *1909-1991*

Victoria Cross of Anzio, Government Minister, Governor General

Major William (Bill) Sidney was commanding Support Company when the 5th Battalion went ashore at Anzio. The Germans launched a counter-attack on the beachhead with great force and a series of fierce hand-to-hand battles ensued.

His headquarters, situated in a gully south-west of the Carroceto bridge, was heavily assailed by enemy infantry who had bypassed a forward position. Sidney collected a mortar crew and led an attack with Tommy guns and grenades, driving the enemy out of the gully. He then, with a handful of men, took up a position on the edge of the gully. Having again driven back an attack by dashing forward with his Tommy gun, he sent most of his party back for more ammunition, keeping only two guardsmen with him. At this point the enemy attacked once more. A grenade struck him in the face and bounced off, killing one of his companions and wounding him and the other. Fed with grenades primed by his wounded comrade, Arthur Wright, he continued to keep the enemy at bay until the ammunition party returned.

As no further assault seemed likely, he retired to a cave to have his wounded thigh dressed, but very soon the enemy attacked yet again. At once he had himself carried back to his post, face down on a stretcher, and continued to engage the enemy for another hour before they were driven off.

General Alexander decorated him with the Victoria Cross with a piece of ribbon cut from the tunic of his father-in-law, Lord Gort VC. He had been a strict commander, and one of his men said of the award, 'Well, if he was as hard on the Germans as he was on us, he deserved it'.

Later he served as a government minister and Governor-General of Australia and was created a viscount and Knight of the Garter.

The Anzio beachhead: the gully is in the foreground with Carroceto behind it.

Counter-Attack on the Beachhead

By 7 February other troops had come up in support and on that evening the Grenadier companies were disposed north of Buonriposa Ridge. That night the Germans sought to isolate the Carroceto salient by three thrusts, the centre of which followed the line of the disused railway embankment. The Grenadier position was the most critical of all. No 3 Company was the first to bear the weight of the assault. One platoon after another was attacked on all sides and whenever they attempted a counter-attack it would coincide with a fresh onslaught from another direction. After a bitter struggle the position was completely overrun. No 1 Company was then given the same treatment, the Germans attacking in greatly superior numbers from three sides, and soon the embankment was cut behind them. Though many small parties

Smiling through: a nasty head wound does not get Sergeant Wilkinson down.

of these two companies tried to cut their way out of the encirclement, none succeeded.

The enemy had also broken through the North Staffordshires on the left. No 4 Company was therefore withdrawn to a position nearer the battalion headquarters in the Gully. No 2 Company was also coming under severe pressure. The Germans were now on top of the Buonriposa Ridge and surged onward. It was at a ditch just short of the Gully that they encountered Major Sidney, commanding Support Company, with half a dozen men, who held them off at this most critical point of the battle. A mere twenty-nine men of the battalion headquarters repelled other attacks in the area of the Gully.

The salient had been held and no further attack followed during the day of 8 February. However, rain fell and quickly turned to sleet. It was bitterly cold and at

Three gallant guardsmen: Lord Gort VC and his son-in-law Bill Sidney flank Sir Harold Alexander before the presentation of Sidney's Victoria Cross. The ribbon was cut from Lord Gort's tunic.

9 pm the German assault resumed. Once again the grenade, the true Grenadier weapon, proved decisive and saved the situation.

The remains of the battalion were withdrawn to the immediate area of the bridges, every Grenadier in the beachhead – drivers, clerks, storemen, orderlies and even cooks – being brought up to help. There they saw off further attacks, and at the end of the night the whole brigade was withdrawn and taken into reserve. 'Now we are back where we started' is the dismal record of the War Diary, 'having inflicted and suffered tremendous losses.'

The Cost to the Battalion

Though pressure on the beachhead increased further and the whole force, even in reserve, was vulnerable to shellfire, the 5th Battalion was not called upon again, except to occupy reserve positions later. They were too weak to fight another battle such as Carroceto. Their casualties were grievous: 61 killed, 232 wounded and 312 missing, of whom most were taken prisoner, many having been wounded. Over the few days since landing they had been commanded by no fewer than four different officers: Lt Col Gordon Lennox, Major Eustace Miller and Major John Nelson, all of whom were wounded, and Lt Col Huntington, who was killed on 9 February.

Principal Source: Nicolson (1)

Grenadier Gallery

REGIMENTAL SERGEANT MAJOR
GEORGE ARMSTRONG
DCM *1910-1978*

Sniper in the Anzio beachhead, winner of the King's and Queen's Medals, electronics engineer

George Armstrong was one of the most remarkable shots the British Army ever had, winning the King's Medal in 1951, the Queen's Medal in 1955 and being runner-up in the Army Hundred in 1949.

He had already proved his worth in battle in the most dramatic way. Landing at Anzio with the 5th Battalion, as Drill Sergeant, he was one of the heroic party, mostly of battalion headquarters staff, who manned the Gully and held off large numbers of Germans at the most critical time of the battle. He is believed to have accounted for thirty of the enemy, sniping in the beachhead, and was justly awarded the DCM.

Armstrong joined the Regiment in 1928 and served with the 3rd Battalion up to the rank of company sergeant major. He became RQMS of the 5th Battalion, the 3rd Battalion and the Guards Training Battalion before being appointed RSM of the School of Infantry in 1960. On discharge in 1964 he became a Yeoman Warder at the Tower of London.

A colleague remarked upon his extraordinary eyesight. He used to analyze his target shooting shot for shot and mark them up. However, before his shot was signalled from the butt he had already recorded the strike. When asked how he did so he replied that he could actually see the flight of the bullet through the air to its point of impact.

He was also at one time signals sergeant of the 3rd Battalion. A brilliant electronics engineer, his ideas of constructing high fidelity equipment were the forerunners of the equipment used in much later years. He was reputed to have been making devices of this kind in the 1930s.

A Gruelling Infantry War in Tunisia and Italy

The three battalions (3rd, 5th and 6th) employed in Tunisia and Italy fought a long campaign, often in the most trying conditions. The following are reflections by some of those engaged:

The British Infantry Weapons

'Under the test of actual experience the weapons of the British battalion were sorted out into categories of usefulness. The basic weapon, the Bren gun, was at first criticized for its slow rate of fire compared with that of the German MG34 or MG42, and for the small capacity of its magazine; but in compensation it had great accuracy and reliability, and its design remained almost unchanged from the beginning of the war to the end. Of the other weapons, the British service rifle was supreme in the field: the 2-inch mortar was found to be less useful than its bigger brothers, the 3-inch and 4.2-inch. The anti-tank rifle was too heavy for a platoon to carry over long distances and was ineffective against all but the lightest German tanks: it was discarded early in the Tunisian campaign. For close fighting the bayonet and the No 36 grenade were as valuable throughout this war as in the last. The 2-pounder anti-tank gun, later replaced by the 6-pounder, was never fully tested: the 3rd and 6th Battalions, in both the Tunisian and Italian campaigns, never had a single opportunity to use them; the 5th but very few.'[17]

Africa Star, Italy Star: the colours of the first represent the desert with a broad red stripe for the army and narrow ones for naval and air forces, those of the second the national colours of Italy.

Bayonets, Equipment, Socks

'Some silly scientist had persuaded the Army that a hat-pin bayonet about eight inches long would kill just as efficiently as the First World War broad-bladed twenty-inch weapon. Fortunately my battalion and several others refused the issue of the Mk 4 hat-pin rifle, and retained our SMLE Mk 1, the bayonets of which were burnished by the guardsmen to shine brightly. When the order came "Charge!" all rifles came down in unison from the high port, flashing in the half light. The intimidation was such that few enemy resisted.

'What should troops carry in the attack or in mobile warfare? Basically personal weapons, ammunition, grenades, entrenching tool (not very efficient), gas mask (until March 1944), water bottle, gas cape (warm at night and a mackintosh in a wet slit trench), small pack with shaving things, mess tin, personal possessions. More than that and the soldier could hardly move, let alone fight. This meant that a high priority was to get picks and shovels forward urgently, to dig slit trenches for protection and to be ready for the German counter-attack which so often followed a successful attack of ours. But we had won ground at dawn – the Germans therefore had to attack in daylight or wait for night when we would be readier. We never occupied German trenches or, worse still, dug-outs. The smell they left behind was utterly revolting.

'The most important item for the mules to convey was two pairs of dry socks per man per day. The slit trenches were a slimy mess. Every man had to take off his boots, massage his feet and don dry socks twice a day. As a result we had no cases of trench foot, a seriously disabling complaint. An American battalion nearby had 140 cases in ten days. Where Harold Lucas, our Quartermaster, found the socks (and how he got them washed and dried) I never found out. Behind a gruff exterior he performed many a minor miracle.'[18]

'One ludicrous idea from the War Office to protect us from allied aircraft was introduced later in Italy. These were recognition panels of shiny orange-coloured fabric with loops at each corner. One loop was to be attached to the top button of the battledress blouse and, when an aircraft was diving towards us to machine gun or bomb, we were to thrust our thumbs into the two other loops and display the triangle to the pilot.... We continued our usual practice of diving into the nearest ditch. We used the material for other purposes.'[19]

The Arrival of Compo

'We were making our first acquaintance with the "composite" type of ration (known as "compo"). This was a completely new departure for the British Army and very

[17] Nicolson (1)
[18] Taylor
[19] Bowley

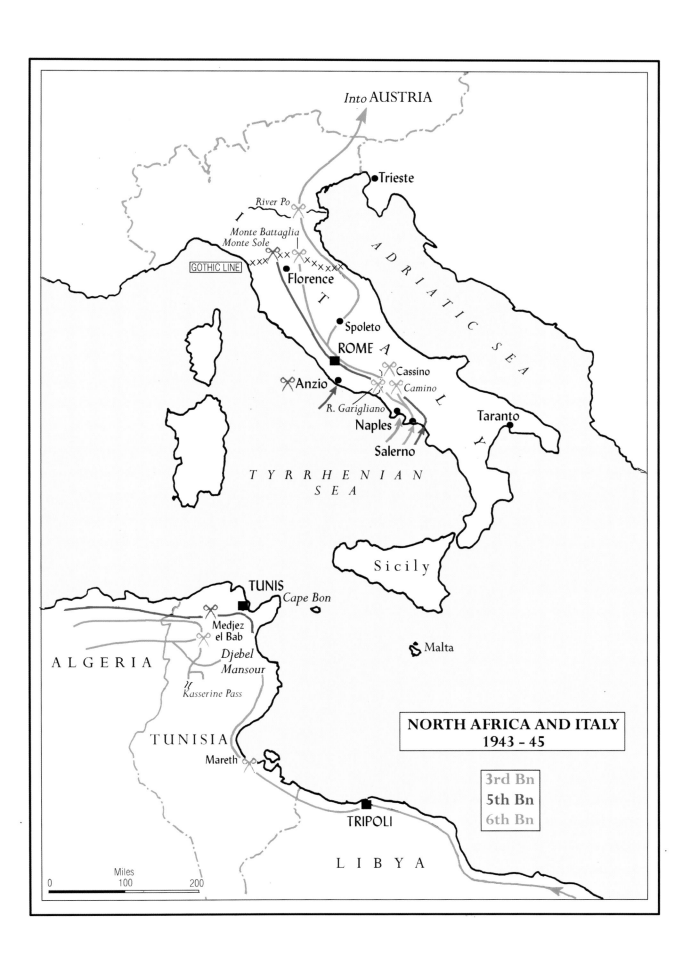

Into AUSTRIA

●Trieste

River Po

Monte Battaglia
Monte Sole

GOTHIC LINE

●Florence

A D R I A T I C   S E A

●Spoleto

ROME *A*

Cassino
■
Camino

Anzio ●

R. Garigliano

Naples *Y*

Taranto ●

Salerno

L

T Y R R H E N I A N
S E A

S i c i l y

TUNIS
■ *Cape Bon*

Medjez
el Bab

✂ Malta

Djebel
Mansour

A L G E R I A

Kasserine Pass

NORTH AFRICA AND ITALY
1943 – 45

T U N I S I A

Mareth ✂

3rd Bn
5th Bn
6th Bn

■
TRIPOLI

L I B Y A

Miles
0   100   200

The battle won: Grenadiers celebrate victory at Cassino.

A poignant memorial: the cairn on Monte Camino built in 2002 by Michael Stirling (nephew of a fallen Grenadier with no known grave), and friends to commemorate their comrades. The intrepid party, no longer youngsters, made many hard and heavy climbs to achieve their objective.

A hotly disputed town: positions and features at Cassino marked on an air photograph.

successful. The rations were in compact wooden boxes, 14 men's rations for one day in each box. There were six varieties, each denoted by a different letter on the box. The rations inside were easily split up into the various meals, and there was a list of contents inside each box. As well as the meals, there was tea, sugar and milk, all mixed in powder form, needing only to be heated in water (admittedly producing rather third-rate tea), also cigarettes, sweets and Bromo loo paper. No bread, only biscuits, so one soon began to exchange biscuits, etc, with the French and Arabs for their bread and eggs. One began to have favourite types of compo. For example, type A had an excellent steak and kidney pudding, whereas type X only had bully beef. Type F, haricot oxtail, were also rather moderate. Some varieties were excellent, especially the puddings, marmalade, plum or rice, the latter amazingly creamy.'[20]

A Hornet's Nest on Monte Battaglia

'In the worst spot they had known since Cassino, the guardsmen held on grimly. Then, one dark night, doubtless judging that days of continuous bombardment must have shattered the defenders, the Germans attacked in force. The guardsmen let them come in. There was confusion as the first Germans fell over the trip-wires and then all hell let loose. For men who for six days or more had been pinned in their trenches there was no need to cry "Up Guards and at 'em!" They were in and among the enemy before the Germans realised just what a hornet's nest they had struck. When the battle was over the guardsmen had taken nearly 100 prisoners and the remaining Germans who had launched the attack were lying dead on the hillside. They did not attack the position again.'[21]

'... it was due to the courageous action of a single man in the leading section, Gdsm R Wood MM, that the attack was repulsed. The man lying next to him was killed at short range and, when Wood started to fire back, his Bren gun jammed after a few rounds. "He picked up the gun," reads the citation, "and knocked the leading German over the head, stunning him. He struck the next one with his fists, and when four Germans attempted to rush the trench, Wood hurled grenades at them at five yards' range, and continued to throw anything he could lay his hands on," including, adds another account, his web equipment.'[22]

The Long, Bloody Slog of Attrition

'Camino remains in the minds of those who fought among its rocks as a memory which will be never blurred. One of them will tell you of the wind and the pools of water streaked with blood; another of the unbearable tension of those nights on Point 819 when they knew not in which direction to hold their rifles in readiness, for the enemy were all around them; while to a third the name "Camino" will recall how he toiled up the goat track night after night with wet loads of food and ammunition, and the shells tore into the hillside at his feet. It is not true to say that the first Battle of Camino was typical of the fighting in the Appennines, for it combined all the worst elements of all battles: extreme danger, intolerable weather, a position inferior to the enemy's, long duration, and, at first, failure. To the Grenadiers Camino seemed so tragic because there was so little to show for all that they had suffered, even after the second battle had at last been rewarded by success. No town was captured, no river crossed, no clean break made in the German line. The enemy was forced back no more than a mile or two to another mountain, and these mountains stretched endlessly up the length of Italy. How, they felt, would it ever end? A clear answer to that question can now be given. The Germans were defeated by the attrition of countless battles, of which Camino remains a striking example; by their losses in dead and prisoners; by the exhaustion of those who survived and the wastage of their war material, by their growing despondency in continual defeat, matched by the growing confidence of the Allied troops. In such a cause, no soldier's life is thrown away in vain.'[23]

The German Soldiers

'The Germans had been told by their officers that the British take no prisoners, or hand them over to the Russians for execution. Is it, then, surprising that they should have fought their hardest to evade capture, and then be overwhelmed with relief to find that they were treated no more harshly than one of our own soldiers under arrest? They never knew us as we knew them. They never saw a billet occupied by the British the night before as we saw theirs. They never handled the litter of

[20] Lambert
[21] Webb
[22] Bozeat, Nicolson (1)
[23] Nicolson (1)

MAJOR GENERAL
Sir JOHN NELSON
KCVO CB DSO OBE MC *1912-1993*

Inspiring infantry
leader in North Africa
and Italy,
Major General at
Horse Guards,
GOC Berlin

*J*ohn Nelson was a superlative infantry soldier. If invited to name the outstanding young regimental officer of the war, few Grenadiers would fail to choose him. A man of lively temperament and passionate enthusiasms, he was famous for his vivid rebukes. But he inspired a fierce loyalty and a determination to excel.

During the Dunkirk campaign of 1940 he commanded the anti-tank company of 1st Guards Brigade. In January 1941 he took over No 3 Company of the 3rd Battalion. He remained with it for two years, but the association was to last as the Nelson Club, formed by the survivors and given his name. He appreciated very early that the infantry war must be won by personal skills and teamwork of the highest order, and mastery of fighting at night. All this he soon trained his company to achieve.

In the Tunisian campaign he led a number of audacious operations, winning a Military Cross but being badly wounded in February 1943. Barely recovered, he went to the 5th Battalion as second-in-command and accompanied it to Anzio, where he took over command, although again wounded, and brought out the survivors. In May 1944 he led the 'Nelson Column' in diversionary operations near Cassino, before returning to his beloved 3rd Battalion in command. He was still only thirty-one. He then led the battalion in the long, bloody haul through Italy, in the process acquiring a third wound and the DSO.

The war over, he commanded the Guards Parachute Battalion for its short life, the 1st Grenadiers in Tripoli and 4th Guards Brigade in Germany, before becoming in succession Major General at Horse Guards and GOC Berlin.

See Nelson

THE REVEREND CANON
DENYS BROWNING
1905-1999

Devoted Chaplain
to the
5th Battalion
in North Africa
and Italy

*D*enys Browning was a sheep farmer in New Zealand before being ordained in his mid-thirties in 1941. The following year he was appointed chaplain to the 5th Battalion, with which he was to remain continuously in North Africa and Italy. When the battalion returned home he remained in Italy as chaplain to the 2nd Coldstream.

Although related to several guardsmen, both Grenadier and Welsh, he was unfamiliar with the exactness of life required in such society. He was a most saintly man and inevitably found some methods of training and strict discipline difficult to stomach, though he was to recognize the value of them in the hard school of war. He was not particularly tidy and an erratic timekeeper. When out of the line, his services were always set for 10am, but would start anything up to ten minutes either side, a risky undertaking for a Grenadier.

However, he made up for such deficiencies by the quality of his ministry. His humility, straight-forwardness, simplicity, courage and support won the hearts of all ranks. He never flinched in action and cheerfully accepted the dirtiest of jobs. He was the recipient of all kinds of confidences which he would never have dreamt of betraying, and was widely regarded as a saint. After the battles in Tunisia he was invited by his Commanding Officer to wear Grenadier shoulder flashes, which he did with pride, to the fury of the Chaplains' Department. It marked the battalion's high regard for him and was also useful when visiting hospital. Wounded guardsmen, Grenadiers or not, would call out for him. They knew his worth.

He continued his ministry in New Zealand and, late in life, was still tearing about on a motorcycle, hair streaming in the wind.

See Browning, Taylor

personal equipment and letters as we handled theirs. The number of prisoners which they took was very small, of deserters none at all. All they knew was that our supplies, our equipment, our morale were apparently inexhaustible, our determination inflexible, our initiative unchallengeable... They did not know what they were heading for: we knew, without a shadow of doubt.'[24]

Courage, Spirit, Endurance, Leadership

'The guardsmen, who won these battles, never wavered in the heat of the fury, the dust and the smoke. It was harder for them, I believe, than for the officers, perennially busy, who had some idea of what was going on. For the guardsman it was endless waiting – "go there, no – the plan's changed – tonight we'll attack – wait – go on stag." They accepted it all with a wry smile, remaining solid, reliable and friends with their officers. I cannot say how much I admired them: and in the 5th Battalion Grenadiers, 90% were conscripts.

'Where does collective courage come from? It was demonstrated time and again in that battle on the Bou. I think one must go back to the Guards Depot. It all starts with drill and discipline and the inculcation of the belief that the recruit has been brought to a centre of excellence, where detail matters. Everyone wants to belong to an organization which patently works, the outward manifestation being smartness of appearance. Pride in personal performance and in the Regiment grows.

'An illuminating conference of psychiatrists ... after the Falklands War ... concluded that no infantryman should be subjected to more than 35 days in the line: no doubt right if he had no motivation. I think that, in my own case, I detected a fall-off of efficiency after about 400 days in the line, but one was so used to everything by then that it was not apparent. And I can number on the fingers of two hands those guardsmen who broke under the strain. Our war experiences marked us ineradicably for the rest of our lives. We knew fear many times but not terror, which warps judgement. Discipline, leadership and a determination never to let a comrade down was the bulwark. We needed no counselling either during or after the war.... It is indisputable that those now claiming and receiving huge cash sums have not experienced a tithe of the stress suffered by our conscripted guardsmen who looked for neither counsel nor compensation and would have derided anyone who did.

'I was duty officer at night. Unexpectedly I had to visit a rifle company. Lieutenant Charlie Lyttelton took my place in the signals office and was killed by a shell. My servant,[25] Guardsman Shaw, lost a leg. In the Regimental Aid Post he smiled at me wryly, "That'll teach you to put me on stag, sir." It epitomized the wonderful spirit of the battalion.

'Perhaps the most important relationship was that between the platoon commander and his men. In those days in the Brigade [of Guards] there was not only a wide social gulf between the two, but also the officers had positively volunteered for the Regiment ... whereas the great majority of the other ranks were "pressed men". So the platoon commander's first task was to build confidence in him personally. He would be leading in battle. If his men doubted his confidence or his bravery, there was little hope of success. Friendship, confidence and respect must be earned. We had a good lot of NCOs when we went abroad but casualties were heavy and once in the line there were no sergeants' or corporals' courses to teach them their trade. Fortunately the stress of war threw up obvious candidates for promotion and I don't think we ever suffered by reason of inadequate NCOs. Moreover, their comrades had seen them perform in action and were happy to serve under them.

'On arrival in UK it was back to Chelsea Barracks for the 5th Grenadiers. Shortly afterwards Churchill rose [in the House of Commons] and announced the surrender of the entire German army group in Italy. A few days later the German war ended. London went wild that night; but the officers dined quietly in the mess. Voluntarily, no guardsman passed the barrack guard. We all had too much to remember, too little to celebrate.'[26]

Faith, Selflessness and Cost

'I place the battle of Monte Battaglia, from a personal point of view, in the same class as Dunkirk and Anzio. In all three situations I felt that the odds against survival were equally heavy and all of us involved needed to call upon every reserve available. Inherent discipline and the fear of being thought a coward helped tremendously, but I am quite certain that it was our Christian faith that was,

---

[24] Nicolson (1)
[25] Officer's orderlies were still then known as 'soldier servants'. In peacetime they were virtually domestic staff. This was not always successful. One was returned to duty with a note saying, 'It appears that the housemaid finds him fascinating but the household extremely trying.'
[26] Taylor

In the mist: a patrol
on its way.

A muddy relief:
up a sticky track
with blanket and
equipment.

On watch: an obser-
vation post with
Bren gun.

Yet another heart-breaking hill: toiling upwards in Italy.

fundamentally, the greatest assistance of all. There was not a single absentee from the voluntary service held on the hillside the Sunday after we came off the mountain.

'The 3rd and 5th Grenadier battalions [after two and a half years of front-line war] were amalgamated at Spoleto in March [1945] and I opted to return to England with all those in either battalion who had been abroad the longest. We, the veterans, had not much reserve left to call upon and ... I considered that the essential spark, which even at this late stage was still vital, would no longer materialise if called upon to ignite .... Losses, mercifully, had been appreciably below the horrifying figures of 1914-18, but they had been bad enough. And they came, as ever, from the ranks of the elite, whatever its status or background. The most patriotic, the least selfish, made the greatest sacrifice .... The less scrupulous, again from all walks of life, remain safely under cover in times of danger only to reappear in full strength after the last all-clear has sounded, their insidious path made easier by the removal of such a high proportion of their more highly motivated compatriots.'[27]

A Hospital Visit

'There was a sudden shout from the door – in rushed a lone figure ... red tabs – the Field Marshal himself, Lord Gort. He almost ran down the ward, came directly to my bed ... sat on one side of it. Spoke to me alone about the Grenadier Guards on Monte Camino and my part in things ... about my wound ... wished me well.... He quickly vanished out of the door as suddenly as he had appeared, having neither spoken to nor looked at anyone else .... From that moment I was the most important person in the ward.'[28]

A Prisoner's Long March to Freedom

'We cleared many mountains before reaching Monte Camino. During the battle I fired at a German soldier ... something came down the hill towards me. It did flash through my mind, "Why is he throwing stones at me?" Of course it was a grenade, Luckily not a stick grenade but a small plastic grenade. Something hit the webbing on my shoulder and my whole arm went dead. The explosion also blew me back into my slit trench – when I got out he was waiting for me. He escorted me round the corner. There were several more captured Grenadiers.

'After being transported into Germany, after many camps, my party arrived at a coal mine in Poland. It was a bit of a joke among my friends when I told them I had joined the Army to get out of the mines.

'We knew the Russians were coming nearer at the end of December 1944. We could hear the rumble of their artillery and all hoped the Germans would leave us there to be liberated by the Russians, but no. At 0500 early on January 3rd they turned us out to start marching. The march west lasted three and a half months and we covered 900 miles, through very bad conditions, bitterly cold weather. We slept at night in old barns and farmhouses. We eventually reached Retensburg on the Danube and were resting in a farmhouse when we were strafed by American Thunderbolts. I was hit in the leg by shrapnel. The Swiss Red Cross lorries picked up all the wounded and took us to hospital in a big POW camp. It was there that we were liberated by the Americans. The British soldiers who were wounded were flown home by Lancaster bombers.'[29]

[27] Nelson
[28] Stephens
[29] Dowding

Nijmegen – A Bridge Just Near Enough

The capture of the road bridge at Nijmegen on 20 September 1944 was for Grenadiers the most dramatic single episode of the campaign in north-west Europe. It was entirely a regimental affair, two battalions acting in concert achieving an extraordinary and fortunate success as part of a greater operation which tragically was doomed to failure.

The *Market Garden* Plan

Operation *Market Garden* was the result of a warm dispute between General Eisenhower, the American supreme commander, and his subordinate General Montgomery, the British commander of 21st Army Group. Eisenhower favoured advancing across the whole breadth of France towards the German frontier, which indeed was done, though insufficient petrol remained for a subsequent assault on the German homeland.

Montgomery advocated a concentrated rapier-like thrust across the river lines of Holland and thence into the North German Plain, which opened the enticing prospect of bringing the war to a close before the end of 1944. The plan was agreed. It involved crossing first the Maas, then the Waal at Nijmegen, and finally the Rhine at Arnhem. This was to be done by the three divisions of the Airborne Corps (Lt Gen Frederick Browning, a Grenadier) dropping to secure the bridges, followed up overland by 30 Corps, in which the Guards Armoured Division took the lead.

The Race to the Bridges

The bridge over the Maas at Grave was taken by American paratroopers and quickly consolidated. It then fell to the Grenadier Group, the motorized infantry of the **1st Battalion** (Lt Col Edward Goulburn) acting in close concert with the Sherman tanks of the **2nd Battalion** (Lt

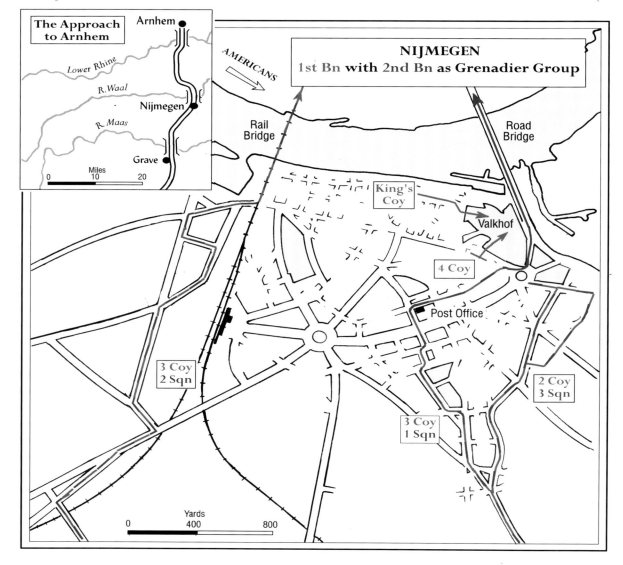

GENERAL
Sir RODNEY MOORE
GCVO KCB CBE DSO PMN *1905-1985*

Command of the
2nd (Armoured)
Battalion,
Major General,
Chief of Staff
in Malaya

*R*odney Moore was commissioned into the Regiment in 1925. His wartime service was largely devoted to the transformation of guardsmen to armoured soldiers and to leading them in that role. He proved to be a commander and staff officer of great ability.

He served as brigade major to both 30th Guards Brigade and 6th Guards Armoured Brigade, and then as GSO1 (chief staff officer) to the Guards Armoured Division, before being given command of the 2nd Battalion at the beginning of 1944. He led it through the entire campaign in Europe from Normandy to the Elbe. His four headquarters tanks were named D'Artagnan, Athos, Porthos and Aramis, after the famous musketeers.

He was not averse to comfort, not to say a touch of grandeur, when out of the line. Caravans were in mode for commanders from Montgomery downwards and Moore, not to be outdone, had a surplus three-tonner beautifully lined and panelled by the battalion pioneers and decorated with small French prints of Napoleon's marshals.

After the war his career continued apace. His commands included 1st Guards Brigade in Palestine and 1st Division and 10th Armoured Division in the Middle East, before returning home to be Major General Commanding the Household Brigade and London District, where his taste for pageantry and ceremonial were given full scope. In 1959 he was appointed Chief of the Armed Forces Staff and Director of Border Operations in the Federation of Malaya, the Malaysian government signifying its gratitude by making him Panglima Mangku Negara (PMN). He became the first Defence Services Secretary and after retirement received many other honours and distinctions.

MAJOR GENERAL
EDWARD GOULBURN
DSO and Bar *1903-1980*

Command of the
1st (Motor) Battalion,
the Grenadier Group
at Nijmegen, and
of the Regiment

*E*ddie Goulburn joined the Regiment in 1924. He was Adjutant at Sandhurst from 1938 and most cadets of that time had vivid recollections of him. He had a great reputation for smartness and absolutely straight dealing.

He took command of the 1st (Motor) Battalion in England in 1942 and was to remain with them for two and a half years. He was a very energetic trainer and his strong views on the handling of his command earned him the nickname 'Tactical Ted', which stuck with him all through his time with the Guards Armoured Division.

He took the battalion to Normandy for the invasion of Europe and the subsequent advance through France, Belgium and Holland. During this time the original grouping of infantry with tanks within his brigade was changed and his infantry companies thereafter operated alongside the armoured squadrons of the 2nd Battalion. The two battalions together were known as the Grenadier Group, under his overall command. It proved an extraordinarily successful combination.

The battle in Nijmegen was the high point of his command. The Grenadier Group had little warning for the operation, which was laid on in a few hours in the middle of the night, but it was in the following muddled day's fighting that Goulburn displayed his full ability as a battle commander, unruffled by unexpected events and incorrect information. The success of the operation was very largely due to his efforts.

Shortly after Nijmegen he was given a brigade and two years later promoted to major general. In 1948 he reverted to colonel in order to command his regiment and later became president of the regimental association.

SERGEANT
PETER ROBINSON
DCM 1915-1999

Winner of the
Distinguished
Conduct Medal for
capturing the
Nijmegen Bridge

Nijmegen: the shattered town with the road bridge in the background.

*P*eter Robinson was the leading actor in one of the most dramatic episodes of the Second World War. He had first served in the Regiment from 1934 to 1938 and was recalled to the Colours on the outbreak of war. He fought with the 2nd Battalion in the Dunkirk campaign and later became troop sergeant of No 1 Troop, No 1 Squadron, when the battalion adopted the armoured role. He crossed to Normandy and in September 1944 was launched into the operation to take the crucial Nijmegen bridge.

After a quick attack the previous day ran into heavy opposition, the Grenadier Group launched a second attack on 20 September and, after hard fighting, were within reach of the bridge. Almost all the Sherman tank troops had been engaged, however, and only Sgt Robinson's remained. At 6.30pm the troop edged forward along the embankment, but it was still too light and they were met by strong anti-tank fire. By 7 pm it was beginning to get dark and the troop fired their guns into the gloom, charged across the bridge and disappeared from sight. Two tanks were hit by anti-tank fire but the remaining two, commanded by Robinson and LSgt Pacey, avoiding the missiles which the enemy were dropping from their perches high up in the girders, reached the far side of the bridge, skidded broadside through a road block, knocked out two anti-tank guns and, a mile down the road, linked up with a party of American paratroopers. It was fully expected that the bridge would be blown at any moment, but it was prevented by the swift and determined action of these Grenadiers.

Robinson received his DCM from the hand of Field Marshal Montgomery, Pacey being awarded the MM.

Col Rodney Moore), to race up to Nijmegen and fight their way to the bridges, which had not immediately fallen to the airborne assault. There were two bridges, road and rail, and both were still intact. The leading platoon and its accompanying troop of tanks were five hundred yards from the road bridge when the German defenders awoke to their danger. Entrenched on a roundabout dominating the slope down to the bridge, they opened up on the approaching columns with everything they had, and for some minutes the fighting was furious. A second column heading for the railway bridge also caught the enemy unawares, but the Germans, in greatly superior numbers, were able to check the attack. A further force succeeded, after a spirited fight, in seizing the Post Office where the German headquarters was situated.

Clearing the Defences

Early the next morning there was no guarantee that either bridge would remain unblown and two companies were launched against the immediate defences. The objective of the King's Company was the Valkhof, a heavily wooded open-air fort honeycombed with underground passages and trenches, from which in 1940 the Dutch had resisted the German invaders for three days. The company climbed a steep bank, cut their way through a wire obstacle and stormed in with grenades and Sten guns. On the right No 4 Company pressed forward over open ground and took a tower which was the focal point of the defences. Tanks were closely involved in support and the fighting was long and severe.

Over the bridge: armour moves across past German dead.

Taking the Road Bridge

At 7 pm, just as the light was beginning to fail, a troop of tanks under Sgt Robinson charged across the bridge and disappeared into the gloom. They fought their way through enemy snipers, anti-tank guns and a road block, and forged on for a mile beyond, on the way meeting up with the remnants of an American force which had made a courageous crossing by assault boat. Meanwhile an accompanying sapper officer,[30] on foot, was cutting every demolition wire he could find and searching the demolition chambers beneath each span. Reinforcements were sent over from the Irish Guards, the bridges secured (the railway bridge had also been taken) and the advanced position hastily prepared for defence.

Why were the bridges never blown? Probably because the Germans were over-confident and never intended to do what every Grenadier expected them to do at any moment. They were in greater strength than had been imagined and probably wanted to reserve the bridge for a counter-attack. But the capture of a great strategic bridge is one of the most exciting of war exploits and it was a fine feat of arms by the Grenadiers.

The Tragedy of Arnhem

Alas, it still could not save our airborne soldiers at Arnhem. The narrow single-track road from Nijmegen was suicidal for armour alone and it proved impossible to reach Arnhem in time. Having been dropped too far from

Three Grenadiers of Nijmegen (from above): Sir Frederick 'Boy' Browning, who had won a DSO at Gauche Wood in 1917 before his twenty-first birthday, commanded the Airborne Corps; Peter, Lord Carrington, was one of the first across the bridge and later became a major figure in politics; Guardsman Walter Meadows was the only Grenadier of the war in that rank to win the DCM, for extreme courage in saving wounded comrades under heavy fire.

the bridge and running into heavy resistance, the paratroopers fought with desperate courage for several days before being overwhelmed, out of ammunition and heavily depleted in numbers. They were only lightly armed, of course, and could not for long match the heavy weaponry of the Germans. Tragically, Arnhem proved to be a bridge too far.

Principal Source: Forbes (2)

---

[30] Capt Tony Jones, who was awarded the MC and later became a brigadier

231

Armoured Grenadiers

The Challenge of Adapting to Armour

While concern was raised about whether guardsmen would fit into tanks, the 2nd and 4th Grenadiers, along with other battalions of Foot Guards, were destined to receive them. The King's Company, however, were regarded as too tall and the 1st Battalion therefore remained as infantry, though motorized. The 2nd Battalion were equipped with Covenanters in 1941, Crusaders in 1942 and finally Shermans in 1943; the 4th Battalion had Churchills.

'The magnitude of the task which confronted them was indeed immense. For every man who knew how to drive a tank, there were a hundred who had never driven a car. For every officer who understood the mysteries of a carburettor or a final drive, there were a dozen who were never quite sure where to find the dipstick in a car engine. To have asked the average man in the winter of 1941 to change a broken tank track would have been like asking a civil servant to mend a railway line.

'First, the five men who make up a tank crew – tank commander, gunner, wireless operator, driver and co-driver – had to be taught how to handle and look after their tank. Then the four tank crews (sometimes three or five) that make up a troop had to be taught

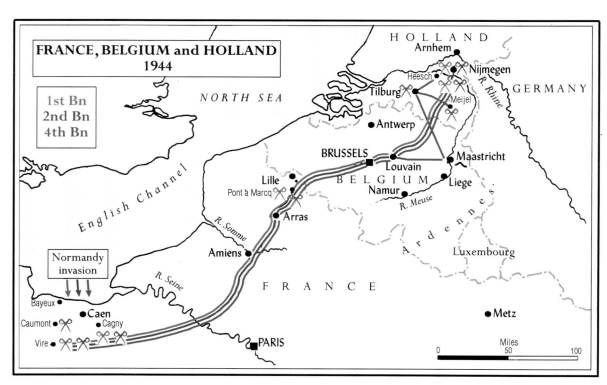

France and Germany Star: the national colours of the United Kingdom, France and the Netherlands.

elementary armoured tactics. Later they had to learn how to cooperate with infantry, and so the process continued.'[31]

The Formidable Panther and Tiger Tanks

'The 2nd and 4th Battalions had been warned time and time again about the giant Panther and Tiger tanks which the Germans were using, but when they actually came to meet them in battle the battalions began to feel an even greater respect for them. They saw their own perfectly aimed shots bouncing off the frontal armour of the enemy tanks like ping-pong balls, and they learnt once and for all that there were only two effective ways of dealing with them: either to move around the flank of the Hun tank and shoot at its sides at a range of no more than five hundred yards, or to call on the medium artillery to deal with it from behind. Furthermore, ... neither the Sherman nor the Churchill (which was the most heavily armoured tank yet produced by either Britain or America) was capable of withstanding a direct hit from a German 88mm anti-tank gun.'[32]

---

[31] Forbes(2)
[32] Forbes (2)

FRANCE, BELGIUM and HOLLAND
1944

1st Bn
2nd Bn
4th Bn

HOLLAND
Arnhem
Heesch
Nijmegen
Tilburg
Meijel
GERMANY
NORTH SEA
R. Rhine
Antwerp
BRUSSELS
Louvain
Maastricht
Lille
BELGIUM
Liege
Pont à Marcq
Namur
R. Meuse
Arras
R. Somme
Ardennes
Luxembourg
Amiens
Normandy invasion
R. Seine
FRANCE
English Channel
Bayeux
Caen
Caumont
Cagny
Metz
Vire
PARIS
Miles
0   50   100

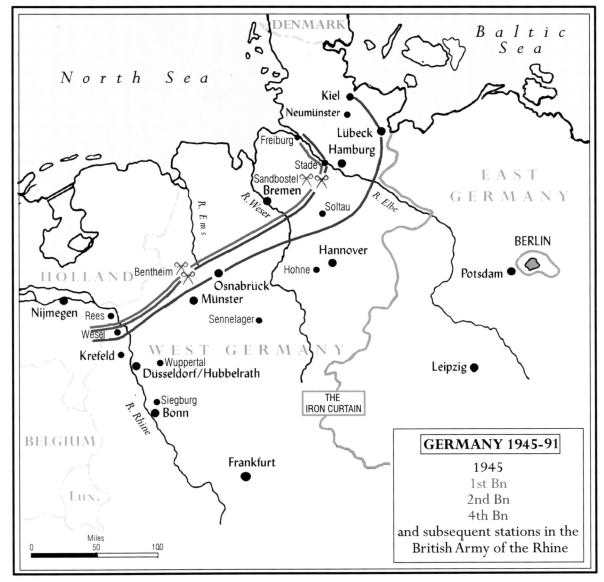

Trapped in a Bogged Tank

'The crews of the tanks bogged in the valley spent a hair-raising night being stalked by the enemy. One in particular was bogged so deeply that the water came into the turret. The enemy surrounded it and told the crew to surrender. When they refused to do so the enemy boarded the tank and tried to open the engine, but the covers were luckily locked and the crew escaped unscathed.'[33]

A Lucky Escape

'Suddenly there was a terrific thud on the side of the [Honey light] tank, which seemed to cause it to leap into the air. Whereupon Sgt Smith shouted, "Reverse, reverse, throw out the smoke". The tank reversed a few yards, then came to a standstill. Whereupon Sgt Smith gave the order to "Bale out!"

'I attempted to lift my hatchway cover but it would only open a few inches and the gun cowling was preventing me lifting the hatch cover. My only escape then was the hatch situated on the floor of the tank beside my feet, which required unlocking two clasps on the back of the seat, pulling the back of the seat around to the front of myself, then turning myself round to release two clips on the base plate of the tank to allow the plates to fall to the ground, then crawling through the aperture.

'The only [sic] remaining exit was via the turret. I had to climb on to the turret floor through a very small opening, between the ammunition rack and the turret

<hr>

[33] Forbes(2)

233

Close knit: four o[f]
Sherman crew of
five take a rest.

Hand in glove: the 1st Battalion on foot and the 2nd in Sherman tanks.

Soldiers great and small:
Grenadiers (though not the
King's Company) managed to
fit into tanks, but it was
helpful to have small and
agile help from the REME to
keep them on the road.

In the bocage: infantry of the 1st Battalion advance in Normandy.

floor supports. It is surprising what you are capable of doing when in a life or death situation. Flames were issuing from both petrol tanks.'[34]

Sang Froid at the 'O' (Order) Group

'These O groups always amused me. Our officers referred to them as OOOOH groups, and it seemed that the longer you could make your OOOO, the higher up the social scale you were. Then you'll remember, they would gather around in a circle, smoking their Turkish cigarettes, regardless of passing bullets, shells, bombs, what-have-you, and discuss just how they were going to win this particular part of the war .... For a very short time there was a lull in the firing and while silence reigned, there was the sound of a voice calling from one of the slit trenches the [Line] infantry were occupying. "Hey, Jimmy, d'yer know who these fellers are standing out there? It's the Guards – we'll be all right now mate".'[35]

A Shelling from Jerry

'Wednesday 28th February '45. Up at 5.00 am .... We sat and read papers and books all day till 4.00 pm .... Jerry sent some shells over, about two fields away. We saw them explode, six, all in a line. I heard some more coming, I

Another move: an officer of the 4th Battalion plans his route.
Christopher Morley

---

[34] Lacey
[35] Holmes (Barney)

All aboard: men of the 6th Airborne Division mounted on a Churchill tank of the 4th Battalion for a gallop into the German heartland.

'He never failed me and he never failed you': Allan Adair and Montgomery in conversation. On the right are Generals Horrocks (30 Corps) and Harding.

looked for cover, I saw a shallow hole at the side of a brick wall, I dived into it, eyes closed. As the shells came nearer, funny smell, then bang, bang, two shells. Dirt fell on me. I opened my eyes and the first thing I saw was a boot with foot still in it...Very cold. On stag 8.30 pm until 10.00 pm. Bed at 10.45 pm (no letters).'[36]

Not forgotten by the young: a Dutch child by a Grenadier grave at Pont à Marcq.

Manna From Heaven

'On the lighter side, we returned to witness a scene of farcical proportions. There was no need for us to have been concerned for the sergeant, as he had turned his misfortune into an advantage. Sergeant Badder's half-track was still ablaze and his section stood in a semicircle, a few yards from the rear of the vehicle. As I watched, a small explosion came from the back of the half-track and a missile cartwheeled into the air, to be instantly pounced upon by the nearest guardsman as it fell to earth. Among the exploding small-arms ammunition came flying tins of all kinds of comestibles, for Sgt Badder's vehicle had been carrying the tinned rations of bacon, beef, stew, rice pudding etc, and here they were already cooked. Fielding at long leg, with the rest of the section placed in advantageous positions, most of the tins were retrieved before their contents could be spilled out on to the parched earth. It was a most unusual meal ... the best we had eaten for a long time.'[37]

The Guardsman's Devotion to Tank and Crew

'I made a mistake in carrying out this task [selecting men from the 2nd Battalion to go to Berlin for the victory march and thus miss the 'Farewell to Armour'

[36] Kennedy
[37] Pritchard

236

parade]. Because there had to be fairly arbitrary choices made if the right numbers were to be achieved, in each tank, in the marching party, men's own wishes were necessarily ignored. This was normal military procedure, of course – a man paraded where he was told. Nevertheless there were susceptibilities greater than I had supposed and I regret my insensitivity. These men – the tank crews – had seen a great deal in these armour-plated, tracked monsters. They had shared fear, privation, bereavement with a handful of others. The tank had been their home, had housed them, protected them, witnessed their emotions. Now some – two out of every tank crew – were told that they could not stay with the machine on its last day.

'We owed everything to these men, our guardsmen – to their patience, their sense of humour, their endurance. I remember one tall, reddish-haired man I knew well – a good soldier, a radio-operator, he had served a long time in one particular tank – and the tank had survived. He was now detailed for the marching party. I happened to pass down the line of tanks in our last harbour before the parade, and saw him. I realized – and cursed myself for the lateness of the realization – that he was deeply distressed. He had just been given his order. Dismounted, he would march on his feet.'[38]

A welcome treat: Nuns supply a fine Christmas pudding in 1944. *Christopher Collins*

Montgomery's Farewell Words

'Monty could still astonish. Ten days after accepting the biggest surrender in history he came to see us [4th Grenadiers], stood on his jeep and called everyone round him. This is what he said:

"I've got news for you. The war is over. No-one is interested in it any more except historians. I've done well and you've done well. Thank you very much. Now what do you want to know? Will you have to go and fight Japan? I can't promise but I hope not. When will you go on leave? Every man Jack of you before the end of July. How will you be demobilized? By age and service. What are we here for? To get the Germans back in their homes, make sure they get the crops in and the coal up. To teach them to be good neighbours."

'That was all. You will not find it in a book about rhetoric, but it says a lot about Monty. How much closer could anyone get to what the troops wanted to hear?'[39]

[38] Fraser (3)
[39] Crosthwaite (2)

SOME STRIKING FIGURES

The Pioneer Sergeant

*I*n the Army only the Pioneer Sergeant is permitted to wear a beard. The custom appears to be a relic from the Crimean campaign. Why the exemption should still apply in his case, except perhaps because he is always too busy to shave, is not clear. At any rate, when appointed to the post, the incumbent cultivates his whiskers with relish and puts up with the jibes of his jealous comrades.

It was the primary duty of a pioneer to clear away obstacles. Equipped with an axe, saw and apron, he carved a path through the countryside for his marching comrades. Today this special activity is

A determined look: the Pioneer Sergeant about to swing his axe. *Gary Gibbs Collection*

recalled by the Pioneer Sergeant, with beard, whitened leather apron and axe, marching on parade at the head of his battalion.

Pioneers are not wholly destructive. Certainly, in their sapper role in the field, they work as assault pioneers, ready to blow up or otherwise destroy whatever lies in their path. They handle the young officer who requests that a square hole should be blown exactly six feet deep and three feet wide,[1] but they also build and improvise. In barracks their job is to make the place comfortable and secure. Their carpenters and plumbers are jacks of all trade, mending and making good, painting signs and generally keeping the place in 'Grenadier order'.

---

[1] Dorney

Getting down to it: the Master Tailor of Victorian days directs his men.

John Southern: tone-deaf drummer who opted for the warmth of the tailors' shop and became a notable Master Tailor.

Ancient tradition: Pioneer Sergeant Joseph Truscott in all his glory at Windsor in 2005. The dog is not part of his equipment, though no doubt it helps. *Roger Scruton*

Immaculate in plain clothes: Sergeant Stephen Devereux, Master Tailor of the 1st Battalion in 2005, wears the blue-red-blue tie of the Household Division. *Roger Scruton*

The Master Tailor

In a profession where appearance counts for a good deal, the Master Tailor and his men play a prominent part. A history of the Ordnance Services gives the intriguing information that in the 18th century 'trousers developed on two distinct lines which approached but did not actually meet'.[2] If a Grenadier has found himself with an unwanted space in this crucial part of his wardrobe – or indeed in any other – the 'Master Stitch' and his crew have been the men to put it right.

The Master Tailor himself has the distinction of taking on a far more modest personal appearance than anyone else in his battalion. Instead of uniform he is permitted to wear a dark suit of plain clothes (clearly of the highest quality and perfectly fitted) topped by a black Homburg hat. His work is reflected in the quality of uniforms worn by others rather than by himself.

In fact, until the early 19th century, little attention was paid to niceties of dress, certainly as far as the soldiers were concerned. Now and then, however, men who had served some sort of apprenticeship as tailors were gathered up by the Quartermaster and set to making general alterations. It was their way of life to get drunk and fight, and sometimes a sentry had to be posted over them to prevent disorder and make sure they kept to the stipulated hours.[3]

Tailors, along with drummers and barbers, who also are nimble-fingered, are often good shots.

Wally Durrant: well-remembered Pioneer Sergeant of the 3rd Battalion.

The Master Cook

The tailors having attended to his outsides, it is up to the cooks to look after the guardsman's insides. Food is, of course, of central importance to any soldier, and the Grenadier is no exception.

Before the days when the Army Catering Corps took charge of regimental messing, the Master Cook was one of the best-recognized figures in a battalion. In sparkling cook's whites, topped by an incongruous forage cap with its glittering peak, he was not to be argued with, either by his own cooks or the legions of fatigue-men who prepared his vegetables and did the cleaning up. He would range up and down the servery, urging his men to greater efforts, and would train the company cooks to feed men in the field under the eye of their Pay Sergeant. One used to chide fatigue men warming their backsides by sitting on the hotplate: 'Get off that – it's for riiii-soles, not rrrrrr-soles.'

Many colourful characters occupied the post of 'Master Scoff'. For special occasions, such as a commanding officer's parade, he would be hauled out of his cookhouse to form up for inspection with the Battalion Staff, decked out in unfamiliar khaki and an even more unfamiliar sword.

Mixing it: Master Cook John Fisher adds the critical ingredient for the Christmas pudding in Sharjah, while his Commanding Officer, David Hargreaves, stirs it in.

---

[2] Forbes, A
[3] Eggington

240

Chapter Eleven

THE ELIZABETHAN ERA
1945-2005

Queen Elizabeth II was destined to give her name to an era longer and hardly less momentous than that of the first Elizabeth. This era is generally, of course, dated from her accession in 1952, but for Grenadiers it had already been running since 1942, when she became Colonel of the Regiment at the age of sixteen. As Queen she then became Colonel-in-Chief. Thus her Golden Jubilee on the throne was also her Diamond Jubilee as a Grenadier. And in 2005 Prince Philip, Duke of Edinburgh, marked his thirtieth year as Colonel. The historical attachment of Grenadiers to the person of their monarch could hardly have endured in a more decisive form.

Post-War Soldiering

An Extraordinary Variety of Activity

The sixty years of peace after the war have seen a new and vibrant type of soldiering, which sent Grenadiers all over the world and offered them every opportunity open to the infantry soldier. It has been a time of extraordinary diversity and variety. The period was similar in length to that of Victoria's reign. But whereas Queen Victoria's guardsmen soldiered almost entirely at home, except where engaged in the occasional major campaign, the Grenadier of the twentieth century spiced his traditional work of ceremonial with constant forays into distant parts. His has become the age of air transport, instant communications and the mass media.

The map and record table in this chapter shows the outline. There have been operations abroad in Palestine, Malaya, Egypt, Cyprus, the British Southern Cameroons, British Guiana, the Gulf and Bosnia. Not all these were distinguished by the award of a campaign medal – they were regarded as run-of-the-mill work in the later stages of empire. There were other places besides for Grenadiers to look after from time to time though, happily, fighting did not prove necessary: Libya, Sharjah, Belize, Hong Kong and the Falkland Islands. There were the long years in Germany before the collapse of the

On a wet square: the Guards Depot, Caterham, in 1952.

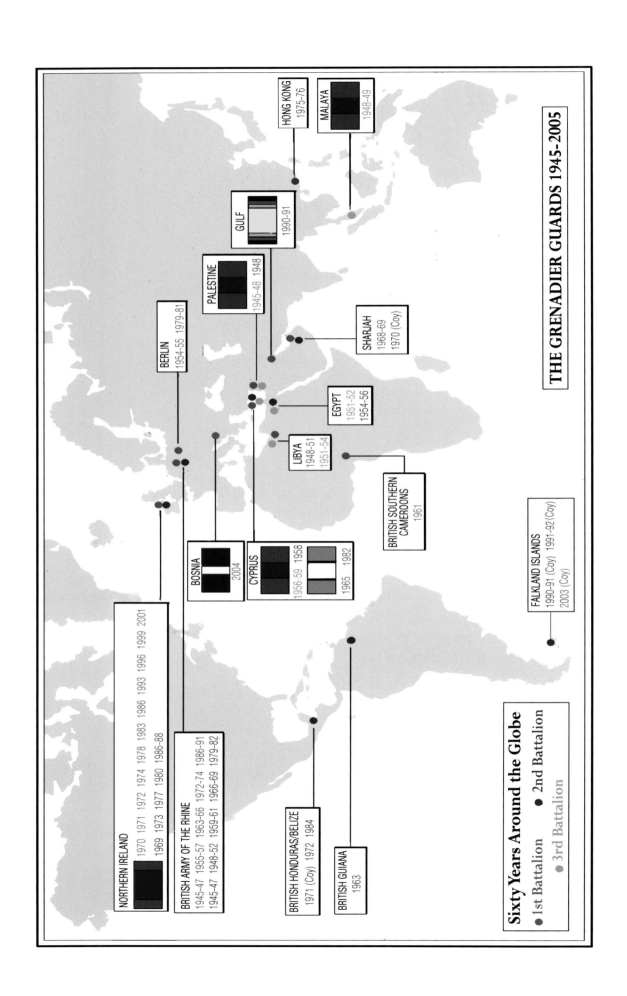

THE GRENADIER GUARDS 1945-2005

HONG KONG
1975-76

MALAYA
1948-49

GULF
1990-91

PALESTINE
1945-48 1948

BERLIN
1954-55 1979-81

SHARJAH
1968-69
1970 (Coy)

EGYPT
1951-52
1954-56

LIBYA
1948-51
1951-54

BRITISH SOUTHERN CAMEROONS
1961

BOSNIA
2004

CYPRUS
1956-59 1958
1965   1982

FALKLAND ISLANDS
1990-91 (Coy) 1991-92 (Coy)
2003 (Coy)

NORTHERN IRELAND
1970 1971 1972 1974 1978 1983 1986 1993 1996 1999 2001
1969 1973 1977 1980 1986-88

BRITISH ARMY OF THE RHINE
1945-47 1955-57 1963-66 1972-74 1986-91
1945-47 1948-52 1959-61 1966-69 1979-82

BRITISH HONDURAS/BELIZE
1971 (Coy) 1972 1984

BRITISH GUIANA
1963

Sixty Years Around the Globe

- ● 1st Battalion
- ● 2nd Battalion
- ● 3rd Battalion

Still a use for the hoof: a radio installation in 1957.

Soviet Union. On our very doorstep was Northern Ireland, to which battalions returned time after time over thirty years to keep the lid on a simmering, and sometimes a boiling, pot.

It was a faithful reflection of what the British army was called upon to do in a rapidly changing world. Only in one year of the period – 1968 – was no British soldier killed in action. At that time the withdrawal from empire had been accelerating and it seemed then that, apart from continuing to face the Soviet Union in Germany (a task to

which no end could then be foreseen) there would be little at home to occupy the military, especially the infantry. There was talk of aid to the civil community and such projects as the training of infantry as mini-sappers. However, as invariably happens, the unexpected dropped in with the solution. In 1969 the troubles in Northern Ireland blew up and for three decades provided occupation enough for large numbers of troops.

In these years also the special strength of the Household troops, and of the Foot Guards in particular,

Glad to be home: marching to barracks from Waterloo station in 1953.

was demonstrated in variety of occupation. Any line battalion of infantry might find itself mechanized in Germany one day, as light infantrymen in a British colony the next, then on the streets of Belfast as policemen or wearing the blue beret of the United Nations in Cyprus. Guardsmen did all this, and more, for it was complemented by the ceremonial role, arising from their treasured and proudly guarded association with the sovereign. Time after time a summer of spring drills and guard-mounting from Horse Guards would come to a stirring crescendo with the Queen's Birthday Parade; and then, silently and unseen by their admiring audience, they would put the Victorian bearskins and tunics into store, assemble their kit, and in a few days be far away on the serious business of the twentieth century.

Enduring 1763 days of captivity: Terry Waite CBE drew deeply on his memories of Caterham when taken hostage in Lebanon.

And at this business, despite the distraction (as some might say) of Royal Guards and other ceremonial duty, they excelled. The distraction might even have helped, for more often than not they came to a new job fresh and eager to learn. Nothing was missed. The technical demands of armoured fighting vehicles, anti-tank missiles, modern communications, night-vision devices and laser training aids all came into their ambit. Many of a particularly adventurous disposition have served in the Guards Independent Parachute Company (now the Guards Parachute Platoon) or Guards Squadron, 22 SAS.

The usual home stations were London, Windsor, Caterham and Pirbright. The nineteenth century barracks in London (Chelsea and Wellington) and in Windsor (Victoria) were rebuilt, as well as the new Elizabeth

Barracks at Pirbright. Caterham, which became a favourite barracks after the Guards Depot moved to Pirbright, was eventually sold to developers. Battalions were also to be found at one time or another at Warley, Tidworth and Lydd, and in the old cavalry barracks at Hounslow, where for a time the 1st Grenadiers languished less than happily under the Heathrow flight-path.

In general the period saw a marked improvement in facilities, both for the soldiers and their families. With the demise of the two-year period of National Service, which had lasted from 1949 to 1962, proper attention was given to better equipment, accommodation and comforts, all of which tended to be most noticeable in the garrisons in Germany. And feeding underwent a revolution. Seemingly overnight, the take-it-or-leave-it regime of splatting potato on to plates and ladling stew over the fingers was replaced by the self-service bar of many choices; it was a touch of civilization well-judged to appeal to the professional, volunteer soldier. In due course, too, regimental cooks were succeeded by those of the Army Catering Corps, who served the battalions with distinction and were quickly absorbed into the regimental family.

Top shot: the Golden Gun, dating back to Victorian times, is still awarded to the champion shot of the 1st Battalion and worn on the tunic on commanding officers' inspections.

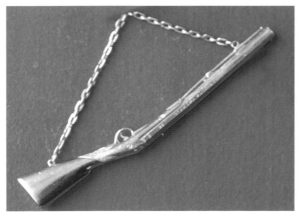

Twice the man: a memorable recruiting poster from the 1980s.
Philip Wright

Married quarters also improved. Even as late as 1956 'our quarter in Stillington Street had been a one-bedroom one on the second floor, each of which had a landing with iron railings. From the outside it looked like a prison; once inside it was quite homely. During the winter months a coal issue arrived on a Wednesday. It would be tipped on to the floor inside the house, then a few hours were spent getting rid of coal dust.'[1]

At home there were periodic descents into quite different kinds of work, largely arising from industrial unrest and strikes. At various times Grenadiers acted as dockers, oil tanker drivers, refuse collectors (a most unpleasant job), ambulance crews and fire-fighters. And, in the face of the threat from terrorists, security alerts, especially at Heathrow airport, provoked swift responses from battalions at Windsor or London.

"DOES THE NOTICE REFER TO THIS BUILDING OR THE WHOLE PLACE?"

A fair question. *Philip Wright*

State Ceremonial and Public Duties

Grenadiers resumed public duties in January 1947, still in the battledress that had been worn since 1940. The duties were then to guard Buckingham Palace, St James's Palace, the Tower of London, the Bank of England by night, the Central London Recruiting Depot and Windsor Castle.

On 20 November 1947 came the marriage of HRH Princess Elizabeth, Colonel of the Regiment, to Prince Philip of Greece. She was given by her regiment a present, subscribed to by all ranks, of several fine pieces of silver. In dreary and austere post-war London the wedding was a refreshing and enjoyable occasion. The 1st

Battalion lined part of the processional route.

In 1952 only three of the ten battalions of Foot Guards were at home and all were under strength. The strain of public duties was considerable and for the first time there were only five guards on the Queen's Birthday Parade instead of the usual eight. In subsequent years, as the number of battalions was reduced to eight, and then to five together with three representative companies, it became common to vary the number of guards on parade according to circumstances.

The pattern of the Queen's Guard also changed as the years passed, as a result of the pressure on resources and the increasing demands of security. Forty-eight-hour guards were introduced and other regiments and corps began to take a turn from time to time. The sentries who used to be posted outside the railings of Buckingham Palace were moved into the forecourt in 1959, as the attentions of the public had become both undignified and oppressive. Though this made the work less rewarding for the guardsmen themselves, the change was inevitable. At night also the duties became more tactical, sentries patrolling in rubber-soled boots and carrying small pocket radios. The mounting of the Tower Guard was joined to that of the Queen's Guard.

A magic little box: one of the new-fangled television sets draws an enthralled audience in the St James's Palace guardroom.

[1] Woodfield

In slow time: the Queen's Colour of the 2nd Battalion trooped in 1984. *Roger Scruton*

Wheeling into place: the Escort to the Colour, found by Inkerman Company, prepares to troop the Colour through the ranks in 2004.
Roger Thompson

All three battalions represented: the Queen's Company, Nijmegen Company and Inkerman Company appear together on Trooping the Colour in 2003.

AUTUMN NUMBER

A wet Troop: the Queen's Birthday Parade of 2001 was conducted in sheets of rain and dee puddles. The effect, however, was not as drastic as *Punch* had feared.

On Horse Guards Parade: new Colours are presented to both 1st and 2nd Battalions in 1992. *Julian Barrow*

The Bank Picquet was discontinued in 1973. In its day it had sometimes been the scene of drama, if not entertainment. The long march through London in tunic and bearskin, in the evening rush hour and ignoring traffic lights, sometimes ended in a new young officer circling the massive edifice of the Bank of England in a vain attempt to find the modest door. On one occasion at least, hopelessly stuck in the traffic, recourse was made to the underground in order to make progress. For the last ten years, however, the picquet became tactical, travelling by vehicle, dressed in khaki and carrying automatic weapons.

The King is Dead: Long Live the Queen

King George VI died in Norfolk on 6 February 1952. Two days later the new Queen Elizabeth II, who had heard the news while in Kenya, was proclaimed at Friary Court in St James's Palace, and on the same day twenty-one men of the King's Company (Major Tony Heywood)

went to Sandringham for duty as bearers and escort. The King's body was brought by train to King's Cross and lay in state in Westminster Hall until 15 February, the coffin being guarded by officers of the Household troops and the King's Body Guard of the Gentlemen-at-Arms. During three cold, wet winter days and nights 300,000 people filed by the catafalque. The King's Company Colour, the Royal Standard of the Regiment, lay at the foot of the coffin, which was then accompanied by the bearer party to Paddington station. On its arrival at Windsor, guards of honour were found at Windsor station and at St George's Chapel by the 1st Battalion, recently arrived in Victoria Barracks. The coffin was drawn to the chapel on a gun carriage, escorted by the bearer party. In accordance with tradition, the small King's Company camp colour was handed to the Queen by Colonel 'Geordie' Gordon Lennox, commanding the regiment, and she placed it on the coffin to be buried with her father.

On 21 February the Queen received the bearer party at

'Fourth bearskin on the right, STAND STILL': shortly before the review of the Queen's Company in 2003 the spectators' seats had been invaded by a swarm of bees. *Patrick McSweeney*

GENERAL
Sir DAVID FRASER
GCB OBE DL *Born 1920*

Commanding Officer
in the Cameroons,
Vice CGS,
NATO Representative,
Historian and Author

*D*avid Fraser is deeply steeped in Grenadier tradition. A descendant of General Alexander Fraser, Lord Saltoun, who commanded the light companies at Hougoumont, he immersed himself in military history and indeed became an eminent historian in his own right.

In 1940 he was hurt, though not seriously, by a bomb dropped on Sandhurst. He fought in tanks with the 2nd Battalion through north-west Europe, eventually as second captain of No 2 Squadron. Thereafter his career advanced at speed, his exceptional ability being daily proved in regimental and staff appointments. With Arthur Bryant, he wrote the pageant for the regimental tercentenary in 1956.

In 1960 he took the 1st Battalion to the British Southern Cameroons. He was said to have written his report on this operational tour on the troopship home, out of his head, and without a single correction. He went on to command 19th Brigade, in the Strategic Reserve, which was deployed to Sarawak during the confrontation with Indonesia, and then 4th Division in Germany. Thereafter he became in turn Assistant Chief of Staff (Policy), Vice Chief of the General Staff, UK Military Representative to NATO and Commandant of the Royal College of Defence Studies.

On retirement he embarked on a new and fruitful career as the author of a number of novels and several military books, including biographies of Alanbrooke, Rommel and Frederick the Great.

He has always been known to Grenadiers as the 'Razor', from his exceptionally sharp mind, his piercing eye and, perhaps, the menacing intake of breath through clenched teeth with which he is apt to greet idle work or sloppy thinking.

See Fraser (3)

Buckingham Palace to thank them for the exemplary way in which they had carried out their duty and presented to each man a signed photograph of them carrying the coffin. On the same day she commanded that the company should now be named The Queen's Company.

Her Majesty became Colonel-in-Chief of the Regiment on her accession. She was succeeded as Colonel by General Sir George Jeffreys, who was followed in turn by Major General Sir Allan Adair in 1960 and HRH Prince Philip in 1975.

The Coronation took place, after lengthy preparation, on 2 June 1953. The 1st and 2nd Battalions were at home and found both street liners and large marching parties in the enormous procession of 8000 men and women from all parts of the Commonwealth. The Queen's Company were on duty at Westminster Abbey and both former and serving Grenadier officers took part in various capacities. In the specially constructed annexe to the Abbey, space for the guardsmen was very limited, and 'Present Arms' was given discreetly by a sword signal, rather than by a word of command, and accomplished directly from the order as there was no room to slope.

Other State Funerals

Queen Mary died in March 1953 and again the Regiment found the bearer party, a guard of honour and detachments for the funeral procession and street lining. In January 1965 Sir Winston Churchill died. His state funeral in St Paul's Cathedral was an enormous occasion, exceeded only by the coronation itself and recalling that of the Duke of Wellington a century before. His widow, Lady Churchill, remarked that it was not a funeral at all, but a triumph. In recognition of his service with the 2nd Battalion in the trenches, which, though short, made on him an indelible impression and instilled his lasting admiration, he was carried by a bearer party of Grenadiers from that battalion. The massive coffin gave his bearers a heavy task, in the most literal sense, but it was discharged with a dignity and bearing that attracted warm tributes from all over the world.

Both the Queen's Company and Nijmegen Company played a prominent part in the funeral of Queen Elizabeth the Queen Mother in 2002 and several officers of the Regiment stood vigil at her lying-in-state.

The Tercentenary Celebrations

In 1956 the Regiment celebrated 300 years since its formation. A week of festivities took place between 29

Borne to his tomb: the bearer party for King George VI represented in bronze by Reginald Gunther.

A heavy burden: Grenadiers of the 2nd Battalion carry the coffin of Sir Winston Churchill in 1965.

An immense procession: the Foot Guards contingents pass beneath Admiralty Arch after the coronation in 1953.

The passing of a great lady: the Queen Mother saluted by a guard of honour of Nijmegen Company outside Westminster Hall in 2002.

Into suspended animation: the farewell parade of the 3rd Battalion at Buckingham Palace in 1960. *Terence Cuneo*

Ours at last: the 2nd Battalion win the Army Athletics Championship in 1984. Lance Sergeant John Taylor collects the trophy; his Army records for the 110 metres Hurdles (Junior 1974, Senior 1983) and Long Jump (Senior 1985) were still unbeaten in 2005.

Last days of the 'Models': the Old Colours of the 2nd Battalion are laid up in St Margaret's, Westminster in 1993. The battalion went into suspended animation the following year.

May and 5 June in London. There was a fine exhibition in St James's Palace, displaying paintings and historical relics of many kinds, which had taken a year to collect. A private view attracted 2000 guests before the exhibition was thrown open to the public.

The 3rd Battalion found the Escort to the Colour on the Queen's Birthday Parade, while the 1st Battalion did the same duty at a similar parade in Germany. The Royal Festival Hall saw a concert and pageant, devised by Major David Fraser (Regimental Adjutant) and Captain Alfred Shaughnessy, and performed by the Band of the Regiment. It was followed by a banquet for 1300 people, one of the biggest given in London since the war. More than one of those attending had fought at Omdurman in 1898.

The 1st Battalion returned to England via Bruges, where it was given a magnificent reception over two days in the city of its foundation. They travelled from Ostend to Dover, as had Charles II and the Royal Regiment of Guards 300 years earlier, and then joined the two other battalions at Windsor, where all three were reviewed together by their Colonel-in-Chief. The 1st Battalion were still in battledress, the others being in tunic and bearskin, and all were formed in mass, the band and the three corps of drums also being in mass, and 1200 old comrades ranged behind. After the inspection the Queen returned to the saluting base and the whole parade marched past her. The final act, after the advance in review order, was an earth-shaking three cheers for Her Majesty, delivered by 2300 Grenadiers before the 6000 spectators. It was the greatest parade of its kind and its equal was not to be seen again.

The Passing of the Third Battalion

The whole army was in a constant state of change. One defence review succeeded another at unwelcome intervals, organizations were varied and modified and, worst of all, reduction, amalgamation, and in some cases downright disbandment, were visited upon many proud regiments.

The Foot Guards were by no means exempt, and in 1960 the **3rd Battalion** (Lt Col Tony Way) subsided into the wonderful condition described as 'suspended animation'. The term was designed no doubt to soothe feelings on the passing of an exceptionally fine battalion and to indicate that, while there was no life left in the body, space for the spirit still remained. Whether it

Grenadier Gallery

ACADEMY SERGEANT MAJOR
JOHN LORD
MVO MBE *1908-1968*

Sergeant Major who overawed his German captors and became a Sandhurst figure of high repute

*J*C Lord won extraordinary renown, not on the field of battle, but in the grim conditions of a prisoner-of-war camp and later at the Royal Military Academy.

He enlisted as a Grenadier in 1933 and left the Army for the police force after his four years. But the war soon found him marching back through the gates at Windsor. His fine qualities were too obvious to ignore and in no time he was a company sergeant major. Yearning for action, he volunteered for parachuting and in a few months was Regimental Sergeant Major Lord of the 3rd Battalion The Parachute Regiment. He was to hold the rank for twenty years. He dropped at Arnhem where, surrounded and out of ammunition, his depleted party was taken prisoner. The two-day journey by cattle-truck to Stalag XIB brought Lord face to face with British troops living in misery and squalor, underfed and packed 400 to a hut, the frequent dead taken to their graves in an old cart.

Lord took the camp by the scruff of its neck. He formed the troops into companies, gained control of the roll-call, insisted on the cleaning of barrack rooms, regular exercise and the organized distribution of food. Funerals – there were fifty in seven months – were properly conducted. The Germans, overawed, did not impede him. When the allied liberators arrived, they were astonished to be greeted by Lord, immaculately dressed and presenting his camp in a high state of morale. For this his MBE was modest recognition.

After the war he moved to Sandhurst, where he remained for sixteen years until retiring in 1963. Here, as the first Academy Sergeant Major, the senior warrant officer of the Army, he became a legend, an unforgettable figure in the lives of over 7000 officer cadets, and of international repute.
See Alford (1)

succeeded may still be debated, but certainly it was a most painful passing, which provoked bitter opposition, especially from the Colonel, Lord Jeffreys. He had always insisted on the sacred standing of the seven original battalions of the Brigade of Guards (three Grenadier, two Coldstream and two Scots). They were the 'Old Brigade'.[2] He asserted that even the 3rd Coldstream, similarly marked for suspension, but dating only from 1897, could not be compared to the 3rd Grenadiers, whose origins lay in the companies of the regiment raised under Lord Wentworth in Flanders. It was the first battalion of the Regiment to be given the right to march through the City of London and was argued thus to be the oldest of the three. It had fought at sea in the Dutch wars and had taken a major role at Waterloo. But there was more to it than the ancient history. It was said (no doubt by a 2nd Battalion man) that the Third Battalion were the maddest, the First the grandest, but the Second the true professionals. The 3rd Grenadiers had certainly acquired a very special character, which they guarded with jealous pride. It was an independence, and a youthfulness of spirit, with which three outstanding wartime commanding officers (Allan Adair, Algy Heber Percy and John Nelson) were fully in tune and to which they brought their own fine qualities.

They had had the longest war, in North Africa and Italy, of any battalion and had suffered accordingly. And little rest was to come with the peace. They were excused Germany, which perhaps did not trouble them, the soldiering there probably being more rigid than suited their temperament. But there was plenty to do in the post-war empire. In 1945, after three months of clearing up in Austria, they went to Palestine and in 1948, after a brief interval at home, to Malaya. Home in the following year, they mounted King's Guard, for the first time since the war in tunic and bearskin, but in 1951 they were off again to Tripoli in Libya, whence they spent some months in the Canal Zone of Egypt. Home once more in 1954, they went to Malta in 1956 with the prospect of joining in the Suez invasion, and from there to tackle EOKA terrorists in Cyprus.

They returned in 1959 to face their demise, marked by a nostalgic farewell parade before the Queen at Buckingham Palace in June 1960. It was a cruel fate and, whatever the logic as seen from high places, undeserved. Happily, a good many Grenadiers were able to continue their service elsewhere. The new **Inkerman Company**,

named after the battalion's famous exploit of 1854 in the Crimea, was formed and sent to the 2nd Battalion early in 1961, whence in 1994 it moved to the 1st Battalion, where as left flank company it remains still to preserve the tradition of the famous 'Ribs'.

The Passing of the Second Battalion

In 1994 came the turn of the **2nd Battalion** (Lt Col Richard Aubrey-Fletcher) together with the second battalions of the Coldstream and Scots Guards. After the fashion of many defence reviews, the decision to cut all three battalions was taken without a chance to assess with any accuracy what the results might actually be. Many other regiments were facing extinction. The Foot Guards could hardly be left with two battalions when other regiments were losing the only one they had. But the arithmetic was not done in advance and the government eventually had to concede that there were too few men in the remaining five battalions of Foot Guards to do the work. Thus the 2nd Grenadiers were to some extent kept alive by the formation of **Nijmegen Company**, named in honour of their most famous battle in 1944. This company was independent of the 1st Battalion, though closely associated with it and chiefly employed on public duties. Inelegantly described as a 'public duties increment', it was composed largely of the youngest guardsmen, straight from basic training, who were thereby given valuable early experience in ceremonial before moving to the 1st Battalion. This scheme, suitably varied by training and overseas exercises, has proved very successful.

Happily Nijmegen Company was able to retain a more tangible emblem of its origins than had proved possible for the 3rd Battalion. In 2001 it was presented by the Queen with new battalion Colours, the old ones being laid up in Bristol Cathedral. It was a suitable mark of respect for the 'Models', as the Duke of Cambridge had once described them. Their going was as painful for the Regiment as that of the 'Ribs', for they had a proud record indeed. From the first battle at Steenkirk in 1692, through to Waterloo, where they had fought alongside the 3rd Battalion, and then to the world wars and beyond, they had made an indelible mark. The 'Models' were the first Grenadiers to go to war in 1914, and endured the early

[2] Jeffreys (3). Hence the popular wartime song: 'Send for the boys of the Old Brigade/ to set Old England free./ Send for me farver and me bruvver and me muvver/ but for Gawd's sake don't send me'

Brown and green: Kenya has proved popular for training excursions.

Heavy going: the snows of Canada and the mountains of Norway make heavy demands on fitness and strength.

An extraordinary achievement for foot soldiers: in 1962 the Grenadier polo team reached the final of the inter-regimental tournament, almost certainly the only non-cavalry team ever to do so. The four officers (left to right) Nigel Corbally-Stourton, Fitz Abel Smith, Peter Thwaites and Lindsay Moorehead, were at last beaten by the Blues.

Every kind of activity: guardsmen enjoying adventurous training in Canada.

Down the slopes: skiing at Army representative level.

At the summit: a team of climbers on Mont Blanc.

Well disguised: though this sniper is not quite in tune with his particular surroundings.

Into the smoke: a vivid silhouette in training.

the true professionalism for which they were renowned, they got to grips with the new mechanical world of track and sprocket. Their fighting record in north-west Europe spoke for itself.

In 1969, at short notice on *Spearhead*, they were the first to be sent to Londonderry on the outbreak of serious unrest in Northern Ireland. There were several subsequent visits. Worldwide, in British Guiana (Guyana), British Honduras (Belize), Hong Kong and the Falkland Islands, they reached more distant points on the globe than either of the other battalions.

Their sporting record, particularly in athletics, was an enviable one. Despite the constant interruptions of movement, training and operations, they were runners-up in the army championship nine times, and in 1984 they won it. The 'Models' were greatly mourned, but the stature they had acquired was to be successfully passed on.

Training at Home and Overseas

In the battalions, training steadily became more varied and interesting as the years went by. There were exercises in many parts of the world, the USA, Canada and Kenya featuring

weeks of Mons, the Marne and the Aisne. In 1941 they adopted tanks, noisy, greasy monsters till then regarded as inconceivable for guardsmen but, with

frequently. Many of these were spread over several weeks and provided a real tonic to those otherwise confined to the small and over-crowded training areas at home. Adventurous training also grew in importance. Once seen as an activity open only to enterprising officers who could wangle themselves long stretches of leave, its value in promoting self-reliance and practicing leadership was soon recognized. There were plenty of opportunities at home, in the wilds of Scotland or the more balmy reaches of Devon, climbing, trekking and canoeing, or sailing in the Household Division's *Gladeye*. But it was abroad that the greatest excitement and challenge was to be found. Expeditions climbed in the Alps, the Rockies and the Andes, explored the Sahara, swam, dived, skied, canoed, parachuted and marched great distances. This all might have been taken by a cynic as extended holidays, arranged for the amusement of otherwise bored soldiers, but those who were concerned knew better. Large numbers of successful young leaders were greatly to benefit from this kind of activity.

All at sea: Grenadiers have a special affiliation with HMS *Illustrious* and visits to the ship are made regularly. The Regiment also has a formal alliance with the Canadian Grenadier Guards, the 1st Battalion the Royal Australian Regiment and the Trinidad and Tobago Regiment.

THE RECORD 1945-2005

Major Regimental Events		Regimental Headquarters		1st Battalion
Date	Details	Name	Station	Name
		■ Lieutenant Colonel ■ Regimental Adjutant ■ Superintending Clerk ■ Director of Music		■ Commanding Officer ■ Adjutant ■ Sergeant Major ■ Quartermaster
1945 (May)	HRH Princess Elizabeth Colonel since 1942 Farewell to Armour (1st, 2nd & 4th Bns) 5th Bn disbanded (6th Bn having disbanded in 1944)	Col RBR Colvin DSO Maj Sir Arthur Penn MC WO1 AG Douglas MBE Capt FJ Harris MBE Maj PAS Robertson	GERMANY Stade Berlin Bonn	Lt Col PH Lort-Phillips DSO Capt M Dawson RSM FH Dowling MC Capt FEJ Carver RSM GC Hackett Capt AEP Needham Capt JE Bolton
1946	4th Bn disbanded		Keil Berlin Neümunster HOME Pirbright	
1947	First King's Birthday Parade after the war (in khaki) 1st Bn take part Marriage of HRH Princess Elizabeth to HRH Prince Philip	Maj ECWM Penn MC	Chelsea Windsor	Capt JFD Johnston MC RSM AJ Spratley MM Lt Col CMF Deakin
1948		Col EH Goulburn DSO WO1 HE Clarke MBE	(PALESTINE) LIBYA Tripoli	Capt AG Douglas
1949	3rd Bn mount the first King's Guard in Home Service clothing since the war			Capt MS Bayley RSM LE Burrell
1950		Maj Hon GNC Wigram MC		Lt Col EJB Nelson DSO OBE MC
1951	New Colours to 3rd Bn – Buckingham Palace 3rd Bn Troop the Colour 3rd Bn Old Colours laid up in Manchester Cathedral	Col GC Gordon Lennox CVO DSO	HOME Windsor	Capt IM Erskine
1952	Death and Funeral of King George VI Queen Elizabeth II Colonel in Chief General Lord Jeffreys appointed Colonel	Col TFC Winnington MBE	Wellington	Lt Col PW Marsham MBE
1953	Death and Funeral of Queen Mary The Queen's Company Colour presented at Windsor Castle New Colours to 1st and 2nd Bns – Buckingham Palace Coronation of HM Queen Elizabeth II 1st Bn Troop the Colour 1st Bn Old Colours laid up in St Mary's Nottingham 2nd Bn Old Colours laid up in Liverpool Cathedral	Maj FJC Bowes-Lyon MC WO1 EC Weaver MBE		Capt MGP Stourton RSM AD Dickinson Lt LE Burrell

Sixty Years of Service

Date	2nd Battalion			3rd Battalion		
	Station	Name		Station	Name	
		■ Commanding Officer ■ Adjutant □ Sergeant Major ■ Quartermaster			■ Commanding Officer ■ Adjutant □ Sergeant Major ■ Quartermaster	
1945 (May)	GERMANY Freiburg Seigburg	Lt Col JNR Moore DSO Capt AG Heywood RSM M Young Capt CE Stedman Capt DW Fraser Lt Col CMF Deakin Capt BH Pratt		AUSTRIA (PALESTINE)	Lt Col PT Clifton DSO Capt WS Dugdale MC RSM W Hagell MBE Capt EV Philpott MBE RSM HJ Wood DCM RSM J Baker Capt F Dowling MC	
1946	Lübeck Neümunster Berlin Wuppertal	Lt Col HRH Davies			Capt AN Breitmeyer RSM RE Butler RSM HJ Wood DCM Capt CE Stedman	
1947	HOME Caterham	Lt Col GC Gordon Lennox DSO Capt FJ Jefferson RSM GC Hackett			Lt Col HRH Davies Capt HN Lucas MBE	
1948	BAOR Sennelager			HOME Windsor (MALAYA)	Lt Col TFC Winnington MBE RSM RE Butler Capt GRM Sewell	
1949		Lt Col TP Butler DSO		Chelsea	Capt AJ Spratley MM	
1950	Krefeld	Capt GW Lamb				
1951		Capt GC Hackett RSM AG Everett		LIBYA Tripoli (EGYPT – Canal Zone)	Lt Col PAS Robertson Capt HF Hamilton-Dalrymple	
1952	HOME Chelsea	Lt Col C Earle DSO OBE				
1953		Capt RMO de la Hey			Capt RE Butler RSM WLA Nash	

THE RECORD 1945-2005

Major Regimental Events		Regimental Headquarters	1st Battalion	
Date	Details	Name	Station	Name
		■ Lieutenant Colonel ■ Regimental Adjutant ▪ Superintending Clerk ■ Director of Music		■ Commanding Officer ■ Adjutant ▪ Sergeant Major ■ Quartermaster
1954			BERLIN	
1955		Col Sir Thomas Butler DSO OBE Maj DW Fraser	BAOR Hubbelrath	Capt JPB Agate Lt Col Hon GNC Wigram MC (G)
1956	Regimental Tercentenary Celebrations 3rd Bn Troop the Colour			Lt Col RH Whitworth MBE
1957			HOME Chelsea	RSM LC Drouet Capt BC Gordon Lennox Lt Col R Steele MBE
1958	The Queen's Company inspected at Buckingham Palace	WO1 PWE Parry Maj HW Freeman-Atwood		
1959		Col AMH Gregory-Hood OBE MC Maj Sir Hew Hamilton-Dalrymple	Tidworth	RSM A Dobson Capt A Dickinson MBE Capt DV Fanshawe
1960	Major General Sir Allan Adair appointed Colonel 3rd Bn Troop the Colour 3rd Battalion placed in suspended animation The Guards Depot moves from Caterham to Pirbright	Capt RB Bashford		Lt Col DW Fraser
1961		Col AG Way MC	(BRIT SOUTHERN CAMEROONS)(D)	
1962	Last National Servicemen leave The Queen's Company inspected at Buckingham Palace	Maj DW Hargreaves	Chelsea	Capt DHC Gordon Lennox Capt ST Felton Lt Col JFD Johnston MC
1963	2nd Bn Troop the Colour	WO1 LG White	BAOR Hubbelrath	RSM J Bing
1964		Col FJ Jefferson Maj PJC Ratcliffe	Wuppertal	Capt RG Proes Lt Col MS Bayley MBE RSM T Pugh
1965	Death and funeral of Sir Winston Churchill	WO1 JR Dann	(CYPRUS-UN)	Capt FJ Clutton MBE MM RVM
1966		Col AN Breitmeyer	HOME Caterham	Capt GA Alston-Roberts-West Lt Col DW Hargreaves
1967	New Colours to 1st Bn – Buckingham Pal. 1st Bn Troop the Colour	Maj CJ Airy WO1 TH Astill		RSM PA Lewis

Sixty Years of Service

	2nd Battalion		3rd Battalion	
Date	Station	Name	Station	Name
		■ Commanding Officer ■ Adjutant ■ Sergeant Major ■ Quartermaster		■ Commanding Officer ■ Adjutant ■ Sergeant Major ■ Quartermaster
1954	(EGYPT – Canal Zone)	Capt PJC Ratcliffe	HOME Chelsea	Lt Col AMH Gregory-Hood MBE MC Capt GEV Rochfort-Rae
1955		Lt Col Hon MF Fitzalan Howard MC (A) Lt AG Everett RSM ST Felton Capt JRS Besly	Windsor	RSM C White
1956	HOME Pirbright Windsor		(MALTA) (B) **CYPRUS**	Capt WLA Nash
1957	Lydd	Lt Col FJC Bowes-Lyon MC Capt CJ Airy		Lt Col PC Britten Capt SJ Loder RSM VC King (C) RSM A Stevens
1958	(**CYPRUS**)	RSM FJ Clutton MM RVM		Capt JP Smiley
1959	BAOR Hubbelrath	Capt GW Tufnell	HOME Wellington	Lt Col AG Way MC
1960		Lt Col AG Heywood MVO MC Capt EC Weaver MBE	3rd Battalion placed in suspended animation The Inkerman Company formed, and joined the 2nd Bn in 1961	
1961	HOME Caterham			
1962		Capt JFC Magnay Lt Col FJ Jefferson RSM D Randell		
1963	(BRITISH GUIANA) (E)	Capt LC Drouet		
1964	Windsor	Capt MLK Healing Lt Col AN Breitmeyer		
1965				
1966	BAOR Wuppertal	Capt HS Hanning RSM RP Huggins Lt Col PGA Prescott MC Capt A Dobson		
1967		Capt J Baskervyle-Glegg		

NOTES

General

In each case the year shown is that in which a change of station took place or an appointment was assumed.

Active Service stations (for which a medal was awarded) are shown in bold type, thus:

CYPRUS

Emergency unaccompanied tours are shown in brackets, thus:

(N IRELAND) (EGYPT)

Particular

(A) Later Duke of Norfolk
(B) In preparation for the Suez operation 400 reservists recalled
(C) Died in office
(D) Later Cameroon
(E) Later Guyana
(F) Later Belize
(G) Later Lord Wigram

THE RECORD 1945-2005

Major Regimental Events		Regimental Headquarters	1st Battalion	
Date	Details	Name	Station	Name
		■ Lieutenant Colonel ■ Regimental Adjutant ■ Superintending Clerk ■ Director of Music		■ Commanding Officer ■ Adjutant ■ Sergeant Major ■ Quartermaster
1968	1st Bn Old Colours laid up in Lincoln Cathedral The Queen's Company inspected at Buckingham Palace		(THE GULF Sharjah)	Capt JVEF O'Connell
1969	New Colours to 2nd Bn – Buckingham Palace	Maj DHC Gordon Lennox Col PGA Prescott MC WO1 CH Jenkins		Capt LG White Lt Col NH Hales Pakenham Mahon RSM W Williams BEM Capt JWH Buxton
1970	2nd Bn Old Colours laid up in Worcester Cathedral	Col DW Hargreaves Maj JP Smiley Capt PW Parkes	Chelsea (N IRELAND – Magilligan)	
1971	2nd Bn Troop the Colour	WO1 BE Thompson BEM	(N IRELAND – Belfast)	RSM GR Whitehead RVM Capt HA Baillie Capt TH Astill Lt Col GW Tufnell
1972			BAOR Munster (N IRELAND – Londonderry)	RSM BT Eastwood
1973		Col NH Hales Pakenham Mahon Maj GA Alston-Roberts-West WO1 VG Jewell		Capt CXS Fenwick
1974	Regimental Headquarters moves to Bloomsbury Court while Wellington Barracks rebuilt		(N IRELAND – Londonderry) HOME Chelsea	Lt Col BC Gordon Lennox MBE
1975	HRH Prince Philip appointed Colonel 1st Bn Troop the Colour	Maj PH Cordle		Capt Hon J Forbes Capt JFM Rodwell
1976	The Queen's Company inspected at Windsor Castle	Col GW Tufnell	Pirbright (N IRELAND – Armagh)	Lt Col DHC Gordon Lennox RSM DT Ashworth
1977	Silver Jubilee of HM The Queen	Capt DR Kimberley MBE WO1 BD Double		Capt GR Whitehead RVM RSM PF Richardson Capt GF Lesinski
1978	New Colours to 1st and 2nd Bns – Buckingham Palace 2nd Bn Troop the Colour	Maj OJM Lindsay Col DV Fanshawe OBE	(N IRELAND – Armagh)	Lt Col MF Hobbs MBE
1979	George Cross awarded posthumously to Captain Robert Nairac, killed in N Ireland in 1977 1st Bn Old Colours laid up in Derby Cathedral 2nd Bn Old Colours laid up in Ely Cathedral	Maj PAJ Wright	BERLIN	RSM DR Rossi Capt REH Aubrey-Fletcher
1980		Col DHC Gordon Lennox WO1 AS Cameron		Capt BT Eastwood Lt Col J Baskervyle-Glegg MBE
1981		Maj HA Baillie	HOME Hounslow	Capt AD Hutchison

Sixty Years of Service

2nd Battalion		
Date	Station	Name
		■ Commanding Officer ■ Adjutant ▨ Sergeant Major ■ Quartermaster
1968	Münster	
1969	HOME Chelsea (N IRELAND – Magilligan)	Lt Col PH Haslett MBE Capt TM Pugh RSM TR Day Capt DM Braddell
1970	Caterham (No 2 Coy to Sharjah with 1 Scots Gds)	
1971	(The Inkm Coy to British Honduras (F))	Capt PA Lewis Capt EJ Webb-Carter Lt Col JRS Besly
1972	(BRITISH HONDURAS (F)) Windsor	RSM WR Clarke
1973	(N IRELAND – Belfast)	RSM MPB Walker Capt PR Holcroft
1974		Lt Col DV Fanshawe
1975	HONG KONG Stanley	RSM DJ Webster Capt D Mason Capt TH Holbech
1976		Lt Col DH Blundell-Hollinshead- Blundell
1977	HOME Chelsea (N IRELAND – Londonderry)	Capt JFQ Fenwick
1978		RSM BE Sheen Capt WR Clarke Lt Col HML Smith
1979	BAOR Münster	Capt JS Lloyd
1980	(N IRELAND – Fermanagh & Londonderry)	
1981		Lt Col AA Denison-Smith MBE Capt ET Bolitho RSM MJ Joyce

Grenadiers who became Generals and Field Marshals, serving from 1945		
Field Marshal	the Earl of Cavan KP GCB GCMG GCVO GBE	1865-1946
General	the Lord Jeffreys KCB KCVO CMG	1878-1960
General	Sir Andrew Thorne KCB CMG DSO**	1885-1970
Field Marshal	the Viscount Gort VC GCB DSO** MVO MC	1886-1946
Major General	FG Beaumont-Nesbitt CVO CBE MC	1893-1971
Lieut General	Sir Frederick Browning GCVO KBE CB DSO	1896-1965
Major General	Sir Allan Adair GCVO CB DSO MC*	1897-1988
Major General	PGS Gregson-Ellis CB OBE	1898-1956
Major General	GL Verney DSO MVO	1900-1957
Major General	Sir Julian Gascoigne KCMG KCVO CB DSO	1903-1990
Major General	EH Goulburn DSO*	1903-1980
General	Sir Rodney Moore GCVO KCB CBE DSO	1905-1985
Lieut General	Sir George Gordon Lennox KBE CB CVO DSO	1908-1988
Major General	CMF Deakin CB CBE	1910-1992
Major General	Sir John Nelson KCVO CB DSO OBE MC	1912-1993
Major General	the Duke of Norfolk KG GCVO CB CBE MC (formerly the Hon MF Fitzalan Howard)	1915-2002
Major General	RH Whitworth CB CBE	1916-2004
Major General	Sir James Bowes-Lyon KCVO CB OBE MC*	1917-1977
General	Sir David Fraser GCB OBE	b 1920
Major General	LAD Harrod OBE	1924-1995
Major General	BC Gordon Lennox CB MBE	b 1932
Major General	Sir Christopher Airy KCVO CBE	b 1934
Major General	MF Hobbs CBE	b 1937
Major General	J Baskervyle-Glegg MBE	1940-2004
Lieut General	Sir Anthony Denison-Smith KBE	b 1942
Major General	Sir Evelyn Webb-Carter KCVO OBE	b 1946

THE RECORD 1945-2005

Major Regimental Events		Regimental Headquarters	1st Battalion	
Date	Details	Name	Station	Name
		■ Lieutenant Colonel ■ Regimental Adjutant ▨ Superintending Clerk ■ Director of Music		■ Commanding Officer ■ Adjutant ▨ Sergeant Major ■ Quartermaster
1982	Regimental Headquarters re-established at Wellington Barracks (The Falkland Islands campaign)	Col ATW Duncan LVO OBE		RSM SR Halford Lt Col A Héroys
1983	The Queen's Company inspected at Windsor Castle 1st Bn Troop the Colour	Maj TJ Tedder WO1 MB Holland	(N IRELAND – Armagh)	Capt DJ Webster
1984	2nd Bn Troop the Colour	Maj TH Holbech WO1 CE Kitchen		Capt CTG Bolton RSM DW Ling Capt NP Sanford
1985		WO1 S Tuck BEM Maj CJE Seymour		Capt EF Hobbs Lt Col EJ Webb-Carter
1986			BAOR Munster (N IRELAND – dispersed)	RSM M Nesbittt
1987		Lt Col A Héroys Maj RJ Parker WO1 P Harris		Capt MJ Joyce Capt DJH Madden RSM DJ Hardman
1988		Maj SA Watts		Lt Col EH Houstoun MBE
1989	Regimental Council established	Maj Gen BC Gordon Lennox CB MBE WO1 RJ Le Louet BEM		Capt GK Bibby RSM CC Savage
1990		Lt Col TJ Tedder	(THE GULF –	Lt Col RG Cartwright
1991	The Gulf War 2nd Bn Troop the Colour	WO1 J Lenaghan	OP GRANBY) HOME Wellington	Capt TA Rolfe Capt JPW Gatehouse Capt JA Sandison QGM
1992	HM The Queen 50 years a Grenadier The Queen's Company inspected at Windsor Castle New Colours to 1st and 2nd Bns – Horse Guards 1st Bn Troop the Colour 1st Bn Old Colours laid up in the Guards Chapel	Capt PE Hills		RSM D Beresford
1993	The Guards Depot becomes Army Training Regiment Pirbright 2nd Bn Old Colours laid up in St Margaret's Westminster		(N IRELAND – Armagh)	Lt Col ET Bolitho Capt RL Fanshawe
1994	2nd Bn Troop the Colour 2nd Bn placed in suspended animation Nijmegen Company formed			Capt BMP Inglis Capt GV Inglis-Jones RSM S Swanwick

Sixty Years of Service

2nd Battalion		
Date	Station	Name
		■ Commanding Officer ■ Adjutant ■ Sergeant Major ■ Quartermaster
1982	HOME Chelsea (**CYPRUS** partly UN)	Capt N Collins
1983		Lt Col JVEF O'Connell RSM TA Rolfe Capt GVA Baker
1984	(BELIZE)	
1985		Capt AJ Fraser RSM DA Moore Capt DR Rossi MBE Lt Col AJC Woodrow MC QGM
1986	**N IRELAND** – Ballykelly	
1987		Capt MB Holland RSM BMP Inglis Capt EC Gordon Lennox Capt PT Dunkerley
1988	HOME Caterham	Lt Col AMH Joscelyne
1989		RSM KR Fairchild Capt GPR Norton Capt CE Kitchen MBE
1990	(The Inkerman Coy Group to Falkland Islands)	Lt Col GF Lesinski
1991	(No 2 Coy Group to Falkland Islands)	Capt RD Winstanley RSM DJ O'Keefe
1992		Lt Col REH Aubrey-Fletcher
1993		Capt GJ Rocke RSM S Swanwick Capt BMP Inglis
1994	2nd Battalion placed in suspended animation Nijmegen Company formed	

Successively Regimental Lieutenant Colonel from 1989 (from top left): Major General Bernard Gordon Lennox CB MBE (through the Dukes of Richmond and Gordon, a direct descendant of Charles II), Major General Sir Evelyn Webb-Carter KCVO OBE, Colonel Edward Bolitho OBE. In 1989 regimental manning responsibilities were assumed by the Ministry of Defence, the duties of the Lieutenant Colonel thereby being confined to the interests of the Regiment itself. The part-time post may be filled by a serving or retired officer.

Lieutenant Colonel Quartermasters and Directors of Music		
(QM)	GFG Turner OBE DCM	1898-1968
(DOM)	FJ Harris OBE	1900-1997
(QM)	BH Pratt OBE	1906-1987
(QM)	AJ Spratley MBE MM	1910-1978
(DOM)	RB Bashford OBE	1917-1997
(DOM)	DR Kimberley MBE	b 1931
(QM)	GR Whitehead RVM	b 1932
(QM)	WR Clarke OBE	b 1936
(QM)	DJ Webster	b 1938
(DOM)	PE Hills	b 1947
(QM)	RAJ Phasey BEM	b 1950
(QM)	CE Kitchen MBE	b 1951
(QM)	P Harris MBE	b 1951
(QM)	S Tuck BEM	b 1951

THE RECORD 1945-2005

Major Regimental Events		Regimental Headquarters		1st Battalion	
Date	Details	Name	Station		Name
		■ Lieutenant Colonel ■ Regimental Adjutant ■ RQMS ■ Director of Music		■ Commanding Officer ■ Adjutant ■ Sergeant Major ■ Quartermaster	
1995	Nijmegen Company moves to Windsor	Brig EJ Webb-Carter OBE Lt Col CJE Seymour		Lt Col JP Hargreaves RSM AJ Green Maj RAJ Phasey BEM	
1996		RQMS RM Jolly BEM	N IRELAND Ballykinler	Capt JDMcL Wrench	
1997				Lt Col AD Hutchinson RSM VJ Overton Maj P Harris	
1998		RQMS N Bould	Pirbright	Capt JJR Hunt-Davis	
1999		RQMS MG Harding	(N IRELAND East Tyrone)	RSM RM Dorney Maj SD Marcham	
2000	HRH Prince Philip 25 years as Colonel Nijmegen Company moves to Wellington Barracks	Col ET Bolitho OBE RQMS DA Harrison		Lt Col DJH Maddan	
2001	New Colours to Nijmegen Company – Buckingham Palace		Windsor (N IRELAND Belfast)	Capt JMH Bowder RSM M Gaunt Maj D Beresford	
2002	HM The Queen 60 years a Grenadier Death and Funeral of Queen Elizabeth the Queen Mother 2nd Bn Old Colours laid up in Bristol Cathedral Recruit training moves from Pirbright to Catterick	Maj D Burton		Lt Col GPR Norton MBE RSM BF Broad	
2003	The Queen's Company Troop the 1st Bn Colour The Queen's Company reviewed at Windsor	RQMS DA Felton	No 2 Coy Gp to Falkland Islands	Capt ARG Cartwright Maj AJ Green	
2004	Inkerman Company Troop the 1st Bn Colour	RQMS JR Keeley	(BOSNIA- HERZEGOVINA)	Lt Col DJC Russell-Parsons RSM G Gask	
2005				Capt OGC Saxby Maj VJ Overton	

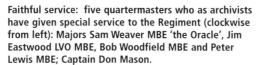
Faithful service: five quartermasters who as archivists have given special service to the Regiment (clockwise from left): Majors Sam Weaver MBE 'the Oracle', Jim Eastwood LVO MBE, Bob Woodfield MBE and Peter Lewis MBE; Captain Don Mason.

The most noble order: Grenadier Knights of the Garter with the HM the Colonel-in-Chief and HRH the Colonel in 1990. They are (left to right): Lord Carrington, the Earl of Cromer, Viscount de Lisle VC, the Duke of Grafton and the Duke of Norfolk. Lord Kingsdown later joined their number.

Boxer and bobsleigher: Jack Gardner (right) won the Army, Imperial Services and ABA Heavyweight titles in 1948, followed by the British and Empire title in 1950 and the European title in 1951. Robin Dixon, later Lord Glentoran, took the Gold Medal in the two-man bobsleigh, with Tony Nash, in the Winter Olympics of 1964.

Germany – The Defence of Western Europe

After the war Germany became a long-standing destination of Grenadiers. Hubbelrath, Wuppertal and Münster[3] became particularly familiar homes to the 1st and 2nd Battalions, though not to the 3rd Battalion, who never went there at all. Still, it was not then the semi-permanent posting that it was later to prove for a large part of the army, particularly for armoured and artillery regiments. Many of those soldiers passed virtually the whole of their careers there and there were a few officers who reached general rank with their uniforms unadorned by a single medal ribbon. For most of the period the British Army of the Rhine in West Germany (the Federal Republic) contained an entire corps of three divisions, besides numerous army and garrison troops. It was by far the biggest permanent deployment of British troops ever seen in peacetime. And they were the best equipped and trained, and the best provided for in terms of comforts and facilities, and in provision for the families, who were there in large numbers.

The training was on a scale unimaginable in the close confines of Salisbury Plain, the Pennines or Wales. Not only were there the abundant training areas (Sennelager, Soltau and Hohne) where the Nazi armies had been honed, but in the most free and easy days whole brigades and divisions of BAOR would go out after the harvest on enormous autumn exercises, steaming blithely over farmland and through woodland in tanks and armoured carriers, dossing down in the barns and clogging up the roads, secure in the knowledge that any damage they did would be mended and paid for in their wake. Though it was not to last, it was a very satisfying way of flexing military muscles.

Clearing Up After the War

The work of reconstruction in Germany was immense. The economy was in ruins, refugees and displaced people were everywhere, German troops had to be disarmed and taken into POW camps. The infrastructure was battered. Germany was divided into four zones, administered by the British, Americans, French and Russians. Battalions had large areas of the country to control and administer, and moved around frequently from place to place. There was little or no time for training or exercises and a constant coming and going of men, many of the older ones returning home for discharge and younger ones arriving. The turnover was enormous, over 3000 Grenadiers leaving the battalions in the last months of 1945. Fraternization with the population was forbidden and not much sought anyway, once the hideous evidence of the concentration camps came to light. Many soldiers, however, were moved by the plight of the women and children, and were able to help them in discreet ways.

The Dropping of the Iron Curtain, NATO

Times were changing rapidly. The Soviets erected an enormous barrier of wire, concrete, ditches and mines down the whole length of the western boundary of their

---

[3] See map on page 233

Well protected: a MILAN anti-tank missile detachment emerges from its FV432 protected against nuclear, biological and chemical attack.

On the alert: FV432 in woodland.

Man and machine: landrovers on the Allied Forces Day parade, Berlin.

Packing a punch: Warrior's 30mm RARDEN gun goes through its paces.

zone of Germany, also cutting off Czechoslovakia and Hungary. It was designed not as protection against the West, but as a fence to keep their own people in, especially those of East Germany, which became a satellite of the Soviet Union and was given the name of the (far from democratic) German Democratic Republic. They blockaded Berlin and did not concede failure until the Allies had supplied the city by an immense airlift over several months. The Soviet empire thus dug itself in and the West responded by the formation of the North Atlantic Treaty Organization. NATO and the Soviet Bloc were to face each other across the Iron Curtain for over forty years, attaining an uneasy balance by powerful ground forces and the threat of nuclear weapons.

As the Soviet Union replaced Germany as the potential enemy, civilized relations with the Germans themselves were steadily restored. Indeed, the German army was reconstituted, though on a much more modest basis than before, and joined the NATO allies in defence of their own country. The Germans buckled down to restore their economy and did so with such energy and speed that those accustomed to post-war rationing at home (which persisted into the early 1950s) were astonished to see the abundance of butter and sugar on the German shelves. BAOR settled down to a proper pattern of training and military life. The 4th Guards Brigade, in which battalions of Foot Guards were almost invariably to be found over many years, was formed.

Backwards and Forwards to Germany

Germany was becoming a good posting. The occupying army had become protectors against a common threat. The people, especially the millions of refugees from the east, were more than happy to be hosts to British soldiers. They were comforted by seeing them out on huge training exercises near the eastern border. Grenadier families moved into good requisitioned houses or the increasing number of married quarters built to order. Good schools and NAAFI shops were established. The ban on fraternization was quickly becoming history as soldiers found German girlfriends and wives.

New equipment arrived. The 7.62mm self-loading rifle and general purpose machine gun came into army service to replace the faithful .303in rifle and Bren gun, the SLR causing interesting modifications to drill. Mortars, however, still came in inches. Mechanization began to appear in the form of the Humber 1 Ton armoured carrier, a horribly uncomfortable metal box useless off the roads and christened – with feeling – the Pig. The MOBAT anti-tank gun appeared on the scene with its huge squash-head shell and a monstrous propulsive bang that turned its gunner to jelly. Nuclear, biological and chemical protection started to enter the syllabus, but it was only talk. An amphibious exercise in the Baltic caused some excitement and a good deal of sea-sickness. But they were good conditions in which to enjoy sport and Grenadiers often excelled, particularly at athletics. There were some talented gladiators who managed to train on the track or field all summer and on the ski slopes all winter, without making much contact with their uniforms.

In 1967 a great step forward was taken with the adoption of the FV432, a tracked vehicle which, though most unimaginatively named, constituted a quantum improvement on its wheeled predecessor and was actually able to keep up with a tank.

The even pace of life was badly interrupted by the needs of Northern Ireland, to which battalions were often diverted during their time in Germany. In such circumstances it was impossible to train successfully in mechanized skills. And, with increasing prosperity and confidence, and seeing the clear success of the deterrent strategy, the mood of the German people was changing. Farmers were no longer prepared to have soldiers exercising on their land. Money to repair damage to property or to replace worn-out tracks was short. Progress was made in other directions, however. Battle groups were formed of a mixture of tanks and mechanized infantry, and combat teams similarly composed at a lower level. This led to more imaginative tactics and training became more imaginative in turn, especially with the establishment of the British Army Training Unit at Suffield, near Calgary in Canada. Here the endless plains gave full scope to large-scale manoeuvres, despite the absence of trees or any easily recognizable feature. There was plenty of ammunition and infantry, tanks and artillery were able to work together without hindrance. Vehicles were kept permanently in Canada and a whole battle group at a time would go out, pick them up, exercise and then wind down with such diversions as adventure training in the Rockies.

In the late 1980s a new rifle appeared, the 5.56mm SA80 individual weapon, with its complementary light support weapon. There was a new light anti-armour weapon and the MILAN guided anti-tank missile, both large and cumbersome and taking some time to make friends with. There were new optical sights and night vision devices. Most of all, there was a fine new armoured

Grenadier Gallery

LIEUTENANT GENERAL
Sir ANTHONY DENISON-SMITH
KBE DL *Born 1942*

Commanding Officer and General with long experience of soldiering in Germany

*A*nthony Denison-Smith joined the 2nd Battalion, via Harrow and Sandhurst, in 1962 and was soon in the jungles of British Guiana with Inkerman Company. After being Adjutant of the Guards Depot he commanded No 3 Company of the 1st Battalion in lively visits to Belfast and Londonderry and emerged with the MBE. He was then in turn Captain of the Queen's Company, Brigade Major 7th Armoured Brigade, instructor at the Staff College and, in 1981, Commanding Officer of the 2nd Battalion in Münster, in London, and for six months with the UN in Cyprus.

He was in his day a fine sportsman, playing cricket for the Army and rugby for his Battalion, but was perhaps less happy with horses. Once, returning to barracks from the Mall after commanding the street liners, torrential rain and a clap of thunder caused his mount, well in charge, to carry him at full gallop across the bridge of St James's Park.

He went on to BAOR as chief of staff of an armoured division and clearly enjoyed keeping the Warsaw Pact at bay, for he later commanded an armoured brigade, became Chief of Staff 1(BR) Corps and, in due course, commanded 1st (UK) Armoured Division. He was proud that the MOD claimed him for a single appointment only, as Director General Doctrine and Training.

His final appointment was GOC Southern District in Aldershot. In 1992 he was also appointed the first Colonel of The Princess of Wales's Royal Regiment, the amalgamated Queen's and Royal Hampshire Regiments. For seven years he was a staunch member of the Grenadier Council and on retirement from the Army became Chairman of the Army Cadet Force Association.

Plenty of room: armoured manoeuvres on the Canadian prairie.

fighting vehicle, the Warrior, which the 1st Battalion had been chosen to bring into service. It was a high compliment.

Warrior was large, expensive, fast and well-armed with the 30mm Rarden cannon and 7.62mm machine gun. The introduction lasted a year, in a complicated programme encompassing every aspect of training, maintenance and tactics. The battalion was besieged by official visitors anxious to see the wonderful new vehicle in action and getting in the way. The result was a triumph. Warrior was brought fully into service with great success, which was to be seen only too clearly in the Gulf War shortly afterwards. Grenadiers had become the acknowledged experts and their credit stood extremely high.

It was a fine point at which to bring to a close the many

Warrior: a silver model of the fine fighting vehicle.

years that the Regiment had spent in Germany. For, with astounding suddenness, first East Germany and then the Soviet Union simply fell apart. The Communist system was proved to have feet of clay. With almost no violence, it crumbled. The threat from the east, which had for so many years seemed inevitable and immutable, no longer existed. It was not long before the Iron Curtain itself was swept away and the whole of eastern Europe opened up. British forces in a reunited Germany were to be greatly reduced. Henceforward the NATO and old Soviet Bloc nations were to be allies in a new global war against terrorism.

The Running Sore of Berlin

Nowhere was the collapse of Communism more vividly apparent than in Berlin. The Regiment had served in the city twice since 1954. In 1961 refugees had poured into the west at a great rate and in August a wall was built to keep them in. This loathed construction was a hundred miles long, round the western sectors of Berlin,[4] creating an island to which access was allowed only under stringent conditions. It was guarded by a line of watch-towers from which many attempting to escape were shot out of hand. For twenty-eight years the wall was the most visible and notorious mark of Soviet repression.

---

[4] Roughly equivalent to the M25 around London

Around the Eastern Mediterranean

Turmoil in Palestine 1945-48

In August 1945 the 3rd Battalion, having returned from Austria in July, was at Hawick in Scotland. They had been warned to go with 1st Guards Brigade to finish off the war against Japan, but thankfully the Japanese surrendered following the atom bombs on Hiroshima and Nagasaki. Instead, the brigade was diverted to Palestine. The situation was a familiar one. The Jewish population, now much inflated by immigration following the Nazi persecution, was determined to entrench with little regard to the Palestinians. The British were mandated to keep the peace, and thus were in their familiar role of trying to satisfy both parties while preventing bloodshed and destruction. The High Commissioner was that most famous Grenadier Field Marshal Viscount Gort VC, though he was a sick man and died from cancer in 1946.

In November 1945 the **3rd Battalion** (Lt Col Peter Clifton and later Lt Col John Davies[5]) in 1st Guards Brigade (commanded in turn by Grenadiers, Edward Goulburn and Rodney Moore) went into Camp 260 on the coast seven miles north of Acre. Operational duties were not very demanding to begin with, though there was serious trouble elsewhere, the Jewish Stern Gang having murdered seven soldiers of the Parachute Regiment at Tel Aviv. In June 1946 three trains were blown up south of Haifa. This was followed by a number of cordon and search operations, frequently launched by a hurried awakening and briefing in the middle of the night in order to secure cordon positions before dawn. Searching was a long and laborious business, taking several hours.

In the early months there had been time for leave and relaxation and a few had managed to travel to Cyprus and Lebanon for this purpose. But in June all this changed and thereafter many never left

General Service Medal 1918-1962: sixteen clasps were awarded, including Palestine.

their camp. An enormous search and arrest operation, involving most of the 100,000 British troops in Palestine,[6] resulted in 600 weapons being found, but the terrorists replied by blowing up the King David Hotel in Jerusalem, killing ninety.

Because of the sensitive political situation British troops were not able to take really offensive action, and there was some time left for training. One large exercise took place in Transjordan (now Jordan). On return it was the battalion's lot to prevent illegal immigration by cordoning the Haifa docks. It was an unpleasant task, for many of those in the ships were Jews who had survived the Nazi holocaust and were expecting to be welcomed

---

[5] HRH Davies
[6] About equivalent to the entire strength of the British Army projected for 2008

EGYPT and PALESTINE

Ready to mount:
a section on the
roadside in Palestine.

On the move again: at
the quayside in Haifa.

A lonely spot: Camp 260. *James Denny*

in their 'promised land'. But the sympathies of the British soldiers lay more often with the Arabs, who had lived in Palestine for centuries and, in order to accommodate the Jews, were in danger of being turned out.

In January 1947 the battalion, over 800 strong, moved closer to the action in the turbulent district of Lydda. Near Tel Aviv Guardsman Donald Roberts was fatally injured when an armoured car was blown up by a mine and landed on him. Disturbances often resulted from the execution of terrorists and security had to be imposed by guards and road blocks. In June there was another move, to Nathanya (now Netanya) where the Jews were mining roads. A large operation was mounted following the abduction of two British sergeants. Two Grenadier officers were among the first to see their bloody bodies hanging from trees with typewritten charges pinned to their chests. One of the bodies was booby-trapped and a large explosion was set off as it was cut down, mercifully without causing serious injury.

At this point the Arabs and Jews started to concentrate more on fighting each other than the British. The decision of the UN to partition the country inflamed them further and the British government decided that they were not prepared to enforce any such policy and would withdraw troops by May 1948 when the mandate expired. But the

last few months were far from easy. An attack was made on the main entrance of the camp at Nathanya. Guardsman Ken Taylor was killed by a sniper after the battalion had moved south to the area of Jaffa/Tel Aviv in January 1948.

In April 1948 the 3rd Battalion returned to Windsor. It was succeeded by the **1st Battalion** (Lt Col Peter Deakin[7]), who went first to Nathanya and then to Haifa. The final withdrawal was under way, but it was turbulent and violent. Lance Sergeant PR Clarke and Guardsman Fred Howlett were killed and five others wounded in various actions. No further attempt was made to prevent inter-communal fighting and 1st Guards Brigade concentrated instead on keeping the camps protected and the roads open. This sometimes meant smashing road blocks with tank fire. The brigade was the last to leave the country, still harassed by snipers and machine-gunners. They drove to the docks on flat tyres, shot out by the Jews.

It was the end of a thankless task. In the light of subsequent history, it is all too clear how impossible it had been to succeed. The new state of Israel was declared by the Jews and ever since that time, for over half a century, Israelis and Palestinians (supported from time to time by various Arab nations) have fought, sometimes in

[7] CMF Deakin

major wars using aircraft and tanks, constantly by guerrilla methods and most recently by terrorism and suicide bombing. This bitter dispute probably has the oldest and deepest roots of any in the world and, as we move into the twenty-first century, there is still little sign of it being resolved.

Libya, Egypt and the Suez Campaign 1948-56

The base installations maintained by British forces in Egypt were still regarded as critically important. They helped to enable the security of the Suez Canal, which almost a century earlier had provoked military action in Egypt. Now the importance of links to the Far East and the increasing dependence on oil from the Middle East made the need as great as ever. It was thought that the eastern Mediterranean (and thence these crucial interests) could be dominated by stationing British forces in Libya, Malta and Cyprus. Thus it was that in June 1948 the **1st Battalion** (Lt Col Peter Deakin and later Lt Col John Nelson) went straight from Palestine to Tripoli in Libya, which was administered by the British with King Idris as nominal ruler until such time as the United Nations decided its future.

The routine was straightforward enough and a welcome relief from the trials of Palestine. After settling in

and a 'Flag March' to impress the inhabitants of Tripoli, training got under way. The winter brought a surprise in the form of severe weather. Snow fell for the first time in living memory, but as it melted and spring broke out the conditions in the hills became very pleasant. Life was varied and a number of wives and children came out to join the men. Most of the guardsmen were National Servicemen. There was sport of all kinds and expeditions into the desert – one was actually taken for German and shot at.

In August 1950 the battalion visited Malta to take part in a large-scale exercise. They were due to return home in April 1951, and looking forward to it, when told that their stay had to be extended. The 3rd Battalion, coming out in 1st Guards Brigade to relieve them, were warned to be ready to go instead to Iran, where yet another scare had brewed up. British soldiers were entitled to return home after three years abroad, so the delay was very irksome and caused some serious tetchiness. The summer dragged on, plagued by sandstorms, which lasted for several days, and the resulting frayed tempers. At last, in September and to their great relief, they came home to Warley in Essex.

The **3rd Battalion** (Lt Col Patrick Robertson) arrived in Tripoli in July 1951 and prepared for adventures in

Ceremonial not forgotten: the Queen's Birthday Parade at Moascar in 1955.

Iran. These, however, did not come off. Instead, trouble arose in Cairo. The battalion prepared to drive, if necessary, along the coast to secure vital installations, but eventually were flown into the Canal Zone itself, going into camp at Tel-el-Kebir near Suez, the scene of the famous victory in 1882. Their job, as part of a force of two brigades, was to protect the vast installations there, the principal one being a huge ordnance depot, containing most of the ammunition and stores for Middle East Land Forces. Its perimeter was twenty-five miles long and the professional pilferers extremely skilful. Their techniques 'included carrying out their raids virtually naked, with their bodies covered in grease, which made capture difficult'.[8] Equipment was constantly being stolen.

There were the inevitable guards to do, leavened by such diversions as unloading kippers from a refrigerated ship. Grenadiers in the docks of Port Said worked at four times the speed of the regular dockers. More serious trouble then broke out and some large cordon and search operations resulted. Two guardsmen, Fred and Alwyn Smith, were tragically killed by British mines while rewiring the Tel-el-Kebir perimeter. In February 1952 the battalion was moved to Deversoir at the northern end of the Great Bitter Lake, and much of the rest of the year was taken up with guard duties. Though life in camp was dreary, training was excellent and it was possible to exercise on a large scale with armour, artillery and engineers. A few wives managed to join their husbands.

The Coronation celebrations in June 1953 were, predictably, modest, but a detachment was able to return to London for the occasion. And at last, in February 1954, the battalion returned to Chelsea Barracks.

In the following month the **2nd Battalion** (Lt Col Charles Earle and later Lt Col Hon Miles Fitzalan Howard) arrived at Port Said to be greeted by the Grenadier commanders of the two Guards brigades in the Canal Zone, 'Geordie' Gordon Lennox and Peter Deakin[9], and then travelled up to Fanara on the Great Bitter Lake. After taking part in the Queen's Birthday Parade on the polo ground at Moascar they settled down into a routine similar to that followed by their predecessors. In December they moved into Golf Course Camp at Port Said, where they began to undertake trials on the new 7.62 self-loading rifle. In 1955 the Regimental Colour was trooped at Moascar at a Queen's Birthday Parade containing more guards than in London that year.

However, the days of the British military presence in

Egypt were numbered. Despite the importance of the Suez Canal, the base itself was now so cumbersome as to be a liability and the government decided to pull out. The battalion left in April 1956, picking up further families in Tripoli on the way home to Pirbright.

But the Egyptian adventure was not quite over. In June 1956 Colonel Nasser became president and promptly nationalized the canal, threatening to block its use. The government decided to intervene, with the French, by launching an attack from Malta and Cyprus. On 3 August the **3rd Battalion** (Lt Col Alec Gregory-Hood) was mobilized, 400 reservists being drawn in, and quickly sailed to Malta. Thrown into an appalling camp, they then suffered frustrating uncertainties as the operation was repeatedly postponed. And there was almost nothing to do. This proved too much for a number of reservists, anxious for their families and jobs left behind. Going out to fight was all right, but hanging about in miserable conditions was not. There was unrest, which the press got wind of and gleefully blew up into a full-scale mutiny. It was not difficult to do, as the whole Suez adventure was highly controversial anyway.

However, the trouble quickly subsided and on 29 October the attack on Egypt was launched. Several Grenadiers of the Guards Independent Parachute Company dropped successfully on Port Said. The vehicles and stores of the 3rd Battalion were loaded into ships, but only the machine-gun platoon reached Egypt, being landed from a minesweeper after a dreadful voyage, and almost at once being re-embarked.[10] The whole adventure had come to a sorry conclusion. The Americans refused to support the action; the short campaign fizzled out after a few days and the UN were left to clear up the mess. It had been an inglorious episode.

Cyprus – The Emergency 1956-59

As a result of the difficulties in Palestine and Egypt it was decided to transfer Middle East Headquarters to Cyprus, an important base for British forces. This provoked opposition from the Greek Cypriot leader, George Grivas, who not only wanted the British out, but also sought union with Greece, a proposition to which the large number of Turks on the island were implacably

[8] Paget
[9] Who had succeeded yet another Grenadier, Algy Heber Percy
[10] Just after the ceasefire a Grenadier parachutist was transfixed by what appeared to be a mirage: the machine-gun platoon sergeant, properly dressed in best battledress, forage cap and sash, supervising the defence of the brigade headquarters (Maxfield)

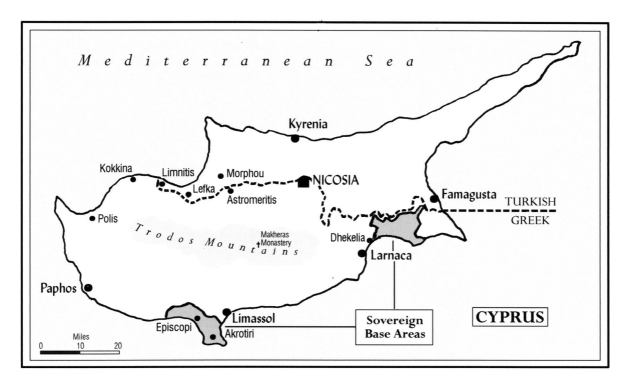

hostile. Once more, therefore, the British were drawn into the unpalatable situation of having to suppress civil strife as well as protect their own legitimate interests. Between 1954 and 1956 Grivas's EOKA terrorists were increasingly active, murdering several servicemen.

The **3rd Battalion** (Lt Col Alec Gregory-Hood and later Lt Col Pat Britten) were nearby in Malta. After the disappointment of Suez the reservists and many National Servicemen whose time was expired had returned home. In December 1956 the battalion disembarked at Limassol and were ordered into another dreadful, water-logged camp near Nicosia; fortunately, however, they were soon able to move into a better one near the airport.

Their duties were familiar ones: to be ready for internal security operations, rioting in particular, and to mount the interminable guards. Early in their time they took part in an important operation near the Makheras Monastery at the eastern end of the Troodos mountains, with the purpose of flushing out Gregoris Afxentiou, Grivas's lieutenant. Here, after sweeping through undergrowth, the accompanying 1st Duke of Wellington's discovered a hide, from which four terrorists emerged. Afxentiou suddenly appeared, firing a Sten gun

General Service Medal 1918-1962: sixteen clasps were awarded, including Cyprus.

and killing one of the DWR, and then bolted back inside. A seven-hour siege ensued, watched by the Grenadiers, and eventually he succumbed to a combination of grenades, explosives, tear gas and petrol, the DWR finding his charred body in the hide. It was the culmination of several months of operations in which eleven out of sixteen terrorist gangs had been dealt with and sixty-nine EOKA killed.

In March 1957 a ceasefire was declared, to allow political negotiations to proceed. It allowed some relaxation and it was possible to run rest camps by the sea. But it did not last. In January 1958 the battalion came under command of a new brigade and prepared to be ready for deployment anywhere on the island. This was a far more worthwhile and exciting role than static guards and road blocks. Operations by helicopter were practised for the first time, tracker dog teams and a reconnaissance troop in Ferret scout cars were formed. Companies were frequently deployed to cordon and search villages, establish observation points and patrol. In March the murders resumed and in June a particularly nasty atrocity occurred when several Greek Cypriots, who had been released from arrest and were on their way home, were intercepted by Turkish Cypriots and murdered, evidently

Megaphone, mule and men: operations in Cyprus.

A little tenderness: guardsman and lamb in Cyprus.

Needle in a haystack: making a search in Cyprus.

with axes. Some were decapitated. The bodies were found by Grenadiers who then had to collect the dead – a grisly and distressing task. Within the hour the entire battalion had deployed and cordoned off the area.

There were occasional accidents, both to terrorists and guardsmen. On one occasion a Grenadier was mistaken for a terrorist owing to a misunderstanding, but fortunately neither his company commander nor CSM, both of whom shot at him from close range, managed to hit their target.

In August there was an unexpected and highly distinguished visitor, Harold Macmillan, the Prime Minister. He had fought in the Regiment during the First World War with Colonel Britten's father and was clearly moved at being among Grenadiers again. He told the press on return to England, 'I ask you to assure your readers that the Brigade of Guards is not in decline, particularly the finest regiment of the Brigade'.

Further operations continued, but in February 1959 a compromise was reached by the Greeks and Turks and peace was restored. The battalion embarked for home in July, having spent almost three years in the eastern Mediterranean and facing the gloomy prospect of being placed in suspended animation.

The **2nd Battalion** (Lt Col James Bowes-Lyon) had meanwhile been languishing at Lydd, on the bleak and draughty shores of Dungeness. In June 1958 they were

United Nations Force In Cyprus: a similar medal was given for many other UN operations.

greatly cheered by the news that they also were to go to Cyprus. Some of the drummers, however, were told that they were too young to be sent. They vented their annoyance with true drummer verve by burning down the gymnasium, for which they were forgiven by a sympathetic commanding officer.

The battalion was off in forty-eight hours. It was the first complete move of a battalion by air. They were in 1st Guards Brigade as part of the strategic reserve and their eventual destination was supposed to be first Lebanon, then Jordan and then Khartoum. As it was they stayed in a bare camp at Limassol, though diverted by a major exercise set by their Grenadier divisional commander, Maj Gen 'Geordie' Gordon Lennox. Not after all being required elsewhere, they joined in the operations on the island. Two big and successful ones were launched, resulting in the arrest of nine wanted Cypriots and the discovery of a large amount of arms and ammunition. In December 1958 they returned home and soon afterwards moved to Germany.

Cyprus – The United Nations 1965-83

But the story of Grenadiers in Cyprus was not yet over. The declaration of the Republic of Cyprus in 1960 had resulted in an uneasy peace. The government machinery quickly broke down and President Makarios agreed to admit a peacekeeping force, which became the United Nations Force in Cyprus (UNFICYP) and operational from

Colours and drums: battalion and company camp colours on proud display with the blue berets.

June 1964. Containing Canadians, Irish, Danes and Finns, as well as British, it monitored the 'green line', dividing Greek and Turkish Cypriots, and there were numerous potential flashpoints in isolated areas.

In March 1965 the advance party of the **1st Battalion** (Lt Col Michael Bayley) left Germany, having exchanged their berets for light blue ones with the UN badge. There was no time to lose as there had been inter-communal fighting and the Greek and Turkish Cypriots were in a state of confrontation. It was the purpose of the UN to separate them, keep them apart and intercede where there were difficulties. It was not a fighting force and could not open fire unless its soldiers were attacked or vital property threatened.

The battalion was based at Polemidhia camp on the northern outskirts of Limassol. Guards and observation posts were established and a scheme of patrols arranged. An ugly incident in May, where a strong platoon of the Greek Cypriot National Guard broke into Turkish Cypriot houses in Limassol, provoked acute tension which was happily defused by prompt action and persuasion. Negotiation was the name of the game, and many hours were spent by the Grenadiers soothing injured pride and inflamed tempers.

There was also some time for relaxation, which was greatly enjoyed in the delightful surroundings that the island had to offer in abundance. But in July an Irish battalion was withdrawn and the Grenadiers had to look after the area of Lefka and Polis as well as Limassol. This district was more troublesome and the battalion thinly spread. Supply along the narrow mountainous roads of the Troodos was a complicated and often nerve-wracking business. And shortly before leaving in September everything was changed again, the battalion for two short weeks being given the Paphos district, another sensitive part of the island, with all the attendant difficulties of setting up and supplying new camps, not to mention making the fresh contacts necessary to make the peacekeeping succeed. Fortunately the blue berets were generally welcomed, and the Grenadiers, in the fashion of the British soldier, were adept at making friends and establishing friendly, though well respected, relations. It was a rewarding job, and well done.

And it was to be done again. This time it was the **2nd Battalion** (Lt Col Anthony Denison-Smith) who returned to the island in November 1982. Turkey had invaded Cyprus in 1974 and had sliced it in two. They now controlled the north and the Greek Cypriot government

In the service of peace: a lance corporal in UN operational order 1983. *Christopher Morley*

the south; a buffer zone separated the two and in it the UN forces operated. The battalion was based near Nicosia. Two companies occupied the buffer zone to the west of the capital, the other half battalion being in Dhekelia under separate command (Lt Col Conway Seymour) and charged with the security of the Eastern Sovereign Base Area (SBA).[11] These were able to train and enjoy the exceptional sporting facilities available. Halfway through the tour the companies changed over.

There were no serious incidents and the peace was successfully kept. More, real improvements were made. On Grenadier initiative, and after long and patient negotiation, many of the fields in the buffer zone were reopened to cultivation and sensitive issues of water supply resolved. It was a cheering and positive way to end a long and often disturbed history of soldiering in that beautiful and troubled island.

[11] The Western SBA was based on RAF Akrotiri

Into Jungle Green

Bandits in Malaya 1948-49

In June 1948 a State of Emergency was declared in Malaya. Communist guerrillas, some of whom had fought against the Japanese during the Second World War, now had ambitions on the country itself and were attacking rubber estates and isolated planters. The Commissioner of Police had known the 3rd Battalion in Palestine and, when offered troops in support, asked for them specifically. Though they were long overdue for home service, this was agreed. Thus the **3rd Battalion** (Lt Col Patrick (TFC) Winnington), including a fourth rifle company made up mostly of guardsmen barely out of training at the Guards Depot, sailed from Liverpool in September as part of 2nd Guards Brigade, which had been formed specially for the purpose. On arrival they travelled 200 miles by train up to Kuala Lumpur and marched to Sungei Besi camp. Sergeant Major Reg Butler, one of the first to arrive, saw a small gunner sitting with his rifle on a large pile of canvas. 'Where's the camp?' he enquired. 'I'm sitting on it,' was the reply.

The job of the battalion was to restore confidence and round up bandits, as they were termed. Like other battalions there, they had no experience whatever of

General Service Medal 1918-1962: sixteen clasps were awarded, including Malaya

jungle conditions. They were welcomed in the Communist propaganda by: '600 red-hair pigs have recently arrived in Sungei Besi; they are not used to the heat and tropical storms and a great many have fallen sick of a tropical fever and have been daily carried out for burial. This is owing to their non-acclimatisation and excessive drinking of whisky.'[12]

To guard the rubber plantations was relatively simple, but the bandits hid in their familiar jungle in well-constructed camps, cleverly protected. In the Kajang area they were particularly active. To get the better of them, in that extremely difficult country, without helicopters or even radios that would work except after setting up antennas in camp, was a formidable task. However, assisted by Dayak trackers, the initial short patrols (usually of some fifteen men) were extended to a week or more as experience increased. Each patrol had to be entirely self-sufficient, which meant carrying loads of sixty pounds or more. Under bad conditions it was not possible to cover more than a mile a day. Until air supply and helicopter

[12] Paget

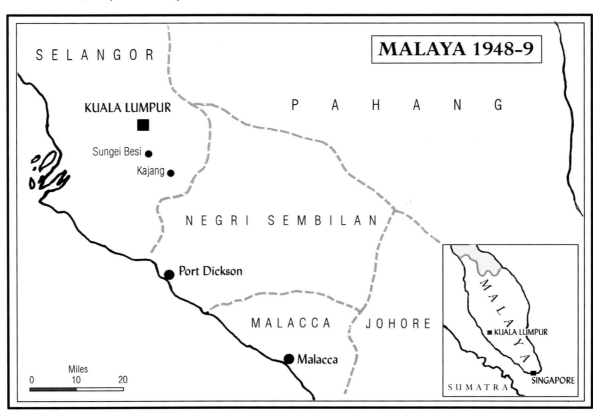

Guardsmen and tracker: a group in Malaya in 1948.

support appeared, wounded had to be carried out on stretchers, a task of dreadful difficulty which involved a change of bearers every few minutes.

The area of operations was so close to camp that it was possible to be on a dangerous patrol one night and eating a good meal and watching a film the next. In March 1949 Lieutenant John Farrer was killed going round his sentries. Failing three times to respond to a challenge, he was taken for a bandit and shot through the head. Later in the month a platoon of twenty men under Captain David Hargreaves, driving up a track, was ambushed by some fifteen bandits, carefully dug in. Despite reacting instantly

and chasing the bandits out of their position, five Grenadiers, Lance Corporal Joe Chriscoli (who had won the MM at Mareth) and four guardsmen, J Ryan, AE Martin, JR Hall and VT Herrett, were killed or died of wounds, and Hargreaves with two guardsmen wounded. It was the single serious loss of the tour.

No 2 Company had two particularly lively operations. In one most of the company were already deployed, but in response to a sudden opportunity a small scratch force was quickly assembled from those still in camp to tackle a party of bandits reported on a nearby rubber estate. After rapidly establishing a rather leaky cordon, they saw sixteen to twenty men wearing khaki uniforms and packs emerging from the estate. Unfortunately these were taken for police, who were known to be in the area, and fire was not opened before the mistake was recognized. The bandits melted into the jungle and only two of them were killed. On another occasion a camp was approached with the usual difficulty, from two different routes, and two further bandits killed after a confused fight. For their courageous part in these engagements the company

Into the jungle: ready for an arduous trip. *Christopher Morley*

Hot tin guardroom: the guard turns out in Sungei Besi camp.

commander, Major Tony Heywood, was awarded the MC and Lance Sergeant Basil Clutton the MM.

Many patrols inevitably saw no action and contacts were usually the result of extraordinary luck or good intelligence, which was not easy to come by. Nevertheless, in the Kajang area alone, between 19 May and 19 June, eleven armed bandits had been killed or captured, or had surrendered, and nine others wounded. In those early days there had been no time, or indeed inclination, to develop a policy of 'hearts and minds' that became so important in later internal security operations. If a Chinese village was found empty it was assumed that the people had fled because they were sympathetic to the bandits, and the huts were burnt. However, the ham-fistedness was understandable enough at the time. The work was dangerous, frightening and extremely uncomfortable, especially for western soldiers in a most unfamiliar environment. The Grenadiers had undoubtedly done well.

The British Southern Cameroons 1961

In 1961 it was the turn of Grenadiers to visit a remote country in West Africa which nobody has heard of, before or since. It was an extraordinary adventure which resulted in the death of a guardsman in battle but was not regarded as worth a clasp to the General Service Medal, being considered run-of-the-mill work for an imperial nation. It was the British Southern Cameroons (since Cameroun), overseen by Britain as a province of Nigeria under a mandate of the League of Nations (the predecessor to the United Nations). Early in 1961 the commanding officer of the **1st Battalion** (Lt Col David Fraser) was told in great secrecy that his battalion was to go there. Within an hour a Pakistani contractor appeared at Tidworth with the same information, asking to go too. In May they sailed in the troopship *Devonshire* and on arrival established themselves in the country, based at Buea, with companies at Kumba and, 280 miles and eighteen hours away by road, at Bamenda in the north.

Their job was to prevent rebellion in the neighbouring French Cameroun Republic spilling over the border. The country, a mixture of forest, plantation and jungle and, in the north, a high plateau with rolling grasslands, had the

Tragic journey: the body of John Lunn is brought down on a Fulani pony.

Cameroon shelter: a primitive home in the wettest country in the world.

highest rainfall of any country in the world (between 5 pm and 6 pm sharp daily) and the battalion were there in the rainy season. The roads, like the weather, were bad and flights by the three twin-engined Pioneer aircraft of the RAF frequently interrupted. While being prepared to undertake familiar internal security operations, it was important for the battalion to get to know the people and inspire confidence. The Queen's Birthday Parade in Bamenda, probably the most bizarre ever seen, was an early opportunity. In front of an extraordinarily colourful audience, which was loud in its appreciation of the drama, The Queen's Company, together with No 2, produced a fine performance.

Patrols then started in earnest. Much of the country was extraordinarily difficult, with swamps and deep ravines, and parts were not mapped at all. The giants with white faces, appearing suddenly in a village that was hardly out of the Stone Age, caused predictable astonishment. In places men would return from patrol, hardly recognizable with red blotchy faces from the bites of 'banana flies and everything else in creation'. There were alarms. Twelve plantation workers were found murdered and tied up in bundles of three. Their killers were not found.

There was one major operation. The British Government agreed that a troublesome terrorist camp on the border, perched high in the Bambutos Mountains, should be attacked and its occupants captured. It was necessary to declare a state of emergency in order to allow this. After a reconnaissance the two companies at Bamenda set out. The approach was difficult and the enemy clearly alert and well protected. A twelve-hour approach, in constant heavy rain, across deep ravines, streams and bamboo jungle, led to the vast, grey and forbidding mountain on top of which was the objective. Everyone was sliding and stumbling in the mud. The stops were in position as dawn broke and the assault group made its final approach. The enemy opened fire at fifty yards and Guardsman John Lunn was killed instantly. The group stormed into the camp, but there was now no sign of anybody. Two terrorists were shot by the stops and the camp was destroyed. In the evening it was abandoned. It took twenty hours to carry Lunn's body out to the roadhead, even with the assistance of Fulani ponies used by the reconnaissance platoon. Little had been gained militarily, but the determination of the British to take risks had been demonstrated and this undoubtedly helped the subsequent political negotiations to bring about a peaceful transfer of power. The battalion withdrew the day after independence was finally granted.

Gdsm David Westbury wrote: 'For most Grenadiers the 1961 tour was the greatest adventure of our lives.

Most of us National Servicemen and short-term regulars had never been abroad before. The sight and smell of Africa were unbelievable and they lived with me for years afterwards.'

British Guiana 1963-64

British Guiana (now Guyana) was a small British colony, though larger in area than Great Britain, on the north-east coast of South America. Its population of some half a million was largely a mixture of Indian and African stock. Political unrest arose in 1962 and rioting between the two communities ensued. Military help was called for. The **2nd Battalion** (Lt Col Francis Jefferson) left in June 1963 to succeed the 1st Coldstream, who had had a rough tour. Rioters who had posed a direct threat to the lives of a party of guardsmen had been shot. An attempt to lay a charge of murder against a Coldstream officer had happily failed, but the incident had demonstrated how fine were the judgements necessary in difficult and dangerous circumstances. The Grenadiers were only too aware of this.

In the area of the capital, Georgetown, there were several alarming incidents where Grenadiers were faced with crowds of excited young men armed with machetes and knives, but steady nerves, reinforced by memories of the Coldstream response, proved enough to restore calm and order. Up in the country the battalion provided parties to protect vulnerable estates and ambushes were laid on mud tracks, though arsonists were seldom caught. The local people, almost invariably, were friendly. The presence of British troops in fact proved very effective

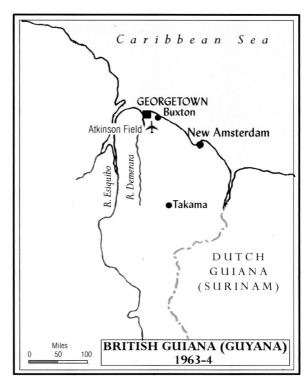

and the state of emergency that had been imposed was eventually lifted.

This allowed the battalion good opportunities to make the best of the tour in the form of adventurous training, long before it became common in the army. Each platoon undertook some kind of enterprise, making the best use of the numerous rivers, dodging flesh-eating piranha fish, trekking through the jungles and seeing a wide variety of wildlife. In perhaps the most hair-raising expedition, ten

Afloat on the Demerara: the end of an exciting trip in British Guiana.

A roof over the head: making a home in Belize.

Grenadiers went 110 miles down the Demerara River on a raft made of 24-gallon oil drums, surviving unexpected rapids and other hazards, and narrowly avoiding being swept out to the Atlantic at the journey's end. In March 1964 the battalion returned home.

British Honduras/Belize 1971-72 and 1984-5

In 1971 the **2nd Battalion** (Lt Col Richard Besly) again interested themselves in the Americas. This time it was British Honduras, later to become Belize. Here the threat was quite different, not the usual internal security but the possibility of invasion by neighbouring Guatemala, which had claims on the territory. For some time there had been a small garrison in the country, of a company group only. It was one of the most delightful postings on offer. In 1971 the 2nd Grenadiers became the designated 'Caribbean' battalion. They had under command S Company Scots Guards,[13] who went first to the colony for six months. In August 1971 it was the turn of the Inkerman Company Group (Maj Richard Corkran). The company was based at Airport Camp, some six miles from Belize City. The country was beautiful, and of astonishing variety. Reefs and sandy islands offshore gave way to a coastline of mangrove swamp and then in turn to open country and jungle and, in the mountains, parts that were hardly distinguishable from the Brecon Beacons, both in appearance and weather. The people

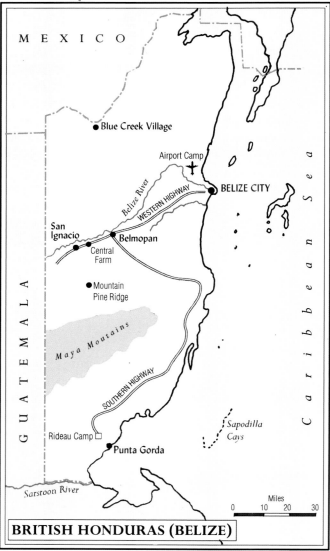

BRITISH HONDURAS (BELIZE)

---

[13] The residue of the 2nd Scots Guards when it was first reduced to a single company. The battalion was restored in 1972 only to suffer the same fate a second time (along with the 2nd Grenadiers and Coldstream) in 1994

were very poor. They imagined the arriving Grenadiers to be from Grenada and expected them all to be black.

Operational and protective duties were not heavy and full use was made of the fine training opportunities in different parts of the small country. There was jungle-bashing and navigation, and excellent field-firing up at 2000 feet in the hills at Mountain Pine Ridge. There were 'hearts and minds' patrols, relaxation on the coast and some travel further afield.

It was planned that the Inkerman Company would be succeeded by No 1 Company and that the whole battalion would re-unite for an exercise during the changeover period. Just at that time, however, the Guatemalan drums began to rattle menacingly. Invasion was thought to be imminent and in January 1972 the battalion took off early, having hauled everyone off leave. The six-week exercise became a seven-month tour and, if the Guatemalans had ever seriously considered invading, they quickly changed their minds.

But it was not the last to be seen of the country. In 1981 it had become the independent state of Belize, but it was reluctant to rely on its own resources to deter the Guatemalans, so the British government agreed to continue support. Internal troubles in Guatemala had suggested that the leadership might attempt an adventure into Belize as a means of drawing popular support, as President Galtieri of Argentina did later by invading the Falklands in 1982. Accordingly, the **2nd Battalion** (Lt Col John O'Connell) returned in August 1984, fresh from their triumph as army athletics champions. They found a well-established force, now supported by guns and aircraft, of 2000 men. Two battle groups were formed, one covering the western border from Mexico to the Western Highway, and the other, based at Rideau Camp near Punta Gorda, on the Southern Highway. Battalion headquarters were again at Airport Camp.

The programme, as before, was patrolling, observation and jungle training. One observation post in the south-west, perched high on a pinnacle of rock on which a Union flag flew bravely, could be reached only by helicopter. It was feared that the Guatemalans might occupy one of the numerous cays, or islands offshore, in order to provoke an international incident, and the southernmost of the Sapodilla Cays, thirty-five miles from the coast, was therefore held by a party of eight Grenadiers.

Test exercises were conducted over some of the most difficult jungle in the world and later the battalion were

In the land of the Maya: patrolling in Belize. *Christopher Morley*

called upon to help combat drug smuggling, which was beginning to pose a worrying threat to stability. This resulted in a number of operations, which were not always popular, as the impoverished farmers often had no reliable means of support other than to grow marijuana, which everywhere flourished like weeds. By way of relaxation, leave and adventurous training parties travelled widely to other parts of Central America and to the USA.

One Grenadier wrote later: 'For me Belize offered a glimpse into the world of the old Empire, where duty called and good men took up the White Man's burden: the foot patrols, moving from village to village, among people whose prized possession was a machete or a football. With bare-breasted women and barefoot children, we entered the prehistoric world of wooden huts thatched with palm leaves. It was a far cry from the unyielding gravel of Horse Guards and a rare chance to put the clock back a hundred years when a Briton was a demi-god with his pale face and high technology.' It was a memory well recognizable to the many Grenadiers who have served in such places in the last fifty years.

Furthest East – Hong Kong 1975-76

There was one more visit into the furthest reaches of the old empire and it was quite different to the others. It fell again to the **2nd Battalion** (Lt Col David Fanshawe and later Lt Col Dermot Blundell-Hollinshead-Blundell), who in January 1975 went to Hong Kong for a two-year tour. They were based at Stanley Fort, a fine barracks which in December 1941 had seen the last stand of British and Canadian troops against the invading Japanese.

The life was extraordinarily diverse and there was a great deal to do. There had been serious riots in the 1960s and the Grenadiers had to be ready to support the police. There were ambitious exercises in counter-revolutionary operations, struggling across the beautiful though harsh countryside, toiling up the mountains, flying by helicopter or skimming about in assault boats, in pursuit of 'guerrillas'. The battalion had probably never been so fit, nor the training so realistic. Each company took a turn training in the Brunei jungle. There was even drill, the Queen's Birthday being celebrated by a parade in a football stadium in sweltering heat. The UN Honour Guard platoon in Korea was found for two months, the guardsmen learning to respond to the American command, 'Stand slack, soldier!'

But the principal work took place on the Chinese border between Crest Hill and Sha Tau Kok. This progressively occupied more and more time, and made heavy demands on the families, though at the outset there were six British and Gurkha battalions to take their turn. The Chinese themselves were not a threat, the Communist regime of Chairman Mao (who died in 1976) being perfectly content to let Hong Kong alone. It would eventually return to them in 1997 when the ninety-nine-year lease on the New Territories ran out, and did. But

the extraordinary prosperity of Hong Kong was a magnet to the impoverished Chinese and, had they been allowed, they would have swamped it utterly. They had to be kept out. It was a curious situation for a Grenadier who was familiar with Germany, especially Berlin, where every encouragement was given to refugees to come over from behind the Iron Curtain. Now he had to man observation points along the twenty-kilometre border and patrol the barbed-wire fences. When illegal immigrants were caught, they were well treated but had to be returned. It was not pleasant work, as there was plenty of sympathy for the unfortunates, whose desperation was only too evident. They would cut themselves to ribbons over the wire and corpses were sometimes pulled from the sea supported by pathetically inadequate makeshift floats. Still, the job had to be done and it was done well.

In most respects Hong Kong was a wonderful place to be. There was a leave camp on Lantau Island. The sport and recreation were unrivalled, the food magnificent, the shopping stupendous. There was the occasional typhoon to be dodged. Most of the wives and families greatly enjoyed themselves, though several found the strangeness of the East very startling at the outset. Many a Chinese emporium was to be set up in married quarters at Chelsea Barracks when the battalion returned home at the end of 1976.

Amphibious exercise: on a landing craft in Hong Kong waters.

Northern Ireland – Thirty Years of Trouble

In early August 1969 the 2nd Battalion was unexpectedly placed on the *Spearhead* list, to be ready at short notice for operations anywhere in the world (anywhere but Northern Ireland, they were told), and accordingly busied themselves with drawing up khaki drill and preparing for a hot winter abroad. A few weeks later, and only seventy-two hours after dismounting Queen's Guard, they were on the streets of Londonderry. Expecting to be in the province for a few weeks, they eventually left after five months. It was the beginning of recurrent visits by both battalions to Londonderry, Belfast and the open countryside, which were to stretch over thirty years with loss of life and much injury. Several Grenadiers were also to serve with the locally raised Ulster Defence Regiment, most often with the 8th Battalion. The troubles as a whole were to claim over 3000 lives, including many women and children and several hundred of the security forces

General Service Medal 1962: over 130,000 have been issued for service in Northern Ireland.

The Troubled Province

The roots of the Irish troubles ran deep, over many centuries. Grenadiers had not been there since Victorian times, when stationed at Dublin on ordinary garrison duties. Dublin, since partition in the early 1920s, was now the capital of the deeply Roman Catholic Irish Republic. Six northern counties had remained as part of the United Kingdom, in the separate province of Northern Ireland.[14] For the most part it was staunchly Protestant, though there were considerable numbers of Catholics, in whom by 1969 there was a rising sense of grievance and injustice at the hands of the Protestant majority. This erupted into demonstration and riots, and eventually into open violence by the Irish Republican Army, a terrorist force intent on bringing about the collapse of the province and its unification with the Irish

---

[14] Often familiarly, though inaccurately, known as Ulster, which in fact was an ancient Irish province including nine counties rather than the six Northern Ireland. Protestants often liked to be known as Ulsterman

The outbreak of trouble: a guardsman in riot order in the early days of 1969. *Christopher Morley*

Republic as a single state.

There was real danger of civil war. The hard-liners of the two parties formed up in bitter opposition and hatred: in the Green corner the Republicans, Nationalist and Catholic; in the Orange corner the Unionists, 'Loyalist' and Protestant. In the ring as referee was the British government with its security forces, the Royal Ulster Constabulary and the Army. The difference with this contest was that the antagonists fought the referee as well as each other, and often among themselves. There were several terrorist organizations, with different titles, the 'Loyalists' being every bit as unpleasant as the Republicans, though the IRA, in various guises, caused more death, injury and destruction. The politics of the situation were extremely complex and constantly shifting. They were dark times.

It was not a happy position for a soldier to find himself in. His enemy was ill-defined and elusive. Reason and logic counted for nothing to those intent on violence. However much they themselves suffered, the good opinion of the ordinary people for the army was easily lost. Force had to be used with great care and fine judgements made at high speed. Too slow in reaction and a soldier lay dead. Too quick and a charge of murder might be laid. Everything was done in the eye of the media.

Early Riots in Londonderry and Belfast

Thus it was that the **2nd Battalion** (Lt Col Philip Haslett), only four months returned from Germany, crossed the Irish Sea in LSL *Sir Tristram* and sailed into Londonderry. On arrival the Inkerman Company was instantly deployed into the city under command of the 1st Queen's Regiment. The rest of the battalion went into a weekend, summer training camp at Magilligan. In September they were off to Belfast to support another battalion who had spent two nights trying to separate two communities firmly entrenched behind barriers of lorries, paving stones and builders' rubble. Here also, burnt-out factories, houses and shops indicated how serious the situation had become.

Both in Londonderry and Belfast the soldiers were at first made welcome, especially in the Catholic communities who feared Protestant extremists and to whom the almost wholly Protestant RUC were anathema. Tea and sandwiches were dispensed by old ladies. But it did not last – the extremists were quick to see to that. Lines were established to prevent their constant raids. For the soldiers it was frustrating and exhausting. But it had not yet proved necessary to use incapacitating gas or to fire live ammunition and tension gradually subsided.

They were succeeded in Magilligan by the **1st Battalion** (Lt Col Nick Hales Pakenham Mahon), who seemed at first to be in for a quiet time. But it was not to last. Over Easter 1970 there were three days of violent rioting. Over 3000 Catholics marched to the centre of Londonderry and some tried to break into the RUC barracks. No 3 Company piled into the fray, almost every man being hit by some kind of missile. The battalion advanced deep into the Bogside in the face of vicious crowds of screaming rioters. Twenty-six were arrested, most of them subsequently receiving six-month prison sentences. Well over half the battalion received cuts and bruises.

After five months they returned to London. Shortly afterwards, in Belfast, grenades were thrown into a platoon of soldiers. An immediate curfew was followed by house searches and the discovery of a large cache of arms. The shooting war was about to begin.

Better prepared: equipment had been much improved by the 1980s.

After the riot: missiles and debris all over the road.

Burning streets: a vehicle on fire.

At the ready: Charles Woodrow (second from right) was to win a Military Cross and Queen's Gallantry Medal, as well as the OBE, for many years of outstanding work in Northern Ireland.

At speed and well covered: in the dangerous streets of the province.

Bullets, Bombs, Mortars and Rockets

In August 1971 the **1st Battalion** (Lt Col Greville Tufnell) returned, this time to Belfast. Two companies were in North Ardoyne and the third in Ballymurphy, whence it later went to Londonderry as brigade reserve. All of them saw a great deal of action and they were several times under fire, happily without serious results. Internment without trial had been introduced in the province. It was a deeply resented measure, which proved anyway to have questionable benefits, and the anger arising from it was inevitably vented upon the security forces in the front line.

In November 1972 they were back in Londonderry. Within hours of arrival the Commanding Officer made a spectacular catch in the form of a Russian-made RPG-7 rocket and launcher which terrorists had hastily abandoned. The following four months saw incessant activity. The company in the Creggan recorded an RPG-7 and two mortar attacks on the camp, eleven sniping attacks on patrols and one by Claymore mine. There were twenty-three serious riots, six bomb hoaxes and numerous bomb scares. In the battalion as a whole several men were wounded, but it was a successful tour. They had found fifty-eight weapons, 9128 rounds of ammunition, 692 lbs of explosive and twenty-five

terrorists. But it was the worst year for the army as a whole – 103 soldiers were killed.

In 1973 came the turn of the **2nd Battalion** (Lt Col Richard Besly). In March they were deployed to the province for a short two weeks to cover the plebiscite, and returned again in July for a full tour in Belfast, starting with the large and provocative Orange Day parade in the Protestant Shankill Road. Companies were in the Catholic Ardoyne and Bone districts as well as the Shankill. They followed a parachute battalion, who had had a very rough time, incurring several killed or seriously wounded. However, intelligence-gathering had greatly improved and the results were noticeable. Fortunately, although there were several shooting incidents, the battalion was not seriously provoked.

In March 1974 the **1st Battalion** (Lt Col Bernard Gordon Lennox) took over responsibility for the Creggan estate in Londonderry. In the first eight weeks there were four serious injuries from attacks on Land Rovers (protected by rather ineffective macrolon light armour) and Saracen armoured carriers and, in one instance, from a booby-trapped flat. On one occasion a 'hot pursuit' close to the camp led to the find of a considerable amount of ammunition and explosives. Cooks and clerks, rapidly deployed, joined in a gunfight that went on for fifty minutes.

In October 1976 the **1st Battalion** (Lt Col David Gordon Lennox) took over responsibility for the rural area of North Armagh, in December the area being widened to include Dungannon, thus bringing some 1800 men under command. Out in the country conditions were rather different. Here there was no contact with the local people, as in the towns, for there was no middle ground. The two sides were clearly delineated, the Republicans against the security forces, and thus the work was rather more straightforward. It was a cold Irish winter and the tour became a constant round of patrols, guards and observation duties, enlivened from time to time by a find or an arrest.

November 1977 saw the **2nd Battalion** (Lt Col Dermot Blundell-Hollinshead-Blundell) back in Londonderry, responsible for the whole city west of the Foyle. It was much quieter than in 1974, although there were still several incidents, including a number of armed robberies. The battalion took care not to provoke and the result was an overall decline in tension. It was even possible for twenty-five children to visit the Creggan camp on Sundays to play football and eat a big tea – something unheard of in earlier years.

The Bandit Country of South Armagh

South Armagh was the most notorious part of the province, in which seventy soldiers had been killed over ten years. They had included the Grenadier Captain Robert Nairac, murdered in May 1977 and awarded a posthumous George Cross. This nasty spot became the next destination of the **1st Battalion** (Lt Col Michael Hobbs) in November 1978. The battalion was based at Bessbrook, company locations including Crossmaglen and Newtownhamilton. Most movement between posts in the border area was by helicopter as the roads were too dangerous. Bessbrook assumed the character of a busy airport.

Sergeant RG Garmory was serving with No 2 Company. He wrote: 'Crossmaglen was rather like the Somme that December with duckboards and mud everywhere. We were all living on top of each other; morale was very good – the strange thing with guardsmen is that the worse the conditions, the better they do. No army vehicle was about – all movement was on foot or by helicopter..'

On 21 December Garmory was patrolling in Crossmaglen with three guardsmen, Graham Duggan,

Dressed for the dark: a patrol sets out in the countryside.

Kevin Johnson and Glen Ling, when attacked by terrorists hidden in the back of a van. All three young guardsmen died and Garmory was awarded the Military Medal for his brave and decisive conduct. It was the worst single loss that Grenadiers were to suffer in Northern Ireland.

The Later Years

By 1980 there were far fewer incidents in Northern Ireland, though the IRA were operating on the mainland of Britain and overseas. It was possible for the RUC to begin resuming primary responsibility for security in large parts of the province. The tour of the **2nd Battalion** (Lt Col Martin Smith) in Fermanagh between March and July 1980 was much quieter. The battalion was scattered, at one time being in ten different places under four different commanding officers. It was a clear indication of how things had changed that the Creggan estate, once consuming the energies of an entire battalion, was now overseen by the Corps of Drums alone, based in the Rosemount police station.

It was, however, at this time that Captain Richard Westmacott, a former 2nd Battalion officer, was killed while commanding a troop of the SAS engaged in

rounding up an IRA team armed with an M60 machine gun in Belfast. This team had been responsible for many attacks, resulting in several deaths, and was a serious menace. The operation was a complete success, though the terrorists escaped from the Crumlin Road jail five weeks after their capture. Westmacott was awarded the Military Cross – the first ever given posthumously.

The **1st Battalion** returned to a much quieter Armagh in October 1983 under Lt Col Alexander Heroys, and again in September 1986 under Lt Col Evelyn Webb-Carter. The second tour coincided with the first full residential visit by Grenadiers. The **2nd Battalion** (Lt Col Charles Woodrow) spent two full years at Ballykelly from January 1986. This was far more like a standard posting. Though there were still constant operational duties, normal training could be done and, most important of all, families could lead a settled and enjoyable life. Ballykelly was a fine barracks, situated in a beautiful place. It was the last visit of the 'Models' to Northern Ireland.

But the dangers were by no means over. It was necessary to train for operations in Northern Ireland with the usual thoroughness, and to be fully alert and professional while there. Chances were not to be taken.

Thus, while the **1st Battalion** (Lt Col Edward Bolitho) were in the course of taking over once more in Armagh in September 1993, two helicopters were attacked by machine guns at Crossmaglen. The subsequent large-scale operation, in which the battalion advance party played its part, saw over 2000 shots fired and all the weapons recovered, though the terrorists themselves were able to make their escape. The town was still the most dangerous in the province, and in December Guardsman Daniel Blinco of the Queen's Company was hit by a sniper's 0.5 inch high-velocity bullet while on patrol and died almost at once.

There were several other serious incidents in the six months before the battalion returned home, covered in honour. Two of them were well out of the ordinary. In Crossmaglen one night the Borucki sangar (named after a Parachute Regiment soldier who had been killed there) was sprayed with fuel and then ignited. A huge fireball erupted and engulfed the sangar for several minutes, but mercifully the four occupants were unhurt. On another occasion a Lynx helicopter was struck by a mortar bomb while on the point of landing in the Crossmaglen base. It caught fire and ammunition on board exploded in all directions before the flames were subdued, at a cost of only a few minor injuries.

In January 1996 it was the turn of the **1st Battalion** (Lt Col Patrick Hargreaves and later Lt Col David Hutchison) for a long residential tour in Ballykinler, County Down. By this time further political progress had been made and, as the 2nd Battalion before them, they were able to live, for the most part, an enjoyable and well-balanced life, with a wide variety of operational commitments. However, while terrorist activities were much reduced, there were new stirrings from the Orange side. Loyalist Orangemen insisted on making an annual march through the staunchly Republican area of Drumcree in Portadown and in each of the two years the battalion had to join a large security operation to control it. It was tense and delicate work, but successfully accomplished.

June to December 1999, just thirty years after the troubles started, saw the **1st Battalion** (still under Lt Col David Hutchison) based in East Tyrone but widely deployed in a now happier province. In April 1998 the Good Friday Agreement had been signed and the violence diminished as political activity took its place. The Drumcree parades came round yet again in 1999, but much heat had been taken out of them.

It was in November 2001 that Grenadiers undertook their last emergency tour of the period. This time the **1st Battalion** (Lt Col David Maddan) was in Belfast. The desire to make political progress dominated the posture on the streets and the Police Service of Northern Ireland (formerly the RUC) requested less support than in previous years. In comparison to some earlier Grenadier tours it was a quiet one, but few of the battalion left the province feeling optimistic about the prospect of early reconciliation between the communities.

Close observation: well equipped for manning a hide.
Christopher Morley

Desert and Desolate Places

Sharjah 1968-70

The Trucial States, on the sharp north-eastern point of the Arabian peninsula, was another area of British interest. The increasing importance of the Gulf (an anodyne term used to avoid the contentious 'Persian Gulf' or 'Arabian Gulf') led to a British undertaking to protect the sheikdoms from external aggression, and a garrison was established at Sharjah, together with the Trucial Oman Scouts nearby, who were largely led by British officers. Thus the **1st Battalion** (Lt Col David Hargreaves) flew out in August 1968 to take their turn for a nine-month tour. They had trained for the job on the soggy green sponge of Sennybridge in Wales where, though it was summer, the weather was atrocious and very cold. Men would keel over from exposure on the hillsides one day and try to learn about heatstroke the

next. A fine, lively platoon from the Welsh Guards was attached, mostly named Williams, Evans and Jones.

The fierce climate took some weeks to get used to. Thereafter the rifle companies went out in turn across the desert to the *jebel* (mountains) on the east coast. Supplied by air and to some extent by the tortuous roads, they set up camp and exercised in the desolate rocky wastes, picketing the heights, building protective rock sangars and falling into *wadis* (dry water-courses). It was arduous and thirsty work. The Queen's Company decided to march seventy miles across the desert. 'Frankly, it was bloody hell,' recalled one guardsman. 'Yes, the company made it, but, oh dear! That journey burned on everyone's soul.'

There was fine support in the form of Army light helicopters, Wessex helicopters, Andover transports and

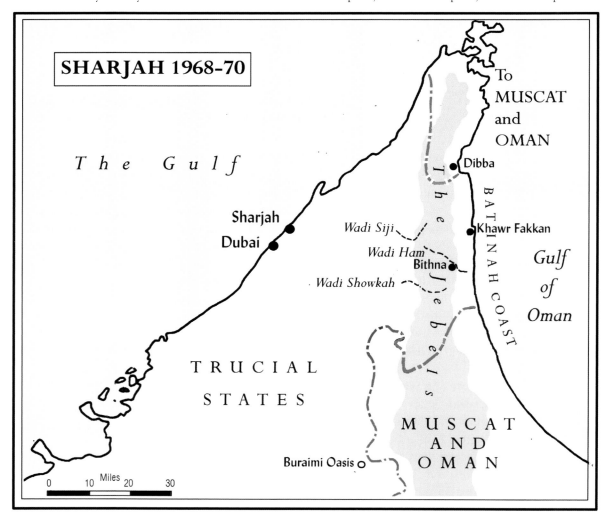

Sartorial in Sharjah: what the well-dressed Grenadier was wearing in the Trucial States.

Hunters of the RAF, a squadron of armoured cars and a battery of light guns. Back in camp there were the usual amusements, including a cheerful Christmas, sport and swimming nearby. The towns were only beginning to develop and nothing approaching the oil-sated pleasure-domes of the present day. To avoid offence to the people it was necessary to be properly covered when walking out. The Commanding Officer approved. 'The British Empire,' he liked to say, 'was won by men in trousers and lost by men in shorts.' And Sergeant Major Peter Lewis enjoyed teasing the airmen by declaring on the Forces radio his dislike of short shorts and long hair.

In 1970 the experience was repeated by **No 2 Company**, **2nd Battalion** (Maj Dermot Blundell-Hollinshead-Blundell), who were attached to the 1st Scots Guards. These were the last days of the British presence in Sharjah and departure was celebrated by a grand searchlight tattoo and a noisy firepower demonstration that alarmed Dubai, ten miles away.

The Falkland Islands 1990-2003

In 1982 the Falkland Islands had been liberated from Argentine occupation by an astonishing amphibious operation, thousands of miles from home and launched with extraordinary speed. Neither Grenadier battalion took part, though they followed with the closest interest the landings at San Carlos and the subsequent battles, watched with admiration the skill and courage of the Scots Guards on Tumbledown Mountain and grieved with the Welsh Guards on their tragic losses in the bombing of *Sir Galahad* at Bluff Cove. And a number of Grenadiers were there with the SAS, working close to the enemy in pursuit of crucial information and living rough, as they were wont to do, in conditions of danger and extreme discomfort.

After the war a stronger garrison was required, both to deter any further Argentine ambitions and to reassure the population, and three times Grenadiers were able to take their turn in that desolate place for some four months. In November 1990 it was the **Inkerman**

Company Group, **2nd Battalion** (Maj Edward Bolitho), 230 strong in five platoons, drawn from all the rifle companies. They were part of a garrison of 2000, including a formidable RAF presence. The emphasis was still very much on operations, with patrols and guards, especially of the airport, alternating with training and recreation. Ammunition was plentiful and danger areas, in the huge open spaces, of little account. Great distances were covered in patrols across country, visiting outlying farms and settlements, and often delivering supplies. Some of this work was done on four legs in the form of the 'Inkerman Light Horse' using animals lent by farmers. Boats were also employed. A party visited South Georgia, 800 miles and three and a half days steaming from the Falklands themselves. In both places the country was desolate and inhospitable, but it was also wild and beautiful, and in the summer months of the southern hemisphere there were many delights. The change from a winter of public duties in London was not to be missed.

In October 1991 **No 2 Company Group**, **2nd Battalion** (Maj Patrick Hargreaves) flew down to the south, several of the guardsmen embarking on a second tour with relish — four summers running was an appealing prospect. The regime was very similar to that of the previous year. Patrols lasted four days at a time, being dropped by boat or helicopter and living in light tents, and this time there was more scope for adventurous training also — canoeing, wind-surfing, waterskiing and rock climbing (including ice work and crevasse rescue). The fishing was 'unbelievable'.

In July 2003 it was the turn of **No 2 Company**, **1st Battalion** (Maj Simon Soskin). There were regular visits to the battlefields and plenty of time to hear again and reflect on what can be expected of the British soldier, and on the importance of always being fit and ready to take up the burden. There is no better place to appreciate this than in the Falkland Islands.

Rocky places: up in the hills of the Falkland islands, where history had been made in 1982.

The Gulf War 1990-91

The Liberation of Kuwait

Twenty years after their visits to Sharjah Grenadiers were back in the desert, but the circumstances could hardly have been more different. This time it was to make war and there really were tanks to be fought. The high technology of the army in Germany was transported to the bare deserts of Saudi Arabia. It was military adventure on the largest scale, spiced with every sort of uncertainty – including chemical warfare.

In August 1990 Saddam Hussein of Iraq invaded Kuwait, to which he had long laid claim. The Americans at once responded by sending heavy forces to Saudi Arabia in preparation for recovering the small but oil-rich state. The British joined in and an entire armoured division was dispatched. It was a colossal and unprecedented

Gulf Medal: the sands of the desert flanked by the colours of the three armed services.

undertaking, only possible because of the sudden collapse of the Soviet Union. The whole of BAOR was ransacked for troops, equipment and spares.

The **1st Battalion** (Lt Col Euan Houstoun and then Lt Col Robert Cartwright) were about to leave for home, after four years in Münster. However, they were the acknowledged experts in Warrior, the new armoured fighting vehicle. They had brought it into service and were clearly more experienced in its use than anyone else. It was now to be tested in war and their skills would be crucial. The tragedy was that the battalion would be split up and distributed all over the Gulf force.

7th Armoured Brigade was quickly chosen to go out to the Gulf, and 4th Armoured Brigade (which contained the Grenadiers) called upon to bring other battalions up to strength with both men and vehicles.

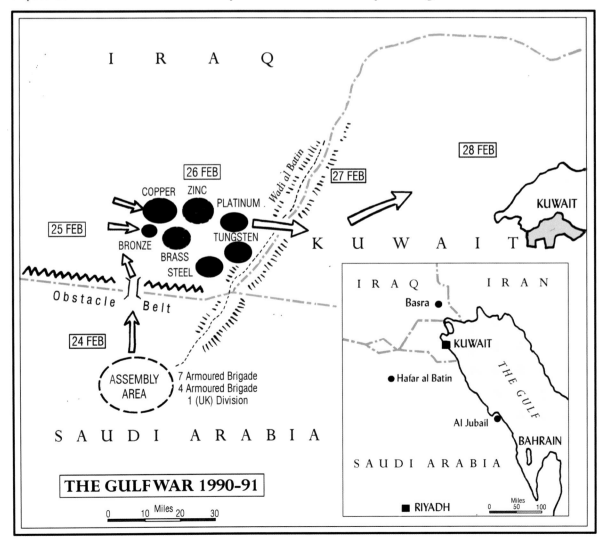

Waiting to move up: guardsmen and Warrior.

When, a little later, it was decided to employ the whole division, and 4th Armoured Brigade was pulled together again, the 1st Grenadiers had already been so spread about that they were beyond reconstitution. Having given up their own Warriors, they had now to acquire them from other sources. This was a dreadful shame for the battalion, but, as it was, their members were to make an important contribution in a myriad different ways. The Queen's and No 2 Companies were each brought up to a strength of 148 and sent respectively to the 1st Royal Scots (later to 14/20 Hussars) and 3rd Royal Regiment of Fusiliers. A platoon went to the 1st Staffords. By early February 1991 some 500 Grenadiers were dispersed between fourteen different units.

Preliminary training had already been done in Germany with great urgency and once in the desert there were several further weeks of preparation. Warriors had to be given extra armour against shoulder-launched anti-tank weapons. This required precision-drilling and much hard work. It had to be done in appalling weather, which made the use of power tools dangerous. Finding the way around, especially when confined in a steel box, was clearly crucial, and some satellite navigation systems were supplied, though they were unreliable at certain times of day.

Every kind of unpleasant hazard had to be prepared

for and casualties, possibly heavy ones, were expected. Saddam had used chemical agents in the past and seemed quite ready to do so again. He had some ninety

Flying the flag: battle order in the Gulf in 1991. *Christopher Morley*

brigades, of unknown quality, in the area of Kuwait and they were expected to be well dug in, with minefields, barbed wire rigged with booby traps, tank traps, sand barriers and ditches flooded with oil that could be ignited at a moment's notice. The coalition was assured of air supremacy, but the Iraqis had plenty of artillery and rocket launchers. As a body of soldiers the Grenadiers were supremely confident, but they perceived that they had reached the edge of an abyss and were unable to see what lay ahead.

The ground offensive opened on 24 February 1991. Several lanes were cleared through the obstacles and then the British division headed for its objectives, for 4th Brigade *Bronze*, *Brass*, *Steel* and *Tungsten*. The guardsmen of the Queen's Company (Maj Grant Baker) seldom had to leave their vehicles as the enemy did not fight from dug-in positions, many of their vehicles were unmanned and they offered little resistance. Bunkers were not cleared, for fear of booby traps and prisoners were made to remove their clothes in case they were concealing explosives on their bodies and preparing to use them in suicide attacks.

On *Steel* No 2 Company (Maj Andrew Ford) collected about 150 prisoners, many of whom were severely wounded. 'The guardsmen displayed a typically generous attitude and distributed carefully conserved chocolate.' Two of the Fusilier vehicles had been destroyed by a misdirected American air strike, but the guardsmen were not unduly shaken as they imagined the battle still to be in the early stages and that much worse might yet follow.

The Grenadiers with 1st Staffords went for *Platinum*. A guardsman wrote: 'We were told to debus and get them [the surrendering Iraqis]. The enemy position was a maze of bunkers, buildings and vehicles. Suddenly the Iraqis fired a RPG-7 rocket which passed through Private Moult before hitting my Warrior. I saw my trousers were alight and that my vehicle commander was on fire and unconscious. I knocked him hard to bring him round. The whole Warrior was in flames until I got a fire extinguisher to put them out. I felt desperately that I must find my steel helmet. The face of the dead Private Moult was perfect but he had lost the side of his body and both his arms had blown off. The lads on each side of him were in shock.'

Warrior, camel and sunset. The small camel that posed for this painting was eaten later but the meal did not go down well with either animal or diners.
Julian Barrow

On the 28th the battle-groups crossed the Wadi al Batin and tore on in an exhilarating gallop towards Kuwait, covering some sixty kilometres in two hours. In all the division had advanced over 300km, destroyed most of three armoured divisions and taken over 7000 prisoners. Three days after the battle opened a ceasefire was announced. Some had a feeling of anti-climax, but there was also deep relief. Much worse had been expected.

The war was over and the return home began in mid-March. Forty-seven British servicemen had lost their lives, many in accidents. Major Ford afterwards wrote: 'I believe strongly that Grenadiers did not suffer significant casualties during or after the conflict on account of our strong code of discipline. During the war we did not dismount our guardsmen to do something that turret crews could do from behind the protection of armour. Similarly, after the conflict we did not allow our guardsmen to collect equipment and run the risk of encountering booby-trap devices. There were very few negligent discharges with personal weapons. Professional military practice, particularly by our NCOs, helped ensure that everyone who deployed to the Gulf returned safely to Germany.'

It had been a deeply unsatisfactory time for the battalion, dispersed over the battlefield as they had been, but for Grenadiers as individuals and in smaller groups, it had been a triumph. 'The Gulf' is now proudly inscribed on the Colours.

Bosnia-Herzegovina –
Nursing a Nation Back to Health

British soldiers first arrived in the former Yugoslavia in 1992, as part of the United Nations Protection Force (UNPROFOR). They were plunged into bloody conflict as the vast swathe of the Balkans, confederated by Tito's Communist party after the Second World War, shook itself apart. Though initially escorting aid convoys and ameliorating the suffering generated by the wars in Croatia and Bosnia-Herzegovina, they found themselves increasingly embroiled in the fighting. They were given no power, however, to enforce the decisions of the United Nations Security Council and as a result became mere observers of atrocity, impotent to intervene.

British troops would ultimately be deployed into Croatia, Kosovo and Macedonia, but Bosnia-Herzegovina was most central to British intervention in the Balkans. From 1992 to 1995 this republic of the former Yugoslavia descended into a vicious civil war between Bosnian Serbs, Bosnian Croats and Bosnian Muslims. It took American airpower to force the parties to the negotiating table at Dayton, Ohio, and forge an uneasy truce – the General Framework Agreement for Peace. This arrangement was guaranteed by international troops, first the Implementation Force (IFOR), then in 1996 the NATO Stabilization Force (SFOR), and in December 2004 the European Union Force (EUFOR).

NATO Medal: it bears the clasp 'Non-Article 5' which indicates operations outside the territory of a NATO nation.

The **1st Battalion** (Lt Col David Russell-Parsons) spent six months in Bosnia, from mid-September 2004, as part of Multinational Task-Force North West, one of three multinational task-forces in the country. The period was characterized by transition: from the twilight of SFOR to the salad days of EUFOR, from the sweltering heat of late summer to the freezing cold of a Balkan winter, from disarming the civilian population to countering organized crime. It was a very different Bosnia to that immediately after the fighting. Blood was no longer flowing, but the scars of the conflict were still much in evidence upon both landscape and people.

Multinational Task-Force North West was a mixture of British, Canadians, Dutch, Chileans, Bulgarians, Swiss, Romanians, Austrians, Norwegians and New Zealanders. Within this tower of Babel the Grenadiers joined with a company of Dutch infantry to form the Multinational Battle Group, the principal manoeuvre component of the force. Support Company, however, was divided between liaison observation teams, living in the Bosnian community and keeping a careful finger on the pulse. After eight years SFOR could justly be proud. The grip of the former warring factions around each other's throats had been prised apart and a resumption of hostilities was now highly improbable. Efforts had also been made to regenerate the country and reduce the prevalent gun culture.

The Grenadiers caught the tail-end of this legacy in the form of so-called *Harvest Plus* operations from September until December 2004. The arrival and intent of the battle group would be announced in advance, before it moved into urban areas across an area the size of Wales. Under the mandate of the Dayton Accord premises would then be entered and searched for arms. The results were continually staggering. The

Snowy post: an isolated radio broadcast station manned by sections for a week at a time.

In the sights: telescopic sights are a great aid to observation for this Grenadier.

disrupt fuel smuggling and other illegal traffic across Bosnia's poorly policed borders. The days were arduous, often requiring rifle companies to man vehicle check points in icy blizzards, while customs officers examined cargo and checked papers. It was thankless work and the men, yearning for tangible results, were not easily comforted by the thought that they were deterring smuggling. It was not a soldier's job, but there and then in Bosnia, only soldiers could do it.

The Grenadiers were left with the impression of a traumatized country whose wounds were no longer bleeding but were not yet healed. The rehabilitation of Bosnia-Herzegovina has been a gradual and exhausting process, which will doubtless continue for years to come. It is often said that, in order to notice progress, one has to leave Bosnia and visit it again after some time, like returning to a lawn in need of cutting after a holiday. The battalion, in the winter of 2004, often found success hard to quantify, but undoubtedly seeds were sown and in due course the harvest should be reaped. Every man who served there in those cold months could return home knowing that he had helped a deeply troubled country up the steep and precipitous path out of dreadful pain and into a new future as a European nation.

Principal source for all except Bosnia: Lindsay (1). Also (for Gulf War) Baker, Tidswell

houses and barns of Bosnia seemed to contain an inexhaustible supply of weapons and ammunition, from Soviet machine guns to American missiles and, everywhere, thousands of hand grenades and land mines. Neatly arranged and unloaded by the guardsmen, the haul at the end of a two-week operation resembled a jumble sale, piled high with curious but lethal clutter.

Shortly before Christmas 2004 the residents of the major urban areas awoke to find the same men and the same vehicles, but now bearing the blue and gold European Union insignia rather than that of SFOR. EUFOR was in control and the Grenadiers, the first British regiment to serve under the European banner, were keen to drive the message home: the insignia may have changed, but the guardsmen remain the same. The most traditional of regiments had again led the way.

This transition was accompanied by a complete change in the character of operations, in a freezing Bosnian winter. As the chance of new conflict had receded, so in proportion corruption and organized crime had taken hold. It fell to the battalion to take the lead in this new quasi-police role, in a series of actions to

A large haul: weapons of all kinds found by the Queen's Company during their searches.

A FAMILY AFFAIR

A newly enlisted Grenadier very soon finds himself part of a family. This starts with the comradeship essential to survive the rigours of the barrack room, the square and the training area, and often endures as a lifelong attachment. The family feeling is to be found at several different levels, at each of which the characteristic behaviour of siblings and cousins is to be found: cheerful rivalry always, squabbling occasionally, but a solid closing of ranks against threats from outside.

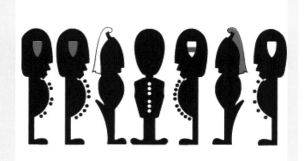

Septem Juncta in Uno: the two regiments of Household Cavalry and five of Foot Guards joined in the unity of the Household Division, though each with distinguishing plumes and button arrangements (left to right): Coldstream, Irish, Life, Scots, Welsh Guards, Blues and Royals, Grenadiers. The Life Guards and the Blues and Royals are now formed into a single operational regiment, the Household Cavalry Regiment and, for ceremonial duties, the Household Cavalry Mounted Regiment. *Henry Hanning*

The Household Division

The first level is the whole company of troops whose privilege it is to serve the monarch and the royal household in a direct capacity. These are the Household Cavalry and the Foot Guards. The Foot Guards were originally the three separate regiments of First (Grenadier), Coldstream and Third (Scots) Guards. In Victorian times they were formed for administrative purposes into the 'Brigade of Guards', later being joined by the new regiments of Irish Guards in 1900 and Welsh Guards in 1915. Battalions of these regiments were grouped for operations in Guards brigades as occasion demanded, and in both world wars a whole division of such brigades was formed, the Guards Division in 1915 and the Guards Armoured Division in 1941. In 1968, when all

regiments of infantry were brought into administrative divisions, the Foot Guards became the Guards Division. The Household Cavalry fight in tanks or armoured cars with regiments of the Royal Armoured Corps, but for regimental and ceremonial purposes they were brought alongside the Foot Guards to form the Household Brigade in 1950, the name being changed to the Household Division in 1968. This comes under the Major General at Horse Guards, who also commands the London District.

This family might have been even larger. In 1916 a proposal was made to form battalions of 'Imperial Guards' from picked men of Canadian, Australian and South African regiments. The idea was examined again after the war, one of the suggestions being that they would wear a red, white and blue plume in the bearskin cap, but the scheme eventually foundered. It is interesting to reflect on how a wider family of guardsmen might have been created.[1]

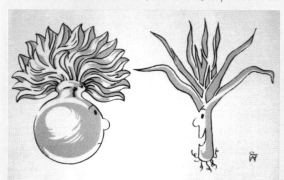

'I've discovered this simply marvellous diet': Welsh Guardsman to Grenadier as one vegetable to another. *Philip Wright*

---

[1] Paget

Smiling with royalty: HM the Colonel-in-Chief and HRH the Colonel meet guardsmen and their families.

Long line-up: a large gathering of past and present Grenadiers at Littlecote House in 2002.

In the States in 2001: a party of the Association with their wives in the USA. Visits to old battlefields and war cemeteries are a regular feature of the Association's programme.

A sea of colour: the 75th anniversary of the Grenadier Guards Association celebrated by a garden party at Buckingham Palace in 1988.

Long and faithful service: Captain Barry Double (pictured when Superintending Clerk), was General Secretary of the Grenadier Guards Association for twenty-two years. The Association is an active body to which many former Grenadiers belong and the largest of any single regiment in the Army.

All the girls love a uniform: these bridesmaids are no exception. *Roger Scruton*

'Yes, Harry; strange though it may seem, the ones below are horses': a view from ground level. *Philip Wright*

The Regimental Nicknames

Grenadiers have been known, for an obscure reason, as **Bill Browns**.[2] The 1st Battalion used to be known as **The Dandies**, the 2nd Battalion as **The Models** and the 3rd Battalion as **The Ribs**. Of these three, the first is understandable enough, though of uncertain origin, the second is a reported compliment by the Duke of Cambridge, and the third has been attributed to the early role of the 3rd Battalion as marines ('the ribs of a ship'), their disposition ('a ribby lot'), and other sources. No 1 Company of the 3rd Battalion bore the proud name of **The Rocks**, attributed to various origins, including their conduct at Gibraltar in 1704, an incident in Italy in 1944 and the idiosyncrasy of a company commander in the 1920s.[3] Sometimes this nickname was applied to the 3rd Battalion as a whole.

Sons and Brothers

In a regiment of this kind there is also, inevitably, a strong tradition of family connection, a tradition which, however, may be called upon by the newest member.[4] There are countless instances of son following father, sometimes over several generations, and there are usually several sets of brothers to be found in a battalion at any one time.

---

[2] The equivalent nicknames for the other regiments of Foot Guards have been **Lilywhites** (Coldstream), **Kiddies** or **Jocks** (Scots), **Micks** (Irish) and **Taffs** (Welsh)
[3] Fraser (4)
[4] A candidate for the army was once asked why he wanted to join. 'Family tradition,' was his reply. 'Don't recall the name; which of your family served before?' 'None of them.' 'Well, how can you possibly be joining from family tradition?' 'I'm starting it,' he said

An annual remembrance: leading the 2003 march from Wellington Barracks to the Horse Guards Memorial on Regimental Remembrance Day are Captain Trevor Rolfe (left) present General Secretary of the Association, and Lieutenant Colonel Conway Seymour, Regimental Adjutant. *Nick Panagakis*

Chapter Twelve

INTO THE TWENTY-FIRST CENTURY

This book has sought to march with the men of the First or Grenadier Regiment of Foot Guards down a road three hundred and fifty years long. There they have met with every kind of fortune: glory, suffering, uncertainty, disaster, despair; death, wounds and sickness; harrowing hardship, brilliant victories, desperate retreats, glowing ceremonies. With their comrades of the other regiments of Foot Guards they have been in the darkest morasses of the battlefield and in the footlights on the ceremonial stage.

We have seen them, with other grenadiers of the army, master those fearsome first grenades. We have followed them tramping the endless fields of Flanders and living like animals in its sodden trenches. We have sailed with them in cramped, stifling troopships to the burning wilderness of Africa and the freezing plateau of the Crimea. We have accompanied them to the field of Waterloo where, barely conscious from exhaustion, they rose to throw back Napoleon's Imperial Guard and win a new name. We have lurched with them, backwards and forwards in the murk of the Sandbag Battery at Inkerman. We have struggled with them in the dunes of Dunkirk, the stony plains of Tunisia, the unforgiving hills of Italy, the bocage of Normandy, the burning houses of Nijmegen, the featureless wastes of the Arabian desert. We have faced with them the abuse and the bullets of their own countrymen on the streets of Northern Ireland.

The Milestones

In 1706, fifty years after their formation towards the end of a vicious civil war, they were fighting with Marlborough at Ramillies. 1756 saw the 2nd Battalion off to Germany for a long campaign at the beginning of the Seven Years War. In 1806 Napoleon had not long been Emperor and the 1st and 3rd Battalions were on their way to garrison duty in Sicily, at the beginning of the second half of the twenty-two-year contest with France that ended so decisively at Waterloo nine years later. In 1831, the exact halfway point to 2006, the Coldstream and the

Beneath the Colours: the officers at lunch in Windsor. *Roger Scruton*

newly named Scots Fusilier Guards joined in adopting the bearskin cap to which the whole Grenadier regiment had been entitled since 1815. The bicentenary arrived in 1856, but much of the Regiment's strength was still in the Crimea and the celebration was put off for four years, the 200th anniversary of the restoration of Charles II.

The 250th anniversary in 1906 was the first major milestone to be enjoyed in peacetime. Despite rumbling noises from the continent, it was a time of grandeur, prosperity and high confidence. Grenadiers were only just emerging from going out on exercise in tunic and bearskin, and many wore medals from Omdurman and South Africa. There was no inkling of what awaited them in 1914, only eight years ahead. By the time the tercentenary had arrived in 1956, the great two-part struggle against Germany was over and won. Those proud to call themselves Grenadiers now numbered thousands upon thousands, and thousands more were lying in the war cemeteries or counting the cost of painful and crippling wounds.

Looking to the Future

The nature of military demands will certainly bring new surprises. Nobody understood in advance the harrowing demands of the Crimea or the tenacity and skill of the Boers. The First World War was unimaginable, the Second, only twenty years later, inconceivable. Who foresaw the thirty-year engagement in Northern Ireland or a huge amphibious operation in the Falkland Islands? Who seriously imagined that we would be engaged, with an entire armoured division, in liberating Kuwait or, a few years later, in taking Basra and then holding down a nasty insurgency in Iraq?

The last century has witnessed the greatest triumphs of human endeavour and the deepest pits of human depravity in recorded history. For Grenadiers, as for others, it has seen the very best in progress and the very worst in loss and suffering. And so it may continue. There is plenty of trouble now, and round the corner plenty more.

People of the United Kingdom can seem very unready to meet such challenges. They have never been so prosperous, but long years of peace have led many into a way of self-indulgence, reckless debt, chaotic family life, obsession with celebrity and amusement, and reluctance to take responsibility.

Fortunately, those in the Armed Forces see things very differently, though it is often a difficult life for both servicemen and their families. They take pride in their profession and themselves, they look after each other, they do not accept the second rate or second best. They are unsurprised by the accidental and the unexpected. They endure danger and hard conditions.

Television, radio and the press are always ready to applaud the soldier, certainly when there is some dramatic action to report. That is good to see, but there is still very little real understanding of the military life among most of our people, including (it must be said) our political leaders, very few of whom have tasted it. The last National Serviceman of 1962 will soon be drawing his pension and is probably already a grandfather.

The Regiment is now smaller than it has ever been: well under 1000, of a population of sixty million. If now established in the same proportion to the six million population of 1660, it would be over 10,000 strong. Yet, compared to most other regiments of infantry, who, even where they have survived, have suffered one amalgamation after another, Grenadiers can count themselves fortunate. And the experience of two world wars has taught that a small glow, if preserved and cherished, can burst into a vivid flame in times of great national emergency. Numbers can quickly be multiplied without dilution in quality, if training is based on a good human organization and high professional standards, and rooted in a deep tradition.

Grenadiers will continue to enjoy their customs, bizarre and inexplicable though some may be, and no doubt will invent more. They will continue to relish their rivalry with that other English regiment of Guards, the Coldstream, in sure knowledge that the compliment will be returned. This is not likely to reach a higher intellectual level than in the past. 'Not a bad fellow,' a Grenadier was once heard to remark, 'but rather "Coldstreamy".'[1]

---

[1] *Household Brigade Magazine*, Winter 1928-9

'Memoranda' in 2005: new arrivals are welcomed to the 1st Battalion in Windsor, (left to right) Capt Oliver Saxby (Adjutant), Lt Col David Russell-Parsons (Commanding Officer), Sgt Martin Howlin, Gdsm Christopher Shread, Gdsm Sarjo Kuyateh, WO1 Gordon Gask (Sergeant Major). *Roger Scruton*

The life of a modern Grenadier: the twenty-first century offers the versatile guardsman unrivalled scope, from enacting the splendour of ancient ceremony to the mastery of modern weapons, vehicles and equipment. He may find himself fighting or keeping the peace on operations and will certainly exercise in a variety of conditions. He will relish his sport and adventurous training. He will enjoy the comradeship afforded by one of the oldest, most proven and best known regiments in the world. His are the proudest of traditions and the most tempting of opportunities.

Eyes right; the Colour passes before the Queen on Horse Guards Parade.

In Service to the Sovereign

In the Armed Forces of the Crown the soldiers of the First Regiment of Foot Guards take a special place. Raised by a king in exile, they were a primary component of the first standing force, and their standards and practices were those subsequently applied to the regiments of a much greater army. By taking the title of 'Grenadier' in 1815 they have represented and preserved the memory of those dauntless, chosen men of many infantry regiments who stood on the right of their battalions and led the most desperate assaults. The Sovereign's Company has the special and most personal duty of bearing monarchs to their grave.

The future of the Regiment was only once seriously threatened, when (with the unfortunate exception of its

Colonel) it refused to break its loyalty to James II in 1688. Happily he did not insist on it to the point of armed resistance, and William III did not disband the First Regiment of Guards on his succession, as he might very well have done. Charles II's creation could easily have vanished into a dusty archive, of later interest only to researchers into deep military mysteries of the past.

But it survived, to win great renown over three and a half centuries. And in 2006 the Regiment is deeply proud that the 350th anniversary falls in the year when their Queen celebrates her eightieth birthday. As Colonel and Colonel-in-Chief she has worn the insignia of 'My Grenadiers' for no fewer than sixty-four years, a period longer than the entire reign of her great ancestor, Queen Victoria.

Startling contrasts; the Band of the Regiment in Bosnia.

Kings, Queens and Colonels
In the History of the First Guards

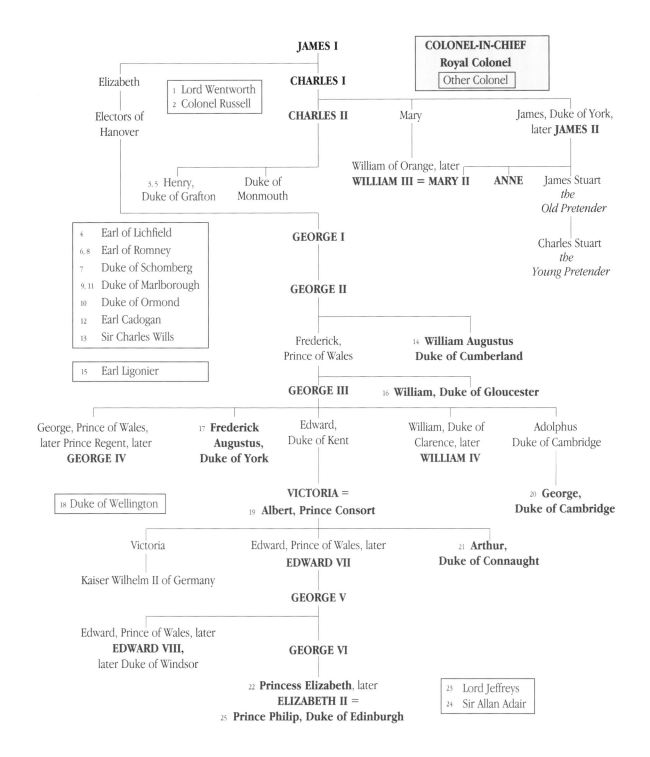

Annex B

Decorations for Gallantry
from 1914, other than VCs

Victoria Cross (VC)
Instituted 1856. The highest military award for gallantry.
Open to all ranks

* * *

Crimea
Lt Col Lord Henry Percy, Lt Col Russell,
Pte Palmer, Pte Ablett
1914-1918
LCpl Fuller, Pte Barber, LSgt Rhodes, Capt Paton (post),
Capt Pryce (post), Lt Col Viscount Gort, Pte Holmes (post)
1939-1945
LCpl Nicholls, Maj Sidney

George Cross (GC)
Instituted 1940. The highest civil award for gallantry.
Open to all military ranks where military honours
not normally granted.

* * *

1979
Capt Nairac (post)

Distinguished Service Order (DSO)
Instituted 1886 for officers. In 1993 Conspicuous Gallantry
Cross (CGC) replaced DSO and DCM as gallantry award
for all ranks

* * *

1914-1918   61 awarded
with bar – Lt Col Bailey, Lt Col Viscount Lascelles, Lt Col
Lord Henry Seymour
with two bars – Lt Col Viscount Gort, Lt Col Thorne
1939-1945   21 awarded
with bar – Lt Col Clive, Brig Goulburn, Lt Col Heber
Percy, Lt Col Lort-Phillips

Distinguished Conduct Medal (DCM)
Instituted 1854 for NCOs and men
Withdrawn in 1993 when CGC instituted

* * *

1914-1918   161 awarded
with bar – Sgt Rhodes
1939-1945   27 awarded

Military Cross (MC)
Instituted 1914 for junior officers and warrant officers.
Opened to all ranks in 1993

* * *

1914-1918   149 awarded
with bar – Capt Adair, Capt Fryer, Maj Neville, Capt Pryce,
Capt Simpson, Capt Spence
with two bars – Capt Cornforth
1939-1945   72 awarded
with bar – Capt Jones, Maj Baker, Maj Bowes-Lyon,
Maj Gregory-Hood
1949 Maj Heywood   **1979** Maj Woodrow
1980 Capt Westmacott (post)

Military Medal (MM)
Instituted 1916 for NCOs and men.
Withdrawn in 1993 when MC opened to all ranks.

* * *

1914-1918   625 awarded
with bar – CQMS Baker, Sgts Burke, Driver, Greenwood,
Jeanes, Nottage, Webb, Wharmby, LSgts Jackson,
Robertson, LCpls Bryant, Jeffreys, Keggin, Lucas, Spouge,
Ptes Askey, Bailey, Bagot, Coton, Crick, Halls, Lowe, Smith,
Spur, Voce, Warner, Wilding
1939-1945   126 awarded
with bar – CSM Barnes, LSgt Rose
1949 Sgt Clutton
1974 CSgt Matthews

Albert Medal (AM)
Instituted 1866 for gallantry in saving life. Replaced by
George Cross

* * *

1914-1918
LSgt Warwick, LSgt Meredith

Queen's Gallantry Medal (QGM)
Instituted 1974 for military of all
ranks and civilians

* * *

1975
Maj Woodrow
1981
WO2 Sandison

311

BIBLIOGRAPHY

(PP – Privately Published, PM – Personal Memoir)

Adair, Sir Allan, *A Guards General: Memoirs* (Ed Oliver Lindsay) – Hamish Hamilton 1986

Adkin, Mark, *The Waterloo Companion* – Aurum Press 2001

'Advice', *Extracts from Advice to the Officers of the British Army with Some Hints to the Drummer and Private Soldier* – Published 1787

Alford, Richard (1), *To Revel in God's Sunshine* – PP 1981

Alford, Richard (2), *On the Word of Command* – Spellmount 1990

Arrowsmith, Harold, *Images From the Trenches* – Grenadier Gazette 1984

Asquith, Raymond, *Life and Letters* – Collins 1980

Aubrey-Fletcher, HL, A *History of the Foot Guards to 1856* – Constable 1927

Baker, Grant, *The Queen's Company, Operation Granby 1990-1991* – PM undated

Ball, Simon, *The Guardsmen* – Harper Collins 2004

Baring Pemberton, W, *Battles of the Boer War* – Batsford 1964

Barthorp, Michael, *British Infantry Uniforms since 1660* – Blandford Press 1982

Bashford (1), Rodney, *Is It the Call I'm Seeking?* – Grenadier Gazette 1981

Bashford (2), Rodney, *Karl Heinz Gustav Schauenburg* – Grenadier Gazette 1983

Blades, Geoffrey, *Backs to the Wall* – Grenadier Gazette 1993

Bond, Derek, *Steady, Old Man, Don't You Know There's a War On* – Leo Cooper 1990

Bowley, Alfred, *Assorted World War II Anecdotes (3rd Bn)* – PM undated

Bozeat, Len, *The Battle Mountain* – Grenadier Gazette 2002

Bridges, John, *Mareth Diary* – PM 1943

Britten, Charles, *Memories of My Life* – PP undated

Brown, Cecil, *Hell on Earth* – PP 1997

Browning, Denys, *Why the Grenadiers?* – PM 1986

Buchanan, John Nevile, *Family Records* – PM

Burnaby, Edwyn, *An Account of the ... 3rd Battalion ... at the Battle of Inkerman* – Staunton and Son 1874

Calvert, Horace, *How and Why I Enlisted in the Grenadier Guards Sixty-five Years Ago* – PM 1980

Carman (1), William, *Richard Simkin's Uniforms of the British Army* – Webb and Bower 1985

Carman (2), William, *see* Fosten

Carr-Gomm, Anthony, *see* Compton

Carrington, Peter, Lord, *Reflect on Things Past* – Collins 1988

Carter, Charlie, *A Brave Grenadier of Mons* (Ed Frank Clark) – PM undated

Chambers (1), Barbara, *John Collett and a Company of Foot Guards* (2 vols) – Barbara J Chambers 1997

Chambers (2), Barbara, *The Men of the 1st Foot Guards at Waterloo and Beyond* (2 vols) – Barbara J Chambers 2003

Chandler (1), David, *Marlborough as Military Commander* – Batsford 1973

Chandler (2), David (Ed), *A Journal of Marlborough's Campaign, by John Marshall Deane, Private Sentinel in Queen Anne's First Regiment of Foot Guards* – London 1984

Chandler (3), David, *Sedgemoor 1685* – Spellmount 1995

Chandos (1), Lord (Oliver Lyttelton), *The Memoirs of Lord Chandos* – Bodley Head 1962

Chandos (2), Lord (Oliver Lyttelton), *From Peace to War: A Study in Contrast* – Bodley Head 1968

Chapman, M, *Intelligence* (sketch quoted in Ponsonby Vol 2)

Clark (1), Frank, *Borne to the Grave by Heroes* – PP 1994

Clark (2), Frank, *Through Hell to Immortality* (Ablett VC) – Leiston Press 1996

Clark (3), Frank, *The Good Soldier and the Bad Soldier* (Ablett VC, Palmer VC) – Grenadier Gazette 1998 and PP undated

Cliff, Norman, *To Hell and Back With the Grenadiers* – Merlin Books 1988

Colville, JR, *Man of Valour* – Collins 1972

Compton, Hugh and Carr-Gomm, Anthony, *The Military on English Waterways 1798-1844* – Railway and Canal Historical Society 1991

Craster (1), JM, *Fifteen Rounds A Minute* – Macmillan 1976

Craster (2), JM, *Suakin 1885* – Grenadier Gazette 1978

Crosthwaite (1), Ivor, *Least Said...* – Robert Maxwell at BPCC 1983

Crosthwaite (2), Ivor, *A Charmed Life* – TWM Publishing 1996

Crowe, Ted, *The Worst Few Days of My Life* – Grenadier Gazette 1991

Dalrymple-White, Sir Godfrey, *How to get on in the Regiment (1947)* – Grenadier Gazette 1994

Dawnay, NP, *The Badges of Warrant and Non-Commissioned Rank in the British Army* – JSAHR Special Publication No 6 1949

Deane, John Marshall, *see* Chandler (2)

Dorney, Richard, *An Active Service* – Helion and Co 2005

Dowding, R, *Personal Memoir* – PM 2004

Egginton, Mark, *A Stitch in Quick Time* – Grenadier Gazette 1996

Felsted, CS, *Personal Letter* – PM undated

Fletcher, Frank, *Personal Memoir* – PM 1990

Forbes, A, *A History of the Army Ordnance Services* – Medici Society 1929

Forbes, Nigel, Lord, *Challenge* (extract) – PM undated

Forbes (1), Patrick, *6th Guards Tank Brigade* – Sampson Low, Marston undated

Forbes (2), Patrick, *The Grenadier Guards in the War of 1939-1945 Vol I* – Gale and Polden 1949

Ford, Sir Edward, *Personal Memoir 1936-1945* – PM 2003

Fosten, Bryan and Carman, William, *Uniforms of the Foot Guards from 1661 to the Present Day* – The Pompadour Gallery 1995

Fraser (1), Sir David, *The Grenadier Guards* – Osprey – Men at Arms Series 1978

Fraser (2), Sir David, *And We Shall Shock Them* – Hodder and Stoughton 1983

Fraser (3), Sir David, *Wars and Shadows* – Allen Lane 2002

Fraser (4), Sir David, *Dangerous Ground* – Household Brigade Magazine Autumn 1962

Fraser (5), Sir David, (Ed) *An Ensign at War* (The Narrative of Richard Master, First Guards 1815) – JSAHR LXVI

Fraser, Mark, *see* McInnes

Freyberg, Paul, Lord, *Bernard Freyberg VC, Soldier of Two Nations* – Hodder and Stoughton 1991

Fryer, ERM, *Reminiscences of a Grenadier* – Gale and Polden 1965

Garrett, Bill, *A Drummer's Nightmare* – Grenadier Gazette 1995

Gascoigne, Sir Julian *A Modern Major General* – PP 1992

Gleichen, Count, *With the Camel Corps up the Nile* – Chapman and Hall 1888

Gow, Sir Michael, *Trooping the Colour* – Souvenir Press 1988

Grenadier Guards (1), *Short History of the Grenadier Guards* – Published by Authority 1917

Grenadier Guards (2), *The Grenadier Guards Tercentenary Year 1956* – WS Cowell 1956

Grenadier Guards (3), *The Grenadier Guards, A Tercentenary Exhibition* – Catalogue 1956

Grenadier Guards (4), *The Sovereign's Company* – Gale and Polden 1928

Grenadier Guards (5), *The Sovereign's Company* – Benham and Co 1945

Grenadier Guards (6), *The Colours of the Grenadier Guards* – Cowell 1958

Grenadier Guards (7), *The Grenadier Guards* – Sisley 1915

Grenadier Guards (8), *The Colours of the First or Grenadier Regiment of Foot Guards* – 2005

Gronow, Rees, *The Reminiscences and Recollections of Captain Gronow* – John C Nimmo 1889. Also abridged version by John Raymond – The Bodley Head 1964

Hamilton, Sir Frederick, *History of the Grenadier Guards* (3 Vols and corrigenda and addenda) – John Murray 1874

Hare, Geoff, *see* Melvin

Harris, Sgt SW (Ed Maj John Harris), *The Nile Expedition of 1898 and Omdurman* – JSAHR 2000

Hawkesworth, John, *Aspects of War* – PM 2002

Haythornthwaite (1), Philip, *British Infantry of the Napoleonic Wars* – Arms and Armour Press 1987

Haythornthwaite (2), Philip, *Invincible Generals* – Firebird Books 1991

Headlam, Cuthbert, *The Guards Division in the Great War 1915-1918* (2 vols) – John Murray 1924

Hibbert, Christopher, *Wellington – a Personal History* – Harper Collins 1997

Higgins, AH, *Soudan* [sic] *Campaign 1898* (Transcribed Brian Lane) – PM undated

Higgins, Harold, *The War Diary of Private Harold Higgins* – Grenadier Gazette 2000

Higginson, Sir George, *Seventy One Years of a Guardsman's Life* – Smith, Elder 1916

Hill, *see* Rosse

Holmes, Barney, *see* Crosthwaite (2)

Holmes, Richard, *Redcoat* – Harper Collins 2001

Hussey, Marmaduke, Lord, *Chance Governs All* – Macmillan 2001

Jay, Bernard, *The Adventures of a Romantic* – PP 1999

Jeffreys (1), George, Lord, *Letters and Diaries* – PM

Jeffreys (2), George, Lord, *Diary of the Nile Expedition* – PM

Jeffreys (3), George, Lord, *'Letter from Poona'* – Letter to Col Guy Rasch, Commanding Grenadier Guards, 22 August 1932

Jeffreys (4), George, Lord, *Guards Depot instructions 1914* (Historical Summary)

Johnston, Brian (1), *Happy Days* – Grenadier Gazette 1981

Johnston, Brian (2), *Letters Home* (Ed Barry Johnston) – Weidenfeld and Nicolson 1998

Johnston, Sir John, *Memoirs of a Tank Troop Leader 1942 to 1945* – PP 2002

JSAHR, *Journal of the Society for Army Historical Research* – from 1921

Kennedy, DJ, *6th Guards Tank Brigade Reminiscences* – PP 1993

Kersh, Gerald, *They Died With Their Boots Clean* – The World's Work 1941

Kipling, Rudyard, *The Irish Guards in The Great War* (2 vols) – Macmillan 1923

Lacey, Laurie, *see* Smith

Lachouque (1), Henri, *Waterloo* – Arms and Armour 1972

Lachouque (2), Henri, *The Anatomy of Glory* (translated Brown) – Arms and Armour 1978

Lambert, Sir John, *Personal Memoir of the Tunisian Campaign* – PM undated

Lawrence, Brian, *Letters from the Front* (Ed Ian Fletcher) – Parapress 1993

Lewis, Peter, *The History of the Quartermaster* – Grenadier Gazette 1996

Lindsay, Donald, *Forgotten General* – Michael Russell 1987

Lindsay (1), Oliver, *Once a Grenadier...* – Leo Cooper 1996

Lindsay (2), Oliver, *The Crimean War* – Articles for the Guards Magazine 2003 to 2005

Lloyd (1), Sir Francis, *First or Grenadier Guards in South Africa* (2nd Battalion) – Keliher 1907 (with 3rd Battalion – see Russell)

Lloyd (2), Sir Francis, *Letters and Diaries* – PM

Longford, Elizabeth, *Wellington: The Years of the Sword* – Harper and Rowe 1969

Lucas, James, *The British Soldier – Experiences of War* – Arms and Armour 1989

Lyttelton, Humphrey, *Take It From the Top* – Robson Books 1975

Lyttelton, Oliver, *see* Chandos

Macmillan, Harold, Earl of Stockton, *Harold Macmillan Remembers* – Grenadier Gazette 1988

Magnus, Philip, *King Edward The Seventh* – John Murray 1964

Malle, Harry, *Letter of 4 June 1900*

Marshall, Colin, *British Grenades* – Royal Military College of Science 1982

Martin, F, *History of the Grenadier Guards 1656-1949* – Gale and Polden 1951

Maxfield, Ron, *Dropping in on Suez* – Grenadier Gazette 1993

McInnes, Ian and Fraser, Mark, *Ashanti 1895-96* – Picton Publishing 1987

McNair, Robert French, *The Colours of the British Army* (The Grenadier Guards) – London 1869

Melvin, Ronald, *The Guards and Caterham* (Ed – with Geoff Hare and John Tilbury) – Guardroom Publications 1999

Mitchell, Norman, *6th Battalion Grenadier Guards From Caterham to Cape Bon* – PM undated

Montgomery, Viscount, *Memoirs* – Fontana 1960

Moore, Sir Rodney, *The Battle of Heesch* – PM undated

Nelson, Sir John, *Always a Grenadier* – PP undated

Neville, The Hon Henry and The Hon Gray, *Letters written from Turkey and the Crimea 1854* – PP 1870

Nicolson (1), Nigel, *The Grenadier Guards in the War of 1939-1945 Vol II* – Gale and Polden 1949

Nicolson (2), Nigel, *The Grenadier Guards in the War of 1939-1945* (shortened paperback version) – Gale and Polden 1946

Nicolson (3), Nigel, *Long Life* – Weidenfeld and Nicolson 1997

Paget, Sir Julian, *The Story of the Guards* – Osprey Publishing Ltd 1976

Paine (1), David, *Crimean Medal Roll of Grenadier Guards* – Grenadier Guards 2000

Paine (2), David, *John Forryan* – PP undated

Pakenham, Thomas, *The Boer War* – Weidenfeld and Nicolson 1997

Park, Dennis, *Tales of a Grenadier* – Alba Publishing 1993

Percy, Algernon, *A Bearskin's Crimea* – Pen and Sword 2005

Ponsonby (1), Sir Frederick, *The Grenadier Guards in the Great War 1914-1918* (3 vols) – Macmillan 1920

Ponsonby (2), Sir Frederick, *Recollections of Three Reigns* – Eyre & Spottiswood 1951

Pritchard, Jack, *Seven Years a Grenadier 1939 to 1946* – Forces and Corporate Publishing 1999

Regiment, Military Heritage Collection, *The Grenadier Guards 1656-1994* – Issue 4 1994

Rickwood, Archie, *The Memories of an Ordinary Man* – PM 1997

Ross, TJ, *What Did You Do In The War, Grandad?* – PP undated

Rosse, the Earl of, and Hill, Col ER, *The Guards Armoured Division* – Geoffrey Bles 1956

Russell, Alick, *First or Grenadier Guards in South Africa* (3rd Battalion) – Keliher 1907 (with 2nd Battalion – *see* Lloyd)

Sale, Nigel, *Wellington's Waterloo Secret* – Alden Group 2005

Sarkar, Dilip, Guards VC, *Blitzkrieg 1940* – Ramrod Publications 1999

Scott, HG, *Autobiography of a Dabbler* – PP undated

Seale, Thomas, *Memoirs (1919 to 1945)* – PP undated

Smith, EA, *Recce Troop Memories (May 1943 to May 1945)* – PP undated

Smith, Wilfrid Abel, *Letters and Diaries 1914-1915* – PP undated

Springman, Michael, *Sharpshooter in the Crimea* – Pen & Sword 2005

St Aubyn, Giles, *The Royal George* – Constable 1963

Stephens, Samuel Harry, *Memoirs 1939-1945* – PM undated

Steevens, GW, *With Kitchener to Khartum* (sic) – Blackwood 1898

Stockton, *see* Macmillan

Strachey (1), Lytton, *Eminent Victorians* (Florence Nightingale) – Chatto and Windus 1918

Strachey (2), Lytton, *Queen Victoria* – Chatto and Windus 1955

Taylor, AR, *The Second World War* – Articles for the Guards Magazine 1995 to 2000 – PM undated

Tidswell, John, *War in the Gulf* – Grenadier Gazette 1992

Tilbury, John, *see* Melvin

Tipping, Alfred, *Letters from the East during the Campaign of 1854* – Egerton Skipwith

Waite, Terry, *Taken on Trust* – Hodder and Stoughton 1993

Waring, Lawrence, *Duty Calls! (with the 6th Bn in North Africa)* – Avon Books 1998

Warner, Philip, *Army Life in the 90s* – Country Life Books 1975

Webb, George, *see* Lucas

Webb-Carter (1), Sir Evelyn, *RSM Arthur Hill (Great Grenadiers)* – Grenadier Gazette 1996

Webb-Carter (2), Sir Evelyn, *William Garton (Great Grenadiers)* – Grenadier Gazette 1999

Webb-Carter (3), Sir Evelyn, *Randolph Beard (Great Grenadiers)* – Grenadier Gazette 1991

Wells, Christopher, *Memories Irrelevant and Irreverent of BAOR 1945-1947* – PM undated

Westmacott, Guy, *Memories* – PP 1978

Whitworth (1), RH, *Field Marshal Lord Ligonier* – Oxford University Press 1958

Whitworth (2), RH, *The Grenadier Guards* – Leo Cooper – Famous Regiments series 1974

Whitworth (3), RH, *William Augustus, Duke of Cumberland* – Leo Cooper 1992

Wigram (1), Neville, Lord, *1st Bn Grenadier Guards May 1940* – PM undated

Wigram (2), Neville, Lord, *Training for War* – PM 2001

Wood, Norman, *Once a Grenadier, Always a Grenadier* – Old Mill Books 1997

Woodfield, RG, *Duty. Service. Games. Fun* – PP 2003

Ziegler, Philip, *Omdurman* – Collins 1973

INDEX

Macmillan, Harold, 171
Maddan, David, 293
Magersfontein, 132
Mahdi, the, 120-123
Maitland, Augustus, 50
Maitland, Crichton, 116
Maitland, Peregrine, 56, 58-65
Makgill-Crichton-Maitland, Mark, 157, 170
Makarios, President, 277
Malaya, 279-281
Malle, Harry, 135
Malmesbury, Earl of, 110
Malplaquet, 28
Malta, 273-275
Mann, Sergeant, 98
Mareth, 199, 213-215
Marines, 14, 29
Marlborough, Duke of, 16, 21, 23-29, 164
Marne, River, 147
Martin, AE, 280
Mary, Queen, 248
Mary II, Queen, 19
Mason, Don, 265
Maubeuge, 158
May, Quartermaster, 133
Mayor, Private, 109
Meadows, Walter, 231
Medjez el Bab, 200
Meijel, 207
Mercer, Captain, 64
Meredith AM, William, 142
Methuen, Lord, 127-131
Middleditch, William, 54
Miller, Eustace, 219
Miller, George, 84
Minor, Sergeant, 94
Modder River, 131-132
Monck, General, 10
Monmouth, Duke of, 13-14, 24
Mons, 145-147
Monte Battaglia, 203, 223, 225
Monte Camino, 200, 222-223, 227
Monte Sole, 202
Montgomery, Viscount, 194, 201, 207, 211, 228, 236-237
Moore, Sir John, 52-55
Moore, Sir Rodney, 203, 229-230, 271
Moorehead, Lindsay, 253
Morris, John, 94, 98
Moult, Private, 299
Murray, Lieutenant, 116

Nairac GC, Robert, 291
Namur, 18-19
Napier, Sir William, 98, 110
Napoleon *see Bonaparte*
Nash, Bill, 139
Nash, Tony, 265
Nasser, Colonel, 274
Neerwinden, 18
Nelson, Horatio, Lord, 51
Nelson, Sir John, 202, 219, 224, 252, 273
Neuve Chapelle, 148, 163
New York, 34
Ney, Marshal, 62, 64
Nichol, Captain, 141-142
Nicholls VC, Harry, 208-210
Nightingale, Florence, 85, 92
Nijmegen, 207, 228-231
Nive, 56
Nivelle, 56
Norfolk, Duke of, 265, 274
Normandy, 203
Northern Ireland, 269, 287-293
Norton St Philip, 16

O'Connell, John, 285
O'Hara, Sir Charles, 18
'Old Pretender', 29, 35
Omdurman, 123-126
Orange, William Prince of *see William III*
Orange, Prince of, 48, 50
Ormond, Duke of, 28
Osman Digna, 121-123
Ostend, 50
Oudenarde, 27

Pacey, Lance Sergeant, 230
Palestine, 271-273
Palmer VC, Anthony, 95-96, 98
Parsons, Private, 147
Passchendaele, 156-157
Paterson, Joseph, 138
Paton VC, George, 150, 159
Payne, Quartermaster, 138
Pearce, Bob, 211
Pearl Harbour, 199
Peninsula (Iberian or Spanish), 52-57
Péronne, 67
Percy VC, Lord Henry, 96-97, 114-115
Phasey, Andrew, 139
Philip, Prince *see Edinburgh*
Phillips, Drummer, 109
Pilcher, William, 157, 173-174, 187

Plancenoit, 64
Po, River, 203
Ponsonby, Sir Frederick, 114
Pont-à-Marcq, 207, 236
Port L'Orient, 23
Port Said, 274
Portugal (*see also Peninsula*), 78
Powell, William, 91
Pratt, Bernard, 211
Prembeh, King, 116
Prescott, John, 194, 210
Prince Imperial, 114
Prince Regent *see George IV*
Prince of Wales *see Edward VII, Edward VIII*
Proby, Lord, 57
Pryce VC, Thomas, 159, 174

Quatre Bras, 58-60, 66
Quilter, Lieutenant, 135

Raglan, Lord, 86, 89, 92
Ramillies, 26-27
Rasch, Guy, 157-158
Reeve, John, 75
Reresby, 17
Reynardson, Edward Birch, 93, 97
Rhine, 207
Rhodes VC, John, 146, 149
Ricardo, Captain, 109
Roberts, Donald, 272
Roberts, Lord, 105, 132, 135-136
Roberts, Paul, 46
Robertson, Patrick, 273
Robertson, Sir William, 143
Robinson, Peter, 231-232
Rolfe, Trevor, 305
Rommel, Field Marshal, 199
Romney, Earl of, 18
Rooke, Admiral, 23
Roundway, Lord *see Colston*
Royal Ulster Constabulary, 288
Ruggles-Brise, Sir Harold, 160
Rundle, General, 137
Russell, Charles, 30
Russell VC, Sir Charles, 96, 98
Russell, Hon John, 11-13, 20, 117
Russell, William, 85, 90
Russell-Parsons, David, 300, 307
Ryan, J, 280

Sackville, Colonel, 14
Salamanca, 54, 56
Salerno, 200

319

PORTUGUESE INSURGENTS   CANADIAN DISSIDENTS   RUSSIANS

EUROPE

○ 1890·1

1897

ATLANTIC
OCEAN

AFRIC

THE CRIMEA
1854 - 5

SOUTH AMERICA

GERMANS   GERMANS   • T H